I0878759

Peasants, Power, and Place

UKRAINIAN RESEARCH INSTITUTE
HARVARD UNIVERSITY

Harvard Series in Ukrainian Studies

HURI Editorial Board

Michael S. Flier
George G. Grabowicz
Lubomyr Hajda
Serhii Plokhy, *Chairman*

Marika Whaley, *Manager of Publications*

Cambridge, Massachusetts

PEASANTS, POWER, AND PLACE

Revolution in the Villages of Kharkiv Province, 1914–1921

Mark R. Baker

Distributed by Harvard University Press
for the Harvard Ukrainian Research Institute

The Harvard Ukrainian Research Institute was established in 1973 as an integral part of Harvard University. It supports research associates and visiting scholars who are engaged in projects concerned with all aspects of Ukrainian studies. The Institute also works in close cooperation with the Committee on Ukrainian Studies, which supervises and coordinates the teaching of Ukrainian history, language, and literature at Harvard University.

Publication of this book has been made possible in part by the generous bequest of Paul Sawka.

© 2016 by the President and Fellows of Harvard College

All rights reserved
Printed in the U.S. on acid-free paper
Library of Congress Cataloging-in-Publication Data

Names: Baker, Mark R. (History professor), author. | Harvard Ukrainian Research Institute.
Title: Peasants, power, and place : revolution in the villages of Kharkiv Province, 1914-1921 / Mark R. Baker.
Description: Cambridge, Massachusetts : Distributed by Harvard University Press for the Harvard Ukrainian Research Institute, 2016. | Series: Harvard series in Ukrainian studies | Includes bibliographical references and index.
Identifiers: LCCN 2016014321 | ISBN 9781932650150 (pbk. : alk. paper)
Subjects: LCSH: Kharkiv (Ukraine)--History--20th century. | Ukraine--History--Revolution, 1917-1921--Social aspects.
Classification: LCC DK508.95.K53 B35 2016 | DDC 940.3/4775--dc23
LC record available at https://lccn.loc.gov/2016014321

Cover photograph: No. 0-183046 from the H. S. Pshenychnyi Central State Archives of Films, Photographs, and Sound Recordings of Ukraine. Used with permission.
Revised portions of this book originally appeared in *Canadian-American Slavic Studies* and *Journal of Ukrainian Studies*. Used with permission.

Contents

Acknowledgments

THIS BOOK HAS BEEN unusually long in coming, so there are too many people to acknowledge. At the same time, I do not wish to bore anyone with a very long list, so here I note only the most significant contributors to the final product. First, I want to thank my advisors, two leading historians of Eastern Europe and Ukraine: professors Roman Szporluk and John-Paul Himka. I thank them for all their attempts to try to make me into an East European historian. I want especially to thank John-Paul for his patient attention, advice, and friendship throughout my post-graduate life. He is the very model of a mentor.

I would like to acknowledge the many graduate student colleagues, now mostly university professors, for all their help, chats over coffee, and patience with my rants about Ukraine, Russia, Eastern Europe, and peasants. Chris Hilliard, Carolee Pollock, Patrice Dabrowski, Andrew Port, Barbara Keys, Graham Tan, Eric Lohr, and Alex Dillon were my most gracious listeners. I want to point out in particular the friendship and sage advice of Andrew Port, who has helped me from earlier on, reading drafts of some chapters, applying his very sharp mind to my messy thinking, discussing various aspects of social history, and welcoming me into his Ann Arbor home on my sojourns across the United States.

In Ukraine, I want to thank all the unnamed people who helped me wade through the chaotic, confusing web of post-Soviet archives and libraries. Iurii Ivanovich Shapoval and Hennadii Boriak were instrumental in obtaining access to the central archives. In Kharkiv, Viktoria Vikorivna Reznikova, the then director of the Kharkiv regional state archive (DAKhO), was not only kind and ready to assist at all times, but made *her* archive a wonderful place to work. In DAKhO's reading room, I wish to thank Liubov Anatolivna and Larysa Polikarpovna, who everyday made my sometimes exciting, sometimes boring, archival work considerably easier. I would gladly water their plants any time. I wish also to thank my Kharkiv historian colleagues for all their help and lively conversations, especially Serhiy Posokhov and Volodymyr Kravchenko. I want to thank Professor Rex A. Wade (George Mason University), whose good name in Kharkiv opened the doors to these many friendships and who has been most encouraging of my research on this topic. Finally, I want to express my gratitude to Ostap and Viktoria Sereda for all their assistance (and friendship) while adjusting to life in Lviv, Ukraine, where I taught my first year after graduation.

Among my Ukrainian nonacademic friends, I want to acknowledge particularly the consistent support and loving kindness of Raisa Alekseevna Strutinskaia and Anton Antonovich Strutinskii. For quite unknown reasons, this couple welcomed me into their home, made me a part of their little family, and taught me so much about Ukraine's more recent past, recounting their stories of war, loss, sorrow, youthful exuberance, joy, and frivolity around the kitchen table. Sadly, Anton did not live long enough to see the publication of this book; Anton was that rare person who helped anyone who asked without question, as several other graduate students who stayed with them can testify. I miss him terribly.

I also want to thank my colleagues at California State University, Bakersfield. It is very difficult to imagine a more supportive department in which to begin as a recent PhD graduate. Cliona Murphy brought me into the department and set an example of scholarly excellence and teaching enthusiasm. Miriam Raub Vivian was my confidante on many an occasion, her door always open for me to come and complain about this or that mishap in my California academic and personal life. Charles Litzinger, though emeritus by the time of my arrival, continued to play a crucial role in creating community among the department's colleagues; he also provided Mary and me wonderful trips to his seaside home in the early years of our time in California. Alicia Rodriquez and Doug Dodd helped me a great deal in adjusting to life in Bakersfield, were great department colleagues, and hosted wonderful department parties. Jeanne Harrie and Oliver Rink were also incredibly encouraging senior colleagues, always supporting and defending the junior faculty, especially in clashes with the administration. I want to thank Jean Stenehjem for her ready assistance throughout my time at CSUB. Finally, I want to thank Beth Rienzi, a voice of warmth and reason in CSUB's sometimes bureaucratic administration. I also miss her very much.

In the fall of 2008, I took up a new position at Koç University in Istanbul, Turkey. Again, I was fortunate to find helpful department colleagues in Dilek Barlas, Yonca Köksal, and Aslı Niyazioğlu. Can Nacar soon joined the department, and as a labor historian with similar research interests, he became a close intellectual and personal friend. I want to thank him in particular for all his helpful advice, chats over lunch, and for putting up with my rants on all and sundry.

In all my travels and studies across Eurasia, I have often thought how fortunate I am to have such a caring family, a home base to which I can return when I need to. I am lucky enough to consider all my siblings—Beth, Phil, Sandy, Tim, and Dan—my friends. This home and these good fortunes are largely due to the tireless and loving efforts of my parents, Robert Leonard Cecil and Loretta May Baker, who have taught me mostly by their examples how to be a good person. I want to thank them all for their loving support and help along the way.

Finally, I want to thank my own young family. Over the course of reworking this book, Mary and I had two children, Lily and Jasper. More than anyone else, these two bright lights have been able to turn my frowns upside down; there is nothing as inspiring as coming home from a relatively difficult day to hear their stories of the many places and times they have visited in their books, imaginative play, and other learning. Finally, and most important of all, I want to thank my soul mate Mary Elizabeth McCue, without whom I would not have finished graduate school, let alone, created two amazing children, traveled and lived all over the place, and completed this book.

Introduction

At its most basic level this book is an investigation of the interactions between the rural inhabitants of Kharkiv province (now a part of Ukraine) and the numerous governments that claimed authority in the region and across the crumbling Russian Empire over the period from 1914 to 1921. Essentially, it is an attempt to tease out of a wide variety of archival documents the most representative experiences of these people, their encounters with the authorities, other outsiders, and with each other. Focusing as much as the documents will allow on villagers' actions (as opposed to what was said about them or in their name), this study yields two main conclusions: first, peasants acted above all in pursuit of their perceived economic interests, although perceptions were often tied to villagers' own sense of what was fair and just. Whether they strove to stop the Stolypin land reform, protest tsarist officials' efforts to force set prices on their produce, seize lands and forests, or resist the attempts of various governments and occupying armies to requisition their grain, they were primarily motivated by what they took to be best for their economic well-being. The second and, perhaps, more striking conclusion is that despite the integrative effects of the Great War and several governments' attempts to get them to sacrifice for larger conceptions of community, peasants acted largely in a very local manner, reflecting their parochial understanding of the world. If we are to judge by their actions, it would seem that these mostly Ukrainian-speaking rural inhabitants thought of themselves mainly as members of one or another village and not as members of any oppressed "nation" or "class."

This book thus joins a few monographs whose findings have begun to curb the post-1989 enthusiasm to find nationalism at almost every historical turn, stressing rather the localness of people's social and political identities. In her monograph about the ordinary people of Kazan and

Nizhegorod provinces, Sarah Badcock argues that "localism overwhelmed national interests in 1917."[1] Kate Brown asserts in her study of the borderlands between Poland, Ukraine, and Russia in the interwar period, that "to call the villagers in the borderlands Ukrainian or Polish is beside the point. They were, as they often described themselves, simply 'local.'"[2] Kharkiv province has been described as a border region, although I do not think peasants' sense of place was primarily determined by their villages' locations along the border between Russian- and Ukrainian-speaking regions. Rather, I consider localness to be a very common, important, and human characteristic across place and time. In the course of world history it is those who did not think locally that were, in fact, the exception. It is much easier to identify with people one knows personally, works alongside, celebrates with, sees regularly, or at least gossips about than with such abstract notions as nation and class. Local identities, of course, continue to be a major feature of most societies, although, unlike the subjects of this monograph, we modern industrialized citizens tend to think of ourselves primarily as members of a broader group, nation, class, ethnicity, race, or people.

To be focused on a local, tangible world was not simple, nor was it easy for outsiders to understand. Indeed, a key theme revealed in this study is the inability of tsarist officials, revolutionaries, nationalists, Bolsheviks, and communists to understand these peasants' preference for the local. My findings suggest that these villagers did not think of themselves *primarily* as the tsar's subjects, or Ukrainians or Russians or workers or Orthodox or only poor or only "backward," or "kulaks." They were people who had rarely traveled farther than the nearest market town, infrequently felt the fear of outsiders, seldom had to engage non-locals (especially non-peasants), or to explain their context to others. Village life was profoundly contextual, seemingly simple to an outsider, but incredibly intricate to villagers. And the historian's problem is that this context is rarely visible in the extant documents.

Exactly because the majority of peasants of the Russian Empire were illiterate at the time of its collapse, I was forced to employ mostly documents composed by these very outsiders – the officials of those governments who ruled the region over this period: The Russian Imperial Government, the Provisional Government, the Ukrainian Central Rada, the Soviet of People's Commissars, the Hetmanate and its German helpmates, the Ukrainian Directory, the Communist-led Provisional

Worker-Peasant Government, General Anton Denikin's Volunteer Army (often called the "Whites"), and finally the Worker-Peasant Government of Ukraine (also Communist-led). Such a problem with sources is not easy to overcome. My method has been to read these sources very closely and critically, taking into account their creators' biases and paying special attention to accounts of peasants' actions and their direct speech (although recorded by others), in order to get as close to peasants' experiences of this period as possible. The result is an imperfect but still informative and useful portrait of how these villagers experienced this very tumultuous period and interacted with the various governments that claimed to rule over them. And the most consistent pattern to emerge from this examination is villagers' rejection of the various wider conceptions of community that these diverse governments proposed; in the face of numerous life-changing events, they sought refuge in their individual village communities, where at least they knew everyone's name.

*

The historiography on the revolutionary period in Ukraine bears the marks of a politically driven, polarized debate. For much of the post-revolutionary period, interpretations of the revolution were determined by the political requirements of the Ukrainian national and Soviet perspectives.[3]

Histories of the Ukrainian national revolution—from Volodymyr Vynnychenko's socialist-oriented and very personal account to Dmytro Doroshenko's more scholarly, state-building-focused contribution—have never agreed on all aspects of the revolution, but they have shared what Himka calls "a common narrative framework." This shared sense of "the events" results from the very basic rule underlying the national approach to history: whatever promotes the national cause is by definition historically relevant. Seeking to portray in particular those events and people that carried the national cause forward, toward statehood, these historians neglect most other phenomena. The result is a history of a nationally conscious elite and its activities in *making* the Ukrainian revolution; great attention is paid to declarations and political bodies claiming legitimacy over the Ukrainian people, an amorphous mass that is often invoked but rarely investigated.[4] Certainly, a considerable amount of intelligent and informative history has been written within the national paradigm, and the historical controversies over the national roles of the successive

Ukrainian governments have led to some lively debate.[5] But like the interpretative framework that gave rise to them, these controversies have been confined to a quite narrow set of events, institutions and people, an institutional, top-down, political interpretation that leaves almost everything else out. Declarations such as the Four Universals and the actions and debates of the Central Rada (Council) have been examined in great detail. Yet, few historians of the Ukrainian national revolution studied the peasantry, its reactions to the appeals of various governments, or its participation in the revolution.[6]

However, Ukrainian national historiography was far more open, honest and useful than Soviet historiography on the revolution, which Himka aptly describes as the "elaboration of a founder's myth," ideologically driven and quite unreliable as far as the evidence is concerned. Within this myth all those people deemed sufficiently relevant to write about were divided into "revolutionary" pro-Bolshevik forces and "counter-revolutionary, bourgeois-landlord" or "petty-bourgeois nationalist" forces; nothing bad could be said about the former, nothing good about the latter.[7]

Perhaps the saddest aspect of this monumental Soviet effort to fashion a history of the birth of the first socialist state was the failure to create a useful social history. Over the Soviet Union's seventy-year existence, Soviet academics managed to erect a history purportedly about the triumph of "the masses," while largely leaving them out. Although Soviet historians had greater (though limited) access to the sources, and though in Marxism (one could argue) they even possessed the ideological preconditions to write such a history, they instead produced a history of the Communist Party and its (often exaggerated) role in "the events," as defined by the party itself. Some Soviet historians discussed the peasantry in Ukraine during this period, but their work was confined to the type of interpretations prevalent in Soviet historiography in general. For example, I. V. Khmil′ carried out research in nine different Soviet archives and perused numerous Bolshevik newspapers, but came to the same conclusion professed by Lenin in 1917: that the union of the poor peasantry and the workers, led by the Bolshevik Party, was "the necessary condition for the victory of the socialist revolution in our country."[8]

Both these historiographical traditions selected which events, people, and institutions were worthy of inclusion according to a preconceived understanding or philosophy of history; for Soviet historians it was class struggle; for national historians it was national struggle. One assumed that people's primary form of identification was their class, as determined by their relations to the means of production; the other that people mainly thought (or, at least, *should* have thought) of themselves as members of a nation. Bringing these very different philosophies of history to their research and writings about the revolution, both Soviet and national historians tended to ignore or mention only in passing those people who did not take some active part (positive or negative) in "the struggle." Considering their numbers and importance to the revolution's outcome, peasants have been without a doubt the most neglected group.

In the immediate post-Soviet period, most historians in independent Ukraine embraced the national paradigm. "Sacred texts" such as the Four Universals and the Central Rada's other decrees and debates have been examined in great detail and lavishly republished.[9] These texts are an important part of the history of Ukraine and should be made known to the country's citizens. But in this period there clearly emerged the unbalanced privileging of these texts, and especially those who composed them, over everything else as part of a new "founder's myth." Instead of Lenin and Stalin, we were presented with Symon Petliura, Vynnychenko, and above all Mykhailo Hrushevs′kyi (to be sure, in a much more sophisticated and honest way).[10] A 2004 historiographical review asserted that the revolution's "most controversial question" is the "evaluation of the state-creating potential of the ideological doctrines of the Ukrainian leadership."[11] While Ukraine's citizens are becoming familiar with some formerly unknown and important aspects of their past—the national leaders, their institutions, and numerous decrees—Ukrainian historians are only beginning to write a viable and even-handed social history of Ukraine's peasants' experiences of the revolutionary period.

More recently, some Ukrainian historians have turned to the peasantry, recognizing, as Hrushevs′kyi did already in 1918, that Ukraine's fate has always been intimately linked with the peasantry.[12] Although this new attention is relatively limited, it has proven sufficiently significant to warrant a scholarly journal, *Ukraïns′kyi selianyn* (Ukrainian peasant), which began publication in 2000 and devotes significant attention to peasants during the revolutionary period.[13] These pioneering studies have focused on three aspects of the subject: some studies strove to find among the peasantry the "formation of a social base of the national revolution."[14] My perusal of those studies reveals that this support was insubstantial and fleeting. This study's findings also question peasants' support for the Ukrainian nation, as do some more recent studies discussed below.

A second group of historians have focused on the Bolsheviks' efforts to impose communism and totalitarianism on Ukrainian peasants. In this interpretation, the Bolsheviks are portrayed basically as evildoers, bent on subordinating all peasants to their control and brainwashing them with their ideology.[15] These studies are in some ways more convincing; they tend, however, to give the Bolsheviks too much credit and power. In a few words, the relationship between peasants and Bolsheviks was not simple or purely antagonistic; at times, peasants supported the Bolsheviks, even called themselves "Bolsheviks" and fought for them, while at other times they resisted (both passively and violently) the Bolsheviks and their policies. This study will also present considerable evidence that totalitarianism had not yet been established in the villages of the Ukrainian Socialist Soviet Republic in the early 1920s.[16] The establishment of Soviet power, as defined by the center, was an uneven and protracted process.

The third and most promising trend in the historiography involves some younger historians, who have turned to the peasant insurgent uprisings from 1917 to 1921, I believe, out of a desire to find a more inspiring story than that of an oppressed nation (Ukraine) and its oppressor (Muscovites/Bolsheviks).[17] While these studies still originate from within the national narrative, their findings are beginning to shift the focus elsewhere. Most important for this discussion, these studies reveal that the majority of peasants who rose up against the communist regimes in Ukraine from 1917 to 1921 valued above all their local interests; most were not struggling for the "building of independent Ukraine,"[18] but rather to be left alone to farm their fields and live their lives in peace.

One can track this more promising direction through the work of Ol'ha Hanzha, who initially focused on Bolshevik evil and assumed that peasants possessed national consciousness. In her most recent publication, a 2006 effort to summarize post-1991 work on the "peasant insurgent movement," she notes that most peasant insurgents were not led by political parties or motivated by any particular ideology. Their dominant slogans were "Peace to [our] houses, war on the palaces!" and "Land to the peasants!" Although she still assumes that peasants were unequivocally "anti-communist," she concludes that most supported the slogan of "all power to the soviets," though their intent was to implement this idea "only in their native village or county." That is, their idea of "soviet power" was profoundly local. This statement is, in fact, doubly significant, because it appears in a book that is a sort of "official history" of the Ukrainian peasantry, published by the Institute of History of Ukraine of the National Academy of Sciences. Hanzha seems to bemoan this localness as some sort of archaic defect, blaming the peasantry's "overall low political literacy."[19] By contrast, I will argue neither for or against peasants' localness, but rather chart its prevalence and importance to them in these turbulent times.

This book, thus begins to remedy a serious deficiency in our understanding of Ukraine's past. By focusing on the ways peasants experienced the world-shattering events of World War I, the revolutions, and the Civil War, I hope to widen our understanding of this crucial period in Ukrainian history and to bring into question longstanding assumptions about peasants' identities. More broadly, the book challenges our understanding of the ways in which people experience revolutionary change by suggesting that the most representative experiences are not always those of the "vanguard," fighting for their political and economic liberation, but those of common people, struggling for their daily existence.

*

One might look to studies of the Russian Revolution for alternative approaches to a social history of the revolutionary period. Despite the wealth of research and debate that historians have brought to the history of the revolution, there remain in this broader and more intensely studied body of work at least four surprisingly significant, neglected areas: (1) the provinces; (2) the peasants; (3) the non-Russian territories; and (4) events before and after 1917.

Although most social historians of the revolution justify their work as an attempt to uncover the experiences of the "masses," they have focused largely on a minority: the proletariat of the empire's main cities. The provinces, where most subjects of the tsar lived, have been neglected. In Murray Frame's quite comprehensive bibliography of sources on the revolutionary period from 1905 to 1921, the section on "Revolution in the Provinces" contains only 31 citations (of 4304).[20] Although Donald Raleigh's studies of the revolution and civil war in Saratov province help to fill in this gap, there are relatively few similarly focused studies.[21]

While more work has been done on peasants, they are still a largely neglected group in comparison to workers and the leading political groups of the revolution. As John Channon suggests, this bias towards workers is due primarily to many Western social historians' Marxist leanings and their general bias towards "the urban revolution."[22] In Frame's bibliography one can find about 110 citations of works focused on peasants; of these only 21 deal with the period from 1914 to 1921; by contrast, of the 110 listed studies of workers, more than 50 deal with the same period.[23] Although considerable work has been done since this bibliography was published, the gap between the peasants' proportion of the empire's population and the historical works on their experiences of war and revolution is still wide.

One exceptional study, Orlando Figes's *Peasant Russia, Civil War: The Volga Countryside in Revolution (1917–1921)*, strives to compensate for the lack of both regional and peasant-centered studies, providing a sophisticated analysis of the peasantry's actions and reactions during the revolution. By examining a region of central importance to the Bolsheviks' victory in the civil war in European Russia, he also sheds light on the reasons for their victory. He argues that the support of the peasantry was "essential to the conduct of any military campaign." Both the Red and White armies included a significant number of peasants; both armies were fed and transported by peasants; most of their footwear, saddlery, and clothing was made by peasant craftsmen; and the peasants carried out labor service for these armies, clearing snow from roads and rail lines, breaking ice on rivers, and digging fortifications and graves.[24] Figes asserts that strategic advantages and superior political skills were not enough to explain the Bolsheviks' victory. Rather the determining factor was the Bolsheviks' ability "to integrate lower-class elements into the construction of the Soviet regime through the local soviets and mass-membership organizations."[25] This study will show, however, that such an integration did not take place in the villages of Kharkiv province or in much of the UkSRR; village cohesion trumped the limited advantages the new regime proffered in the Ukrainian countryside.

A third major gap in the literature on the Russian Revolution is the treatment of the non-Russian nationalities of the multinational *Rossiiskaia imperiia*. Ignoring the multiethnic composition of the empire,[26] many social and political historians have portrayed the revolution as "the Russian Revolution," somewhat unconsciously treating the Russians' experience as the overall revolutionary one. Certainly some Western historians have examined the plight of the non-Russian nationalities during the revolution, but with a few important exceptions these studies have not been the work of historians of the Russian Revolution. Rather, as in the Ukrainian case, historians of the non-Russian nationalities have (understandably) focused on the national struggles coincident with that revolution, and interpreted the latter as "a national war of Russians against minorities, the center against the peripheries."[27] The result has been a bifurcated scholarship of mutual unintelligibility: "Whereas much of the new social history depicts the revolution in the central Russian cities as a struggle between increasingly polarized social classes, or at least an intense pulling apart of the *verkhi* (top) and the *nizy* (bottom) of society, historians of the revolution in the borderlands have traditionally emphasized ethnic rather than social struggles."[28]

Finally, one should note the great attention historians have paid to the year 1917. Apart from a few general surveys, social histories of the revolution tend to focus almost exclusively on that year, ignoring both the impact of World War I and the Civil War. Although some recent studies carry through to 1921, few historians have attempted to traverse the period from the beginning of large-scale violence in July 1914 to the more conclusive end of the Civil War, when most peasants stopped openly resisting the regime's efforts to impose its control over them.[29]

*

This book then, while contributing to our knowledge of the provinces and the peasants, spans the revolutionary period from 1914 to 1921, and presents a quite different picture of the revolution among non-Russians. Following Figes, I seek to move the historiography beyond 1917, the capitals, and the workers, but at the same time I strive to explain how some non-Russians experienced the revolution. While bringing out the importance of peasants' perceived economic interests in their actions and reactions to these tumultuous events, and how these actions helped and hindered the efforts of various governments and armies to assert their power over Kharkiv province, the book shows how locally peasants thought. Their *primary* form of identity through much of this period was neither "their class" nor "their nation" (they may not have even thought that they had one), but rather their village, at most their volost (approximately equivalent to a small county). Hence, when some peasants supported one government, this did not mean all did, nor did it suggest a lasting commitment.

Among the mostly Ukrainian-speaking peasants of this province I have found little evidence of sympathy for Ukrainian nationalism. The Ukrainian national revolution of 1917–1921 was for these peasants only the beginning of their exposure to the national idea, the start of a long and halting process that, it could be argued, has yet to be completed in contemporary, independent Ukraine. Hence, this study of peasants in a non-Russian province of the empire challenges our understanding of peasants' role in the revolution, of the process of revolution outside the central Russian provinces, and of the importance of nationalism in non-Russian areas of the empire.

Historical Background on Kharkiv Province and its Peasants

Before beginning the main narrative, some background on Kharkiv province and its peasants before the Great War is in order. Founded as a military defense post in the mid-seventeenth century, Kharkiv lost this function as the empire sprawled beyond the town's environs in the eighteenth century. Simultaneously, the town took on the growing administrative tasks of a regional center. In 1765 the Cossack administrative system of Slobids′ka Ukraine, still enjoying considerable autonomy, was abolished and replaced by *Slobodsko-Ukrainskaia guberniia* with its capital in Kharkov (Russian spelling). In 1780 this *guberniia* became the Kharkov general-government (*namestnichestvo*) and in 1836 the region was renamed Kharkov province (Khar′kovskaia guberniia), remaining so up to 1920. By the outbreak of World War I, Kharkiv had evolved from a frontier outpost to an important administrative, trade, educational, and industrial center of the Russian Empire.[30]

In early Muscovite documents the original settlers of the region were referred to as "Cherkasy." They migrated mainly from the villages of Kyiv, Volhynia, and Podilia provinces, seeking land not dominated by the great Polish land magnates of Right-Bank Ukraine. They spoke a Ukrainian dialect, were from the beginning primarily interested in cultivating the land, and were not exactly admired by the newly arriving imperial authorities. The region's main military commander at the time, Voevoda Ofrosimov, referred to the settlers as "riffraff" and "country bumpkins [*muzhiki derevenskie*]."[31]

In the nineteenth century, trade and administrative Russification policies brought a large Russian population to the region's center, Kharkiv/ Kharkov, leading many urban Ukrainian-speakers to learn Russian. The abolition of serfdom, the development of industry, and the construction of railroads, with Kharkiv as a regional hub, accelerated Russian migration to and Russification of the city. According to the first empire-wide census of 1897, in Kharkiv city 109,914 declared themselves to be Russian speakers (63 percent), whereas only 45,092 acknowledged themselves as Ukrainian speakers (26 percent).[32] Surrounding this quite Russified urban population was a great mass of Ukrainian-speaking peasants. Those who declared their native tongue to be Ukrainian (*Maloross*) numbered 2,009,411, or 80.6 percent, of the province's total population; those claiming Russian as their native tongue numbered 440,936 (17.7 percent).[33] Of the latter group, about one-third lived in the cities of the province, while only ten percent of declared Ukrainian-speakers lived in the province's urban settlements.[34] Bearing in mind the gradual, but quite incessant, Russification of the city and administration, reaching out to the countryside, it is not surprising that most of these Ukrainian-speaking peasants came to equate becoming literate and educated with learning to speak, read, and write in Russian. When peasants composed appeals to the authorities or addressed outsiders, they did so in Russian, the language of district government officials, the police, grain merchants, the city, the governor, and the tsar.

The overwhelming majority of these peasants little resembled the mythical independent yeoman farmer often portrayed in the national historiography on Ukrainian peasants and now seemingly revived in independent Ukraine.[35] Most peasants of Kharkiv province were in fact active members of the repartitional commune. From 1877 to 1905, the amount of privately owned agricultural land in the province actually decreased by 52,000 desiatynas (des.), while the amount of land held in communal ownership increased from 57.7 percent to 59.2.[36] These communes were certainly not without internal conflicts, but the majority of peasants seem to have preferred the commune's powerful formal and informal rules for spreading the risks of harvest failure and checking the attempts of the few to disrupt larger collective interests to the more dangerous prospect of striking out on their own individual farmsteads.[37]

Over this same period, the number of communal households dramatically increased by about 40 percent (from 261,400 to 364,100 households), while the number of communes slightly decreased. The peasant population rapidly outpaced the land area held by these communes: the number of des. held per peasant household fell from 9.8 in 1877 to 7.3 in 1905. Although the gentry in this period sold off much of their land (almost 40 percent), few peasants were able to purchase it; by 1905 only 10,757 peasant households (just three percent) owned land privately, though each of these households owned about 24 des. Moreover, in 1905 almost one quarter of all agricultural land in the province was still owned by non-peasants (1,084,116 of 4,497,271 des. or 24.1 percent).[38] This is not the place to enter into the long-standing debate over whether the Great Reforms were overall beneficial for peasants or not, but there is much evidence (and more to come) that they did not believe themselves to have benefited. As their numbers continued to rise at an accelerated pace, they increasingly resented the non-peasant landowners in their midst, especially because most of the latter did not work the land with their own hands, but hired peasants as rural laborers at low wages or rented it out to them at exorbitant rates.

Not surprisingly, the peasants of Kharkiv province took quite an active part in the rural disturbances of 1902–1903 and 1905–1906, plundering property and seizing land from the landlords' estates, non-peasants' properties, and even from other peasants.[39] According to one soviet source, there were as many as 885 peasant disturbances (*vystupy*) in the province between 1905 and 1907. These disturbances took the form of attacks on landlords' estates, seizures of landlords' and other peasants' lands, and refusals to submit to local authorities.[40] Peasants' actions took on their most organized form in the province's northern district of Sumy under the charismatic leadership of A. P. Shcherbak, returned Californian emigrant and radical rural activist. Leading the Sumy district peasant union, Shcherbak encouraged local peasants to take decisive actions to establish their own sort of "peasant rule" in several of the district's volosts. At large assemblies in the fall of 1905, peasant union activists called for political reform, better education for peasants, and above all "the expropriation of gentry and church lands for equal distribution among the laboring masses."[41] Shcherbak and his followers advocated nonviolent actions rather than brute force to achieve their demands, such as strikes of peasant laborers working on the estates and refusals to pay taxes or to provide men for the army. Indeed, "peasant rule," of which some historians have made much, mostly involved peasants refusing to obey local officials' orders.[42] Eventually, in mid-December 1905 the government violently suppressed the Sumy peasant union, arresting Shcherbak and other "instigators."[43]

Out of the fire and violence of the first revolutionary outbreak, the begrudging and hesitant moves of Tsar Nicholas and his ministers toward compromise, and then the conservative step back of June 1907, peasants did not come close to fulfilling their dream of the great Black Repartition (*chornyi peredil*)—a radical, equal redistribution of all lands among those willing to work it with their own hands. Instead, the tsarist government under the guidance of Petr Stolypin offered peasants a land reform primarily intended to insure order in the countryside. Striving to overcome the assumed "backwardness" of peasants' farming methods, mainly by reorganizing the "farrago of land patchworks and strips" into separately consolidated farms, Stolypin's reform sought to transform communally minded, risk-averse peasants into loyal, landowning farmer-citizens with a greater stake in the established order.[44] In effect, though not in word, the reform was an assault on the commune. Unfortunately for Stolypin and the agrarian reformers, many peasants quickly perceived this and did all they could to resist.[45]

In Kharkiv province the reforms made very little progress in their early stages. By May 1908 only 13,700 (about four percent) of the province's peasant households had declared the desire to have their land consolidated as private property. In addition, many of these households probably belonged to land-poor peasants, desiring to consolidate their tiny allotment plots only in order to sell them immediately and move to urban areas.[46] Thereafter, a more substantial number of the province's peasants seem to have warmed to the government's efforts. According to the research of V. S. Maistrenko, by 1 January 1914 more than 94,000 of the province's peasant households (about 27 percent) had declared a desire to gain title to or consolidate their communal strips (about 500,000 des. in all). It should be noted, however, that by this date only 14,352 (about four percent) of these households had actually accepted the certification acts necessary to carry out their declarations.[47]

Nevertheless, because a relatively large number of the province's peasant households did declare a desire to take part in the reform, we must dwell briefly on the nature of these "consolidations" and what they say about the peasants' attitudes toward their commune and community.[48] Those peasants who applied to receive title to their plots did not for the most part intend to leave the commune, but only to secure permanent ownership of the plots that their household already held. In effect this aspect of the Stolypin reforms forced peasants to decide between "fixing the land currently in their possession and as a consequence sacrificing any future claim they had on commune land, pressing for a repartition, or waiting to see how events would unfold."[49] The more risky act of consolidating one's land into a separate farm (*otrub* or *khutor*) was attempted only by the daring or reckless few, and the panic such acts evoked among co-villagers proved to be *the* driving force behind many village-wide consolidations. Indeed, most of the declarations to consolidate in Kharkiv province were village-wide. For example, in the village of Slaviansk, Kharkiv province, the decision of just 18 households to enclose their land provoked the village's other 607 households to join in the consolidation. The province's leading land reform officials observed at the time that a crucial feature of land reorganization was that "individual separations are transformed into commune-led enclosures."[50] Judith Pallot has convincingly argued that these commune-led enclosures were motivated by peasants' fears of receiving the worst plots of land or losing access to pasture lands, as well as their desire to regain for the commune some degree of control over the otherwise government-enforced redistribution of their limited resources. The land reform legislation stipulated that all commune-wide consolidations required the approval of the commune's assembly, while granting no "override" to land reorganization officials; if the commune petitioned for consolidation as a unit, it could then delay the process indefinitely.[51] Hence, the relatively large number of peasants and villages in Kharkiv province who proclaimed their intention to consolidate their land does not suggest that many of them desired to farm independent consolidated plots, nor to leave the commune. Many commune-wide declarations were in fact quite rational attempts to stave off the worst effects of the reforms' implementation.

Structure of the Book

As the first two chapters of this book will show, the Great War and the revolutions of 1917 (which the war in part provoked) laid bare the fragility of the Stolypin land reform effort and the resilience of the commune. During the war many peasants in Kharkiv province, particularly *soldatki*—the wives of mobilized soldiers—openly resisted attempts to continue the land reform's realization, eventually forcing the government to halt the land reorganization committees' work altogether in May 1915. But peasants' newly found activism did not end there; they protested local officials' repeated attempts to impose low prices on the produce they brought to market and local authorities' efforts to enforce those prices. The February Revolution freed peasants to reorganize their lives and land relations as the majority desired. One of the first actions of many village communities was to reabsorb—sometimes voluntarily, sometimes violently—those few who had separated from them. As members of their village community, peasants then embarked on an attenuated version of their long-unrealized Black Repartition. Their semilegal and illegal seizures of the lands of non-peasants soon provoked numerous intervillage conflicts over the redistribution of their newly acquired resources. Indeed, much of peasants' behavior in 1917 and thereafter revealed their very strong sense of local identity, as expressed not only in these numerous intervillage conflicts, but also in their unwillingness to sacrifice for larger ideas of community. The Bolshevik coup in October 1917 forced Kharkov/Kharkiv into a contested position between two conflicting visions of revolution, one in Kyiv and one in Moscow. Lenin's Soviet of People's Commissariats chose to solve this conflict by violent and undemocratic means. The Ukrainian Central Rada, after several pleas for compromise, responded in kind, eventually resorting to the Central Powers' "assistance." In chapter 3 I demonstrate that this "assistance," in effect an occupation, proved to be a fundamental turning point for the revolutionary process in Ukraine. The occupation cut off the Ukrainian People's Republic's new citizens from the brutal side of Soviet power to the north, while presenting a nasty version of an "independent," "Ukrainian" state to its citizens; they soon rejected not only the Hetmanate, but also its successor, the reformed Ukrainian National Republic, now led by the Directory, and poorly represented by Petro Bolbochan's forces on Left-Bank Ukraine. Chapter 4 will show how the civil war of 1919 brought anarchy and greater brutality to the countryside and hunger to the city. The Soviet government of that year attempted to force collective agriculture on the peasants and employed ruthless methods to requisition their grain, inciting many peasants to open revolt. This revolt facilitated the arrival of General Denikin's Volunteer Army (VA) in June 1919, as it pressed on towards Moscow. The VA's occupation policies and its unwillingness to alleviate peasants' fears about its "restorationist" and "counter-revolutionary essence" made the

Soviet regime's return in December palatable to many peasants. Indeed, as chapter 5 will show despite the numerous mistakes of the Soviet government of the previous year, the province's peasants in early 1920 expressed a great willingness to compromise with the new Soviet regime and the new leaders of the reorganized Communist Party (Bolsheviks) of Ukraine. But when those leaders refused to listen to peasants' conciliatory requests for local autonomy, free trade, and an end to requisitions, and attempted to impose their rule over the province, peasants again resisted, refusing to give up their grain to the city or their men to the army. This regime responded with more violence and few carrots, provoking numerous increasingly broad-scale disturbances across the province. In fact, the regime's attempts to requisition peasants' excess grain and to create a base of support in the village failed almost entirely, until it belatedly and begrudgingly implemented the New Economic Policy. Even then, many peasants continued to resist the regime's efforts to consolidate its power in the village, openly until at least 1924, when the "struggle against banditry" was officially declared completed, and in more covert forms throughout the 1920s.

*

This book undoubtedly provokes questions about the representativeness of Kharkiv province and its peasants. So few studies of a similar kind have been done that comparison is difficult. In addition, the variegated geography and history of Ukraine and Russia make it hard to see how any one region could be considered representative of the overall experience of the revolutionary period. Kharkiv peasants shared with the majority of the empire's peasants the repartional commune as a land management system. The rich, black soil of the region made the province a net exporter of grain (mostly to the north); it thus had more in common with other grain-producing areas. Ukrainian historians may try to dismiss this study's findings, claiming that Kharkiv province's location near Russian-speaking regions and long period under Russian control transformed its peasants into a peculiar Russo-Ukrainian amalgam, and hence somehow less representative of Ukrainian peasants. Alternatively, Russian historians may discount this work as focused on a "Ukrainian province," not representative of Russian peasants' experiences. Both would be wrong.

Indeed, I would argue that dividing peasants into national categories obscures more than it helps understanding.

While these peasants certainly possessed many local peculiarities, there are important ways in which their experiences were similar to other peasants across the empire. Over the period from 1914 to 1918, all the empire's peasants endured the mobilizations and hardships of World War I, and then took part in the revolutions of 1917, especially the seizures of land and forest. The German occupation of 1918 changed much of this. But even then, peasants' experience of the second Soviet government in 1919, its brutal and crude attempts to bring about communism in the countryside, bore close parallels to Russian-speaking peasants' experiences of the previous year. The attempts to introduce the Committees of Not-Well-Off Peasants (KNSs) also bear striking resemblance to the introduction of Committees of Poor Peasants in the RFRSR in 1918, although the Ukrainian communists proved far more persistent in this regard. In addition, Kharkiv peasants' continued resistance to the attempts to requisition their grain and mobilize their men, sometimes leading to large-scale uprisings, bears similarities to other areas, especially in Tambov and Saratov provinces. Moreover, as I note at various points in the book, the localness of peasants' identity seems to have been a common feature in quite disparate parts of the empire. Recent studies of the peasant insurgencies of 1917–1923 in other provinces in Ukraine reveal the localness of these insurgents' identities; Graham Tan's work on peasants of Right-Bank Ukraine also confirms peasants' attachment to their village community (*hromada* in Ukrainian). In addition, Sarah Badcock's study of Nizhegorod and Kazan provinces, two provinces quite distinct in geography, industry, and culture from Kharkiv province, demonstrates that the tendency for local self-identification was not particularly Ukrainian. Hence, though more studies are necessary to make more solid generalizations, it appears that peasants' localness was quite a widespread phenomenon across the crumbling Russian Empire.

1 The Social Effects of the Great War in Kharkiv Province

As in all belligerent countries,[1] but perhaps to an even greater degree in the Russian Empire, World War I's direct and indirect exactions tore apart the very fabric of society, making any return unthinkable. And this was not only the case in those areas near the front lines or in the empire's capitals, but in such remote places as Kharkiv province, where not even the faint rumbling of artillery guns could be heard. First of all, the war brought important economic changes to the province's villages. Though the evidence is less than complete, it is clear that the mobilizations of men and livestock impoverished many peasant households, forcing them to decrease their sown areas, or give up on farming altogether. In addition, the number of peasants able to engage in wage labor outside their farms, in order to supplement or replace their declining harvests, sharply decreased. At the same time, some better-off peasant households continued to do well during the war and some even prospered.

The resultant growing economic disparity within the village did not, however, lead directly to class conflict. Instead, from the very start of the war, conflicts broke out over the continuing implementation of the Stolypin land reforms between a minority of (usually) better-off peasants, who wished to separate from the peasant commune, and the rest of the villagers, who did not wish to have their communal allotments redistributed. In these disturbances, *soldatki*—the wives of men fighting in the active army—played an important part, reflecting the war's impact on gender roles. In fact, during the war women led almost all large-scale actions in which peasants participated, though they rarely acted alone. These actions eventually forced the government to put aside the land reforms, but these newly empowered villagers did not stop there. In the spring and summer of 1916, rampant inflation and local officials' attempts to curb it served as critical catalysts, provoking significant disturbances at local markets. Though in the period leading up to the February Revolution they largely dissipated, these conflicts left deep wounds and underlying animosities in the village and in the marketplace, which would reemerge, once peasants began to learn of the tsar's abdication in the spring of 1917.

The Economic Impact of Mobilization

For most of the inhabitants of Kharkiv province, the unprecedented large-scale mobilization of working-age males declared by Tsar Nicholas II on 17 (30) July 1914, was the most profound and personal result of the war.[2] As was true across the empire, the overall impact was greater in the countryside, whence, over the course of the war, 339,678 men were mobilized, representing 50 percent of all working-age men of the province's peasant households (in 1917).[3] Of course, before World War I men had been drafted into the army, but never on such an extraordinary scale. For every ten pre–World War I peasant households in Kharkiv province there were on average about fourteen working-age men; by 1917 there were only seven.[4] During the war, the labor of these drafted men was replaced by that of women and of men too young or too old to serve; by mid-1917 these groups comprised 64.3 percent of all able-bodied work hands in the province's peasant households.[5]

In reality, however, men were not drafted so evenly across households. By 1917 in Kharkiv province 36.4 percent of peasant households (168,383 of 462,923) had no adult male workers.[6] The remaining 294,540 households shared among themselves 341,392 working-age males (about 12 for every 10 households). The uneven and often corrupt methods of mobilization provoked considerable discontent among rank-and-file soldiers. For example, in the spring of 1915, trench soldiers from Nyzhnia Syrovatka volost, Sumy district, complained in a letter to General M. V. Alekseev, Chief of the Russian Imperial General Staff, that even more offensive to them than the brutal way that government officials were treating their wives (about which more below) was that some of the better off men subject to call-up had managed to remain at home. The soldiers listed a number of men by name (mostly merchants and their sons) and declared, "Here is the source from which the district police superintendent gains [*nazhil*] hundreds of thousands [of rubles], thanks to the patronage of the

Marshal of the Nobility." Declaring this to be a great crime, the soldiers concluded that they would lay down their weapons and give themselves up as prisoners to the enemy in protest.[7]

Not only men were mobilized. Livestock, especially horses, were requisitioned on a grand scale with dire consequences for the typical one-horse peasant farm. Data from the Mobilization Department of the Imperial General Staff and the Ministry of Internal Affairs indicate that about 2,760,000 horses were mobilized, requisitioned, or purchased from the entire rural population of the empire for the army over the period from August 1914 to September 1917.[8]

On the surface, peasants of Kharkiv province do not seem to have suffered too badly from this massive mobilization. In 1913 the 330,900 peasant households (including all districts except Starobilsk) held 375,700 head of work horses;[9] by 1916, 358,767 households held 377,494 horses;[10] and in 1917 there were 392,742 households with 386,745 working horses.[11] Thus, the province's peasants suffered a relative decrease in horses per household from 1.135 to 0.985 over the course of the war, but this was not that substantial, especially when compared to the proportions of human mobilization.

As with the mobilization of men, however, procurement of horses was not carried out evenly. According to the law on horse mobilization, even those households owning only one horse could have it mobilized, while those owning several had to give up only half of them, less if they owned an odd number of horses. The Soviet historian, A. M. Anfimov, argues that this law placed most of the horse mobilization burden on the poorer peasant households, while rich "kulaks" and landlords were able to hide their better horses from requisition. For example, Aleksei [most likely Oleksii] Piavko, a rich peasant from neighboring Poltava province owning 30 horses and two farmsteads [*khutory*] in two adjacent *volosts*, moved his horses back and forth between them, depending on which one was carrying out a mobilization.[12] Such violations appear to have been widespread. In a perlustrated letter one landowner complained that "many of the landowners and peasants absolutely do not present their good horses" during mobilization; no one was willing to speak out against such behavior. At the same time, he noted the detrimental impact of repeated mobilization on poorer peasants: "in Zmiïv [Kharkiv province], for example, during the first mobilization they took the one horse a peasant owned; he bought another one and they took that; he bought a third—it is registered [to be mobilized]. Or if there were two horses, they took one in the first mobilization, the second in the next."[13] In addition, the price paid for mobilized horses, set by the government back in 1911, was not sufficient to replace their value, especially after the first horse mobilization, when prices on horses began to rise rapidly. Lieutenant Colonel Adamovich, sent out in March 1916 to investigate the causes of the horse shortage, reported that when their horses were mobilized, peasants lost not only the work time they then had to spend finding another horse; in addition, the former owners would have to raise twice the miserly amount paid by the army to purchase another. They were thus forced to buy new horses on credit, and then these newly purchased horses were often also mobilized in exchange for the earlier mobilized and now exhausted ones. As a result of these mistakes and problems, Adamovich concluded, peasants had lost the possibility and desire to acquire good horses, "and as a majority they do not consent to the delivery of horses to the troops."[14] Government-set prices for horses were not raised until 15 May 1916, after two million head had already been mobilized.

The requisition of cattle was also a considerable burden to peasants. In fact, from 1914 to 1916 the Ministry of Agriculture mistakenly assigned Kharkiv province to deliver more cattle than it should have, because the ministry overestimated the province's total cattle stock in 1913 (949,000 head, when in fact there were only 758,567). The error was multiplied by repeated mobilizations. The ministry received numerous petitions from the Kharkiv provincial and district zemstvo officials to lower the assigned quotas. In early July 1916 the chairman of the Valky district zemstvo, Dublianskii, telegrammed the Minister of Agriculture, A. N. Naumov, complaining that the War Department had responded to the provincial zemstvo's numerous petitions to reduce the monthly livestock norms by increasing them. If the norms continued to be filled at their assigned rates, the population of Valky district would soon find itself in a critical situation, both from the absence of nutrition from milk products and from the lack of livestock to work the land. Recently, the zemstvo had calculated that the district possessed almost no reserves of livestock, and thus, the completion of the government's orders threatened "the complete requisition of all available livestock." The ministry finally reduced the province's norms in late July 1916, though by then much of the damage had been done.[15]

Putting aside Anfimov's ideologized rhetoric, it does seem that he was basically correct to argue that the poorer members of the village suffered most from these livestock mobilizations. A comparison of the yearly overall livestock figures for the province from 1910 to 1917 reveals that the worst impact of these requisitions was felt in the first year of the war, after which the province *as a whole* seems to have recovered.[16] However, we must keep in mind that these mobilizations were not carried out uniformly and that considerable corruption exacerbated the situation. By 1917 there were 157,579 households (35 percent of the province's 450,650 households) with no *working* livestock: 84,605 farms had no livestock at all, and 72,974 owned work animals that were either too young or too old, or for some other reason could not be used to work the land.[17]

On an empire-wide scale, the province's villagers were comparatively hard-hit by the livestock mobilization. Comparing the livestock holdings of thirteen provinces for which prewar data is available with that of the 1917 agricultural census, Anfimov found that the number of farms without any working livestock increased from the prewar period: from 25.7 to 30.7 percent, still five percent less than in Kharkiv province.[18] In addition, 167,870 of the province's peasant households did not own a single cow by 1917.[19]

*

It is not easy to evaluate the economic consequences of these mobilizations of men and animals. One would expect a significant decrease in the land area peasant households were able to cultivate. Table 1 below provides some indication of the changes felt by the peasants of the province through 1917.[20] Because the 1913 figures quantify area sown, while the 1917 numbers refer to arable land, the dramatic increase in land-poor households from 1913 to 1917 may have been even more pronounced than these statistics suggest. Clearly, one of the most important effects of the war was to increase substantially the number of peasant households not farming any land at all. Moreover, by 1917 the number of households farming three desiatynas or less had increased by more than 50 percent since 1913, from 134,456 to 204,984 households. According to official zemstvo investigations in Kharkiv and Poltava provinces, no less than three desiatynas of sown land was necessary in order to feed an average peasant family (5–6 people) and its livestock. Employing traditional farming methods, which

Table 1. Number of households by amount of arable land sown or plowed.

1913			1917		
Sown land (in desiatynas)	**No. of farms**	**Pct.**	**Plowed land (in desiatynas)**	**No. of farms**	**Pct.**
none	46,812	14.0	none	99,048	22.0
0.1–1.0	15,690	4.7	0.1–1.0	22,018	4.9
1.1–3.0	71,954	21.4	1.1–3.0	83,918	18.6
3.1–4.0	68,110	20.3	3.1–5.0	75,993	16.9
4.1+	132,808	39.6	5.1–10.0	102,816	22.8
			10.1–15.0	37,019	8.2
			15.1+	29,832	6.6
TOTAL	335,374	100.0		450,644	100.0

Note: A desiatyna equals 2.7 acres.

were especially prevalent among those farms holding such small amounts of land, these peasants would have been hard-pressed to provide sufficient nutrition for themselves and their dependents.[21]

One might suggest that these small farms supplemented their meager harvests with other sources of income. Indeed, according to the 1913 provincial zemstvo census, those districts with less land per peasant household reported higher percentages of peasants working outside their own farms, mainly as day-wage agricultural workers on gentry estates, but also in small rural industries—on the railways, in mines, and as construction workers, haulers, and domestic workers. However, by 1917 the number of peasants supplementing their farms' production in this way had declined by 62.8 percent (from 514,389 in 1913 to 191,342 in 1917), suggesting that peasant households were increasingly deprived of the opportunity and labor resources to do such work. Moreover, it seems that those hardest-hit were the poorest farms: the substantial drop in the number of women working outside the farm—from 162,958 to 84,367 (a drop of 48.2 percent)—indicates that the overall decrease was not caused only by the direct mobilization of men, but that many women were forced to give up supplemental wage- or piece-work in order to farm their small plots, while continuing to feed and raise their children.[22]

*

While these statistics suggest that many peasant farms were impoverished by the war's exactions, there are also indications of continuing prosperity among some of the province's rural inhabitants. First of all, the overall harvests from 1913 to 1916 did not substantially decrease, though 1917 witnessed a sharp decline, largely due to the revolutionary events of that year.[23] At the end of the 1916 growing season the province was still producing 90 percent of its prewar grain output in the major crops grown there (and it should be noted that the unusually good harvest of 1913 somewhat distorts the prewar figures upwards).[24] In addition, it is very likely that, as was the case across the empire, a significant portion of the decrease in production came from landlords' estates, which, because of the lack of work hands, sharply decreased their production during the war.[25] Other data reveal that there was no substantial reduction in land area sown between 1916 and 1917, showing a decrease of only 1.3 percent (22,734 desiatynas).[26] Thus, it would seem that the much lower harvest yields of 1917 had far more to do with the events of that year than with the effects of the world war. In addition, peasants significantly underreported their 1917 harvests, worried about being forced to sell their grain at low government-regulated prices to local food supply committees in a year of rampant inflation.[27]

One other important, if more subjective, piece of evidence comes from a survey conducted by the Kharkiv provincial zemstvo in 1917. One of the questions to which the zemstvo's peasant-correspondents were asked to respond was: "Is agriculture getting better or worse in this locality and what are the causes?" Their replies reflect not only their perceptions of their real situation, but the revolutionary optimism of 1917 and the economic position these literate men likely held in their respective village communities. Of 359 responses, 280 (about 78 percent) reported that agriculture was improving in their village; 55 (15 percent) reported that it was getting worse and 24 (7 percent) that the situation remained unchanged.[28] These peasant-correspondents most often attributed their economic improvement to technological innovations—in particular, the use of more advanced farming tools and machines (most often mentioned), changes in the traditional crop-rotation system, the advice and knowledge of local agronomists, the examples set by local model farms and fields, the use of fertilizer, and, finally, their separation from village communes onto privately owned farms, called *otruba*.[29] A few correspondents mentioned the war as a factor improving their farms' productivity. Three reports from Okhtyrka district noted that they were benefiting from "the high prices of the current moment"; one from Izium district mentioned the great demand for foodstuffs at reasonable prices from government and military food supply agencies; another that land rent prices had decreased.[30] Nonetheless, these few comments were outweighed by the numerous times correspondents mentioned the war's negative effects. In ten of the province's eleven districts the war was mentioned at least once as the cause of a drop in agricultural production. Overall, 35 correspondents complained that the scarcity of work hands and livestock, caused by the mobilization, was the reason that their productivity was not increasing.[31]

One cannot deny the peasant-correspondents' overwhelmingly positive response to the zemstvo's question, but how reliable and representative were these correspondents? In the preface to its questionnaire, the zemstvo itself noted that sometimes in the past, when it had attempted to implement measures in the localities based on the correspondents' reports, it had discovered that the latter's information "deviates from reality." Stressing the negative effects that such inaccurate reporting had on its work, the zemstvo appealed to its correspondents "with a most humble request to report only entirely accurate, trustworthy information. It is better absolutely not to provide an answer than to provide an inexact, incorrect [one]."[32] It is also clear that these peasant correspondents were not representative of the peasant community as a whole. Not only were they unusual because they were literate and willing to disclose valuable, local information to "outsiders," but most of those correspondents who reported positive economic progress appear to have been *otrubshchiki*—that is, peasants who had separated from the tradition-bound peasant commune in order to farm privately owned consolidated plots, though they may have continued to live in the village.[33] A correspondent from Okhtyrka district claimed that local peasants now living on consolidated farms had improved their agricultural output fivefold, while in the commune no improvement was noticeable; another boasted "with pride that farming among *us* stands equal with that of the estates," while the communes "remain far from the [agronomic] teachings [*daleko ot znanii*]."[34] One correspondent from Valky district reported that "on correctly established farms improvement is noticeable, but on farms with old-fashioned ways [*s dedovskimi priemami*] there is no improvement."[35]

It would seem, then, that many of these peasant-correspondents subscribed to and were active participants in what Kimitaka Matsuzato has called the "agro-technological revolution." Inspired by the Stolypin reforms that began in 1906, government and zemstvo officials across the empire strove to improve the farming methods and knowledge of all peasants, though in practice they mainly focused on those who had consolidated their plots. Agronomists argued that agricultural improvement was easier in regions where the land reforms had been carried out, because they could organize the consolidated farms anew, without worrying about past land uses, customs, and traditions. They also asserted that their efforts were more effective on those farms, because "the energetic and progressive people very often end up on the restructured farms."[36] To these farms, agronomists and other land reorganization workers brought an "agro-technological revolution" of new metal tools, crop rotation methods, fertilizer and agricultural knowledge. The peasant-correspondents' reports to the zemstvo clearly reflect this attitude toward improvement and the Stolypin reforms. These peasant-farmers were the optimistic, hopeful, and prospering few, proud of their accomplishments to date, and annoyed by the reluctance of the overwhelming peasant majority to follow the path of "improvement" and "progress." Thus, while their reports tell us something about the situation in the village during the Great War, they cannot be taken as representative of peasants' experience as a whole.

*

What then can we conclude from these statistics and reports? Many Western historians have for a long time ignored economic differences within the village in discussing the war's economic impact on the peasantry. Lumping all the peasants together, they have assumed that general prosperity in the countryside meant prosperity for all. On the other hand, Soviet historians, following Lenin, overemphasized "differentiation" within the village during WWI, and more importantly, assumed that this differentiation would necessarily in itself lead to "class struggle." The analysis presented above falls somewhere in between. Some peasants, very likely the same ones who were improving their lot before the war, continued to fare well; some even profited from wartime demands for food supply and changes in the ways food was collected. Prices on agricultural products increased significantly, despite local authorities' attempts to control them, and the army provided a large, reliable, and constant demand for peasants' produce. At the same time, those peasants living closer to subsistence level before the declaration of war—and there were far more of them—were considerably impoverished by the war's exactions. The mobilizations of men and animal labor took from them their only male adult worker, their only horse, and in numerous cases deprived them of the possibility to farm the very small plots they did have or earn supplemental income outside their farms. The clearest and crudest indication of their plight during the war was that the number of peasant farms holding three desiatynas or less increased by more than 50 percent from 1913 to 1917, comprising 45 percent of all peasant farms by 1917. It should be stressed that overall grain production did not significantly decrease until after the February Revolution, but in the midst of a generally prospering countryside, a large segment of each village fell into greater poverty.[37]

The Stolypin Reforms and the Rise of the Soldatki

Although Soviet historians often assumed that such economic changes in themselves determined peasants' behavior, the increasing disparity between rich and poor in the village during World War I did not lead to open class struggle, although its effects were manifested indirectly in some of the conflicts that did arise. There are many different understandings of the term "class struggle," but I have in mind here the classic Marxist definition, in which members of a class, as defined by their relations to the means of production, become conscious of themselves as a class (become a "class for itself") and struggle against another "class," which they perceive to be their oppressor.[38] I am questioning two aspects of this definition: that peasants were conscious of themselves in class terms that transcended the borders of their village; and that they viewed the oppressing class—landlords—as their main enemy. Of course, Marx and Engels themselves recognized that "classes" were a prominent feature only in capitalist societies ("class itself is a product of the bourgeoisie"), and the economic relations in the Ukrainian countryside could hardly be described as capitalist. Indeed, my findings on this issue would not be of great import, had Soviet historians not for seventy-odd years portrayed all the conflicts to be discussed below as "class struggle." Contrary to such claims, the cases below reveal that the war imposed other circumstances that more directly led to social conflict in the village.

First of all, the removal of such a large number of men dramatically (if temporarily) transformed gender roles in the countryside.[39] Men were forced to leave their homes, families, and farms, travel to far-off, unknown places to fight in a war about which they knew (besides what patriotic propaganda told them) only that the chances that they would ever return were not great. As Alan Wildman has shown, soldiers' experiences at the front were not only horrific, but life-changing.[40] From the letters they wrote home, it is clear that many soldiers were radicalized and emboldened by the war; numerous soldiers expressed the intention that when they returned home, they would seize the landlord's land.[41] The mobilization also deprived many men of their traditional authority as heads of peasant households and forced women to take on work and other responsibilities that had previously been strictly within men's domain, both in the factories and on the fields. This led women to rethink who they were, what roles they should play in society, and with whom they most clearly identified.

Perhaps the clearest expression of these shifting gender roles was the rise of the soldatki, women so named because their husbands were called into active military service. Soldatki were not a phenomenon particular to World War I. Throughout the nineteenth century they were marked and primarily defined by their loss; though they were not yet widowed, soldatki harbored little hope of seeing their husbands again and were often treated as unwanted guests in their in-laws' homes.[42] However, it was only during the Great War that these women began to act collectively and became a serious and formidable force within the village, to a large extent because there were suddenly so many of them, and because the war affected them in particular ways. The soldatki abruptly became a relatively well formed social group, and began to take independent and forceful actions in defense of their perceived interests.

There was a quite vibrant feminist movement in prerevolutionary Russia, but this was a movement among mostly upper-class and professional women, who confined their activities to furthering "the interests of the women of the intelligentsia, though, given the pious canons of Russian social reform, this was seldom admitted."[43] There were some halting attempts to lighten the burdens of factory women, and the latter did play important, sometimes leading, roles in some strikes, especially in St. Petersburg. But these women never emerged as a major social force until February 1917.[44] The soldatki were quite a different sort of group; they did not forge collective ties with other soldatki beyond the confines of their village. And their rise was relatively brief—they fell back into obscurity in the violent turmoils of the revolution and civil war. Yet their fleeting appearance constitutes a remarkable and important part of World War I's impact on the homefront.

The first collective actions occurred soon after the soldatki's men first trudged off to war in the summer of 1914. At about 7 a.m. on 22 July in the village of Stativkin (Pavlovska volost, Starobilsk district) thirteen peasant women appeared at their village's parish school, the temporary residence of the newly arrived land surveyor, F. S. Shpital′nyi. All but one of these women were soldatki; the other, Elena P. Pugacheva, was the mother of two new recruits. Arriving at the parish school, the women began to curse at the surveyor shouting, "Go away you son of a bitch, or we will kill you!" They then started to smash the window shutters and frames of the parish school with wooden stakes and broke into the apartment, convinced that Shpital′nyi was hiding inside. But the surveyor had escaped through a back window and ridden off to nearby Pavlovka village. Not finding him inside, the soldatki became enraged, tore up his clothes and scattered his surveying instruments about the apartment. One eyewitness even reported seeing some of the women chasing Shpital′nyi out of town, waving their stakes in the air and hurling threats at him.[45]

Why were these women so angry? Local police officials investigating the incident claimed that the soldatki's attack was instigated by three male village elders, vehement defenders of the communal form of land ownership, who had, during the announcement of the mobilization in the village, supposedly told the soldatki, "They have taken our men to war, and he [the land surveyor] will cut up the land into *otruba*—we must kill him!" As their numerous reports reveal, the police never quite believed that women could plan, instigate, and carry out such provocative, decisive, and sometimes violent actions without male leadership. During their interrogations, all these soldatki claimed that they themselves had resolved to confront the surveyor without any provocation from others and had come to Shpital′nyi in order to demand from him documents explaining who had sent him and for what reasons. They admitted that they had cursed at him and demanded that he leave the village and not cut up the land into *otruba*, because they feared that "with their men away at the front they would receive worthless land and thus their children would be deprived of their daily bread." The district constable had the three male elders and Pugachova arrested and asked the provincial governor, M. K. Katerinich, to subject them "to administrative punishment in the highest degree [*v vysshei mere*] for incitement to hooliganism." In the end only the three men were sentenced to imprisonment.[46]

On 19 July 1914 in the village of Shaparskoe (Bilokurakynska volost, Starobilsk district) a crowd of forty or fifty soldatki, shouting and making a great din, broke into the yard of the house where the land surveyor, G. I. Malianovskii, was staying, and demanded that he appear for an explanation. Coming outside, Malianovskii asked the soldatki what they needed, to which they replied by shaking their sticks at him and shouting: "They have taken our men off to war, and we demand that you [*ty*] leave our village right now, and if you [*ty*] do not leave voluntarily, then we will kill you." Proving unable to quiet the crowd, Malianovskii retreated into his apartment and locked the door. The soldatki then hammered on the doors and windows, until the house's owner, with his sons' help, managed to force them out of the yard. Even then, the women continued to raise a racket, rapping their sticks on the gate and demanding that Malianovskii again come outside. Finally, he reappeared, but refused to give in to the soldatki's demands, categorically declaring that he would not leave their village, but would continue the work entrusted to him. Eventually, after more cries and threats to kill him, the soldatki dispersed. Part of the crowd went off to quarrel with the local *otrubshchiki*, and the rest returned to their village, Eremin, intending to remove the boundary markers placed by the surveyor on their land plots.[47] Returning to their village, the soldatki came upon the peasant Nikita Kiiashchenko. Recalling that he had helped Malianovskii to place the markers, they began to curse him and chased after him, intending to beat him.[48]

On 22 July, Malianovskii invited Eremin's village *starosta*,[49] also named Kiiashchenko, to his office, where he attempted to convince the latter to renew survey work the next day. Kiiashchenko, likely a close relative of Nikita, refused to assist the surveyor, stating that he needed to call a village gathering in order to find out what the people are saying, "that is, to decide whether to continue the land survey work or to stop it." Malianovskii demanded "that the starosta not call a gathering, since all matters are in order; the work was begun long ago and must continue." Kiiashchenko did not listen to him. At the gathering the peasants told Kiiashchenko not to help Malianovskii and resolved that the survey work be stopped, which resolution Kiiashchenko then transmitted to Malianovskii, requesting the latter's appearance at the gathering.[50] The surveyor refused to appear.

Police investigators claimed that the crowd of soldatki had arrived from Eremin under the leadership of fellow villager Dmitrii Fedorovich Ignatenko, but that the real leader of the crowd was the soldatka Lukiia Antonovna Lavrenkova, whom the investigator described as "a woman not having children, of wild [*buinyi*] character and possessing significant strength." It is very likely that the investigator extracted this characterization of Lavrenkova from one of the soldatki-participants, Anastasiia Cherednichenkova, who, attempting to avoid responsibility for the riot, characterized Lavrenkova as "a strong woman, who does not have children, [and] has a wild character; more than the others she rioted [*buistvovala*] and demanded that without her permission none of the women could go home."[51] Lavrenkova was the first to break into the yard and bang on the windows of Malianovskii's temporary residence. The district police chief asked Governor Katerinich to subject her to the same punishment as the two male villagers who were accused of incitement to violation of the law.[52]

On the evening of 20 July 1914, the senior land surveyor of Kharkiv province, Vladimir S. Dmitriev, temporarily working in the village of Rudov (Pavlovska volost, Starobilsk district), heard a noise in the yard outside his room and saw a crowd of men and women approaching. Going out to investigate, Dmitriev was met at the door by Elizaveta Panchenkova, who insistently and rudely demanded that the surveyor not divide up her husband's plots into *otruba*, and threatened him with murder if he did not comply. Assuring Panchenkova that he would not divide her land into *otruba*, Dmitriev appealed to the village starosta, Ihor Borovenskii, and the village elders, asking them what they wanted. The elders replied that they had come to ask him not to divide the land into *otruba*, especially those strips near the local pond, declaring that they would categorically forbid him to do so and complaining that Dmitriev did not consult with them, the *obshchinniki*, when dividing the land. Having stated their case, the peasants withdrew from the yard, except for Vasili Fomenko, who then demanded from Dmitriev five rubles for vodka. When Dmitriev refused, Fomenko made some signal with his hand to the crowd standing outside the yard's gate, and the women rushed back in. Two soldatki, Marfa and Fedos′ia Grutovaia, approached Dmitriev, repeating the same demand not to divide up the land and threatening to kill him. They feared that the better land would be given to the *otrubshchiki*, leaving the poor land to the commune; with this land they could not feed their children. Rejecting their demands, Dmitriev insisted that he would divide up the land according to the law and authorities, and not listen to the arbitrary will of the peasants. The women responded by thrusting the babies they held in their arms at Dmitriev and shouting, "here is all the law and authority you need."[53] They began to tug at his clothes, attempting to pull him off the porch and begging that he not pay any attention to the authorities or law and leave their village at once. Then, Fomenko attacked Dmitriev, who managed to duck back inside his apartment and lock the door. Someone then threw a rock through one of the windows and the broken glass cut Dmitriev's eyes and forehead. The crowd again began to bang on the windows and demand that Dmitriev leave immediately, and this continued until ten that evening.[54] As in other cases, the police suspected above all the local village elders, strong supporters of the communal form of land ownership, of inciting the soldatki to action, though during the investigation, the soldatki claimed no one had sent them and that they had come for their children's sake.[55] Four village elders were arrested and sentenced to between sixty and ninety days' administrative arrest, while Panchenkova was given only thirty days. Marfa and Fedos′ia Grutovaia were simply called to the police administration's office and warned about their behavior.[56]

Taking such deliberate actions to protect their own and their children's interests strengthened soldatki's consciousness of themselves as a group, and the kid gloves with which authorities often treated them can only have reinforced their sense of being special. In most instances, these anti-land reform protests did not lead to serious violence, though the threat of violence was invariably present.[57] In one case, however, this violent undertone broke through the surface of social quiet in rural Kharkivshchyna.

In the village of Nyzhnia Syrovatka, Sumy district, on the morning of 12 April 1915, a market day, members of the land reorganization commission and local police officials arrived at the volost administration building in order to resolve their misunderstanding with the "husarki" (the local name for soldatki),[58] who had on the previous four days repeatedly protested against the redivision of their commune's land into *otruba* while their men were away at the front. Of the 1200 households in the village, only 106 had expressed a desire to separate from the commune. Alarmed by the large and already boisterous crowd (mostly composed of women) quickly growing outside the administration building, the officials inside decided to put off the redivision to an undetermined time in the future[59] and asked the representatives of both the *otrubshchiki* (those who had separated from the commune) and *obshchinniki* (those who wished to remain in the commune) to inform their respective constituents. Coming out onto the porch, the representatives attempted to explain that the redivision work had been laid aside, but the crowd refused to listen, silencing them with shouts and noise. The crowd continued to grow, gradually surrounding the administration building and numbering about 3,000 people. The local land captain, Petrishchev, and commission member, Sebriakov, then came out and tried to quiet the crowd. But, paying no attention to the officials' exhortations and drowning their words in a great din, the enraged women forced their way into the building en masse. The village constable and his guards, attempting to block the entrance, were summarily seized and beaten; some peasants even tore off the coat and ankle boots of district police supervisor Khizhniakov. Police officials do not, however, appear to have been the principal game of this mob's hunt.

Representatives of the *otrubshchiki*, brothers Kyrylo and Ivan Stakhno and Ihor Ptashnik, had in the meantime locked themselves in a room inside the administration building. The *obshchinniki* had for several years been cultivating a hatred toward these three *kulak*s (in Ukrainian *kurkuli*), as they called them. Unfortunately for them, the enraged crowd, storming through the building, broke into the room where they were hiding, killed Kyrylo Stakhno and Ptashnik, and severely beat Ivan Stakhno. Then, the "completely enraged crowd" began to roar with joy, to shout "Hooray," and smash all the furniture and windows, while outside other peasants began destroying the building's foundation. The mob then turned on the police, breaking into the tax-collector's room, where the injured, bootless, and humiliated supervisor Khizhniakov, his deputy Lavrovskii, and three other police officers were hiding. Only with the help of a few friends among the crowd was one local constable saved from a lynching (*samosud*) and taken to the hospital. Khizhniakov managed somehow to escape and hid in a nearby church, where the land captain Petrishchev had already taken refuge. Lavrovskii was not so lucky and was badly beaten by the crowd.

For some time the police were unable to contact the district center, Sumy, to call for reinforcements, because the peasants had cut the telephone wire. Eventually, someone managed to send a telegram from the local railroad station, and at about 3 p.m. a police detail arrived and put an end to the disturbance. At eleven in the evening, Vice Governor Masal′skii arrived by emergency train from Kharkiv, also accompanied by a substantial police detachment. Having learned of the alarming events of the day, Masal′skii ordered the immediate arrest of the main "instigators"; on that night thirty-four persons were arrested. The next morning he called the village's entire population to assemble in the village square. From among those gathering that morning, a small group of peasants, probably women, approached the vice governor and presented him with the traditional greeting of bread and salt. But Masal′skii refused to accept these gifts, exclaiming to the crowd that he could not accept bread and salt from people who "in such a difficult year for the motherland [*rodina*], would riot [*buntuiut*] to the joy of Russia's enemies, kill their fellow villagers, and attack government officials." Reportedly, in response to Masal′skii's bold admonishments, the crowd fell on its knees and begged forgiveness. The vice governor explained to the peasants the illegality of their deeds and the seriousness of the crime they had committed. Apparently, his reprimands had such a profound impact on the people that they themselves began to point out the instigators of the riot. Masal′skii then supervised their arrest and handed them over to the judicial authorities.[60] The peasants' rapid return to submission following Masal′skii's reprimand is not very surprising. Once the authorities applied serious force, peasants often retreated into "customary shows of abject repentance."[61]

The events in Syrovatka soon became widely known, and the details often exaggerated. On 13 April 1915, 200 soldatki gathered in the yard of the Okhtyrka volost administration building and demanded that two surveyors who had recently arrived to survey the land not divide up the commune's land until their husbands returned from the front. They became angry when a local peasant, Aleksei M. Romanika, shouted, "some good lashes would not be bad for the soldatki [*soldatkam ne meshalo-by dat′ khoroshikh pletok*]." The soldatki attacked and beat Romanika. An injured soldier, David G. Shapovalov, then shouted from the crowd, "Do not allow them to divide up the land and separate onto *otruba*; beat the land surveyors, who will cut up the land; I myself will kill [*ulozhu*] five of them and we will do the same with them as was done in Syrovatka." Romanika barely escaped with his life. The village starosta, Petro Tyshchenko, then came out of the administration building and explained that the surveyors would not carry out the survey and redivision work until the end of the war, after which the soldatki quieted down and eventually went home.[62] Informing the chief of the provincial gendarme about these alarming events, Captain Mkurnali concluded that "the vast majority of the population (especially the soldatki) in the districts under my authority [Sumy, Okhtyrka and Lebedyn] relate not only negatively, but hostilely toward the work of the land reorganization commissions, because a large part of the peasant men are at war and in their absence only a few want to restructure the land."[63]

In the spring of 1915, peasants launched several other similar (though less violent) protests, eventually provoking Governor Katerinich to suspect—quite mistakenly—that some sort of revolutionary underground organization, the so-called Kharkiv Ukrainian Socialist Collective, was agitating among the peasantry against the government.[64] Such a collective did in fact exist: a small group of students at Kharkiv University bearing that name printed a pamphlet entitled "*Z selians'koho zhyttia* (From Peasant Life)" that described the events in Nyzhnia Syrovatka in April 1915. Major General Rykovskii, head of the Kharkiv provincial gendarme administration, did not share Katerinich's suspicion, noting that the pamphlet was not "revolutionary in character" and that only a few copies of it had been distributed around Kharkiv *after* the disturbance. Moreover, he pointed out that the riot in Nyzhnia Syrovatka "was not provoked by revolutionary propaganda among the peasantry of the named village, but was the result of an intense displeasure against those peasants desiring to separate off onto *otruba*, which [displeasure] was not understood by the land reorganization commission, appearing during wartime to resolve the peasants' land questions."[65] Rykovskii's deputy, Lieutenant Colonel Levanevskii, blamed "the tactless actions of the land reorganization commission," and noted that such actions were "intensifying among the peasant masses a consciousness of the justice of the demands presented, and at the same time the necessity to support these demands with force." According to Levanevskii, peasants were so convinced of the righteousness of their actions in Nyzhnia Syrovatka that they believed that Governor Katerinich was dismissed from his post shortly after the riot because of his poor handling of this very matter.[66]

On 5 May 1915 the minister of agriculture, A. V. Krivoshein, dispatched a circular letter to all governors. Noting that he had received many petitions from peasants, the majority of which cited their family members' absence at the front and called on Krivoshein to suspend the land reform until their return, he ordered the cessation of all land reorganization work, though describing this as a temporary reprieve necessitated by wartime conditions.[67] Some peasants interpreted Krivoshein's decree as the revocation of the land reform and called for all *otrub* and *khutor* plots to be reintegrated into the commune. At the same time, some officials continued to carry out land survey work, further provoking soldatki, though these were largely isolated cases.[68] More important, although it would seem that villagers' main motivation for such disruptive actions had been removed by administrative fiat, they continued to act collectively, take part in and often lead other protest actions.[69]

A Different Moral Economy

As the war progressed, peasants increasingly participated in protests and riots against inflationary prices brought on by the war.[70] More than their actions against the Stolypin reforms, these protests reflected villagers' sense of "moral economy"; those they attacked were violating what they believed to be a mutually understood sense of fairness in the marketplace.[71] In this moral economy, however, peasants could end up on either side of the fence, depending on whether they were buying manufactured goods or selling their farm produce. Here again the war's impact was instrumental, creating inflationary pressures on manufactured items, though peasants as consumers were far more likely to blame local storeowners, whom they often called "speculators," and the police, than the scarcities brought on by war.

One case in particular exemplifies this type of action. On 17 May 1916 about three hundred women, mostly soldatki, working on the Leshchinskii estate, Sumy district, incensed by the estate manager's announcement that their meager wages would be decreased from fifty to forty-five kopeks per day, quit their work, declared that they would not work under such conditions, smashed up some of the estate's property, and marched off to the local market town, Iunakovka. Picking up other women and youngsters along the way, the women complained to each other about the inflated prices on basic goods, especially sugar. When they arrived at Iunakovka, they gathered around two local shops and accused the store owners of raising prices artificially. Soon they smashed the stores' windows and streamed inside, damaging property and stealing goods; then they went home.[72]

The violence might have ended there were it not for the police, who the next day arrested seven soldatki implicated in the riot. On 19 May a larger, angry crowd of women gathered around the Iunakovka volost administration building, demanded the release of their sister soldatki, and began throwing rocks through the building's windows. Volost chief constable Khizhniakov (the same one humiliated and beaten in Nyzhnia Syrovatka) ordered all of his seventeen officers out into the yard to disperse the crowd, but the women met them with a hail of rocks, injuring a sergeant major. Not wishing to worsen the situation and noting that the crowd had now reached about four thousand people, Khizhniakov decided to release the detained soldatki and, seeing that this somewhat quieted the crowd, attempted to convince them to go home. During his exhortations, however, a portion of the crowd drifted away from the administration building to one of the shops ransacked two days past and began to break in again. The police raced to the store and attempted to disperse the crowd, but the rioters shouted to each other: "Do not leave! Beat the police!" They threw rocks at the police, eventually forcing them to take cover in the administration building. Several policemen, including Khizhniakov, were injured in the attack. The crowd then broke into the store, stole much inside, and plundered another store. After the arrival of another police detachment, the rioters gradually dispersed.

The scale of this riot was great enough that the governor himself soon arrived by emergency train from Kharkiv. Although he had five rioters arrested, the police report claimed that the main cause of the riot was "the artificial inflating of prices on goods in general and sugar in particular," pointing the finger at the local traders and storeowners. The governor ordered an infantry company from Sumy to Iunakovka and reinforced the local police force with officers from other districts, but also took measures to provide the population with essential goods at reasonable prices; the city administration was directed to take this branch of trade into its own hands.[73]

A similar incident occurred in the village of Ulianovka, Sumy district. On 15 June 1916 about three hundred soldatki, claiming dissatisfaction with a decrease in their pay, refused to continue working on an estate belonging to the sugar magnate Kharitonenko and marched off to their village, again collecting other women and youngsters along the way. Gathering around two stores, the angry crowd began to complain about the high cost of staples and manufactured goods. When the police arrived, several soldatki shouted, "Give us our men!" A window was broken and five rubles stolen, but, because of the quick arrival of the district police chief with several officers, the crowd quieted and soon went home. Interestingly, the Kharitonenko estate's administration claimed that it had not decreased the soldatki's daily wage, but rather that the women had demanded a raise from 55 to 70 kopeks per day. Even then, they had not waited for the estate manager to arrive for negotiations, but had instead immediately left for Ulianovka. If this is correct, it only reinforces the impression that these soldatki were acting deliberately as a group and that they felt quite empowered to challenge both their employer and the storeowners' prices. Noting that the mood in general was anxious, gendarme deputy chief Levanevskii dispatched ten more officers to Ulianovka.[74]

The disturbance in Ulianovka inspired Levanevskii to write a second report to his superior in Kharkiv about the people's mood in those districts under his jurisdiction—Sumy, Lebedyn, and Okhtyrka. He reported that the recent rapid increase in the peasants' dissatisfaction with the rising cost of manufactured goods was accompanied by the increasingly popular conviction that shopkeepers, in order to justify their high prices, were presenting false accounts from their manufacturers, and that the government was doing nothing to alleviate the situation. He warned that the population in general exhibited an extremely nervous mood, which "could lead to highly undesirable phenomena."[75]

Although the soldatki were the main actors in many of these disturbances, they rarely acted alone; their ranks were often reinforced by other peasant women, youngsters, elders and returning or injured soldiers. Women, however, were and remained the initiators and main actors in the various riots sparked by hyperinflation and the local government's attempts to control it; their prominence in these riots is quite understandable. Even though women often worked in the fields alongside men, they were also traditionally expected to prepare food for their households, and thus felt they had a more direct interest in this crucial aspect of daily life. Moreover, with their men away at war, women had to take on total responsibility for providing for and nourishing their children both in the field and in the marketplace. Thus, it is not surprising that women were not only the leading protesters against inflationary prices on manufactured goods, which they could not produce themselves, but that they were also the principal demonstrators against local administrations' attempts to control the high prices on the foodstuffs that they did produce to sell at market.

The government's wartime acquisition policies, the army's disruption of the transportation system, and speculation increasingly affected the prices at local markets across the empire. Town administrators most often cited transportation problems as the main cause of inflation, though speculation was also usually mentioned. Although these factors played some role, Lars Lih has convincingly argued that the government's policy of setting fixed prices for army food supply purchases was crucial. This policy created a "dualism" between the government price and the unregulated market price, forcing the latter to rise rapidly, "because the producers and the millers made up for losses on government purchases by overcharging the civilians."[76] Responding to complaints about rising prices, fears of possible disturbances, and encouragement from Petrograd, city and town administrations across the empire almost from the beginning of the war attempted to employ their limited powers to impose tariffs (called *taksy*) on the local market prices of staple food products.[77] As in many cities and towns across the empire, in Kharkiv province the tariffs' effects proved less than satisfying to the authorities. In a November 1915 report to the Ministry of Internal Affairs, Kharkiv gendarme chief Rykovskii commented that the regulation of prices on necessities had provided some benefit, undermining the "speculative strivings" of some merchants. For the struggle with the rising cost of living, however, these set prices proved to be only "palliative measures," because not all necessities were included. Moreover, Rykovskii admitted, only the working class and the relatively "insignificant urban population" truly were suffering from the high cost of living. "The peasants, a large part of whom are selling necessities, not only do not suffer from these high prices themselves, but on the contrary have the full possibility of profit."[78]

Rykovskii's overestimation of most peasants' earning potential aside, many peasants greatly resented the imposed tariffs, and as the war's exactions placed them in increasingly difficult economic circumstances, they began to circumvent the tariffs. According to the data from a survey carried out by the Union of Cities, the majority of the eighty-nine cities that responded to the more detailed questions reported some form of circumvention of the tariffs. Most cities openly admitted that they lacked the authority and resources to enforce observance of the tariffs, and thus control "amounted to a fiction of real control."[79] In a sense these peasants were acting on their perceived understanding of a "moral economy," though their position within that economy was the almost very opposite of E. P. Thompson's English crowds. Whereas the latter organized, threatened violence, and rioted in order to keep food prices down in times of dearth, these peasant women rose up against local officials' attempts to regulate food prices, that is, to keep prices down; Their primary goal was to protest the authorities' intervention in their economic lives and, indirectly, the latter's attempts to place the needs of town-dwellers over their own. They perceived the tariffs as unnecessary interference in and violations of their moral economy, and brazenly ignored them. That these peasants felt justified in selling above the tariff rates is clear from their reactions, when local police attempted to enforce the tariffs.

In the early morning of 30 May 1916 at the bazaar in the district center of Starobilsk, Matrena Syrovatkina, the wife of the city bailiff, asked to buy ten eggs from Ekaterina Grigorenko, a peasant woman from the nearby village of Chmyrivka, at the established tariff rate of 25 kopeks. Grigorenko refused to sell the eggs to her for less than 35 kopeks. Syrovatkina appealed to police officer Iasenko, supervising the marketplace, who, discerning that "Grigorenko did not want to believe in the existence of the tariff, invited her to the police station." Grigorenko's arrest provoked great irritation at the bazaar, where an angry crowd of about a thousand peasants, "predominantly peasant women" from the surrounding villages, gathered together and then quickly headed off to the police station. As Iasenko, Grigorenko, and Syrovatkina were approaching the station, two peasants from Chmyrivka attacked Iasenko, seizing him by the leg and beating him; but somehow he managed to escape and run into the police station, dragging Grigorenko along with him. After arriving at the police station, the large crowd began to yell at police chief Koronatskii, who had come out of the station to disperse the crowd; they demanded that he release Grigorenko and hand over Iasenko for retribution. Koronatskii released Grigorenko but refused to deliver Iasenko, further aggravating the crowd. Grigorenko then began to spread rumors that Iasenko had beaten her while she was in custody. The peasants started to press in around Koronatskii, but then thirteen mounted police arrived and temporarily scattered the crowd. As soon as Koronatskii stepped back inside the station, the crowd returned and threw rocks through its windows into his office, and then did the same at the police officers sent out to stop them. The latter were forced to retreat, because they were not permitted to use their weapons even to defend themselves. The peasants' demands were clear: they shouted, "Smash the police and the stores! The *pany* set tariffs on our products, but in the stores they sell goods for whatever they want!" The crowd then spilled out over the city, smashing the windows of some stores and private apartments, including that of the bazaar's starosta; several women also broke into and ransacked Iasenko's apartment. Eventually, with the help of the district military chief, colonel Kozlov, and his troops, Koronatskii managed to convince the crowd, little by little, to go home.[80]

In Valky on 19 June 1916, M. Z. Kristalenko provoked a similar demonstration when he stepped on Khristina P. Zhmailova's eggs because she refused to sell ten to him at the tariff rate. A large group of women tried to punish Kristalenko for his act, but he somehow escaped, further antagonizing the women, who then began to express their dissatisfaction with the absence of sugar for sale and the high prices on various manufactured goods. Ignoring the orders of a police detachment that had arrived at the market, the crowd refused to disperse and instead demanded that the police release two women accused of selling their produce above the tariff rate. The police were forced to release the women, after which the protesters dispersed.[81]

With such incidents in mind, it is not surprising that one of the provincial gendarme's leading officials declared in June 1916 that "the tariffs in general provoke extreme bitterness among the peasants absolutely in all districts." Pointing out the complete absence of tariffs on manufactured goods (especially sugar) in stores, peasants declared, "not just as individuals, but as a mass," that "the *pany* allow merchants to rob us, and at the same time they force us to sell at the tariff rate."[82]

Even when local police attempted to control prices on some manufactured goods the results could be unsettling. On 19 August 1916, a market day in the district center of Bohodukhiv, the local police's market supervisor, Vilchinskii, observing the prices on foodstuffs at the bazaar, demanded that peasants sell their produce at the tariff rates. The peasant-sellers retorted that merchants and traders (*kuptsy*) were selling other items at whatever prices they desired, and the police had taken no notice of them. A woman approached Vilchinskii and informed him that one trader, a Jewish refugee named Kaplun, was selling soap at more than double the tariff rate. Vilchinskii immediately went to Kaplun's shop and demanded that he sell the soap at the prescribed rate and return any excess money he had received. Then Vilchinskii himself began to sell the soap at the tariff price to the large crowd gathered around the shop, forcing Kaplun to close up and leave quickly. Vilchinskii then headed to other shops with the growing crowd of peasants close behind him, but seeing the crowd approaching, traders hurriedly closed their shops to avoid selling at the tariff rate. More important, Vilchinskii's actions seem more to have emboldened the crowd than to have won it over. When the peasants spotted Bohodukhiv's entire police force along with part of the cavalry command arriving to the bazaar to quell the disturbance, they shouted, "Beat the police! And beat the traders so that they will not sell dear!" The crowd began to throw apples, pears, and rocks at the police, and it was not until the district chief constable arrived and quieted them down that the peasants finally dispersed.[83] One might note that this was the only example I have found in which peasants even mentioned the ethnicity of a non-peasant. And there is no evidence that Kaplun or any other traders at this bazaar were beaten. As usual, the police took the brunt of peasants' anger.

As a means of alleviating price inflation, the tariffs proved to be a near complete failure. While some peasants chose these riots as a form of resistance, far more took the less conspicuous and more profitable path of selling their produce in towns where tariffs had not been imposed or were less restrictive. Thus, the locally imposed tariffs often led to local insufficiencies in basic foodstuffs and, ironically, forced unofficial prices to rise on those products remaining.[84]

Social Quiet

Although one might think all these disturbances to be portents of the revolution of February 1917, often dubbed "the people's revolution," and though they suggest that peasants, alongside soldiers, workers, and the intelligentsia, were about to rise up in open revolt against the tsarist government, this did not turn out to be the case, at least in Kharkiv province. As the above accounts from the archives have shown, the war and its effects greatly provoked and emboldened peasants to take audacious and illegal mass actions. In the three and a half years prior to the war's outbreak, there were only eight peasant "disturbances" (which the police usually called *vystupleniia*) for the entire province (1912: 3; 1913: 3; January–June 1914: 2). By contrast, in the first two and a half years of World War I, the province's peasants took part in 53 similarly labeled "disturbances" (July–December 1914: 22; 1915: 19; 1916: 11).[85] And yet, in the months leading up to February 1917, peasants' acts of protest and violence did not increase in number or frequency. On the contrary, they seem to have dropped off. Perhaps, as news arriving from Petrograd became increasingly alarming and the revolution seemed at hand, the attention of local police officials turned more to the center and less to local events and attitudes. But it is doubtful that this could fully explain the complete absence of evidence of any collective peasant actions across the countryside of Kharkiv province from the suppression of the anti-tariff riot in Bohodukhiv in the late summer of 1916 until late April 1917. Even the very well-kept records of the Kharkiv governor's *sekretnyi stol* do not contain a single file about any collective actions by peasants after August 1916.[86] High-ranking police officials noticed a similarly quiet turn among peasants across the empire. In his October 1916 report to the minister of internal affairs, the director of the department of police A. T. Vasil′ev summarized the numerous reports on the public mood he had received from police organs across the empire. He pointed out that, in contradistinction to the very threatening situation in the cities, in the countryside "in the majority of cases, as a result of economic conditions very favorable for the peasants, not only is no state of excitement observable, but there is even noticeable the population's satisfaction and a peaceful, or more exactly indifferent, attitude toward almost everything that so disturbs the urban population."[87]

There are some possible explanations for this change of mood among the peasants. First, the anti-tariff riots of 1916 were, of course, quite particular in time and place. They could only be sparked at those times when peasants were selling their produce at market and local police officials attempted to enforce the tariffs, which the police proved increasingly reluctant to do. In addition, the period leading up to and including the February Revolution coincided with the time of the year when peasants rarely rose up. Historically, most peasant uprisings took place in the spring, before intensive work in the fields began, or in the fall, after the harvest had been brought in. Moreover, it should be noted that the revolution—as much as we define it as the popular uprising in Petrograd leading to abdication of the tsar—took place far away from these peasants, in Petrograd and in the tsar's train car standing at Pskov. Although behind much writing on the revolution there seems to lurk an assumption that the peasant masses in general backed the rioting women and men, soldiers and workers in the capital, this was patently not the case. As across most of the empire, the peasants of Kharkiv province did not help make the revolution in the capital; they learned about it gradually in bits and pieces as the news found its way out to the provinces. Thus, it is perhaps more useful to conclude this chapter by noting how the war's multifarious effects would condition peasants' behavior once news about the revolution reached their villages.

The War's Effects on the Peasantry

First of all, the war significantly increased the disparity between rich and poor peasants in the village. And yet, this disparity was not translated into peasant action, except when it coincided with other more readily apparent differences between peasants, especially the conflicts between *otrubshchiki* and *obshchinniki*. Second, the military mobilization created a uniquely large population of wives of soldiers, who quickly became an important force within the village. After the February Revolution, the soldatki, and women in general, fade away from the documentary sources on peasants, making it near impossible to follow them.[88] This is unfortunate but not surprising. Many of the soldiers fighting at the front returned home in 1917, and even more after the treaties of Brest-Litovsk; no doubt, as in other belligerent countries of World War I, these men pushed women back into more private roles in the household, where those who compose documents rarely tread, especially during times of revolution and civil war.[89]

Third, we must note the long-term local consequences of the numerous riots described above. As Thompson pointed out some time ago, the effects of such violent convulsions on local communities are often calamitous and protracted.[90] The disturbances over the redivision of the commune's land into *otruba* set *obshchinniki* against *otrubshchiki*, exacerbating differences already apparent between these two groups: poorer peasants farming with traditional methods against better-off "farmers" employing new methods and "improving" their farms. In a similar way, after the anti-tariff riots of 1916, town-dwellers and peasants had to continue to live in close proximity and, more importantly, to interact weekly in the marketplace, over which the further threat and lingering animosities of these violent eruptions now hung. The changed and strained relations that followed such outbursts are, perhaps, impossible to measure. But we can posit that the anti-tariff riots, in particular, further estranged peasants from the city and its inhabitants, especially the *pany* and *kuptsy*, and made peasants more reluctant in these increasingly uncertain times to bring their produce to market. Indeed, trying to persuade peasant food producers to do so would become perhaps the greatest problem, which none of the governments claiming authority over the province throughout this period of war and revolution managed to solve until the third Soviet regime, reinstalled in Kharkiv by the Red Army in late 1919, eventually began to encourage free trade and to ensure manufactured goods were delivered to the countryside in late 1921.

Fourth, one should note peasants' increased activism, as this discussion of the impact of World War I on the home front has repeatedly shown. Peter Holquist has convincingly argued that a crucial feature of World War I across Europe "was precisely this self-mobilization of society for the ends of total war."[91] In the case of the Russian Empire, Holquist's statement applies mainly to educated society, but this examination of Kharkiv province suggests that peasants too, in their own way and with different ends in mind, were also greatly mobilized by the war effort.

Finally, the various disturbances discussed above reveal the growing hostility among peasants toward government and police authorities, as well as an increasing boldness in their actions against those authorities. Except for the three *otrubshchiki* attacked in Nyzhnia Syrovatka, tsarist officials were almost invariably the primary object of peasants' wrath. Upon hearing about the revolution in Petrograd, most of these officials hurriedly abandoned their posts, convinced that they would find little sympathy among the peasants and fearing that they might be attacked. But peasants' hostility toward government officials—the authorities—did not end there. They had little difficulty transferring their increasingly brazen contempt for tsarist officials to other figures of authority, whether they represented the Provisional Government, the Ukrainian Central Rada, the Bolsheviks' Sovnarkom, or any other of the governments that would claim authority in Kharkiv province over the next few turbulent years.

In this chapter I have focused quite deliberately on those aspects of peasants' experience that they translated into action during the war, arguing that in these actions peasants expressed most clearly what they wanted. However, the war seriously encouraged peasants' aspirations in one other very important, though less easily documented, way. Some police agents noted that peasants expressed an increasing interest in military events at the front. Newspapers became scarce commodities, anxiously awaited in the village; peasants would gather around local post offices to have the latest news read to them.[92] It is very likely that this new interest, while it may have unintentionally broadened their understanding of the world, was not inspired by a rising sense of patriotism among the peasantry. Rather, it was spawned by the large number of local men now fighting and dying at the front, and perhaps motivated even more by hopes of their return, which peasants increasingly associated with the final fulfillment of their generations-old dream of the great "Black Repartition." In June 1915 Lieutenant Colonel Levanevskii reported to provincial gendarme chief Rykovskii that he had intercepted several letters from soldiers at the front to their families. In these letters, the soldiers complained that the war had completely exhausted them, but that when they returned home, they planned to seize the land from the *pany*.[93] In November 1915 Levanevskii submitted another report on peasants' attitudes, noting that though "everyone is still conscious of the need to bring the war to a victorious conclusion," there was noticeable "a tiredness and desire for peace." He expressed concern that, as a result of the insufficient distribution of newspapers across the countryside, peasants were relying on rumors "often far from corresponding to reality," and on the accounts of returning injured soldiers for their information about the war. And he noted that "although at the present time the land question is not of a severe character, the peasants obviously are counting on some sort of land compensation after the war." What form this aspiration would take, Levanevskii found difficult to predict, but he suggested that it would be expressed in some form of "agrarian disorders."[94] Peasants did not translate their desire to carry out the great Black Repartition into action before the February Revolution, but land seizures would become the predominant form of action in rural Kharkivshchyna, once news arrived of the tsar's abdication and the fall of autocracy. At that point, peasants were left to reorganize their lives and land relations as they saw fit.

2 The Rural Revolutions of 1917, Intervillage Conflict, and the Limits of Villagers' Identities

The rural inhabitants of Kharkiv province were not quick to respond to news of the February Revolution, but once they realized that they were almost completely free to do as they pleased, they embarked on a massive endeavor to transform land and (consequently) power relations in the countryside. Beyond the cultivation of their little *hospodarstvo* (farm), peasants acted above all to acquire more land and forest. And yet, contrary to many interpretations of this agrarian revolution, this was not a "class struggle." Peasants behaved not as an oppressed "class" rising up against its oppressor, but as members of a village or *volost* (county) attempting to obtain what they viewed as a more "just" redistribution of limited resources. They carried out this operation with a surprising degree of orderliness and at least the form of legality, using the newly established land committees, the local organs of which they controlled, to justify and affirm their actions. Often they even left a "just" portion of the seized land for the lord and his family to farm.

Moreover, at least as often as peasants confiscated nonpeasant lands and forests, they squabbled among themselves over the proper apportionment. If they disliked the local landlord, they did not more so than those peasants from the next village, who contested their claim to the newly acquired land. Peasants expressed this localist mentalité not only in numerous intervillage conflicts over land and forests, but in their unwillingness to sacrifice for larger ideas of community. They proved unwilling to sell their crops at low, government-set prices to food supply committees, despite numerous appeals from Kharkiv, Kyiv, and Petrograd for them to save the army, Ukraine, and all of Russia from starvation. Moreover, even the Kharkiv Provincial Soviet of Peasants' Deputies, which claimed to represent them and speak on their behalf, could not enforce its decrees among them and proved unable even to extract enough money from them to fund itself.

This understanding of peasants' attachment to their locale has important implications for a crucial theme of this period: the rise of the national idea in Ukraine, which first found its way into many villages only in the summer of 1917, as the authority and notoriety of the Ukrainian Central Rada spread. Although many historians have studied the Ukrainian Revolution, we actually know very little about how the national idea and its attendant institutions, declarations, and leaders were accepted, supported, rejected, or ignored by peasants. While noting Steven Guthier's laudable efforts to illuminate this dark chasm, I will suggest that even the strongest evidence of a rising popular national sentiment among Ukraine's rural inhabitants is questionable. The large number of votes that peasants cast in the Constituent Assembly elections for parties whose platforms included a demand for some form of national autonomy for Ukraine was not so much an expression of their national sympathies as it was a result of their limited understanding of democratic institutions, the absence of political alternatives, and their belief that these parties would use the Constituent Assembly to affirm, legalize, and protect their land seizures.

*

News of the February Revolution drifted slowly and unevenly out to the villages of Kharkiv province. Not much evidence has survived concerning peasants' initial response to the revolution, although, if we can believe the description of a leading local Socialist-Revolutionary (SR), Volodymyr Kachyns′kyi, the news was announced in a traditional manner. The village elders called all peasants to gather at an assembly, at which a declaration from the Provisional Government or its predecessor, the Temporary Committee of the State Duma, was read. Sometimes the village assembly would respond by drafting and sending a resolution to the higher authorities. For example, on 6 March 1917 peasants from Trostianets, a large village in Okhtyrka district with a railway station nearby, sent a telegram to the newly appointed Kharkiv provincial commissar, P. P. Dobrosel′skii,[1] declaring that they "unanimously resolved to recognize the Temporary Committee of the State Duma as the highest authority." The peasants "quietly and joyously accepted the news of the fall of the old regime," expressed their preparedness to follow the appeals of the government and the Petrograd Soviet, and asked Dobrosel′skii to convey "the passionate greeting of a free people to their chosen ones [*svoim izbrannikam*] and a wish for successful work on the path of truth and justice."[2]

Although some villages expressed such noble ideas fairly soon after the tsar's abdication, actual revolutionary change proceeded much more slowly in the countryside in general. Local tsarist officials sometimes managed to stay at their posts, mainly because of the lack of competent personnel to replace them. As a practical matter, those local educated elites who had welcomed the revolution as embodied in the Provisional Government seem to have accepted back into service numerous former tsarist bureaucrats, and even police officials, who were willing to swear allegiance to the new revolutionary government. On occasion this provoked great concern among peasants. A correspondent for the Kharkiv SRs' official newspaper, *Zemlia i volia* (Land and Freedom), reported on 18 March that peasants were becoming increasingly fearful that "the old regime had still not died and that the Provisional Government was hindering its decisive elimination." From many villages the correspondent had received complaints that members of the old administration remained at their posts. As a result, in some villages peasants were taking matters into their own hands, threatening and arresting various police officials. For example, the peasants of Sinne (Bohodukhiv district) resolved to demand that "the former district police superintendent, Rudenko, immediately leave Sennyi [the Russian name for Sinne], because of the entire population's general hatred toward him, which he deserves, and the possibility from his side of activities, having the goal to provoke disorders."[3]

The revolution moved yet more slowly into districts far from Kharkiv and not situated close to major railway lines. In mid-June 1917 a soldier from the sleepy southern district of Starobilsk returned to find his homeland largely unmoved by the revolution. In a letter to *Zemlia i volia* he reported that local peasants complained to him about the Provisional Government, declaring that they had lived better under the tsar. Tsarist police officials either still served at their posts or had been relocated to serve in neighboring villages, "and none of them had been sent to the front, as was done in other districts." He added,

> For the whole time of my leave nowhere did I see a red revolutionary flag and those soldiers who showed up in the district on leave wearing red bows are called fools here. No meetings or assemblies take place, nothing is explained or read to the peasants about the significance of all that has occurred. For example, in our district land captains still exist, and, as the leaders of committees and the militia, they arrest all those who attempt to explain a little something about all that has happened.[4]

Archival documents on peasants' early responses to the news of the tsar's abdication are few, but there is some evidence that by late April peasants began to take advantage of their newfound freedom. On 27 April, a landowner named Matenkov complained to provincial commissar Dobrosel′skii about "outrages" committed on his estate by peasants from nearby Mykolaïvka village, Izium district.[5] On 2 May landowner M. V. Kondratskii complained that peasants of the surrounding villages in Starobilsk district had plundered all his land.[6] In early May the Valky district commissar informed the provincial commissar about "excesses" carried out by the peasants of Kov'iahy village, noting that such "arbitrary retributions" by local peasants against those suspected of theft had occurred in other villages of the district as well.[7]

Despite these few spontaneous actions, it appears that in the early months of 1917 there was little organized revolutionary activity in the countryside in comparison with urban areas. Whereas workers in Kharkiv took bold actions to ensure the revolution's success in their city by organizing, demonstrating, and electing their own soviet within days of hearing the news,[8] the first clear indication that peasants were beginning to organize (or perhaps, that someone was trying to organize them) on a large scale did not emerge until 3 May with the calling of the First Congress of Peasants' Deputies of Kharkiv province. The initiative to hold this congress, which was mandated to elect the province's Soviet of Peasants' Deputies, came from the Kharkiv Soviet of Workers' and Soldiers' Deputies, motivated by a rather paternalistic yet naive desire to encourage peasants to support the revolution and defend its achievements (as they understood those terms).[9] The documentary evidence concerning this congress is unfortunately incomplete, but it is possible to piece together the main issues discussed, which included national autonomy, the land question, and the grain monopoly.

The National Question

The national question, discussed on the first day of the congress, appears to have been an important and contested issue, but more for the provincial party intelligentsia in attendance than for the peasant deputies themselves. The official publication of the Ukrainian Social-Democratic Workers' Party (USDRP), *Robitnycha hazeta* (Workers' Newspaper), called the peasant deputies "Russified old peasants [*diadky*]" and complained that they "listened distrustfully to the literary Ukrainian of agitators… Only jargon could smash the block of ice covering the heart of the *slobozhanets*."[10] Both in the corridors and at the congress's sessions, "Ukrainian and Russian resounded pell-mell [*vsumish*]. The Presidium carried out the assembly in the Russian language."[11] I do not mean to suggest that Ukrainian SDs' sensitivity to the language problem was unjustified. Kharkiv's liberal Russian-language daily, *Iuzhnyi krai*, defensively labeled their slogan, "Long live Democratic, Autonomous Ukraine," a sign of "the ardent nationalism of the Ukrainian SDs."[12] However, neither they nor anyone else presented evidence that the peasant deputies themselves were sensitive to the language issue. Moreover, the comment about the need to use "jargon" to get through to the *slobozhanets* and the fact that the peasant deputies allowed the presidium to carry out the congress in Russian suggest the opposite.

Despite the apparent lack of interest of the peasant deputies in the matter, the congress took a fairly strong stand on Ukraine's national autonomy, resolving that the best form of government in Russia would be a democratic, federated republic and that "national-territorial autonomy for Ukraine, while ensuring national minorities' rights, was necessary for the complete development of the Ukrainian people." The congress also demanded that the Provisional Government "immediately and openly recognize the Ukrainian people's right to national-territorial autonomy," that all education be in Ukrainian, although again ensuring the rights of national minorities, and that education be free and obligatory for all children of both sexes.[13] While these resolutions suggest that the Kharkiv provincial congress was echoing resolutions recently pronounced in Kyiv, two important differences should be noted: first, the Kharkiv congress's resolutions made no references to the Ukrainian Central Rada, and second, the assemblies and congresses meeting in Kyiv in spring 1917 paid far less attention to the land question.[14]

The Land Question

The most important issue for most peasants of Kharkiv province in 1917 was not the national, but the land question. Party representatives who spoke at this first congress seem to have sensed this, their anxieties heightened by recent news that peasants in some provinces were arbitrarily seizing land and property. Although this was not yet a serious problem in Kharkiv province, the party intellectuals speaking at the congress repeatedly reminded the peasant deputies that "the land question cannot be solved by violent seizures," calling peasants to wait patiently for the Constituent Assembly.[15] The peasant deputies themselves, however, expressed a clear and unequivocal stand on the land question, as summarized by *Robitnycha hazeta*'s correspondent:

> Private property on land must be abolished. Monastery, allotted, state, and landlord land must all be transferred to the people and must be justly distributed among those who work the land with their own labor. The land must be transferred to the people without compensation. The land is God's, the people reaped and protected it for thousands of years. With the institution of serfdom hundreds of thousands of desiatynas of land and hundreds of thousands of people were crushed by the tsars and their favorites—the gentry. Under serfdom peasants watered their native land with sweat and then during the war with blood. And this was a price higher than money. There was not found one peasant who spoke for private property on the land or compensation. They unanimously declared: "All land to the people! We shall obtain land and freedom!"[16]

Although this account suggests that the peasant deputies were united and certain on the land question, the congress's debate proved to be protracted. The controversial issue seems to have been whether the peasant deputies would agree to wait for the Constituent Assembly to solve the land question, to which the party leaders obtained agreement only after lengthy debate, lasting into the early hours of the morning of 5 May.[17] And this was also reflected in the congress's resolutions, which very clearly stipulated "the foundations for the resolution of the land question":

> (1) Private property of individuals on the land is to be abolished forever. All landlord, state, monastery, church and all other lands will become community property [*hromadske dobro*].

(2) Only those who will work the land with their own hands, with their family or in a society without hired hands, can make use of it.
(3) All lands, both of private owners and other types, must be transferred to the hands of the entire people without any compensation.
(4) Local, regional, and central organs of self-government will manage the all-people's land fund.
(5) Underground wealth, woods, rivers, lakes, and other riches are to be made the property of all people. The central legislative organ will issue rules on how they will be used.
(6) The All-Russian Constituent Assembly will establish the basic principles of the land laws. The detailed elaboration of the land laws, with a view to the conditions of local life, will belong to separate autonomous units; in Ukraine, the Ukrainian Seim.[18]

Not only was the Constituent Assembly's role in resolving the land question relegated to one sentence of these "foundations," but the congress also resolved immediately to ban the purchase, sale, and mortgage of all land, to give local self-governing institutions the right to administer all lands left uncultivated, and to abolish all laws that permitted "the consolidation of land in property." Moreover, the congress called on "the organized peasantry to take into its hands the establishment of rules for renting land, hiring of agricultural laborers, and control over the carrying out of agriculture and equally the felling of forests."[19] As these additions suggest, there was at this first congress considerable resistance, very likely from the peasant deputies, to leaving the land question alone until the Constituent Assembly. This was borne out by the events of the summer and fall of 1917.

The Grain Monopoly

The final important issue debated at the congress was food supply. According to "Aronov" [A. Legin], the main political writer for *Izvestiia Khar'kovskogo Soveta rabochikh i soldatskikh deputatov*, the question of introducing a grain monopoly[20] in order to solve the still worsening food supply problem provoked lively debate at the congress. Some peasant deputies were so hostile to the introduction of a state monopoly on grain that they demanded that it not be introduced in any case. One declared, "A partial requisition of grain would be better than a monopoly." Others spoke for the introduction of a grain monopoly, but only if monopolies were introduced on other products as well. Some went still further, citing the excessive increase in the cost of living and demanding the establishment of control over factories, especially those producing textiles and leather goods.[21]

In the end, the congress resolved to consider the law on the grain monopoly the "single correct means that will save the country and army from hunger, ruin, and grain speculation." The congress called for the immediate organization of local food supply committees, composed of people elected on a democratic basis from the whole population, whom peasants would trust and who would be capable of carrying out all food supply measures. It was necessary to remove all middlemen and speculators, to purchase grain, and to distribute all necessities through local community organizations. The congress demanded the immediate introduction of a state monopoly on all items of wide consumption, as well as agricultural instruments and machines. Finally, the congress, which had renamed itself the Provincial Soviet of Peasants' Deputies, resolved that, in concert with the Soviets of Workers' and Soldiers' Deputies, it must "exert all forces and measures, which are only in the hands of the united laboring people, in order to solve the food supply question most quickly."[22]

It is difficult to determine to what degree the congress's resolutions reflected the views of the peasant deputies, let alone their constituents. Some of the resolutions seem to reveal more the opinions and hopes of party representatives than those of the deputies. Though a majority of peasant deputies eventually assented to the proposals of these educated men, one should not assume that their assent meant peasants' support, and especially not long-term support. After the congress closed, these deputies had to return to their villages with no conclusive decision on the land question—just copies of the congress's resolutions—and attempt to convince their fellow villagers to wait patiently for the Constituent Assembly and give up their surplus grain to food supply committee agents, whenever they came around.

Perhaps a more authentic expression of many peasants' aspirations at this time can be found in a list of ten conditions issued by the "Executive Bureau of the representatives of the soldier-peasants from units of the Kharkiv garrison" on 9 May 1917. This organization represented those soldiers who still considered themselves to be peasants to the extent that they had elected their own delegate, Fedor Golchkin, to the All-Russian Congress of Peasant Deputies then taking place in Petrograd. These soldier-peasants instructed Golchkin to stress that all land in excess of "the labor norm" must be transferred "free of charge" to the laboring people. Though the assembly recognized that at present unauthorized seizures of privately owned land were not permitted, it concluded that all land remaining unsown should fall to the command of local food supply committees. Almost all ten of these peasant-soldiers' conditions concerned the land and its cultivation, along with calls for the soviets to stop pernicious speculators, and for the government to establish a monopoly on grain as well as basic manufactured goods (especially farming tools). Not a word was expressed about national autonomy or the war effort.[23] And yet, I am reluctant to place too much weight on such declarations. Decrees and resolutions were a sort of mania of 1917. Many historians of the revolution have assumed that they reflected the opinions of those people whom the institutions producing these resolutions claimed to represent. While I would not argue that these resolutions say nothing about nonurban, uneducated peasants' desires, I want to suggest that we need to look more closely at their concrete actions and less at the resolutions of congresses, assemblies, and soviets, if we want to obtain a clearer and deeper understanding of peasants' attitudes and aspirations.

*

Of course, most peasants spent most of their time in 1917 as they had in previous years, cultivating the soil and tending their livestock to provide themselves with food, clothing, and shelter. Beyond the fulfillment of their households' basic needs, however, peasants took actions above all to obtain more land and forest. Outside the *hospodarstvo*, this was their primary concern.[24] Were it not for the insistence in the current Ukrainian historiography on the importance of the nation, the centrality of this issue would not require further elaboration. There is no point in proving only that one region's peasants aspired primarily to the same goal as many other peasants across the crumbling empire. Thus, in what follows I will focus not so much on peasants' rather obvious aspirations, but instead on the way they went about fulfilling them. It is in this process, the practical and pragmatic steps taken by individual peasant communities, that we will hopefully learn something more valuable about the countryside and its inhabitants in 1917–1918.

Statistical evidence on the agrarian revolution of 1917–1918 is largely unreliable. As Orlando Figes has pointed out, Soviet historians' estimates of the number of peasant disturbances vary widely, because each historian has a different definition of the term "peasant disturbance [*vystuplenie* or *vystup*]."[25] For example, I. I. Mints lists the total number of peasant disturbances for the period from March to October 1917 as 4,285 on one page and 4,246 on another. A. D. Maliavskii gives a figure of 16,298 for almost the same provinces and time period. For Kharkiv province in particular, Mints found 102 cases of peasant *vystuplenie*, whereas Maliavskii found 563. Mints's figures rank Kharkiv province seventeenth among all 84 provinces and oblasts in total number of uprisings, while Maliavskii puts the province in eleventh place.[26] The one Soviet historian who focused on the peasants of Kharkiv province in 1917, P. F. Reshod′ko, found at least 164 cases of peasants independently seizing landlords' arable land over the period from March to October 1917. In addition, the provincial land committee reported at the time that its lower-level committees had over the same period "transferred" to peasants almost 100,000 desiatynas of land not being cultivated by their owners.[27] I have calculated that just for the period from March to June 1917, there were at least 226 cases in which peasants acted in some illegal manner to achieve their goals.[28] Hence, the peasants of Kharkiv province, though not the empire's most riotous in 1917, were among the most active, and certainly among the most energetic in Ukraine.

Such statistics are not very dependable and can be used only as broad indicators; moreover, statistical evidence rarely reveals important qualitative aspects of peasants' actions. Thus I will present much of the evidence on this agrarian revolution by describing specific cases from across the province. This method will reveal both the variegated nature of peasants' actions and allow for some generalization.

One of the most interesting aspects of peasants' actions in this period is that they strove consistently to use newly formed local committees, assemblies, and soviets to carry out and justify their actions. Coming to realize that the tsar was gone, most peasants did not simply begin to plunder and seize what they had long desired. They set up local committees and soviets, drafted protocols, and used them to legitimize their actions, though they often "expanded" the powers of these institutions far beyond the Provisional Government's intent.

An example from Izium district exemplifies this behavior and reveals the process of land seizure and the seizure's eventual confirmation after the October Revolution. On 9 July 1917 two peasants identifying themselves as members of the Mykhailivka volost land committee, knocked on the door of the prosperous landlord A. N. Silin and asked that he indicate how many desiatynas of land he would agree to rent to local land-poor peasants. According to his own account, Silin replied that he thought that most local peasants were sufficiently provided with their own and rented land. Nevertheless, he agreed to compromise with the land committee and to rent to the peasants 215 desiatynas, while complaining that the rental rate proposed by the committee was "extremely low."[29] Apparently dissatisfied with Silin's offer, the peasants left and appealed to the Izium district land committee, which resolved to allow them to take 470 desiatynas from Silin's estate.[30]

On 24 July Silin was served copies of two protocols: the first, from the 2 July meeting of the Mykhailivka volost land committee, decreed that all privately owned land in the volost be distributed among the peasants under the supervision of the committee. The second protocol was from a joint meeting of the Mykhailivka volost Soviet of Peasants' Deputies land committee and food supply committee, who had together resolved to seize 1,000 of Silin's 1,200 desiatynas and rent them to peasants at a rate to be established by the land committee. (It bears noting that in general, peasants tended to treat these new titles—soviets, committees, etc.—emanating from the city, as interchangeable. One should not assume that they attached the same meanings to them as city-dwellers did to their urban counterparts.) This joint meeting also produced a decision to seize all of Silin's cattle and to resell his inventory to peasants at low prices, while forbidding Silin himself to sell the same.

In his 29 July complaint—the first of several—to the Kharkiv provincial commissar, Silin pointed out that these decrees were incorrect, illegal, and contrary to the commands of the Provisional Government. He asked that they be repealed and that the commissar order the Mykhailivka land and food supply committees not to obstruct Silin's ambitious agricultural work, especially his ongoing preparations for winter sowing. He noted that in June the provincial land committee had sent a telegram explaining to both the Izium district and Mykhailivka volost land committees that their earlier decrees on Silin's estate were illegal, but the local committees had ignored them. Silin stressed that the local land committee had issued decrees concerning not only his estate, but also the estates of almost all landowners in Mykhailivka volost, "and thus the immediate repeal of these decrees is necessary first of all in defense of the interests of the state itself." He concluded that, because it was obvious that the district and volost committees did not consider the provincial committee's order obligatory, "the achieved freedom and the state itself were threatened." It was necessary to take "the most energetic and decisive measures, which could prevent the disordering of the national economy, the ruin and elimination of highly-intensive farms and the reduction of the harvest, so necessary to Russia."[31]

The provincial commissar, acting promptly, passed Silin's complaint on to the provincial land committee on 1 August, and asked it to take emergency measures to restore order, noting that the volost land committee's decree of 2 July 1917 "could not in form or content be recognized as corresponding to the current legal situation."[32] A week later the provincial land board, the land committee's executive organ, asked the Izium district land committee to provide an explanation of the circumstances surrounding Silin's complaint and reminded the district board that it is obliged to watch that volost committees do not issue any illegal decrees such as the requisition of inventory and land. "The right of requisition belongs solely to the Provincial FOOD SUPPLY Committee; volost food supply committees can only make proposals on these questions and present them for confirmation to the Provincial Food Supply Committee."[33] Probably, the peasants included the food supply committee in their joint meeting specifically for this purpose—they perceived that such committees had some right to requisition land. On 11 April the Provisional Government had authorized food supply committees to take all uncultivated land on estates under their temporary command to rent out to peasants at a "just price."[34] Indeed, the rate of rent became a controversial question in the Kharkiv Provincial Soviet of Peasants' Deputies, which resolved on 14 June to grant *local* land committees the right to set rent rates on uncultivated lands.[35] This measure gave de facto authority to peasants to set the rate as low as possible, which they proceeded to do in many cases.

Probably because a reply from Izium did not soon arrive, Silin, who seems to have had some influence in Petrograd, had the Minister of Internal Affairs demand from the provincial commissar the resolution of his complaint. In response to the commissar's order, the chair of the provincial land committee sent a copy of his request of 8 August, ordering the Izium land committee to explain the circumstances of Silin's complaint, to which evidently he had still received no reply by 5 September. The provincial committee on 12 September again asked Izium to send information, but had still received nothing by 24 September, when a second complaint arrived.[36]

Silin now complained that on 20 September "in agreement with a decree of the Izium district land committee," and contrary to his will, peasants had arbitrarily seized more than 500 desiatynas of his best land, part of which Silin had already sown with winter crops and part of which was appointed to be sown in the spring of 1918. As a result of these seizures, Silin lamented, his estate's crop rotation system would be ruined for several years and he would be forced to decrease the area he planned to sow in the spring by half. Less sown area meant less grain-feed, and thus, he would have to reduce significantly the number of working cattle and horses he could breed and maintain. Silin stressed that for more than 30 years he had "personally" carried out the most intensive cultivation of his estate, possessing the latest farming equipment, such as steam plows and a steam threshing machine, and had sown yearly between 500 and 750 desiatynas. The peasants, having now appropriated all but 200 desiatynas of his land, lacked the equipment and labor to cultivate all this land in addition to the plots they already possessed.[37] As a result, the seized land would not be sown and this would harm not only him, but also the state. Referring to the government's strict prohibition on the arbitrary confiscation of land, he requested that the Izium land committee's illegal decrees be repealed and that his right to use his land be restored.[38] On the same day, Silin sent an almost identical complaint to the Minister of Agriculture, adding the fairly significant statement that, based on the poor results received from his complaints to the provincial land committee, he was "more than convinced that, without your [the minister's] lofty [*vysokii*] interference in this matter, the district committee will not submit to the provincial, and thus, I most humbly ask You, Gentleman Minister, to render assistance in the repeal of the Izium committee's illegal decree and the restoration of my legal rights to use the land seized from me."[39]

Despite Silin's numerous complaints to the provincial land committee and Petrograd, and the provincial committee's repeated demands, no information from Izium district arrived before the Bolshevik takeover in Petrograd and the Central Rada's declaration of the Third Universal in Kyiv pulled the legal basis out from under Silin's complaints. Declaring the creation of the Ukrainian People's Republic, the Third Universal (7 November 1917) abolished the right of ownership of all landlords and other lands not worked with one's own labor. These lands were declared the property of "all laboring people" and transferred to them without any compensation.[40] Thus, it is not surprising that when the Izium District Land Committee finally reviewed Silin's complaint on 7 December, it resolved to lay it aside and confirm the protocols of Mykhailivka's local committees. In belated recognition of the peasants' actions, the district committee presented the 1,000 desiatynas of Silin's estate to the command of the volost land committee for the formation of a land fund and distribution among the land-poor peasants of that region at a very low rental rate; it also gave that committee control over Silin's cattle and inventory.[41] Having received and confirmed the district committee's resolution, the provincial land board informed Silin on 19 December that "on the basis of the Third Universal of the Central Rada and the consequent changed land relations," the processing of his complaint had been stopped.[42]

One of the examples most indicative of peasants' increasing assertiveness, using newly formed institutions to legitimize their claims to more land and forest, occurred in Vesele volost, Kharkiv district. In May 1917 the Kharkiv Public Committee received two complaints from the manager of Iu. L. Kenig's estate, O. A. Kalnin, that peasants of the villages Vesele and Petrivka were forcibly pasturing their cattle on the estate's hayfields and in its forests, thereby ruining the hay harvest and damaging the growth of young seedlings crucial to afforestation. Kalnin had repeatedly appealed to the volost committee, but to date no measures had been taken.[43] On 17 May the Kharkiv Public Committee sent Kalnin's complaints to the Vesele volost committee, asking for a detailed explanation. In response the volost committee sent back a copy of a 20 May protocol of "the Vesele Land-Forest Commission," describing its investigation of Kalnin's complaints. Examining the estate's supposedly damaged forest and hayfields in the presence of two of Kalnin's employees, the commission found no damage to the forests or fields and "not the slightest trace of pasturing." Instead, it "accidentally uncovered" many large piles of deadfall and brushwood, "which without any necessity are lying there and losing their usefulness, the deadfall for fences and the brushwood for fuel." The commission concluded that Kalnin's complaints were "baseless" and informed the volost public committee about the deadfall and brushwood, suggesting that it be taken for local peasants' use.[44] It would seem that the "Vesele Forest-Land Commission" was under the control of and staffed by local peasants, and that its investigation was largely informed by their attitudes and desires. And they did not stop there.

At the end of July 1917, manager Kalnin received an announcement from the estate's employees informing him that citizens of Vesele "on the initiative of fugitive deserters, have completely destroyed our work on the estate." Local peasants had twice arrested and the second time severely beaten Kalnin's assistant, I. G. Dontsov, and the estate's machinist and blacksmith, S. A. Velichko. Day and night "some sort of hooligans or deserters in military uniforms" would show up at the estate without any reason and stroll about the yard, threatening to smash up the employees' apartments and hurt their families. Under such conditions, the employees concluded that they could not continue to work on the estate. If Kalnin did not take measures to ensure the safety of the employees and their families, they threatened to leave his service.[45]

Provoked by his employees' ultimatum, Kalnin appealed to the Kharkiv provincial commissar. Embellishing the more limited statements of his subordinates, Kalnin complained that Vesele's inhabitants had throughout the summer been committing various violent acts against estate employees, citing the examples of Dontsov and Velichko. Not referring specifically to deserters or hooligans, Kalnin claimed that the "inhabitants of Vesele" had been stealing estate grain, showing up without any reason, threatening employees and their families, and "completely terrorizing everyone on the estate, clerks, skilled and unskilled workers." Under such conditions, the correct management of the estate was impossible; if the employees left, the farm's production would be ruined. Kalnin asked the provincial commissar to send him armed militiamen, whom he promised to supply with food and horses, to watch over the estate and eliminate the violent acts of local peasants, "since the local militia lack the forces to deal with this."[46]

Apparently Kalnin received no help from Kharkiv; on 15 September he again petitioned the provincial commissar. Now local peasants were "intentionally driving their cattle to pasture on the estate's land sown with winter crops, which are knocking down and trampling winter crops and threatening their complete destruction." Noting that this "could affect the well-being of the state" and that the estate's mounted patrol was "in no condition to struggle with this evil," Kalnin requested that the Kharkiv provincial food supply committee send five soldiers to protect the estate.[47] Kalnin also sent a statement from Kenig's attorney, stating that peasants from Ternova, Valky district, were arbitrarily plowing up some of the Vesele estate's land, though it was located in Kharkiv district and appointed by the provincial land committee to be rented and cultivated by peasants of Vesele volost.[48] Kalnin also complained to the commissar about the villagers of Petrivka, who had appeared that morning on the estate's fields, appointed for sowing sugar-beets for 1918, stopped the tractor from plowing the fields, and seized them for themselves. These peasants were also obstructing estate workers' from carrying out fieldwork and gathering brushwood and deadfall in the estate's forests. Because these actions were causing huge losses to the estate and greatly reducing the sugar-beet harvest, Kalnin asked the commissar to order "the immediate elimination of such arbitrary actions from the citizens of the village of Petrivka."[49]

On 22 September the provincial commissar forwarded Kalnin's complaints to the provincial land committee and ordered the district commissar to go out to the estate and resolve these misunderstandings.[50] For its part, the land committee dispatched T. Gotviansky and a representative of the Provincial Soviet of Peasants' Deputies, D. V. Nazorovich, to Vesele. Their report has not been preserved, but existing evidence suggests that their efforts proved ineffective. On 23 October (before the Third Universal was issued) the provincial land board informed the provincial commissar that "all means toward settling the conflict had been exhausted."[51]

As mentioned above, there are many such cases. Though the Provisional Government insisted to its very end that only the Constituent Assembly could solve the land question, peasants managed over the summer and fall of 1917 to acquire much of the land not yet in their hands. They did this by both legal and illegal means, but almost invariably with an attempt to legitimize their claims through these local committees, which they controlled.

Yet one would receive a very incomplete picture by focusing solely on peasants' acquisitions of these lands. Although Soviet and Western historians have concentrated their attention on these seizures, often assuming that this agrarian revolution was a "class struggle" of peasants versus landlords.[52] There were, in fact, at least as many conflicts among peasants as there were with large landowners. In other words, at least in Kharkiv province, the peasant revolution of 1917–1918 was not so much a revolution of the peasants as a "class" with any conscious sense of a collective identity, as it was many tiny local revolutions by individual peasant communities, usually involving the seizure (violent or not) of nonpeasants' land. Moreover, these local revolutions quickly turned into squabbles between peasant communities over the splitting of the disappointingly meager spoils.[53]

First, it should be noted that peasants seized not only landlords' lands, but those belonging to all nonpeasants, including the church, the state, and the tsar's family.[54] As reflected in numerous peasant folktales recorded in the nineteenth century, peasants easily substituted the village priest or the tsar for the landlord.[55] To peasants, these others were basically those who owned land but did not cultivate it themselves. Not surprisingly, many villagers also took back the lands belonging to those who had separated from their communes under the Stolypin reforms. Although a large number of these *otrubshchiki* quite voluntarily rejoined the commune in anticipation of receiving their share of the great Black Repartition, some did resist. Intravillage conflict arose only in those few cases in which there was a sufficient number of *otrubshchiki* to resist the demands and actions of the *obshchinniki* (communal peasants). For example, in April 1917 the Kharkiv press reported on a serious conflict that had arisen between the *otrubshchiki* and *obshchinniki* of the village of Udy, Kharkiv district.[56] More typical, however, were complaints from individual *otrubshchiki* protesting the decision of their former commune (usually under the cover of the volost land committee) to take back their land. For example, the peasant Mikhail T. Vasys complained to the provincial land board about the Bashkinsk village zemstvo's resolution annulling all *otruba* formerly cut off from the commune. Despite several cogent appeals to the current law, Vasys received no satisfaction, largely because the provincial land committee was almost powerless to stop peasants' actions.[57] Although no exact figures are extant, it appears that by the end of 1917 most *otrubshchiki* had—forcibly or not—been reabsorbed into their village communes.[58]

Within peasants' understanding of the Black Repartition, this reabsorption made great sense. Most peasants saw their commune as the main actor in the repartition, and bringing back in the *otrubshchiki* and their lands would strengthen the commune and provide it with more land for redistribution. Moreover, as the country devolved into unrest and as power dissipated to the localities, peasants' tendency to identify primarily with their village community was only intensified. And the numerous intervillage conflicts that then erupted over the proper allocation of all seized lands and forests could only have strengthened peasants' allegiance to their village, making it the true locus of power in the revolutionary countryside.

On 3 September 1917 the Ternova volost land committee (Kup'iansk district) informed the provincial committee that on 15 July it had "taken into account" the land and meadows of Count Sheremetev's estate. The committee somewhat defensively asserted that "by right of the law of the Provisional Government" this property had to be used first of all to satisfy the citizens of Ternova volost, because that was where the estate was located. If any land was left over after that, it could be given to citizens of other volosts. Confident in their "interpretation" of the current law, Ternova's peasants had already started to cultivate this land for winter sowing. Soon after, however, peasants from Iampolsk in neighboring Izium district had begun to seize and rent out strips of this same land without any authorization. Thus, the Ternova land committee asked the provincial committee to intervene on its peasants' behalf.[59]

On 16 September the Kharkiv provincial land board (the provincial land committee's executive) informed the Ternova committee that "there was no instruction of the Provisional Government about issuing land to rent only to peasants of the same volost, and thus, the citation of this nonexistent decree is without foundation." The board asserted that such questions "had to be solved in accordance with the real needs for land," and thus ordered the Ternova committee "without fail to enter into an agreement with the Iampolsk committee."[60]

Evidently the peasants of Ternova volost did not comply with the provincial board's order. On 30 September a commission from the Zakotiansk volost land committee arrived at Sheremetev's estate to investigate the damages that the citizens of Ternova volost had caused to the Iampolsk community's hay harvest. Though the commission claimed it had sent an invitation to Ternova ten days earlier, no representatives from the accused community appeared at the investigation. Apparently, the provincial committee had given the Iampolsk peasants permission to cut 20 desiatynas of hay from the estate's fields, and then 40 desiatynas of aftergrass (hay from a second mowing of a field). Peasants from Iampolsk had cut all this hay and loaded it, but when they began to cart it home, a large group of Ternova villagers (*Ternivtsy*) arrived and forcibly seized all of it without presenting any authorization. The commission calculated that these peasants had caused about 7,200 rubles' damage to the Iampolsk community and asked the provincial committee to help draw them to responsibility.[61] Becoming increasingly aware of its incapacity to enforce its own decrees, the provincial land board in response merely suggested that the Iampolsk community take legal action through the courts to recover its losses.[62]

In early October 1917 the citizens of Ostroverkhivka (Merefa volost, Kharkiv district) appealed to the provincial land committee to restore order on the estate of M. M. Kovtun. Apparently, on 15 August the Merefa volost land committee had taken plowlands and hayfields from Kovtun's estate for Ostroverkhivka's citizens (*Ostroverkhivtsy*). A week later this committee rejected a complaint from Kovtun's former renters about the seizure, resolving in favor of the *Ostroverkhivtsy*. However, soon afterwards the Sokolivka volost land committee from Zmiïv district seized this same land for its land-poor peasants. In their appeal, the *Ostroverkhivtsy* wondered how the Sokolivka peasants could be land-poor at all. In April the *Sokolivtsy* had taken land from the Zhukov estate (Zmiïv district), leaving Ostroverkhivka without any arable land there; and they had not yet sown or even plowed that land. Now, they had taken more land from Kovtun's estate, land which Ostroverkhivka's peasants had already divided up, plowed, and sown. The *Ostroverkhivtsy* asked the provincial committee to restore order, to instruct the Sokolivka land committee to follow orders, and to draw the Sokolivka community to responsibility for leaving the land seized from Zhukov's estate barren—neither working it, nor giving it to others to cultivate.[63] Sending the peasants' appeal to the provincial committee, the Kharkiv district land board asked it to help the Ostroverkhivka community and stressed that the Sokolivka community's demands were late and unjust.[64]

Conflicts among peasant communities arose even when the land in question had been legally transferred to peasants to rent. On 12 September the Committee of the Army's Fourth Reserve Artillery Division, then quartered near Chuhuïv (Zmiïv district), resolved to divide up its military fields among four nearby villages who had recently petitioned to rent this land: to Maslivka, 520 desiatynas; to Malynivka, 340 desiatynas; to Korobchyne, 400 desiatynas; and to Tahanka, 65 desiatynas. The committee warned the peasants not to plow the land allotted to other communities, but three of the four villages proved unwilling to adhere to the committee's decision.[65] On 10 November the Maslivka Village Public Committee reported to the Kharkiv Military-Revolutionary Staff that the Malynivka community had on its own initiative plowed up 470 desiatynas, rather than its allotted 340, thereby cutting into the land granted to Korobchyne. The Korobchyne villagers had in turn seized some of the land given to the Maslivka community, and the citizens of Tahanka, being unsatisfied with a mere 65 desiatynas, had also plowed some of

Maslivka's land. Thus, the peasants of Maslivka were left with a little more than 100 desiatynas, despite the fact that their representatives had paid the military commissar full rent for the whole 520.[66] The Maslivka Public Committee claimed that the peasants of the other three villages had sufficient land, while those of Maslivka, being former landlord's peasants (as opposed to former state peasants), had very little land; and half of that land was swamped. Extremely offended by these other peasants' seizures, the Maslivka peasants warned that "undesirable phenomena" could arise among these villagers: certainly fights, "and perhaps even murders." They asked the Military-Revolutionary Staff immediately to send representatives for the demarcation of the Division's lands among all four communities in order to remove the possibility of violence.[67] The Kharkiv Provincial Land Board merely resolved on 24 November to ask the Zmiïv District Land Board to delegate its members to Maslivka to resolve the matter; if those members found that a surveyor was required, the Kharkiv board promised to dispatch one.[68]

Conflicts among peasant communities, already numerous, increased in 1918.[69] On the All-Russian scale, Figes has stated that, "contrary to the old Soviet myth, there were very few conflicts within the village between richer and poorer peasants. But there were a great many conflicts between neighboring communes, sometimes ending in little village wars, over control of the estates."[70] But the cases provided here are sufficient to illustrate that the great agrarian revolution of 1917–1918 in Ukraine was not a "class struggle" in Soviet historians' sense of that term, or in the sense assumed by some Western scholars. For the most part, peasants acted as members of a community; they acted in a local manner, reflecting their local understanding of the world. This worldview can also be seen in the ways peasants related to broader issues; especially the crucial problem of food supply.

The Food Supply

Immediately after the old regime's collapse, which to a considerable extent resulted from its failure to supply the cities with food, the Provisional Government took serious steps to overcome the food supply problem.[71] In March 1917 the government introduced a monopoly on all grain surpluses, charging local food supply organs to collect the grain and pay set prices, which were soon overtaken by rampant inflation in the summer.[72] As noted above, in early May the first Kharkiv Provincial Congress of

Peasants' Deputies endorsed the grain monopoly, while calling for a monopoly on manufactured goods as well. The Provisional Government refused to implement the latter, leaving itself open to repeated attacks from socialists for being too cautious and from conservatives for interfering too much.[73] Not surprisingly, the peasants of Kharkiv province, as across the former empire, proved increasingly reluctant to give up their grain to local food supply agents at such low prices and in the absence of manufactured goods for purchase.[74] Soviet historians argued that the food supply problem could only have been overcome by the transfer of "All Power to the Soviets," thereby in part justifying the Bolsheviks' coup. Yet, the overthrow of the Provisional Government did little to alleviate the problem, and in Ukraine, where the Central Rada claimed authority, the food supply situation continued to worsen as winter came on.

On 2 December D. Skrypnichenko, the Kharkiv Provincial Commissar for food supply matters, published a panicky "Appeal to citizen-peasants of Kharkiv province," asserting that the food supply situation in the army was becoming "deadly." Almost daily the provincial food supply committee received alarming telegrams from the front with appeals "to save the army" by sending more grain. Unfortunately, the provincial committee not only could not increase grain deliveries to the front, but had, in fact, ceased sending grain altogether, "because the population of Kharkiv province has almost stopped supplying grain to the food supply committees." Skrypnichenko warned that soon it would be too late; starving soldiers would quit their trenches in droves and anarchy would break out: "we free citizens will be made into slaves again and lose all hope of receiving land and freedom." He cautioned the Ukrainian people not to be "deaf and dumb" in this threatening moment, but to help their sons and brothers, dying from hunger at the front. "Only those who desire the destruction of the people's freedom, of the young Ukrainian republic and all of Russia, only they would at this time hide their grain, or sell it not to the food supply committees, but various interlopers and speculators. Let there not be among us one who would keep any surplus grain to oneself. Everyone as one immediately give your grain to the food supply committees. Save your army, Ukraine, and all of Russia from anarchy and ruin."[75] That peasants had not and would continue not to give up their grain is perhaps not only a sign of their economic self-interest, but of their lack of identification with such broader ideas as "Ukraine," let alone "All of Russia."

It is useful here to describe briefly the political situation in Kharkiv province at this time. After the proclamation of the Third Universal on 7/20 November 1917, the General Secretariat—the Central Rada's executive body—had declared its authority over food supply issues across the Ukrainian National Republic (UNR), forming a special food supply council under the Secretary for Food Supply. The Kharkiv Provincial Food Supply Committee then recognized the authority of the Central Rada and General Secretariat. But later, in response to the Bolsheviks' ultimatum to the Central Rada, the Secretariat had ordered the closure of the UNR's borders to the northern and western front and to the rear provinces of Russia, thus cutting off Kharkiv province's traditional trade routes to the north. In response, the food supply committee insisted that the food supply question should stand outside of politics and refused to submit to the General Secretariat's demand not to transport grain to northern, starving provinces. The Kharkiv Soviet of Peasants' Deputies supported this position, even though it had just been informed that Bolshevik troops were approaching from the north. The soviet resolved not to submit to the Central Rada's order to close the borders, while condemning the Soviet of People's Commissars (Sovnarkom)'s interference in the UNR's internal affairs. Such ambiguous positions were typical for Kharkiv during the revolution.[76]

Although the position of Kharkiv Provincial Soviet of Peasants' Deputies on the food supply crisis, expressed at its Fifth Congress in early December 1917, suggested a broader concern for citizens of Russia and Ukraine, the congress's reports also revealed that its constituents did not share this concern. On the second day of the congress comrade Rubinsky, the soviet's representative on the Provincial Food Supply Committee, gave a detailed report on the present situation. Accusing the peasants of not fulfilling their civic duty, Rubinsky claimed that the countryside had received far more in goods from the city than it had given in grain. Kharkiv province was supposed to provide 28 million poods of surplus grain, but only 3.5 million had been received, and this had come mainly from landlords. Dismayed that "the peasants are not giving up their grain," Rubinsky claimed that the grain was now in the hands of "village kulaks, who often meet representatives of the food supply committee with stakes in hand. Poor villages are giving up their grain more willingly."[77] Interlopers from the starving provinces of the north were also greatly obstructing grain collection, because they could pay as much as 15 rubles per pood. Rubinsky called on the peasant deputies to demand that their constituents back home not sell their grain to these interlopers, among whom there were not only those from starving regions, "but speculators, who will then resell the grain at four times the price."[78] At the same time, he noted that the supply of necessities to the population was in "a sad state," mostly due to ruined transport. And, more recently, representatives from the starving northern provinces had announced that their populations refused to fulfill their civic obligation and would not send manufactured goods to Kharkiv province unless they first received grain from there.[79] In the end, the congress resolved "immediately to take all measures to gather surplus grain from the population of Kharkiv province," ordering all local soviets to assist food supply agents in all ways possible, and to "explain to the population the necessity to complete grain deliveries."[80]

Not surprisingly, the soviet and its deputies, once they returned to their villages, were largely unsuccessful in carrying out this resolution, as evidenced by the protocol of the Sixth Congress of the Kharkiv Soviet of Peasants' Deputies, which met from 21 to 23 January 1918. Speaking again on the food supply question, Rubinsky stated that, when starving people from other provinces appealed to the Kharkiv Food Supply Committee, he would become "ashamed of his native province." The province had always provided at least 21 million poods of surplus grain, but in this past year it had only given up four million. He had received "exact data" through the statistical department of the provincial zemstvo "from the peasants themselves," confirming that the harvest had been above average in four districts, average in six, and failed in only two districts. Hence, the surplus grain from the 1917 harvest could not be less than 15 million poods, but by late January 1918 food supply organs had received only four million, most of which came from landlords.[81] Despondently Rubinsky declared, "nothing helps, not the democratic character [*demokratichnost′*] of organizations leading the food supply work, not the requests of the starving, not armed forces. The village consciously holds on to the grain, motivated by the absence of kerosene, manufactured goods and nails." As a person closely involved in the matter, Rubinsky claimed that he could provide exact information that the city could not spare to give any more to the countryside. The city had been "refused in everything," in order to send to the village all possible manufactured goods, which to date totaled 15 million rubles' worth. Of course, this was not enough to satisfy the village, but it was a great sacrifice for the city and certainly worth more than four million poods of grain. Calling for the local soviets to take grain requisition into their hands, Rubinsky stressed that the only way to get grain from the peasants was to provide more manufactured goods, "because the masses will come only to those who give and not to those who take." He noted that there had already been cases when bagmen (*meshochniki*) from starving regions, appearing in the province in search of food, had engaged in armed battles with peasants. Listing the many obstacles to transporting goods to grain-producing provinces and grain to starving ones and seeing no real exit from the crisis, Rubinsky concluded: "I cannot offer any real measures, but anyway, I propose: (1) to organize goods exchanges; (2) to implement freedom of trade; and (3) volost soviets of peasants' deputies must take measures to requisition surplus grain and send it to starving provinces."[82]

As these appeals and protocols suggest, most peasants of Kharkiv province proved quite unwilling to make substantial sacrifices for larger ideas of community, regardless of which government, the General Secretariat in Kyiv or the Sovnarkom in Petrograd, claimed political authority over them. In fact, many peasants hardly noticed the change of authority in December 1917, which is not surprising when one considers the only fine distinctions between these two governments' land policies. To the peasants' way of thinking, both the Sovnarkom's "Decree on the Land" and the Central Rada's Third Universal abolished private property on the land and gave it over to the authority of local land committees, which the peasants themselves controlled. Other aspects of either government's land policies seemed to them details.[83]

It is important to note that food-growers' reluctance to give grain was not at all limited to Ukraine or Ukrainian-speaking peasants. Sarah Badcock describes the great lack of understanding between food supply committee workers (and their superiors) and villagers in Kazan and Nizhegorod provinces as evidenced through fascinating examples of resistance to the grain monopoly, especially in Kazan province. These disputes sometimes led to armed conflict with locally garrisoned soldiers.[84] Peter Holquist's work on the Don region reveals that peasant and Cossack communities alike resisted the removal of grain reserves throughout 1917.[85] In fact, on the eve of its own dissolution, the Provisional Government had become so frustrated with grain producers' reluctance to give up their grain that it was arranging to pull troops from the front lines to help extract food from the countryside.

*

A related and important aspect of peasants' local-mindedness in 1917 was their attitude toward the primary institution that claimed to represent them ever since that first conference in early May 1917: the Kharkiv Provincial Soviet of Peasants' Deputies. Though historians have often invoked the resolutions of provincial soviets as indicators of popular mood, the attitudes of "the people" toward these institutions have almost never been examined.[86] This is understandable. The leaders of the soviets claimed to represent and speak in the name of "the people," whether this meant workers, soldiers, peasants, or some combination thereof. Yet, it is doubtful, at least in the case of the Kharkiv Provincial Soviet of Peasants' Deputies, that the views expressed by this institution's leaders and the resolutions they passed and sent on to Kyiv and Petrograd, reflected the desires of their claimed constituents. In a sense, the soviet's leaders had acquired and employed the language of the popular revolution, but not the support of the people.

Certainly, this is a matter of degree. The provincial soviet's resolutions doubtless reflected peasants' views some of the time. There is considerable evidence, however, that villagers proved increasingly unwilling to support the soviet's efforts to speak and act on their behalf. First, as the above discussion suggests, peasants rarely heeded the provincial soviet's decrees and warnings. The soviet usually passed on conflicts over peasant land seizures to the provincial land committee and supported the committee's decisions.[87] Thus, the provincial land committee's inability to carry out or enforce its commands at the local level or to resolve disputes among peasant communities also reveals the limits of the provincial soviet's authority.

For example, on 15 September 1917, in support of the land committee's efforts, the provincial soviet sent a telegram to the peasants of Matviïvka (Bohodukhiv district) denouncing their illegal plowing of the beet fields of sugar magnate, I. P. Kharitonenko, as "intolerable" and demanding they stop immediately. Not only did the Matviïvka peasants ignore the soviet's telegram, but also Kharitonenko's estate manager soon reported that the peasants of neighboring villages had begun plowing the estate's fields.[88] If peasants supported the soviet, why did so many not heed its appeals (and those of the provincial land committee) to stop seizing land and felling forests and patiently await the Constituent Assembly's resolution of the land question?

Further evidence of peasants' lack of support for the provincial Soviet of Peasants' Deputies can be found by tracking how the soviet was funded, an issue historians have rarely examined.[89] Perusing the protocols of the provincial and district-level soviets, one is struck by how much time their executive committees spent on financial matters, ranging from how much committee members should be paid to the funding of the Constituent Assembly election campaign. At its very first meeting on 7 May 1917 the provincial soviet's Executive Committee (EC) discussed how it should be funded, resolving to entrust its Economic Commission to ask the All-Russian Soviet of Peasants' Deputies from where they were to acquire means and in what form, and to work out a budget for the Soviet.[90] On 16 May the EC examined the Economic Commission's draft budget, but resolved that it was too general and the sums proposed too modest.[91] The next day the EC approved a revised draft budget amounting to 50,000 rubles per month, though entrusting its presidium to revise this figure "in correspondence with developing activities."[92] The EC then requested funding from the Provincial Land Board, the Union of Cooperatives, the Union Bank and the Public Committee.[93] Having exhausted all these possibilities, the EC, which now included a chairman, deputy chairman, secretary, and 26 members, resolved on 11 June "to deem obligatory for the Soviet of Peasants' Deputies the principle of self-taxation [*samooblozheniie*] to cover the costs for maintaining the soviet."[94]

In July the EC embarked on a campaign to collect this self-tax from the peasants. It sent out an appeal to all volost soviets of peasants' deputies, informing them about its decision to ask the peasants to fund "their" soviets at a rate of 10 kopeks per desiatyna per month; households holding less than two desiatynas were to pay 20 kopeks per month. After the land seizures of 1917, the peasants of Kharkiv province held about 2.6 million desiatynas of arable land. If they had paid the self-tax at this rate, it would have generated 260,000 rubles per month, half of which was supposed to be transferred to the provincial soviet—more than sufficient to cover its estimated expenses.[95] The EC asked volost soviets to call assemblies in each village to discuss the self-tax and to take all measures to obtain this money, "since neither the volost, district, nor provincial soviets of peasants' deputies can exist without consistent support from their electors, without the support of the laboring peasantry, who elected the Soviets of

Peasants' Deputies for the defense of their rights and interests." Half of the money collected was to remain at the command of the district soviets, exclusively for the needs of the volost and district soviets of peasants' deputies; the rest was to be transferred to the provincial soviet.[96]

Unfortunately for the members of the EC and provincial soviet, peasants proved reluctant to volunteer funds to support "their soviets," and in particular, it seems, the provincial soviet. In mid-August, the EC discussed a protocol received from the Zmiïv District Soviet of Peasants' Deputies in which that soviet resolved to place all funds generated by the self-tax in its own treasury—in other words, not passing on the obligatory 50 percent to the provincial soviet. At the same meeting a resolution was heard from the Randava Volost Public Committee and Soviet of Peasants' Deputies (Bohodukhiv district), which refused to carry out the self-taxation, stating that local organizations were funded by the peasants' communities (*iz mirskikh summ*). In both cases, the EC resolved to order these local soviets to comply with the self-tax and send the much-needed funds to the provincial soviet.[97] In late August the EC again discussed its continuing search for money and decided to send one of its members to the Union Bank, another to the Agricultural Society and provincial zemstvo, and a third to the Union of Cooperatives of South Russia to petition for funds.[98] On 8 September the EC resolved to ask all district soviets to petition their respective district zemstvos to provide means for the provincial soviet's needs.[99]

At the Fourth Congress of the Provincial Soviet of Peasants' Deputies on 24 September 1917, one of three central issues discussed was self-taxation. Opening the debate, EC member Trebelev admitted that "not everywhere are the peasantry sympathetic to self-taxation." Due to the absence of sufficient means, the provincial soviet was unable to carry out even such important matters as preparations for the elections to the district zemstvos and the Constituent Assembly. Trebelev passionately called on peasants "to support their own peasant organizations."

Trebelev's words provoked a series of speeches from peasant deputies attempting to explain why the self-taxation was going so poorly. The most common reason given was that "the peasantry is insufficiently enlightened about the goals of the gathered money, thinking, for example, that this money will go only to the salaries of members of the Executive Committee." Some deputies claimed that peasants refused to give money voluntarily to the soviets due to "the agitation of the village bourgeoisie."

And a few suggested that peasants either did not know where to send the gathered money, giving it entirely to the local public committees, or had not received the proper accounting books to gather the money. The congress resolved to appeal to the peasants once again to support the voluntary self-taxation, and to explain to the population the necessity and goals of the taxation.[100]

Not surprisingly, the provincial soviet's appeal did not have its intended effect. Neither resolutions and appeals from Kharkiv nor the peasant deputies' efforts back home could convince peasants to pay this modest sum to support "their" soviet. At a meeting of the EC on 2 December, it was revealed that the provincial soviet's financial situation was critical; there were "no means and, apparently, nowhere to obtain them." Public organizations and credit granting institutions refused to give the soviet funds, supposedly "because they are all composed of defensists."[101] The EC resolved simply to ask the city duma for a loan.[102] On 8 December the EC again discussed the soviet's lack of means and passed several resolutions aimed at raising funds: (1) to order the Lebedyn, Kharkiv, Valky, and Starobilsk public committees to give 3,000 rubles each for the Ukrainian Constituent Assembly elections; (2) to ask the Central Rada to give 30,000 rubles for these elections; (3) to demand that all district soviets of peasants' deputies send half of the self-taxation funds immediately to the provincial soviet; (4) to appeal to all zemstvos and cooperatives for funds; and (5) to appeal along with the Soviet of Workers' and Soldiers' Deputies to the Sovnarkom in Petrograd for money.[103] These measures also proved ineffectual. The provincial soviet did not overcome its financial difficulties before invading German troops forced the EC's members to evacuate from the province in late April 1918.[104]

This evidence of the peasants' indifference to wider interests is not conclusive. It is not easy to determine why it was so difficult for the provincial soviet to extract this tax from its supposed constituents. As the peasant deputies suggested, peasants may have been confused about the reasons for the self-tax and unsure of where to send it, though in the context of that fourth congress of the soviet, the reasons offered by the deputies ring somewhat apologetic: they supposedly represented their volosts and were responsible before the provincial soviet for the failure of the tax collection. It is also possible that peasants simply lacked the funds to pay the tax, though this is in part refuted by Rubinsky's statement (mentioned above) that by January 1918 peasants of the province had purchased about fifteen million rubles' worth of manufactured goods and that this amount had not satisfied them.[105] It also seems that in some districts peasants were paying the tax, but that district and volost soviets were not passing on the required 50 percent to Kharkiv (a further indication of peasants' localist tendencies). Moreover, it is doubtful that the amount imposed on any individual peasant household was burdensome. Even after their seizures of land in 1917–1918, most households would have ended up with no more than about six desiatynas each, making their tax "burden" only about 60 kopeks per month.[106] Thus, it is reasonable to suggest that many peasants did not pay this tax because they were not willing to support the provincial soviet, even to this modest extent. This and other already presented evidence of peasants' lack of support for "their" soviet prompt the questions: to what extent did the resolutions and decrees of such higher-level soviets, provincial and above, reflect the peasant masses' attitudes and desires? To what extent did those resolutions come to express attitudes held by those "elected" (under quite unknowable circumstances) to represent peasants? And to what extent did such resolutions reflect the aspirations of these higher-level soviets' executive committees, largely composed of urban, socialist intelligentsia?

The Ukrainian National Revolution

The story presented above of the countryside in 1917 is different from the one Ukrainian historians have traditionally told. Most glaring is the lack of attention to the Ukrainian national revolution, so often discussed and studied before 1991 by Ukrainian historians in the diaspora, and warmly embraced by most historians in Ukraine since independence. There is no doubt that the emergence and spread of the national idea during the revolution in Ukraine had profound long-term historical significance. Above all, were it not for the Central Rada and its leaders' efforts to declare and begin to organize an independent Ukrainian state, it is doubtful that Moscow would have decided to make Ukraine a separate Socialist Soviet Republic. That was in turn a decision which arguably contributed a great deal (despite Moscow's intentions) to the eventual emergence of independent Ukraine. Moreover, I do not wish to suggest that there was no support for the Ukrainian national movement in Kharkiv province in 1917. As in other Ukrainian provinces of the Russian Empire, in Kharkiv province some local Ukrainians strove to create national organizations.

Largely because of the tsarist regime's policies, the Ukrainian national movement was almost nonexistent in the province on the eve of the revolution. In his November 1915 report to the Department of Police, Major General Rykovskii, chief of the provincial gendarme administration, noted that to the present date only students took part in "the Ukrainian movement," despite their efforts to broaden its appeal. Recently, some of these students had attempted to publish a Ukrainian workers' newspaper, *Slovo*, under Volodymyr Vynnychenko's editorship. Providing yet one more example of the authorities' attitude toward any attempts by local intelligentsia to politicize the Ukrainian question, the Kharkiv governor shut the newspaper down immediately after the first issue appeared. Nationally conscious Ukrainian students who tried to move beyond "cultural work" were almost invariably arrested and soon exiled or forbidden to live in the province.[107] Rykovskii proudly concluded that the Ukrainian movement "in general does not embrace the mass of peasant or worker populations of the province and meets sympathy only among an insignificant part of the intelligentsia, mainly in Kharkiv among the students."[108]

Given the prerevolutionary situation, it is remarkable how quickly local Ukrainian intelligentsia began to organize after the February Revolution. On 8 March 1917 about 1,500 representatives of various Ukrainian organizations in Kharkiv gathered in the public library to elect an organizing committee charged with creating the Kharkiv Provincial Ukrainian Rada, soon to be the Central Rada's plenipotentiary. Hnat Khotkevych, a leading Ukrainian figure in Kharkiv, was elected chair of the committee. Indicative of the stage of nation-building in the province at this time, the committee soon issued a broadsheet, "To the peasants," explaining "what a Ukrainian is and what he must do." Its content reflected the Ukrainian intelligentsia's paternalistic attitude toward peasants, as did many of its other activities. For example, the organizational committee conducted a fundraiser, in which Ukrainian peasant girls were auctioned off to urban *intelligenty* to symbolize the hoped-for union between the intelligentsia and the village.[109] In mid-March a congress of credit cooperatives in Kharkiv passed a resolution, proposed by Khotkevych, to Ukrainianize all the cooperatives. The resolution concluded with a demand that all cooperatives on Ukrainian territory "must be only Ukrainian."[110] On 1 April the organizational committee published the first issue of its weekly, *Ridne slovo*, declaring its goal to be the unity of all Ukrainians: "We can be people with various convictions, but let us be united in one thing: we are Ukrainians and want good for Ukraine, good for all Ukrainian people."[111] The editors of this newspaper and its successor, *Nova hromada*, called on Ukrainians to support their work, especially in the form of money to help pay for printing. Over the course of 1917 they would repeatedly refer back to the oppression Ukrainians suffered under the old regime, that this had resulted in a people barely conscious of their own nationality, and that there was much work to do.

Such efforts, resolutions, and appeals can be charted in the newspapers these organizations published, but we are interested in a different question here: how did the overwhelming majority of the province's population—the peasants—receive these efforts? The Ukrainian national movement has been examined at great length from its national leaders' perspectives, but very little has been written on the broader masses' reception of their activities and declarations. Partly because of the lack of access to archives and partly because of the focus of Ukrainian historians in the diaspora, we actually know very little about peasants' understanding of the relatively new idea that they were all part of a much larger "imagined community" called Ukraine. The one historian who has seriously studied this problem, Steven Guthier, found that there was "a popular base" for the national movement among the peasantry. Although prohibited from carrying out archival research in Ukraine, Guthier amassed considerable evidence from newspapers and published documents to support his argument.[112] The archival and newspaper evidence presented here, however, brings into question Guthier's claim that the majority of peasants (at least in Kharkiv province) supported in a serious way the Central Rada and Ukrainian autonomy.

It is important to recall how most Ukrainian peasants spent their time in 1917. Leaving aside the resolutions of congresses and conferences, and focusing on their behavior, we recall that peasants spent most of their time cultivating their plots and striving to obtain more land and forest. In their numerous legal and illegal seizures, often legitimized by the resolutions of local committees and soviets, peasants revealed their priority to be, above all, their perceived economic well-being. Moreover, in their numerous squabbles over the redistribution of seized land, they expressed the limits of their "imagined communities," the borders of their village's fields, at most of their volost. And this localism directly inhibited their willingness to sacrifice for broader ideas, such as "Ukraine." If they were unwilling to make such sacrifices, could they truly be said to support the Ukrainian government or Ukrainian autonomy? Peasants did not in important ways even support the Kharkiv Provincial Soviet of Peasants' Deputies, the one organ that was supposed to represent their interests. This soviet and its executive committee roundly endorsed Ukrainian autonomy, but this did not mean that most peasants did.

Although Guthier discusses some local elections, the main evidence he provides showing peasant support for Ukraine is the results of the Constituent Assembly election in November 1917. Demonstrating that most Ukrainian peasants voted for Ukrainian "populist" parties, scoring "a decisive electoral victory throughout most of Ukraine," he concludes that these results "repudiate the notion that the Ukrainian peasantry lacked national consciousness in 1917."[113] One cannot deny the Constituent Assembly election results, which historians have examined in considerable detail.[114] As in most Ukrainian provinces, most peasants in Kharkiv province voted for the list that included on its platform a call for Ukrainian autonomy. But in order to determine how to interpret these election results, it is necessary to examine in some detail the process leading up to the election and the election itself. In the revolutionary countryside of 1917, where the very idea of free, universal elections was unprecedented and almost unknown, one can hardly draw the kind of conclusions Guthier does.

Constituent Assembly Elections

The promise of the Constituent Assembly was born with the February Revolution. On 4 March, on the first page of the first issue of *Izvestiia Khar'kovskogo Soveta rabochikh deputatov*, the official newspaper of the newly formed Kharkiv Soviet of Workers' Deputies, the central importance of this institution was proclaimed. The newspaper appealed to the Provisional Government to call a Constituent Assembly, elected on the basis of a universal, equal, direct, and secret ballot, which would fulfill the central task posed by the fall of the old regime: "the creation of a new, democratic structure."[115] On 1 April in its first issue, *Ridne slovo* also held out to its Ukrainian readers the promise of the Constituent Assembly. While calling on Ukrainians to welcome all those asking for their votes, the paper demanded that "we must cast our votes only for those who will at the Constituent Assembly stand up for the autonomy of Ukraine and desire to make Russia a federation, a union of autonomous regions." Significantly, the article concluded by linking autonomy with the land question: "And when the Constituent Assembly gives us autonomy, then we can elect our own people from our country and establish our own order. Then, our better elected people will decide that all lands—state, royal, and monastery—will be given to the people, so that there will be no one who has 10,000 desiatynas and another who has none."[116]

Such declarations probably meant little to most peasants. As the above discussion has shown, peasants were quite unwilling to wait for the Constituent Assembly to resolve the issue that mattered most to them: the land question. From the First Congress of Peasants' Deputies to their repeated land seizures and intervillage squabbles, peasants expressed their eagerness to solve this matter as they saw fit, before the elections even took place.

Most of the campaign to "enlighten" the masses about the elections was carried out by the soviets, in this case directed by the Kharkiv Provincial Soviet of Peasants' Deputies. Whatever may have been the soviet's good intentions, it is quite clear that most peasants were only "enlightened" about one political option: the Party of Socialist-Revolutionaries (PSR) in coalition with the provincial soviet. Already off to a late start, on 21 July the Executive Committees of the Provincial Soviet of Peasants' Deputies and the Kharkiv Soviet of Workers' and Soldiers' Deputies met jointly to discuss primarily the election campaign. Noting that the elections were scheduled to take place on 17 September, Comrade Rubinshtein alarmed those assembled with a report on the poor organizational level in the countryside: "One cannot deny the circumstance that the peasantry on the whole are disorganized and not prepared for the elections." In many districts the volost zemstvos had not even been elected yet. He recommended that the soviets train and dispatch as many "instructors" as possible to the countryside to explain what the Constituent Assembly was and how peasants should vote. At this stage, the party leaders in attendance all agreed that the instructors should be nonpartisan and explain the programs of all parties, remaining "completely neutral." But another speaker pointed to the more critical problem: that there simply was not sufficient time to train the instructors or, therefore, to inform the peasants adequately about the elections. The meeting passed no resolution.[117] The elections were soon postponed until November, but the insufficient number of "instructors" would force the Soviet's Executive Committee to streamline their "enlightenment" project along clearly partisan lines.

On the evening of 25 July a meeting of the Executive Committee of the Kharkiv Soviet of Peasants' Deputies, including thirteen representatives from the district soviets and twenty members of the executive committee, was held to discuss the Constituent Assembly elections. Comrade Aivaz'ian called for the creation of a commission of propagandists and agitators, who would be obliged to travel to "every corner of the district" in order to "familiarize the population with the technicalities of the elections and with the conduct of individuals of the revolutionary-democratic tendency." Though the meeting's protocol suggests that committee members discussed mainly how the soviet should better inform the peasants, the actual debate turned to party politics. In the end the committee resolved "not to put forward its own separate list in the elections to the Constituent Assembly, but to vote for the list of the Party of Socialist-Revolutionaries, which must be composed with the participation of representatives from the Soviet of Peasants' Deputies and must contain candidates from the soviet." This resolution was not to be considered obligatory until it was discussed at the soviet's next congress on 30 July.[118] The close interconnection between the soviet's executive and the PSR was also evident at the 29 July meeting of the Executive Committee, which chairman Kachinskii opened with a short argumentative speech "of a clearly party character," justifying his decision to quit his post. His announcement provoked lively debate, a number of orators bemoaning Kachinskii's departure on the eve of the Soviet's Third Congress. But when it was explained that this was a decision of the PSR, the committee quickly moved to elect a new chairman, suggesting that the party's decisions overrode the committee's desires. While moving yet closer to the PSR, the executive committee also revealed its growing distance from the peasants. At the same meeting the committee unanimously resolved that all of its members should acquire weapons to be carried whenever they traveled to the countryside, even agreeing to reimburse those committee members who could not afford to purchase their own weapons.[119]

The PSR's dominance of the Executive Committee seems to have extended to the soviet's deputies. On the following day, 30 July, the Third Congress of the Kharkiv Provincial Soviet of Peasants' Deputies, with 167 deputies in attendance, commenced its activities by unanimously resolving to send its "first word" to the PSR's leader, Viktor Mikhailovich Chernov: "The Congress salutes you, our peasant Minister, and expresses great confidence that in our general struggle for Land and Freedom the final victory will remain with the laboring people." As its second order of business, the congress unanimously resolved to assign 3,000 rubles to the Ukrainian and Russian PSRs for agitation in the countryside about the Constituent Assembly elections. The passing of these resolutions provoked no debate.[120] At its evening session the congress passed the resolution proposed by the Executive Committee on 25 July, that the Soviet would not put forward its own list of candidates to the Constituent Assembly, but would combine with the Ukrainian and Russian Socialist-Revolutionaries on one list. Local soviets were to adhere strictly to this resolution, making sure that "all candidates were acceptable to both the soviets and the parties." Once the congress had composed and confirmed the candidate list, each and every member of the congress was obliged in his volost and district "to explain to the population the necessity to cast votes only for this list and to carry out agitation for this list."[121]

The congress also took a strong pro-Ukrainian stance, recognizing the Central Rada as "the competent authority in Ukraine" and calling on the newly reformed Provisional Government to confirm its July agreement with the Rada's executive, the General Secretariat. Noting that the All-Russian Constituent Assembly would probably take place before the All-Ukrainian one, the congress's deputies resolved to oblige themselves "to take care that the interests of the Ukrainian laboring people will be most completely represented in our list of candidates to the Constituent Assembly."[122]

The Executive Committee's strong pro-SR and pro–Ukrainian autonomy position did not go unchallenged. At its 12 October meeting, the committee discussed the "separatist actions" in Sumy and Starobilsk districts. Though we do not know what these actions entailed, they seem to have challenged the candidate list proposed jointly by the PSR/UPSR and provincial soviet, and thereby provoked a split in the Executive Committee. Committee member Kovbasa announced his solidarity with Sumy district; member Koshura declared that he could not support the Soviet-SR list and therefore resigned his post. When Kachinskii (still very influential, though no longer chairman) questioned Koshura's declaration, the latter replied that he could not vote for the list, because it included many "maximalists."[123] He thereby provoked "the general outrage" of most of the other committee members, who immediately voted for Koshura's removal from the committee and soviet. They also formed a commission to investigate these members' break with the committee's otherwise strong solidarity and resolved to issue an appeal to the peasants of Sumy and Starobilsk districts, which would list numerous "facts characterizing the candidates of the hostile lists."[124]

The most important rift that emerged in the Kharkiv Soviet, however, was provoked by the so-called Soviet of Peasants' Deputies-Soldiers of the Kharkiv Garrison. This other Soviet of Peasants' Deputies, elected by those garrison soldiers who considered themselves to be peasants, had throughout the summer of 1917 led a largely independent existence while trying to acquire seats in the larger Kharkiv Soviet of Peasants' Deputies. Repeatedly snubbed by the latter soviet's Executive Committee, this soviet resolved to advance its own list of candidates to the Constituent Assembly. On 13 October the Executive Committee discussed the soldiers' list, No. 15, and resolved to exclude all of that list's candidates from the PSR and to carry out agitation against that list, despite the fact that Ekaterina K. Breshko-Breshkovskaia, "the Grandmother of the Revolution," headed and supported it.[125] The Executive Committee resolved to carry out the most active agitation against the soldiers' list, sending its members to all district-level congresses of soviets, and resolved to send Chernov a telegram most urgently asking him to come to Kharkiv province to stop discord from breaking out among the peasants.[126] Although this split provoked considerable debate at the provincial and district level soviets, it does not seem to have seriously affected the elections' outcome.

Just a few days later, on 20 October, the Executive Committee finally decided on slogans for its joint Soviet-PSR-UPSR list of candidates for Constituent Assembly elections. The slogans for list number 5 represented the crucial aspects of its platform, from most to least important: "(1) All land without compensation to the laboring people; (2) All power to all the people; (3) Enough blood! Peace to all peoples! (4) Workers' organizations must control factories and plants; (5) An autonomous Ukraine in a Federated, Democratic republic of Russia."[127] Armed with these slogans, the committee's members and other agitators went out into the district centers to rally support for their list.[128]

Only a few descriptions of the district conferences called to rally peasants to list number 5 have survived, but they are worth discussing. One of the more raucous conferences took place on 22 October in Starobilsk, home to a fairly rebellious district soviet. The conference attracted many citizens, "especially peasants, who followed the exchange of opinions with intense attention and very passionately greeted those orators with whom they agreed." The district executive committee chairman, Viretskii, explained that the conference had been called at the request of several volost soviets; Novo-Astrakhan Soviet, for example, had declared that the district soviet's executive committee "is not up to the task and does not defend the interests of the laboring peasantry."[129] Once the conference was opened, a number of peasants stood up and sharply criticized the soviet and especially the executive committee for its inactivity and laziness. Attempting to defend the committee, Viretskii argued that the SRs' policy, and not the committee's lethargy, had prevented peasants from receiving land. The peasants loudly responded with cries: "Enough! Away! We will take the land!" After passionate debate, the conference resolved to vote for list number 5, asking Breshko-Breshkovskaia to revoke her candidacy "for the sake of the unity of the laboring people and its victory over the landlords and bourgeoisie. The conference will call the peasantry to vote only for list number 5 and to refuse their support to all other lists."[130]

In early November 1917 the SR newspaper, *Zemlia i volia*, reported on the congress of the Kup'iansk district Soviet of Peasants' Deputies, the main task of which was to decide for which list, number 5 or number 15, "the laboring peasantry of Kup'iansk district will vote." The supporters of list number 15 sent Breshko-Breshkovskaia and a former government minister, Lebedev, to speak for its list. Kachinskii, along with several other members of the Executive Committee, arrived to promote the Soviet-SR list. After an entire day of debate, 38 of 41 deputies present voted for list number 5. The main reasons given for choosing this list are informative: that this list was chosen by the provincial soviet and the SRs; that Chernov headed the list; and that the list promised the land to the peasants: "V. M. Chernov is the first peasant [*muzhitskii*] minister and we will send him to the Constituent Assembly to get us [*dobyvat′ nam*] land and freedom." The district soviet also obliged all the deputies, upon their return home, to explain to their co-villagers the congress's decision and to "exert all their forces in order that during the elections to the Constituent Assembly all peasants will vote only for list number 5."[131]

Such unanimous decisions at the district level suggest that at the local level matters were decided much more simply. From the evidence available, it seems clear that the peasants were not presented with much of a choice; they were told that they should vote for list number 5, because it "best corresponds to the interests of the laboring peasantry." For example, the Bohodukhiv volost congress of peasants' deputies unanimously resolved on 30 October "to make all efforts among the population in order that voting to the Constituent Assembly will be for list number 5, at the head of which stands the former Minister of Agriculture, V. M. Chernov."[132]

It is difficult to determine how the elections themselves were carried out at the local level. L. G. Protasov, in his study of the elections, has noted that contemporaries themselves gave such contradictory descriptions that one would think they were describing different elections. For example, the Kharkiv newspaper *Zhizn′* reported on 26 November that in Izium district the elections had completely lacked organization: "Staggering absenteeism. People almost had to be dragged by force." On the other hand, the left-leaning liberal daily *Iuzhnyi krai* was first of all struck by "the enormous percentage of voters," citing a figure of 66 percent for the whole province, 76 percent for Izium district.[133]

Few descriptions of the actual voting at the local level remain, but what we do have suggests that the process was less than democratic. Mykola Kurylo, a peasant correspondent from the village of Husynets, Kup'iansk district, reported that already a week before the elections a volost assembly had resolved to vote for list number 5. The elections proceeded quietly over a three-day period from 12 to 14 November; old people and youths all came out to vote, because, according to Kurylo, "each wanted to cast their vote for list number 5." List number 5 won an easy victory. After the elections, the peasants expressed great anxiety that the Constituent Assembly should meet as soon as possible in order "to work out the laws about the land. They desire that the Constituent Assembly will meet promptly, because to wait is already impossible."[134] One might note here that, though Kurylo identified himself as a Ukrainian and was a sort of national agitator in his village, his last statement suggests that his co-villagers mainly expected from the Constituent Assembly the resolution of the land question.

A more detailed description of the election process was provided in the village of Merefa (Kharkiv district). The reporter began by noting that despite the village's location about 15 miles from Kharkiv, few preparations had been made. Only three agitators had appeared and they had not managed to acquire any authority in the village, attracting no more than fifty inhabitants. And yet, the reporter claimed, the voting over a three-day period proceeded "unusually briskly," with about 60 percent of eligible voters casting their ballots. There was a rumor circulating that someone was threatening the people with various punishments and calamities if they did not take part; the reporter did not know who this "someone" was but wished to thank him for the substantial election turnout. Older people complained that they had to go to the polling station and vote in person, claiming that they were too frail or did not have the time. One older woman lamented that she had been foiled by the election official who took her ballot. She claimed that when she told him that she wished to vote for list number 5, the official had her vote put in the urn for list number 1. Her son had discovered this upon her return home, because one voted by tearing or cutting out the list one preferred from the ballot, placing it in an envelope, and putting it in the urn. Returning to the polling station, the woman exclaimed: "What in the world am I to do? I went home and my son saw that list number 1 had been torn out [from my ballot] and began to scold and bawl me out, [saying] that I was not supposed to vote for that list. But I did not know, I am not literate and did not know what to do." Not surprisingly, most peasants in this village voted for list number 5.[135] Such descriptions certainly lead one to wonder whether any sort of democratic elections could have been carried out, especially in the countryside. Although the ballots were composed so as to make voting as simple as possible, one would still have had either to be able to read the names or at least the number of one list or trust that some literate person would indicate the correct list.

The election results in Kharkiv province were fairly predictable, considering the predominance of SRs in the peasant soviets and their central role in propagandizing the elections. List number 5 received over seven times more votes than the second-place finisher; this joint UPSR/PSR-Soviet list received 796,552 votes (72.9 percent); the RSDRP(b)'s list (number 3) came in second with 114,743 votes (10.5 percent); the Kadets (list number 6) finished third with 58,302 votes (5.3 percent); then followed the garrison's soldiers-peasants' list number 15 with 42,329 (3.9 percent); the Union of Landowners with 13,847 votes and the RSDRP (united) with 12,192. Interestingly, in Sumy district, the main district (outside of Kharkiv) where a serious challenge was made to list number 5, that list received proportionally fewer votes than in all other districts.[136]

While these results reveal an impressive victory for the joint UPSR/PSR-Soviet list, they do not prove that there was a social base for the national revolution among peasants. At the beginning of 1917 the peasants of Kharkiv province could have known only very little about the democratic election process. And once they heard of the tsar's fall, they had more important matters to consider and act on. The Provincial Soviet of Peasants' Deputies did what it could to enlighten peasants about the election process, but this was not nearly enough. The soviet and its district level subordinates lacked the means, time, and personnel to inform peasants properly; and, of course, learning to vote in democratic elections takes time and experience. Moreover, most of those peasants whom the soviet's instructors and agitators did reach were thereby "enlightened" about only one candidate list—the joint Kharkiv Soviet-UPSR/PSR list. Of all the names listed on the ballots, this was very likely the only list most peasants would have recognized. Finally, if we are to measure peasants' priorities by their actions in 1917, it seems clear that the main reason peasants voted for this list was that it propounded the slogan: "All land without compensation to the laboring people!" Keeping in mind peasants' localist worldview, as expressed in so much of their behavior in 1917, it is difficult to believe that many of them voted for list number 5 primarily because it called for an "autonomous Ukraine." At the very least, this examination of the Constituent Assembly election process at the local level brings into doubt the assertion that the election's results prove that Ukrainian peasants were nationally conscious.[137]

One should be careful, however, not to confuse a different interpretation of these election results with a dismissal of the Constituent Assembly's importance. Soviet historians often questioned these results in an attempt to justify the Bolsheviks' deliberate, violent, unilateral closure of the assembly. The interpretation presented here does not in any way justify this violent action. Certainly, those deputies elected to the assembly represented a much broader spectrum of opinions and interests than those of the Bolshevik party. Perhaps they would have been able to create a broader consensus, and even to avoid the horrible civil war that led to so much suffering. What I am suggesting here is simply that we must be very careful in drawing conclusions about peasants' consciousness and identities based on the Constituent Assembly elections' results.

*

In conclusion, I would like to stress that I am not arguing that the revolution that raged across Ukraine in the period 1917–1921 was not in part national. I am pointing out that it was *not only* national, and that Ukrainian historians' singular focus on the national aspects of the revolution has considerably obscured our understanding, excluding many people, events, and institutions from the story. For most peasants of

Kharkiv province, as across the crumbling empire, the land question was primary. Outside their essential, daily activities of cultivating the soil and feeding their animals in order to feed their families, peasants acted above all to obtain more land; sometimes legally, sometimes not. This scramble for the land was not merely, or even primarily, a "class struggle" between peasants and landlords. Peasants took land from all nonpeasants and fought among themselves as much as with former owners for the land, revealing the very local identity that they brought to the revolution. Their localness was expressed not only in the numerous intervillage conflicts, but also in their unwillingness to sacrifice for larger ideas of community. They proved unwilling to sell their grains at low government-set prices to food supply committees, despite numerous appeals from Kharkiv, Kyiv, and Petrograd for them to save the army, Ukraine, and all of Russia from starvation. Moreover, even the Provincial Soviet of Peasants' Deputies, which claimed to represent and speak on the peasants' behalf, could not enforce its decrees among them and proved unable even to extract enough money from them to fund itself. This suggests how poorly the provincial soviet represented the views of its claimed constituents, questions the reliability of documents generated by such higher level soviets for understanding peasants' revolutionary aspirations, and more broadly, reveals the ephemeral and fluid nature of power in revolutionary Ukraine, at least in the rural localities.[138]

3 The German Occupation of 1918 in the Ukrainian Countryside

A FUNDAMENTAL LINE WAS DRAWN between Ukraine and Russia at Brest-Litovsk on 9 February (27 January) 1918.[1] When the delegation representing the Ukrainian National Republic (UNR) signed a separate peace treaty with the Central Powers and subsequently invited the latter's armies to assist it in asserting its authority over Ukraine, the republic's new citizens were effectively cut off from events occurring in the rest of the former tsarist empire. The Central Powers' occupation sheltered the UNR from the excesses of Soviet rule—war communism—to the north. At the same time, the brutal and arbitrary actions of the occupying German and Austro-Hungarian armies undermined the legitimacy of the UNR, its ruling body the Central Rada, and even more so its successor, Hetman Pavlo Skoropads′kyi's Ukrainian state, in the eyes of its citizens. Over the course of 1918 these citizens came to view these regimes as a foreign occupation by "Germans" and the "pany," and as "counterrevolutionary." As a result, the separate peace at Brest and the Central Powers' "assistance" discredited the national idea before many peasants in Ukraine while preserving the image of "Soviet power" as benign, local, self-rule by the people.

*

In January 1918 pro-Soviet troops, including detachments from the north as well as numerous local recruits, quickly swept across Ukraine from Kharkiv, taking Kyiv on 26 January 1918.[2] As Andrea Graziosi has argued, the main reason for their "easy victory" over pro–Central Rada forces was that about 300,000 peasant-soldiers from Ukrainianized regiments deserted the Rada's troops, returning to their native villages hoping to obtain their "fair share" in the land seizures.[3] Placed in a desperate situation by the Sovnarkom's violent actions, the Rada's leaders felt forced to sign a treaty with the Central Powers in an effort to preserve their fledgling republic. A few days after the treaty was signed, at the German military command's "suggestion," delegates from the Central Rada signed an appeal to the Austrian and German peoples requesting their assistance in "liberating Ukraine from the Bolsheviks." The German Supreme Command responded on the same day, informing the Emperor and Foreign Office that "military assistance would be furnished without delay, and that two German detachments had already been ordered to Pinsk and Rovno."[4] German forces began marching into Ukraine on 18 February and, sweeping quickly across Right-Bank Ukraine, entered Kyiv on 1 March 1918. Returning to Kyiv with the occupying forces, the leaders of the Central Rada immediately reaffirmed the UNR's law effectively granting all non-peasant arable land to the peasants, as well as the Third and Fourth Universals. They also promised to restore the "order" that had ruled in Ukraine before the Bolsheviks' arrival and attempted to assuage citizens' fears about the arrival of German and Austro-Hungarian troops, against whom many of the new republic's peasant men had been fighting for the last three years. In a February 1918 interview the UNR's president, Mykhailo Hrushevs′kyi, despite his personal misgivings about Germany's intentions, reassured the Ukrainian people that the German troops then entering Ukraine had been ordered not to rob or oppress them. "The German government wants to establish broad and friendly relations between Ukraine and Germany…in order that the Ukrainian people will see the Germans as their friends."[5] Such promises in the name of the Ukrainian People's Republic—of land and friendly German helpmates—likely only increased peasants' eventual disappointment with the UNR and even more so the Ukrainian State of Hetman Pavlo Skoropads′kyi.[6]

The situation in Kharkiv province in early 1918 differed considerably from central Ukraine mostly because German troops[7] did not manage to occupy the province until mid-April 1918, after overcoming formidable resistance from Red Guards and other pro-Bolshevik forces.[8] Hence, in early 1918 the nominal authority in Kharkiv province remained the provincial Soviet of Peasants' Deputies,[9] though it seems to have wielded very little control or influence in the countryside. Peasants continued to seize land, forest, and anything else they could get their hands on through the early months of 1918. In a circular to all district and volost land departments of soviets of peasants' deputies, dated 5 March 1918, the provincial soviet's land department noted, "unfortunately, from many places news is arriving that the population is beginning independently [*samochinno*] to carry out the massive felling of trees in both state and formerly private forests."[10] Noting that "such plundering of the people's wealth" would inevitably have a very negative impact "not only on the interests of the local population, but on the whole state," the land department ordered district land departments to take the most decisive measures immediately to ensure that no trees were cut without the appropriate permission. The department stressed that "permission for felling forests can be issued only by the district and provincial land departments of soviets of peasants' deputies, and hence not [by] volost [departments]," which implies that, as with the land committees of 1917, peasants were employing these local institutions to provide some official cover for their actions.[11] It also seems that peasants were on their own initiative firing the guards hired to protect the forests, because the provincial land department felt impelled to issue a decree stressing that such firings were not allowed, that this too was not within the volost land department's authority.[12]

Kharkiv's soviet authorities also attempted to bring some order to the seizures of the previous year, thereby revealing how rapidly power had diffused to the localities. On 7 March 1918 the provincial soviet's land department ordered all volost land departments "under the supervision of district departments immediately to elucidate all cases of destruction [or theft] of former non-laboring farms," and to compose protocols listing all individuals involved, in order to bring the guilty to legal responsibility before the People's Court. Stolen property, including cattle, forage, and farming tools (land was not mentioned), were to be seized and taken for safekeeping under the district land department's command for "distribution in the usual order for the liquidation of former non-laboring farms."[13] As their insistent and frustrated tone suggests, these decrees were probably almost impossible to enforce at the local level, especially because they aspired to control and limit the power of local peasant-dominated bodies.

No doubt, the great dispersal of power to the localities was not limited to Kharkiv province. In his now well-known report on the situation in March 1918, the German journalist Colin Ross observed that across Ukraine "complete chaos ruled." There was no real central authority.

> The entire country is divided up into a whole series of separate territories, confined to the borders of a district, a city, and sometimes even separate villages and hamlets. Power in these territories belongs to various parties, as well as individual political adventurists, pirates, and dictators. One can find villages surrounded by trenches and waging war against each other over the lord's land.[14]

In such an anarchic situation, the soviet authorities could hardly enforce their decrees, and as pro-UNR and German forces advanced on Kharkiv, these leaders were forced to turn to issues more essential to their own survival. On 5 April the Executive Committee of the Provincial Soviet of Peasants' Deputies discussed its plan to evacuate Kharkiv and executed the plan shortly thereafter.[15] Following a few days of bloody fighting, the last pro-Soviet detachment abandoned Kharkiv. Most of those workers and peasants, who had fought in the Red Army, evacuated the city with the party organization and joined the Tenth Soviet Army.[16]

It is important to describe the first document that most peasants in Kharkiv province would have received from the Central Rada. After German troops and some pro-Rada Ukrainian troops occupied the city, the Soviet's land department was replaced by a provincial land committee. This body soon received an appeal "From the Ukrainian Central Rada to the Citizens of the Ukrainian People's Republic," in which the Rada explained recent events, striving to justify its peace treaty with the Central Powers and the latter's military assistance. The appeal had been issued on 11 March, but the provincial land committee did not receive it until 23 April, probably delayed by the military situation. The appeal stressed that all freedoms established in the Rada's Third and Fourth Universals remained in force. Trade unions and soviets of peasants' or workers' deputies were free to continue working "for the protection of their class [and] professional interests," but they were not permitted to pretend to power, "because there must be only one authority in Ukraine: the Ukrainian Central Rada and its ministers." At the same time the Rada stressed that its authority was only temporary, until the long-promised All-Ukrainian Constituent Assembly was able to meet. In a key passage, the Rada assured citizens that the Germans would not interfere in Ukraine's internal affairs: "They come as our friends and helpers for a short time in order to help us in this difficult moment; they have no intention to change our laws or regulations [or] to limit the independence and sovereignty of our republic." The Rada called on peasants "to take care in particular that the land, which has been transferred to the hands of the laboring people, will all be sown," concluding that "in the grain is our wealth," and that this was crucial "in order that our reborn, free and independent Ukrainian People's Republic will live and blossom."[17]

On 27 April the provincial land committee's executive (the provincial land board) sent to all district land committees copies of another decree, the Central Rada's "Land Order," instructing the committees "immediately to distribute these copies to all volosts of the district."[18] Reaffirming the Rada's temporary land law of 18 January, which had abolished the right of ownership on all lands in the republic, the Land Order stressed that "in the interests of the whole Ukrainian people and state, all lands must be sown immediately" and promised that "whoever sows, keeps [the land]." Volost land committees were obliged to watch assiduously that all land was sown. "One who has not sown the land [already] in his possession does not have the right to additional allotments." Owners of non-laboring farms had no right to interfere in the redistribution of their land among the rural poor and would be severely punished for any attempts at interference. Only when peasants were unwilling to sign an agreement to sow the land granted to them would former landowners be allowed to sow some portion of their former estates.[19] Clearly, the Rada's land policy was not very different from that of its predecessor, except that the primary role at the local level was to be played by the land committees and not the local soviets' land departments. The Rada's great concern that all reapportioned land be sown reflects its fears of not fulfilling its food supply obligations to the Central Powers, while carrying out (or at least attempting to bring some order to) this massive land redistribution project.

It is difficult to determine how widely these documents were distributed, or whether peasants were reassured by their content, mainly because the Central Rada's rule ended just two days later. On the night of 29/30 April 1918 the German military authorities arranged the replacement of the Rada with Hetman Pavlo Skoropads′kyi and his supporters.[20] In his memoirs, Skoropads′kyi later claimed that, if he could have, he would have supported and courted above all the "*khliboroby-demokraty* [farmer-democrats]."[21] In reality, he felt compelled by circumstances to rely on the far more powerful "Union of Landowners" and the occupying troops who placed him in power, neither of whose plans for the countryside corresponded with those of the majority of rural inhabitants. The members of the union strove to reclaim their estates, seized by peasants in 1917, and Skoropads'kyi supported them as much as possible, declaring the restoration of private property in his ascending "Charter [*Hramota*]." It is true that the hetman eventually announced a plan to redistribute some of the great estates' lands to land-poor peasants, but he unequivocally declared that the government would not violate private property rights nor embark on any experiments that could ruin Ukraine's agricultural production in the process.[22] At the same time, the occupying troops who placed him in power, and to whom he had granted as a condition of their support "a free hand in trade and raw materials procurement,"[23] sought to extract from the countryside all they could, plundering where and when they wished and disregarding both the peasants from whom they took and the local hetmanate authorities who protested the troops' arbitrary actions. Peasants sent numerous appeals for compensation or relief from the occupiers' exactions to government officials; these officials pleaded with local German military commanders and sent appeals to Kyiv; central hetmanate authorities appealed to the German general staff; and German commanders ignored them all. One finds it difficult to imagine a regime less acceptable to most rural inhabitants.

As a result of these political and military changes, the first encounter of many peasants of Kharkiv province with the Ukrainian People's Republic was the arrival to their village of a detachment of German troops seeking food and fuel, and wielding the weapons to extract them. For example, on 25 March 1918 a German dragoon regiment passing through the village of Nova Vodolaha (Valky district) demanded from the village's agronomist, A. G. Storozhev, oats and hay for their horses. Storozhev refused, asserting that this forage was for local peasants' cattle. Ignoring his protests, the German cavalrymen forced him to give up about 90 poods of oats and hay, while other soldiers took more oats themselves without asking permission. The soldiers stayed in the village overnight, and Storozhev discovered in the morning that they had taken another 50 poods of various foodstuffs. On their way out of town that morning they also seized the village's breeding bull, worth about 3,000 rubles at the time. For all this, the regiment paid 150 German marks and promised to send an inventory listing everything else they had taken and for which they would pay later. Neither Storozhev nor any of the villagers of Nova Vodolaha ever received the inventory, let alone the promised money.[24]

In mid-April soldiers passing through the village of Popivka (Izium district) requisitioned about 1,770 rubles worth of foodstuffs from the village's cooperative. One can easily imagine that Popivka's peasants feared the worst had come to pass: the Germans, against whom they had sent to fight some of their best sons, husbands, and fathers over the last three and a half years, had won the world war and were now taking possession of their conquered lands. The German troops gave the peasants no money for the food they seized, though they did issue a promise to pay. Over the next six months, representatives of Popivka's peasants repeatedly (at least six times) traveled to Izium and appealed to the German commandant to pay them for the requisitioned foodstuffs. Each time, the commandant refused them, providing one excuse or another and promising that they would be paid the next time.[25] There were numerous such cases, as evidenced by the number of complaints that the provincial starosta, the highest authority in the province under the hetmanate, received over the next eight months.[26]

One of the most informative documents on the situation in the countryside at this time comes from an unlikely source: the chairman of the Graivoron (Russia) district land committee. Part of Kursk province before the revolution, Graivoron district's local leaders had in 1917 petitioned to have their district joined to Kharkiv province. Not having received any directions from central authorities, in early 1918 they decided on their own simply to consider their district part of that province.[27] As a result, in early May 1918 the chairman of the district's land committee wrote a lengthy report to the Kharkiv provincial land committee on the situation in the district, providing a rare glimpse into events at the local level. During the rule of "Bolshevik power," the chairman began, on the basis of provincial and district decrees, a general redistribution of all lands—peasants' and landlords'—was undertaken. The land committee simply added up all the arable land in the district and divided it by the number of people to determine the allotment per person (*dushevyi nadel*). Hence, all the lands and property of peasants (whether they were members of a commune or independently consolidated farmers) were included in this redistribution plan. The chairman noted that this method had greatly increased hostilities among peasants. The emerging situation prompted the chairman to ask the Kharkiv provincial land committee for clarification on a number of questions: Could communal lands be redistributed by the number of persons per household? What were the land committees to do with common pasture fields? How did one define non-laboring farms? What was the area of a "laboring farm"? What was to be done with sugar refineries and the lands they had owned and on which they had grown sugar beets, now that these lands had been redistributed among peasants? What was to be done with the agricultural tools and livestock of the confiscated estates, now under the land committee's control? Livestock presented numerous problems, being expensive to feed and maintain. The chairman insisted that the land committee receive clarification on these questions immediately, because peasants otherwise refused to carry out fertilization or any other fieldwork on their newly acquired lands. He also asked for money to implement and enforce these policies.[28] As across most of Kharkiv province, in Graivoron district the spring sowing had coincided with the arrival of German and pro-Rada troops pursuing retreating Red Army soldiers. The troops had greatly disrupted and delayed the sowing, especially in the northern part of the district, where the Iusipov and Kharitonenko estates were located. German commanders had issued orders to restore these estates to their original owners. Such orders would have realized peasants' worst fears, greatly encouraged by Bolshevik propaganda, that the Germans were coming to restore the estates to the landlords and punish all those peasants who had taken part in the land seizures and plunder.[29] In this restoration, the chairman claimed, the estates' former employees played a crucial role, responding quickly to any German commander's first indication and completely ignoring the UNR's land law. He also reported that the district's total area sown had decreased considerably, due to dry weather, the absence of seeds, and "general agricultural ruin." Noting that the entire spring sowing had been done by peasant communes, societies, and cooperatives (and not individual farmers), the chairman asked for monetary subsidies, since this "would give the laboring people the possibility to become economically stronger."[30]

In all likelihood the chairman of the Graivoron district land committee never received a response to his many queries, let alone any funding. In his "Charter to the Ukrainian People," issued two days before the chairman sent off his report, Skoropads'kyi declared that the Central Rada, the Mala Rada, and all of the land committees "are from this day forth dissolved." Skoropads'kyi's charter would have confirmed the chairman's fears as foreshadowed by the decrees of those arriving German commanders. He declared, "The rights of private property, as a basis of culture and civilization, are restored in complete measure, and all the orders of the former Ukrainian government, as of the provisional Russian government, are rejected and abolished." The charter did mention that "measures will be taken for expropriating lands at their true value from great landowners for redistribution in land allotments to land-poor farmers," but even such moderate concessions remained largely on paper during the hetman's rule.[31]

On 1 May the hetman's government informed the public that it had begun working out a plan of land reform intended to meet the needs of landless and land-poor peasants, in the process revealing its much more conservative approach: "The government does not intend to enter onto the path of violating the right of property, nor on the path of dangerous experiments, which no cultured country has yet known, nor on the path of ruining the farming culture, which has composed the basis of Ukraine's national economy. But the government will not hesitate before any sacrifice in order to create in Ukraine a healthy peasantry, insured with land and capable of raising its productivity in the highest measure."[32] In mid-May the Ministry of Land Affairs, under the leadership of V. H. Kolokol'tsov, decreed the creation of temporary land commissions to replace the abolished land committees. To any informed observer, these commissions' tasks must have seemed truly insurmountable: (1) to return all seized farms to their owners; (2) to help landowners calculate their losses and induce the population to give up stolen property and repay owners for their losses voluntarily; and (3) to resolve misunderstandings between owners and peasants concerning seized or confiscated lands that peasants had already sown.[33]

Although the hetmanate probably lacked the resources even to create these commissions, let alone implement this restoration policy, the hetman's declarations did encourage some landlords to return to Ukraine to reclaim their estates, often soliciting the help of locally quartered German or Austro-Hungarian troops and paying them for their services.[34] The returning *pany* would frequently on their own initiative impose exorbitant "contributions" on the local peasants, the scale of which far exceeded their losses from the previous year. In these actions they were supported by the Union of Landowners, which had done much to help bring Skoropads′kyi to power. The union's leaders expressed no interest in implementing Skoropads′kyi's suggested land reform, and thus, the government moved very slowly on this issue. No land reform was passed into law during Skoropads′kyi's rule, despite the hetman's complete legal authority to issue laws as he saw fit.[35]

Historians of the hetmanate have stressed the enthusiasm with which landlords reclaimed their estates, enlisting the help of German and Austro-Hungarian troops and creating their own "punitive detachments,"[36] but very little evidence has survived of landlords' attempts to regain their estates in Kharkiv province. One document provides an idea of how some owners tried to reassert their property rights. On 15 June the Ulianovska volost (Sumy district) zemstvo (probably operating in the absence of a local land commission) sent out an order to be posted immediately across the volost, informing peasants that all livestock and farming equipment taken from the estates had to be returned by noon on 17 June, or else a punitive detachment of German troops would be called in to extract the stolen goods.[37] In another soviet-published document dated 9 May 1918, the hetman's war ministry informed the de facto commander of German forces in Ukraine, General Wilhelm Groener, that a revolt had broken out in Kup'iansk district, likely sparked by landlords' attempts to reclaim their estates. The ministry claimed that twenty estates had been destroyed and that "the pogrom movement continues."[38] The Soviet historian N. I. Suprunenko also notes that on 9 May the hetmanate government appealed to Gen. Groener "to order German troops to stop the *bunt* in Kup'iansk district" and that on 14 June peasants from Zmiïv district crushed a German detachment arriving to requisition grain from the village.[39] Such documents are, however, most striking for their rarity.

Some evidence of peasants' responses to landlords' attempts to regain their property was provided by a landlord from Kurulka volost, Aleksandr Georgevich Matisen, who complained to the Izium district starosta that "despite the commands of the hetmanate and the German authorities," peasants were "only incompletely" returning the inventory they had seized from his estate. Some peasants were not surrendering the inventory at all, expressing confidence that they would soon be able to seize it back. They were also not giving up weapons, declaring that "only with force" would they hand them over; even then, they promised to "defend themselves with arms in hand." Recently, Matisen observed, "such views and convictions are expressed freely because of the complete absence of power in Kurulka and neighboring volosts, since the local ataman and his assistants are completely inactive." The precinct's chief of militia lived 25 kilometers (about 15 miles) away and had yet to visit any of these volosts. Noting the complete absence of reliable troops in the area, he asked that a German detachment be dispatched to his district.[40] Matisen understood that only the German troops were capable of accomplishing their goals in the countryside. In late September the chief of the province's criminal investigation bureau admitted as much: "without the help of German or other outside forces there would not be any possibility to restore the local estates."[41]

Certainly, the hetmanate gave peasants ample cause to label it a counterrevolutionary and restorationist regime, from its proclaimed land policy to the employment of former tsarist police officials. And yet, the evidence leads one to wonder whether peasants perceived the main evil of the hetmanate to be the return of the *pany*. Most of peasants' complaints to hetmanate authorities focused on the actions not of returning landlords, but of the occupying soldiers. And almost all of these complaints did not concern German troops' role in restoring landlords' estates, but rather two kinds of interconnected impositions: requisitions and contributions.

An illustrative case of the latter began on the night of 22 June 1918 near the village of Sinne, Bohodukhiv district, when an unknown assailant attacked, shot, and seriously injured the district's chief of militia. The next day Bohodukhiv district's deputy starosta and the commandant of German troops quartered in the district visited Sinne and announced the imposition of a 50,000-ruble fine (*kontributsiia*) on the entire village for the crime. In addition, the German commandant ordered the peasants to surrender immediately all weapons still in their possession. The German troops were supposed to confiscate all weapons from the civilian population. They suspected that the Bolsheviks had given out many weapons to the local inhabitants, who were hiding them from the occupying authorities. Although the extraction of these weapons was enforced very unevenly, depending mostly on the energy and thoroughness of locally stationed German troops, the German authorities occupying Kharkiv province expressed great diligence in this regard.[42] If the peasants of Sinne did not surrender these weapons, which the commandant seemed certain they possessed, he threatened to impose another 25,000-ruble contribution. Finally, the commandant ordered the village to give up another 6,000 poods of grain, out of supposedly "available reserves," "because this grain was needed for the starving population of Kharkiv." All these fines were designated the mutual responsibility (*krugovaia poruka*) of the entire village and had to be paid within a three-day period. If the peasants did not make full payment on time, the village starosta was ordered to seize their cattle to sell at current prices up to the value of the fine; hence, the commandant also forbade all villagers to take their cattle out to pasture, or even to leave their yards, on the day appointed for final collection, 27 June 1918.[43]

On the morning of 24 June the village's starosta, V. N. Bardakovskii, and the chairman of the volost's "people's zemstvo," T. F. Shubai, called a village assembly and informed the villagers about the crime committed and the fines that the German commandant had imposed on them. The villagers listened patiently, and then composed their own "opinion," in which they declared that they were "deeply disturbed by the crime of this unknown criminal," but that they were guilty of nothing. They beseeched the district starosta to carry out "the most rigorous investigation" of the crime, promising to render all possible assistance "in the matter of establishing the truth." They insisted that the crime had not been carried out by any inhabitant of Sinne, claiming that the chief of the militia had done no evil against the villagers and that his activities did not concern their village. "The inhabitants completely did not know about the injured chief's trip," nor could they even identify him. They stressed that to punish all the people for a crime they had not committed was very unjust.[44]

The villagers then elected six men as their representatives to travel to Bohodukhiv ("or further") to ask the district starosta, and through him the German commandant, whether "it was just to impose a fine on us, a guiltless people." Concerning the presence of guns in their village, the representatives were instructed to admit that their volost had received 100 rifles during the months of Bolshevik control in order to create a Red Guard detachment. But soon after, most of these rifles had been transferred to the village of Klemovoe to protect the alcohol produced there; German troops had already confiscated those guns. The peasants claimed to have surrendered the rest to the local militia before the German troops' arrival. They admitted that they had also requested two machine guns and ammunition from Kharkiv, but they had not received them before the Bolsheviks had fled. Finally, the peasants asked the starosta to remove the fine of 6,000 poods of grain, arguing that "the population has no grain at all right now, because part of it was consumed and part was requisitioned [already!] by German troops."[45]

It seems that the village's spokesmen received no satisfactory response, because on 2 July they sent an appeal directly to the Kharkiv provincial starosta. Apparently, following an investigation of the matter, the German commandant "orally" agreed to remove the 50,000-ruble fine, and extended the period for surrendering weapons to 1 July. And when one weapon was surrendered on 30 June, the same commandant declared that the 25,000-ruble fine would be remitted. Hence, the villagers were very surprised when the commandant returned with several German soldiers on 1 July, declared a 75,000-ruble fine on the village, and went about seizing the villagers' cattle and horses. The livestock were not systematically collected according to the list that peasants had composed and presented to the village starosta on time, but were taken at random. Sometimes the only cow was taken from a soldier's wife, a widow or orphans; better-off peasants had all their livestock seized, making it impossible for them to gather in their almost ripe harvests. The village elders were not able to determine how many livestock had been taken, but they estimated that it was five to ten times more than the value of the imposed contribution. Noting that the cattle had been herded off to Bohodukhiv, they complained that "obviously, the district authorities had not taken any measures not only in defense of those offended, but even to determine the value of the seized cattle." Disillusioned with the local authorities, the representatives asked the provincial starosta to order the district starosta to stop these illegal seizures and to investigate this matter seriously, "since the facts of the shooting are in great doubt."[46]

Four days later the provincial starosta responded to the peasants' appeal, forwarding their complaint back to Bohodukhiv district's starosta and requesting "detailed information concerning the circumstances of the matter… and also about the bases of imposing the punishment on the peasants of Sennyi [Ukr. Sinne]."[47] The district starosta's response, which he did not manage to send to "His Excellency" the provincial starosta until 27 July, is instructive of the nature of power at the local level under the Hetmanate. The district starosta stressed that he had very much disagreed with the German commandant's decision to impose this contribution on Sinne's peasants and had repeatedly appealed to him to remove the fine. Admitting that it was entirely the German commandant's decision, the starosta reported that the Germans had collected and retained 42,840 rubles from Sinne's inhabitants and that the German commandant justified the contribution as a punishment for the peasants' refusal to surrender their grain and weapons. The commandant's order had had the character of a demand, threatening repressive measures, if the peasants failed to comply. Apparently, the starosta felt quite powerless to countermand the commandant, merely noting that the seized livestock had now been returned, because it had only been confiscated to ensure that the peasants paid the contribution.[48]

The provincial starosta took further action on this matter almost three weeks later, on 14 August 1918, when he sent a letter to the Minister of Internal Affairs; the only piece of correspondence in this case, one might note, that was written in Ukrainian. Merely summarizing the peasants' appeals and the district starosta's report, the provincial starosta added only one significant point: "Presenting the above-described for Your perusal, I, from my side, will add that the laying of contributions on the population by German troops, in general, has a rather wide application, considering which I beg [you] to give me instructions."[49]

Sometimes peasants responded to the German authorities' unjust and arbitrary actions with physical resistance—and suffered the consequences. On 5 June a large horse fair took place in the village of Kolomak, Valky district that was attended by many people, including horse-dealers from as far away as Voronezh and Kursk provinces. At the very height of the horse auction, a group of German soldiers arrived, led by a Lieutenant Safar, who began requisitioning whichever horses struck his fancy from the dealers arriving to sell them. In response, the horse-dealers, most of whom were peasants, began to seize back the horses from the soldiers, including from Safar. The Germans then quickly left the market, but returned moments later with an entire detachment and opened fire. One peasant was killed in the shooting.[50] About ten days later, the district's German commandant, Captain Weiss, sent a telegram to Kolomak, imposing a contribution of 75,000 rubles on the village's inhabitants, "because an attack had been carried out on a German officer and his soldiers by peasants from the horse fair in Kolomak." The contribution had to be paid in foodstuffs (as much as possible) by 24 July and submitted to the German detachment now present there.[51]

The villagers of Kolomak must have protested almost immediately, though no written record of their protest has survived. On 19 July the Valky district starosta wrote to his provincial superior about the incident. He stressed that there was considerable evidence that those who resisted the German soldiers' attempts to requisition the horses were not from Kolomak, that the requisition was imposed without the knowledge of the local police and administrative authorities, and that "the huge sum of the fine is very burdensome for the inhabitants." The district starosta asked the provincial starosta to cancel the contribution, "the more so that ignorant nonlocals from various places, who took cover at the appropriate moment, played the main role in the disturbance."[52]

On 20 July Captain Weiss informed the chairman of the Kolomak volost board that, though "the pranks against German officers and soldiers were in the first place committed by non-Kolomak residents, full responsibility falls on the town of Kolomak, which did not strive to defend German servicemen from these pranks at its fair. Hence, the established contribution cannot be removed as a result of principled causes."[53] A few days later, however, Weiss extended the deadline for payment to 7 August and imposed the fine on the entire volost, which the volost managed to pay by mid-August 1918.[54]

One can get some idea of how Kolomak volost's peasants felt about the situation from an appeal they composed in mid-December 1918. The peasants stressed that many outsiders had come to the horse fair, including many horse-dealers from Voronezh, Kursk, and Poltava provinces. They claimed that the peasants who had accosted Lieutenant Safar were not from their town. Noting that Weiss had recognized this fact and that he had fined them anyway, the peasants pointed out that they could only have prevented these "pranks" if they had known about their preparation in advance. "But the local population did not know about this, because everything took place accidentally, unexpectedly, and quickly ended." In addition, the peasants argued, "the local population should answer only for its own inhabitants; for arriving, unknown people it cannot answer." In fact, as Weiss had admitted, the local population had enjoyed good relations with the Germans, at least until this incident.[55] Eventually, the peasants' appeal inspired the later Kharkiv provincial commissar, Serhii Tymoshenko, the highest civil authority in the province under the Directory's short-lived rule in December 1918, to appeal to the High German Command (which was at that time hurrying to evacuate its troops from Ukraine) to return the money to the peasants, citing all the reasons they had provided. It is very unlikely, however, that the peasants were ever reimbursed.[56]

German troops' arbitrary requisitions and their commanders' unresponsiveness to peasants' appeals for justice were widespread and provoked numerous complaints from and discontent among peasants. On 15

July the Valky district starosta reported to his provincial superior on the discord caused by the German military authorities' recent requisition of horses across the entire district. German soldiers had seized horses from those owning only one, or they had paid only the lowest prices for them, far below market value.[57] Many peasants wrote to the district starosta complaining about the Germans' methods. An interesting example of such an appeal came from Koz′mo E. Iaremenko, a peasant from the small village of Bolhar (Valky volost), dated 2 July 1918. Iaremenko reported that according to the requisition announcement, the German authorities had ordered that each peasant household present one horse, "not younger than four years," to sell at a "voluntary price—by agreement with the horses' owners." Not possessing such a horse, Iaremenko sent along with his father's horse his own little filly, born in May 1916. Violating their own announcement, the Germans requisitioned the two-year-old filly from Iaremenko's father, despite the latter's protests, paying for it a mere 500 rubles, though Iaremenko claimed it was worth at least 5,000 rubles. He had already appealed to the district starosta, but had been refused: "the German authorities considered my horse to be four years old, and so they took [it]." Iaremenko provided the names of many witnesses from his village who could confirm that his filly was only two years old, along with records of the horse's conception and birth certificate, but it is very unlikely that he received any satisfaction.[58] Numerous horse owners appealed to the district starosta, requesting that their requisitioned horses be returned because they were paid so little for them; others demanded to be paid the current market value of their horses. The district starosta had repeatedly asked Captain Weiss to satisfy these peasants' petitions, but the German commandant simply replied that he did not "have the right to return the horses."[59]

One of the most informative documents on German troops' behavior was provided by the Izium district starosta, Kokh, in his 9 August appeal to the chief of the district's German garrison. Noting that as a result of his many conversations with the local inhabitants he had determined that "dissatisfaction toward the German troops is growing," Kokh listed villagers' grievances: German troops were requisitioning grain and other products without following the decrees issued by their commanders; sometimes they requisitioned grain without paying for it; sometimes they seized all the grain, leaving nothing for the family to eat; they carted off the grain without weighing it, merely guessing at the amount by sight;

if they were given inventories of the requisitioned products, these were issued "in extremely slipshod fashion" such that they were almost incomprehensible; in villages near the borders with Kup'iansk and Bakhmut districts, German detachments quartered in different districts were requisitioning in the same villages and paying different prices for the same food items. Stressing that he was motivated by only the best intentions, "sincerely and in every way desiring to support among the people of the district the best attitudes and feelings toward the German troops" and striving to ensure that these relations were based "not only on the threat of arms, but on a consciousness of justice and moral authority," Kokh asked the German commandant to take a whole series of measures to improve people's attitudes toward the soldiers:

- declare definite prices on all goods subject to requisition, and ensure that soldiers adhere to them;
- establish a normal portion to be requisitioned from each peasant household, leaving sufficient food for the household's continued existence;
- as much as possible, pay peasants for the requisitioned food in cash, and issue typed, legible receipts;
- weigh requisitioned goods;
- fix and declare the German mark's exchange rate with the ruble;
- requisition detachments should carry with them documents (in German and Russian) granting them permission to requisition, and these should be presented to the village authorities upon arrival;
- these detachments should also have their own bags for carrying the goods, because these were rare and dear among peasants;
- allocate places of requisition evenly among various German detachments, so that the same village was not subjected to requisition by different detachments;
- inform peasants to whom they could appeal with questions and grievances.[60]

These suggested measures reveal how chaotic the Germans' requisitions were and how little account they took of peasants' needs. Kokh sent his report and recommendations not only to the German commandant, but to the provincial starosta, adding a more alarming note: "recently German troops have been carrying out the requisition of grain and other products so carelessly that they are provoking the general dissatisfaction of the population, which all the more often appeals to me with complaints." Asserting that these complaints were often "well founded," Kokh asked for the starosta's assistance in solving these problems.[61]

Complaints about the German soldiers stationed in Izium district came from other sources as well. In mid-August the chairman of Izium district's zemstvo, Sumtsov, sent an urgent telegram to both the provincial starosta and the Minister of Agriculture reporting that German troops were also requisitioning forage in the district, "completely not considering the needs of the population." Soldiers had arbitrarily requisitioned hay purchased by the zemstvo for its agricultural work and to feed its horses. Stressing that "these actions threaten to undermine at the very root the newly begun work," Sumtsov asked these higher officials to issue immediate orders to stop this behavior.[62]

Into the increasingly complex mess of Izium district then entered representatives from the State Grain Bureau, who categorically declared to Kokh and the population at large that only they possessed the right to requisition anything. Kokh reported that German troops were still very busy carrying out "independent requisitions of grain, forage, cattle, butter, honey, riding equipment, and many other things." Moreover, he noted, these German requisitioners sometimes even presented official documents from their commander. "All my undertakings, both on paper and in person, have not achieved any kind of results. Between the Germans and the population is being created strained relations, which it would be desirable to avoid."[63] The Kharkiv provincial starosta dutifully passed on Kokh's and Sumtsov's appeals to the Staff of the First Army Corps, requesting that the latter issue an order stipulating that forage be requisitioned exclusively at the demand of the State Grain Bureau.[64] It does not seem, however, that the German military staff paid much attention to such requests.

On 19 September 1918 the provincial starosta wrote an appeal addressed, significantly, not to the Ministry of Agriculture, but to the Ministry of Internal Affairs, providing evidence of how widespread such cases were. Citing reports from various district starostas, he stressed that "in many districts the population's general dissatisfaction with the German authorities' actions is progressively increasing." As causes of this growing frustration he cited "various kinds of injustices allowed by them [the German authorities] during the requisition of grain, forage, and other things," and also the imposition of contributions on whole villages for the criminal actions of individuals. Requisitions were being carried out "far too abnormally." Usually, the Germans requisitioned without any kind of plan and "persistently" violated the order of requisitions. Listing all the grievances mentioned by his subordinates (discussed above), he added a few more: German requisition detachments would confiscate peasants' carts, forcing them to haul the requisitioned grain and even German soldiers; peasants complained that soldiers had mowed down their pastures and crops without even asking permission; sometimes they even mowed down meadows rented by village administrations to help the needy. Overall, "the cases of arbitrary and illegal requisitions... are becoming more and more frequent, taking on in places a universal character." The starosta stressed that these German soldiers seemed to be operating without the authority of German commanders, motivated simply by their basic needs and desires. And German commanders were not quick to respond to the numerous complaints of those suffering at their troops' hands; local state officials had great difficulty enlisting local commanders' assistance. In conclusion, the starosta stressed that the German soldiers' actions, and their commanders' unwillingness to discipline them or help local officials, were "bringing to maturity a dark dissatisfaction with the Germans' conduct and in the localities a disquieting situation is being created, which could in the end lead to undesirable forms of separate, hostile conflicts, which would not be without danger for the state order and public quiet." Stressing that the continuation of these chaotic requisitions could have catastrophic economic consequences as well, in particular decreasing deliveries of food to the cities, the starosta called for the introduction of "urgent measures for putting in order the whole requisition matter, in order to pull out at the root the cause of the dissatisfaction...and its possible results."[65]

It seems that the Germans' near universal response to such appeals, whether they came from the peasants themselves, local officials, or the Minister of Internal Affairs, was silence and inaction. German occupation policies in Ukraine were, though in some respects quite confused, clear about their main goal: "Above all, our task in Ukraine consists in acquiring supplies as quickly as possible in order to alleviate the misery in our homeland." The German authorities cared very little about the local inhabitants' objections to the Germans' methods of completing this task. Field Marshal Hermann von Eichhorn, the commander of the German troops in Ukraine at the time, described German policy in April 1918: "If this leads to clashes with the government or the population, then this is to be sure very regrettable, but the German command authorities are from their side to alter nothing."[66] When the German journalist Colin Ross presented his report on the chaotic situation in Ukraine in March 1918 to Chief of the Operations Department of the Eastern Front General Max Hoffman, he listed a series of mistakes made by the German command and its troops. Hoffman simply replied, "Ah, all of Ukraine interests me only to the next harvest. Then, you can do with Ukraine whatever you like."[67] However, in the implementation of this task the German authorities were in the end greatly frustrated, mostly by their own troops, who, left to their own devices, often sought to fulfill their personal needs first of all. Their behavior not only decreased the foodstuffs available to be sent to Germany, but also turned peasants further against the regime and against cooperation with the Germans.[68]

If the local German commander responded at all to the complaints of peasants and Hetmanate authorities, it was generally in a less than adequate form. In late September the Izium district starosta, Kokh, received a reply from the local German commander, Major Giller, concerning one of Kokh's recent appeals. Informing Kokh that troops were absolutely not to requisition hay and other products without leaving some for the peasants, Giller asked for more exact information: the name of the foodstuffs' owner, place of requisition, time of requisitions and the name of troops who carried them out. Noting that specific rules had been established concerning such requisitions, he simply stated that "all troops must requisition exclusively for pay."[69]

Kokh's reaction to Giller's reply reflected his growing frustration with the local German command. Forwarding Giller's letter to Kharkiv, he stated that "in addition to all my requests and reports I again recount: German troops are carrying out extortions and requisitions not only carelessly, but unjustly, bordering on pillage [*maroderstvo*]." Kokh begged his superior to take measures to protect the population "from the unjust extortions [that are] provoking general discontent." Citing Giller's attached letter, he concluded that "the local German command enjoys no especial prestige [among the troops, presumably] and an appeal to some sort of higher instance is necessary."[70]

On 23 September the provincial starosta sent another appeal to the German staff, informing it about the chaos in Izium district and suggesting that such behavior was widespread. He even appealed to the German command's desire to extract grain to send back to Germany, stressing that the German troops' requisitions of forage were forcing those cultivating the land to kill or sell their working livestock, because they could not feed them. Noting that without this livestock much of the crop would not be harvested, the starosta politely asked the German command "not to refuse to take the appropriate measures toward establishing systematic order in the requisition of forage."[71] In a letter to the Ministry of Internal Affairs, two weeks later, the provincial starosta recounted the German staff's response to his appeal. The staff simply replied, "in Izium district requisitions of forage have not been carried out by German military detachments."[72]

At just about this time, German generals and politicians in Berlin began to realize that they were not going to win the Great War. On 3 October, in an effort to stave off possible Allied-imposed internal reform, a new government was formed under the chancellorship of the liberal yet princely Maximilian von Baden. As a condition of accepting this post, Maximilian was forced to affix his signature to the fateful diplomatic note sent to all belligerent countries that asked President Wilson "to take in hand the restoration of peace," accepting in principle Wilson's Fourteen Points "as a basis for a future peace negotiations.... To avoid further bloodshed, the German government requests the President to arrange the immediate conclusion of an armistice on land, by sea and in the air."[73] Thus began more than six weeks of great international uncertainty that eventually led to the armistice; and thus were German soldiers first definitively informed that the war was lost. Maximilian had strongly desired to give a speech in the Reichstag explaining in detail his government's understanding of Wilson's Points, including an assertion that Poland, the Baltic states, the Caucasus, Finland, and Ukraine should not be considered "Russian territory in the strict sense." He was forced, however, to lay such bold assertions aside because of the fear of Supreme Command and Foreign Office that the speech would provoke Wilson to reject the armistice offer.[74]

The diplomatic note and the protracted negotiations that followed put the German forces occupying Ukraine in a peculiar position. Those Ukrainians who had prospered under the Hetmanate, and who realized their dependence on German troops, wanted the latter to remain. In a 6 October secret report, the Foreign Armies Division of the General Staff claimed that "the Ukrainians were developing greater confidence in the Reich, were friendlier than ever before toward the occupation forces, and the prospect of a German evacuation disquieted the pro-Hetman forces."[75] Such claims seem to have reflected prevailing opinion among German commanders in Ukraine, or at least in Kyiv. In a letter to his wife, dated 9 October 1918, General Groener stated that "in Ukraine it is at present so peaceful and quiet that one could live here quite pleasantly, if the uncertainty from other theaters of war and from Berlin were not casting heavy shadows there and here."[76]

Whether Kyiv was as peaceful as Groener believed, Hetman Skoropads′kyi seems to have sensed that matters were more threatening outside the capital. On 1 November the hetman's government formally asked the Entente to allow German troops to remain in the country until it was able to organize a real Ukrainian army. German military leaders then resolved to keep their military forces in Ukraine after hostilities had ceased in the west, so that they might prevent Ukraine "from falling back into chaos and lawlessness," certainly a rather novel understanding of cause and effect.[77]

On 22 October 1918 Skoropads′kyi himself revealed how bad the situation was becoming in Kharkiv province. In a published decree he admitted that recently across the province "predatory attacks of armed bands, murders, robberies, arson, and the blowing up of railway bridges" were occurring at an accelerated rate, violating "the normal conditions of life" and provoking "unrest among society." As a result, in order "to insure order to peaceful communities," he found it necessary to proclaim the province in a state of extraordinary safeguard (*chrezvychainaia okhrana*), presenting sweeping powers to the provincial starosta on the basis of a tsarist law ("Regulations on Decency and Security") published in 1916.[78] Skoropads′kyi seemed quite willing to pass and publish a decree clearly citing a tsarist law, even though the very words "extraordinary safeguard" must have evoked in the minds of many former subjects of the tsar the nastiest features of the old regime.

The newly appointed provincial starosta, S. Shidlovskii, quickly employed his new powers in attempts to eliminate all possible "anti-government" behavior, thereby revealing his anxieties about the current situation On 30 October he forbade "the proclamation or public distribution of any articles or printed information inciting a hostile attitude toward the government." In addition, he forbade the distribution or publication of "untrue information about the activities of government institutions, officials, troops, or military detachments, inciting a hostile attitude," or "inciting public alarm," including "rumors about government commands, public disasters, or other events." Those guilty of such behavior would be subjected to three months in jail or a 3,000 ruble fine.[79] Of course, the degree to which the authorities could enforce these decrees rapidly decreased the farther one traveled away from Kharkiv.

Unfortunately, it is at this very time, when the historian would want most to know more about peasants' attitudes and actions, that the reports from local government officials begin to dwindle. One of the last sources of information on the situation in the Kharkiv countryside in 1918 was provided in a telegram from Shidlovskii to the Minister of Internal Affairs on 11 November. After noting the dreadful situation in Kharkiv itself, Shidlovskii turned to the countryside, citing numerous examples that betrayed the continuing breakdown of "order," such as it was. In Kharkiv district a police officer (*varta*) had recently been killed (probably by local peasants). In the Graivoron district jail prisoners had taken advantage of the small number of guards to take over the prison; disarming and tying up the guards, they then killed the chief jailer and escaped. In Okhtyrka district "bandits" had recently killed the estate owner Trutovskaia and her daughter. In the village of Vendelevka, peasants had arrested the chief of Valky district's police along with his officers and guards. It seems that the district's police officers had seized 140,000 rubles from the villagers as a "security [*zalog*]" until the latter surrendered "a group of criminals"—probably insurgents—hiding in the area. Concluding his list of recent disturbances, Shidlovskii asked that more guns and men be sent to him, claiming that he then could restore peace and quiet to the province.[80]

Shidlovskii never received the personnel, weapons, or opportunity to set his province "right." On the very day he sent that telegram, the armistice between Germany and the Allies was finally proclaimed. No doubt, Hetman Skoropads′kyi now realized that German troops would demand to return as soon as possible to their homeland, and that the chances of his political survival were fading fast. On 14 November he hammered the final nail into his state's coffin with a decree proclaiming Ukraine's new task to be the restoration of "Great Russia." Claiming that, compared to the other parts of "much suffering Russia," Ukraine had received "a more fortunate fate," and that "with the friendly help of the Central Powers, [Ukraine] had remained peaceful to the present day," Skoropads′kyi called on Ukraine's inhabitants to do all possible to restore "on federal principles the ancient might and power of the All-Russian state." Ukraine's first task was to take action for "the creation of an All-Russian federation, the final goal of which will be the renewal of Great Russia."[81]

Considering Skoropadskyi's assertion that this new "Great Russia" had to be a federation and non-Bolshevik, one might question whether his goals differed much from those of most nationally conscious Ukrainian socialists, who, as members of the Central Rada had made similar proposals in the previous year. The latter, however, having been summarily deposed in April 1918, and now united in the Ukrainian National Union, took great exception to Skoropads'kyi's decree and used it as the pretext to declare a general uprising against the hetman.[82] The self-proclaimed leaders of the uprising formed a Directory and issued a decree signed by V. Vynnychenko, calling on "all Ukrainian soldiers and Cossacks to struggle for the state independence of Ukraine, against the traitor, former tsarist hireling, General Skoropads'kyi, [who had] spontaneously seized for himself the right of Hetman of Ukraine." Listing a series of deprivations suffered under the Hetmanate, the Directory forbade all citizens living in Ukraine to help or defend Skoropads'kyi in any way. Ordering all pro-Hetman troops to switch to the UNR's side, the Directory stressed that UNR troops had one goal: "to destroy completely the order established by the Hetman's government, to destroy the scourge on which he has leaned until the present moment."[83]

At this point in the story, Ukrainian historians have usually described the massive peasant uprising that then broke out across Ukraine. On 16 November the most loyal Ukrainian troops, the Sichovi Stril'tsi from Eastern Galicia, who were deployed around the Directory at Bila Tserkva, began to march on the capital. Numerous small peasant bands soon joined them. It would take the insurgents almost a month to capture Kyiv, largely because of the interference of German troops, but also due to the resistance of some pro-Hetman forces. Eventually, on 14 December Hetman Skoropads'kyi relinquished his authority and slipped out of the country, fleeing to Berlin. The massive insurgent peasant army then marched into the capital, carrying with it banners of various kinds. While one cannot deny that this uprising was widespread, events unfolded quite differently in Kharkiv province and across Left-Bank Ukraine as a whole.

For most of Skoropads'kyi's rule, the main non-German military force in Left-Bank Ukraine was the Second Zaporozhian Regiment, stationed in southern Kharkiv province under the command of Colonel Petro Bolbochan.[84] Bolbochan was to play a crucial role in the twist of events played out in Left-Bank Ukraine. Considering himself a true Ukrainian patriot, he feared above all in late-1918 the pro-Moscow forces in Ukraine that were striving to restore the Russian Empire and quash Ukrainian independence.[85] Thus, the hetman's decree of 14 November could only have pushed Bolbochan into the Ukrainian National Union's camp, even though he did not share the socialist leanings of that organization's leaders. Even during the anti-hetman uprising he had "hoped to unite revolutionary democracy with conservative land-owning [*khlibo-robs'kyi*] circles in the person of the hetman for a common struggle against Muscovite intrigues in Ukraine." Apparently, Bolbochan even attempted to explain to the hetman the causes of the National Union's dissatisfaction, before announcing that in the case of an uprising under the National Union's leadership, he and the Zaporozhians "would not be on the hetman's side." Skoropads'kyi, on the other hand, did not think such a union of forces possible, nor capable of defeating Ukraine's many enemies. For this reason he sought support among the victorious Allies, who considered the National Union to be too revolutionary.[86] As the historian Serhii Shemet notes, neither the hetman, who wanted to preserve the Ukrainian state, nor Bolbochan, who wanted to defend Ukraine's independence, attained their goals: "The hetman was mistaken in his hopes for international support; Bolbochan was mistaken in his hopes for [this] understanding and the state-building capabilities of Ukrainian revolutionary democracy."[87]

The circumstances of Bolbochan's conversion to the Directory's side are not entirely clear, but it is likely that the Directory's leaders took the initiative. One of these leaders, Mykyta Shapoval, commented in his memoir that when they began to search for military backing, they asked Bolbochan to come to Kyiv to discuss the matter.[88] During the negotiations Bolbochan insisted that his two Zaporizhian regiments be moved to Kyiv after its liberation "to ensure that peace, order, and legality were preserved" there. As one of his captains, I. Barylo, put it, Bolbochan wished to ensure that in the capital, "the rule of a corrupt otaman [Petliura?] and later anarchy" would not begin again. Bolbochan also demanded that the Directory leave the state-administrative structure in place, only removing those who were clearly hostile to an independent Ukraine.[89] Bolbochan advised the Directory's leaders, Vynnychenko and Shapoval, "to place a military person at the head of the army" who enjoyed great authority. In response, the leaders seem to have promised Bolbochan that they would do all that he requested.[90] Bolbochan then agreed to join the insurgents and he was appointed commander in chief in Left-Bank Ukraine.

On the night of 14/15 November, Colonel Bolbochan arrived in Kharkiv with his Second Zaporizhian Regiment, including 1,600 bayonets, several cavalry companies, and two artillery batteries with twelve light and twenty-four heavy machine guns.[91] The commander of the Seventh Kharkiv Army Corps (pro-hetman troops), General Lihnau, upon inspecting Bolbochan's well-equipped regiment resolved to surrender Kharkiv to the Zaporozhians "for the maintenance of legal order." On the night of 16/17 November the Zaporozhians surrounded all government institutions in the city, including the staff headquarters of Lihnau, who was placed under house arrest. Bolbochan then proclaimed the power of the Directory. "Nowhere did the overthrow proceed with such order as in Kharkiv. The Zaporozhians did not allow themselves any excesses. Any insubordination or misdeeds were severely punished." Under Bolbochan's leadership, the Zaporozhians strove to preserve the state apparatus, leaving most government employees in their place, except for the provincial starosta Shidlovskii, who was replaced by a new provincial commissar, appointed by the Directory, Serhii Tymoshenko.[92]

Outside of Kharkiv, order was not so easy to establish or maintain. A report from an assistant to the procurator of the Kharkiv district court gives us some idea of the chaos in the countryside. On 17 November, a regional chief of the state guard in Izium district received information that a "gang of robbers" had crossed over from Katerynoslav (modern-day Dnipropetrovsk) province to the southern volosts of the district and was robbing and killing state guards and well-off peasants along the way, especially in Oleksandrivka volost. The chief ordered the chairman of the volost administration "to organize a detachments of persons deserving trust and possessing weapons." Once the gang learned that this detachment had come to number about 400 people, it quickly left that volost. However, at about the same time a number of "disorders" began to appear across the district. Peasants were reportedly organizing soviets and proclaiming "Bolshevik power." In Mykhailivka, Serhiïvka, and Prelesne volosts, "insurgent Bolsheviks" had arrested several local chiefs of the state guard, some of their assistants and officers, and other volost officials. In the village of Prelesne, "local Bolsheviks" had formed a detachment of about 150 insurgents and then raided the German colony of Vasylivka and disarmed the colonists, seizing about 25 rifles. Learning that this "band" of Bolsheviks was headed toward his precinct, the chief of the state guard organized a volunteer detachment of officers (about 20) living in Barvinkove, and asked the local German commandant to help them.[93] The Germans agreed[94] and united with the officers "for joint action against the Bolsheviks." This joint detachment then set out to attack the band of "Bolsheviks," chasing them back to Prelesne; eventually, after several hours of artillery and machine gun fire, these "Bolsheviks" were forced to abandon the village, retreating south into Starobilsk district.[95] Along the way, the German soldiers in this joint detachment confiscated a great deal of foodstuffs, money, and other items from village stores as they passed through. Such behavior can only have worsened peasants' attitude toward the Germans and other outside authorities attempting to impose their will.[96]

The archival records here have to be viewed with some skepticism. It is unlikely that a small village in southern Kharkiv province could have been harboring 150 "Bolsheviks," if that term is narrowly defined as members of the RKP(b) or the KP(b)U. These "Bolshevik" insurgents were most likely local peasants who, encouraged by news of Germany's defeat, the beginning exodus of German troops, and rumors about Bolshevik detachments invading from the north, resolved to rise up against the Hetmanate's authorities and local representatives of "German power." They may have called themselves Bolsheviks because many peasants credited the Bolshevik party with granting them the land, ending the war, and proclaiming Soviet power. Moreover, the past year had taught them nothing bad about Soviet power and nothing good about the independent Ukrainian state that had invited the German occupiers to their land. In other words, these "Bolsheviks" were probably local peasants who had obtained the quite common misunderstanding of what the other Bolsheviks, the ones coming from Moscow and other places to the north, meant by the term "Soviet power."[97]

Despite the reports of growing unrest, Bolbochan seems to have done very little to win peasants over to the Directory's side. One attempt was an "Order to the Peasants" issued by the Directory on 21 November which demanded "that everything that was illegally seized by the hetman's government, as well as requisitions and contributions to the landlords' benefit, be returned to the peasants."[98] There is, however, no evidence that this decree was distributed in Left-Bank Ukraine, let alone implemented. Moreover, although Bolbochan issued decrees ordering hetmanate employees to stay at their posts, very few documents from local officials in the countryside have survived, and it is likely that many of them fled in the face of the insurgent peasants. A decree issued by Bolbochan on 25 November suggests that local uprisings and attempts to establish local "soviet power" were quite widespread. Declaring martial law (*voennoe polozhenie*) in Kharkiv, Chernihiv, and Poltava provinces, Otaman Bolbochan—"commander in chief of the armies of Left-Bank Ukraine," as he now began to call himself—forbade the holding of any congresses and assemblies without his permission. "I will not tolerate any soviets of workers' deputies and monarchist organizations, and in general any organizations striving to seize power." Noting that in the Ukrainian Republic the rights of all population groups and nations living on its territory would be ensured, he stressed, "We are fighting for an independent Democratic Ukrainian Republic, and not for a united Russia, whether it is monarchist or Bolshevik."[99] Bolbochan's authoritarian leanings and his failure to distinguish among Russian monarchists, "Bolsheviks" (of any stripe), and anyone with socialist leanings probably contributed much to the Directory's failure to hold power in Left-Bank Ukraine.

A very useful source on the situation in the countryside in late 1918 was provided by deputies elected to an extraordinary provincial zemstvo assembly that took place in mid-December, as reported in the Kharkiv Menshevik newspaper *Nash golos*. It seems that the Directory sought to use democratized zemstvos as its local representative bodies.[100] One deputy reported that German troops had left the town of Sudzhe (Sumy district) already on 22 November. Bolshevik troops occupied the town soon afterward, immediately abolished all zemstvo institutions, and then began to organize Committees of Poor Peasants, with considerable success. In Starobilsk district, another zemstvo deputy reported, "Republican power was established relatively painlessly." The district starosta was forced to flee and work was started to recreate a democratic zemstvo. Then, the starostas of Starobilsk and Kup'iansk districts suddenly appeared with several Cossack detachments to punish the insurgents, eventually restoring the hetman's power there. The newly created democratic zemstvo was dispersed and up to the day the deputy reported—that is, two days after Skoropads'kyi's abdication—the hetmanate authorities remained in control of the district. In Okhtyrka district, the starosta was still at his post, though he was allowing the democratic zemstvo to function. Disturbances had, however, occurred in the northern part of the district, where "several estates had been destroyed." The northern part of Kup'iansk district had also been seized by self-described "Bolsheviks," though here it was admitted that "in most cases" these Bolsheviks were "insurgent detachments," probably local peasants calling themselves Bolsheviks. In Graivoron district the peasants were "expecting the Bolsheviks," and were in a "Bolshevik mood." The representative from Zmiïv district reported that when the district starosta heard that Bolbochan's troops had occupied Kharkiv, he fled. But when newly arrived Republican troops announced a mobilization, "the peasants refused en masse. Many peasants are armed." The locally stationed German troops, alarmed by the "huge influx of peasants," issued an order to stop the mobilization, and arrested and jailed the Ukrainian commandant.[101]

Although these deputies present a chaotic and changing picture of rural Kharkiv province, one thing was quite clear: the Directory and the Ukrainian People's Republic found little support among the peasants. The clearest evidence of this lack of support is peasants' repeated refusals to respond positively to Bolbochan's attempts to recruit them into the Republican army. Such refusals appear in various sources from the period, but the boldest example occurred on 17 December, when a group of about 4,000 peasant recruits arrived in Kharkiv to report to the Republican military commandant. At the time of their arrival, they do not seem to have been aware of "the goals of their mobilization, nor the tasks of the power that had called them up." But when they learned that the Directory had mobilized them, they refused to serve Petliura and walked off, singing revolutionary songs, carrying red flags, and shouting "All power to the Soviets!" They marched to the building where the recently formed Soviet of Workers' Deputies was meeting and summoned its presidium. When the presidium's members emerged, these young peasant men demanded that they "stand up and fight for the power of the Soviets," placing themselves at the Soviet's command. The presidium then arranged a demonstration under the slogan "All power to the Soviets!" A battalion of Republican troops, called in to suppress the demonstration, instead joined the demonstrators.[102]

Peasants' support for "Soviet power" appears to have been quite extensive in Kharkiv province and across the Left Bank. On 11 December 1918, the Belgorod Revolutionary Committee, just northeast of the province, informed the newly proclaimed "Worker-Peasant Government of Ukraine" that its troops were moving toward Kharkiv. Reporting that the formation of new Red Army detachments was going well in the areas now coming under occupation (northern Kharkiv province), the committee called not for more men, but more weapons and ammunition.[103] In a report from the chief of the Republican forces' intelligence department, Lieutenant Colonel Matvienko stressed that up to 15 January (at least) his intelligence agents had found no basis to assert that the pro-Bolshevik troops moving into Kharkiv and Chernihiv province included Russian troops among them. Rather they were "insurgent, Ukrainian detachments" composed of men from Left-Bank Ukraine.[104]

In mid-January 1919 one of Petliura's commanders, Colonel Kapustians′kyi, submitted a detailed report on the advancing Soviet offensive in Left-Bank Ukraine. He stressed, "the Bolsheviks' offensive is finding decisive help among local Bolsheviks and the population." Republican troops arriving to stop the Soviet advance in Poltava province had refused to fight and were sent away for reformation. The commander of Republican troops in Chernihiv and Poltava provinces, Colonel Borys Vasyl′ovych Palii-Neïlo, also admitted the unreliability of his troops, many of whom identified with the Bolsheviks. Noting one case of soldiers refusing to fight against the Bolsheviks, Palii added that this attitude prevailed in other detachments, where soldiers "refuse to move against their brothers, as they say."[105]

Confirming repeated reports from Bolbochan himself, Kapustians′kyi stressed that the Zaporozhian troops were thoroughly exhausted by two months of near constant battle. Those reinforcements that had been sent proved to be "highly unreliable [and] in a Bolshevik mood." In fact, the main problem for Republican forces on the Left Bank was that "the population in general sympathizes with the Bolsheviks and renders them active assistance, providing whole partisan detachments against Republican units." Kapustians′kyi emphasized that "in the villages and in large cities, the population relates hostilely to Republican troops and provides large detachments against them, armed with machine guns.... In general, we cannot with [any] hope of success fight with only our own forces against the Bolsheviks."[106] In his recent study, Pavlo Isakov claims that the reason why Left-Bank Ukraine came under Bolshevik control in February 1919 was "the military aggression of Soviet troops against the UNR [Ukrainian People's Republic]."[107] As this chapter makes clear, however, many peasants welcomed Soviet troops as liberators in early 1919 and eagerly joined their forces in order to bring "Soviet power" (as they understood that concept) to their villages.

*

The German occupation of 1918 marked a major turning point in the revolutionary process in Ukraine. Although there were other factors, German soldiers' interactions with peasants played the crucial role in turning the majority of the population away from the Ukrainian national idea. From the perspective of many peasants, the Ukrainian People's Republic, headed by the Central Rada, had invited the German plunderers into Ukraine; the Hetmanate had done nothing to stop them, and was, in fact, dependent on the Germans for its existence. Subsequently, the Directory, at least in its Bolbochanian form, seemed little different from the Hetmanate, especially because Bolbochan openly strove to retain as many Hetmanate employees as possible, and in his few pronouncements gave peasants much to fear and nothing to cheer about. It is therefore not very surprising that many Ukrainian-speaking peasants in late 1918 came to sympathize with the "Bolsheviks," who they believed had given them the land and whose rule they had yet to experience. Nor is it surprising that many of them came to call themselves Bolsheviks, or that they took up as their slogan "All power to the Soviets," the implementation of which they hoped would finally give them control over their lives and land.[108]

4 The Shifting Allegiances of 1919: Civil War in the Countryside

GREAT AS IT WAS, PEASANTS' MISUNDERSTANDING of the returning Bolshevik-led government's character was not as enormous as that government's inaccurate interpretation of their initially positive reception. Completely misinterpreting why peasants had risen up against the Hetmanate, supported the Soviet Army, called for "All Power to the Soviets," and helped bring them to power in Ukraine in January 1919, the "Ukrainian"[1] Bolsheviks of the newly arrived Provisional Worker-Peasant Government soon did all possible to undermine peasants' support and clear up the latter's misunderstanding of what these "Bolsheviks" meant by "Soviet Power."[2] The second Soviet government's attempts in the spring of 1919 to introduce socialist communes into the countryside, to extract as much food and forage from it as possible, and to draft peasant men into the Red Army provoked numerous uprisings in Kharkiv province, as across Ukraine. These peasant insurgents were only halted by the arrival of General Anton Denikin's Volunteer Army (VA) at the end of June 1919. Surprisingly, though the VA and its political leaders had amassed a great deal of information about what peasants wanted, they did very little to reassure peasants, let alone gain their cooperation. Proclaiming the restoration of private property and that peasants would have to pay for any land they wished to receive, the VA found few friends in the countryside and made fewer efforts to make new ones. By mid-October 1919 the VA's own intelligence agents reported not only widespread apathy among the peasants but open hostility to its rule. Peasants refused to provide recruits or give up grain to supply the faltering army. By December 1919 many welcomed the return of the Red Army and expressed a great (and largely undeserved) willingness to compromise with the third Bolshevik government.

The Second Soviet Government of Ukraine

From the moment of the workers' pro-Soviet uprising in Kharkiv on 1 January 1919,[3] the Ukrainian Soviet Red Army managed to take Kyiv in a little over a month, on 5 February. Graziosi attributes this "one more easy victory" to the massive transfer of the allegiance of numerous partisan groups from Petliura's forces to the side of "Soviet power." In mid-December 1918 Petliura's forces numbered almost 100,000 men; by February 1919 he could count on only about 20,000. Over the same period, the forces of Vladimir Antonov-Ovseenko, Soviet commander of the Ukrainian Front, grew from 8,000 to about 46,000.[4]

The loss of support for Petliura in Ukraine was not very surprising. Many peasants in Kharkiv province, as across Ukraine, welcomed the return of "Soviet power" in January 1919 in light of their recent hardships under the German occupation, and the fact that new Worker-Peasant Government spoke the language of class liberation, including the liberation of all "laboring peasants." Quite a few Red Army soldiers who fought their way across Kharkiv province in early 1919 were peasants from that same province. They had been mobilized into the Red Army in late 1917 or had retreated with that army as the German troops swept into the province. Over the course of 1918 they were joined by those who fled the Hetmanate and the arbitrary actions of the occupying soldiers. Together these men came to form the First and Second Soviet Ukrainian Divisions, trained in 1918 in the neutral zone—the strip of land between the Hetmanate (German occupied areas) and Soviet Russia.[5] Returning to Kharkiv province with those divisions, the majority of these peasant-soldiers actively sympathized with the new government and were willing to lay down their lives for the cause of Soviet power.

It is important, however, to stress the conditional nature of these soldiers' allegiance. A January 1919 report from the Volunteer Army's intelligence agency, Azbuka, noted that compared to Soviet troops fighting in the Don region and in Siberia, "the Ukrainian Soviet Army is very undisciplined and is composed of irregular detachments." Whenever these detachments were dispatched to the front, their numbers decreased "sharply," in the words of the report. Peasant-soldiers arbitrarily moved from one detachment to another, frequently during battle, and there were numerous cases of detachments refusing to go to the front.[6] Even some Red Army commanders worried about the persistent local-mindedness of these peasant-soldiers. In a confidential report to the Red Army's Commander-in-Chief, I. I. Vatsetis, Antonov-Ovseenko cautioned that, although the "so-called Second Insurgent Ukrainian Division" numbered as many as 6,000 soldiers, "they are all from Kharkiv province. They will go gladly only to Kharkiv.... I repeat, the insurgent detachments are tied to their own region, and to take them away from there means to weaken them extremely [*kraine oslabit'*]."[7]

In addition to those peasant-soldiers who had returned to the province in the First and Second Soviet Ukrainian divisions, many peasants living in the province supported the return of Soviet power and sometimes joined the Red Army. An Azbuka report based on captured Red Army orders from February and March states that numerous Soviet detachments had recently been formed in Kharkiv, Poltava, and Chernihiv provinces; in the smaller district centers of Sumy, Zmiïv, and Chuhuïv reserve battalions had also been created.[8] A VA report from March 1919 notes that during the Soviet troops' advance into Ukraine, attempts to sign up volunteers from the local population had had so much success that there were now 500 soldiers per Red Army regiment.[9] Moreover, at this very time the Red Army was advancing rapidly southward, pushing across Kharkiv and Katerynoslav provinces. As Orlando Figes has pointed out, the Red Army's successes could not have come without the cooperation from local peasants behind the front lines: for example, providing food, fodder, and labor services, sometimes for pay, sometimes at the point of a gun.[10]

The leaders of the new Worker-Peasant Government seem not to have understood the nature of the peasants' support, as evidenced by one of their first efforts to gauge and increase that support. On 31 January 1919 the Kharkiv Soviet of Workers' Deputies called the province's workers and peasants to a Provincial Congress of Soviets. Claiming that soviets were appearing spontaneously across Left-Bank Ukraine as the "unbeatable Soviet troops" advanced, the Kharkiv Soviet asserted that there was "an urgent need to unite the work of organizing soviets across the whole province, to bring out the attitudes of workers and poor peasants of Kharkiv province toward the power of the soviets, [and] to make its own decisions on the land question, food supply, and a series of other vital questions." Elections to the provincial congress were carried out at volost congresses at the ratio of one deputy per 10,000 electors in rural areas, and one deputy per 2,000 electors in urban areas. At these volost congresses deputies were to discuss the crucial issues of the day, pass resolutions, and then send to Kharkiv "staunch defenders of the laboring masses, firmly standing for the power of the Soviets."[11]

Upon their arrival in Kharkiv, the deputies were given surveys to fill out; these provide much useful data. Nearly all of them claimed to work with their hands; most were engaged in agriculture, though almost half (164 of 357, or 45 percent) owned no land of their own. Of the 193 who owned some land, two-thirds owned three desiatynas or less. During the civil war the Communist Party often found its strongest rural backers among such landless and land-poor peasants. In addition, more than three-quarters of the deputies held some sort of political position in their village or volost (274 of 357). Most of the deputies had had some elementary education: 287 of 357, or 80 percent. In political terms the deputies were very pro-Soviet and pro-communist: 160 were Communist Party members and 111 were sympathetic to the party; only 22 deputies were members of the PSR (strangely, no distinction was made between Ukrainian SRs or Russian LSRs); 44 declared themselves sympathetic to the SRs' position. The Communists' strong position can also be explained by other statistics the deputies provided: 51 of them came from Kharkiv district; most of these would have been very pro-Bolshevik Kharkiv workers, inspired by their recent overthrow of the Directory. One hundred ninety-one deputies claimed to have worked in the underground, which the Bolsheviks had dominated, especially during the Hetmanate. One hundred one deputies had spent time in prison, probably because of their work in the underground. Finally, ninety-two deputies had served in the military during the revolution; hence they were probably Red Army soldiers and very pro-communist.[12]

Despite their numerical superiority over urban deputies, peasant deputies said very little in the first two days of the conference, during which the chairman of the Soviet of People's Commissariats of Ukraine, Khristian (Krŭst′o) Rakovskii,[13] reported on the government's activities and launched numerous verbal attacks on the Left SRs. The latter responded in kind, leading to heated exchanges, uproars of applause, cries of "Bravo!" or "Enough!" and the chairman's frequent calls to order.

Near the end of the second day, however, one peasant provided a brief glimpse into peasant delegates' views on the proceedings. Encouraged by the very critical speech of one worker, named in the proceedings as Ryzhkov, this unnamed peasant deputy found the courage to stand up and voice his first criticism of the government and the congress itself: that peasant deputies had been elected at the ratio of one for every 10,000 peasants, whereas each worker deputy had been elected by as few as 2,000 electors. Identifying himself as a peasant from the village, and stressing that he represented 10,000 peasants (which statement was met with loud applause and cries of "Bravo"), he pointed out, "we did not travel here in order to fling mud on each other, but to express the will of those who sent us. Comrades, yesterday for about two hours we listened to the representative of the Temporary Government, comrade Rakovskii. We listened to similar speeches at our own congresses and at our volost soviets." The speaker was then interrupted by some worker deputies asking why he was only addressing peasants. He replied that he did not see written on the building of the Kharkiv Soviet of Workers' deputies the letter "K" for "peasants' deputies," implying that the workers themselves were not including peasants. Receiving numerous shouts of "Bravo" (probably from other peasants), the peasant speaker went on:

> Comrades, here all the time they fling mud [a din erupted]. Comrades, we have to resolve the most important questions—the land and food supply questions (correct!). I am not an orator, I have never been in an academy and do not know mathematics (din, shouts, the chairman's bell [ringing for order]). I speak in the language that I know; peasants do not know January or February, but [they know] that spring is coming, [so] give us the land (noisy ovations, shouts of "Bravo"). Comrades, here we do not need to defend ourselves individually; we did not come to defend this or that party. As representatives we need to remember that we were sent by 10,000 electors; we must assert this and openly defend their interests (noisy applauses, shouts of "Bravo").[14]

The congress's presidium, composed of communists and a few other pro-Soviet party leaders, responded by informing this peasant deputy that his time was up. The chairman, P. A. Kin, then announced that the presidium had decided to end the debate on Rakovskii's speech and unilaterally declared that he would allow only "the fractions' orators"—that is, party leaders—to speak. As far as we can tell from the stenograph, Kin's declaration was not met warmly,[15] though a majority of deputies did vote for the communists' resolution on the government: "The First Kharkiv Congress of Soviets completely approves the internal and external policies of its government and promises its complete and unconditional support."[16] Incidents such as the speech by the unnamed peasant, however, reveal that some peasants even at this very pro-communist congress did not feel that their attitudes and input were being given serious consideration by party leaders; moreover, the presidium's reaction reinforced this view.

The next day the congress discussed the food supply question. The communists' resolution stated that the most basic goal of Soviet food supply policy was "the replacement of commodity exchange with socialist products exchange." In essence this entailed a state monopoly on the procurement of grain and other essential food products at set prices, the establishment of set prices on all other products and essential finished goods, and "the nationalization of trade." According to the resolution, the practical implementation of this policy could be ensured "only by food supply organs of class struggle, constructed on the strictly maintained principles of the dictatorship of the proletariat and poor peasantry." Naming in particular the food supply organs in the cities and the committees of the poor in the countryside, the resolution also called for a union with middling peasants to fight "a merciless struggle with the kulak" and resolved to organize state requisitions and confiscate from "the kulak" all grain surpluses "in those cases when he remains deaf to the suffering of starving brothers and surreptitiously sells grain to speculators." The final reading of this resolution was, according to the published stenograph, greeted with several "noisy ovations."[17]

Although this resolution was passed by a majority of the deputies present, there were voices of dissent. One Left-SR received shouts of support when he pointed out that in Russia "village kulaks" had "infiltrated" the committees of poor peasants, rendering them useless. And there was stormy applause whenever a speaker mentioned that manufactured goods must also be nationalized and that workers had to do all they could to supply the countryside with goods. Seemingly sensitive to this issue, the People's Commissar of Food Supply, O. G. Shlikhter, just before introducing his resolution, stressed that goods for peasants were already on their way from Russia. Yet, on this question so crucial to peasants, only party leaders were allowed to speak. Indeed, this seems to have been the party leadership's solution to the grumbling and disorder created on the previous day, when one worker and one peasant had been allowed to speak ever so briefly. Ordinary deputies, whether communists or not, were simply not given the chance to voice their opinions. The deputies' role in the congress was reduced to that of a muttering, confused audience, now and then called on to vote on the party's resolutions.

From the communists' perspective, this solution worked in the short run. All the communists' resolutions were passed by a majority of deputies. The newly elected peasant deputies, fresh from experiencing or even taking part in the Red Army's victories, and inexperienced in the city, in party politics, and in speaking their minds in front of large groups of people, seem to have accepted the communists' position on most issues and, by their votes, expressed support for the new regime. However, the debate on the most important question discussed at the congress—that is, the land question—did evoke some interesting remarks, a sign that the communists' support was not as strong or enduring as they seem to have assumed.

The communists' proposal on the land question reflected their most idealistic dreams of a quickly realizable, socialist society. Private property on land was abolished. Lands, forests, water, and natural resources were proclaimed "all-people's property." Landlords and their nonlaboring renters were to be immediately evicted from their estates and farms; the estates and their properties were to be inventoried and put under the control of the soviets' land departments. In the words of the proposal, this land and property was to be used above all for "the transformation from individual farming to collective. Soviet farms, communes, the public working of the land and other forms of collective land use are the best means for achieving socialism in agriculture; thus, it follows to consider individualistic farming as temporary and moribund." All confiscated lands were to be used "in the first place for collective, public farming; and in the second place for the needs of individual land users."[18] The provincial and district land departments were entrusted to determine which confiscated estates were suitable to serve as model "cultural-industrial soviet farms and communes," to be organized immediately. Local soviets were obliged to guard very carefully all former landlord estates' properties, "not in any case allowing the arbitrary seizure and dividing up of this all-people's property to the benefit of separate individuals." Only the land not used for collective farming could be subject to "temporary, equal redivision among individual farms," and all land departments were obliged "energetically to explain and bring into life the organization of public cultivation even of these lands." At the same time, this remarkably ambitious document informed land departments that their "first obligation" was to increase the area sown: "Not a single desiatyna should be left empty in this time of hunger and ruin, provoked by the world war."

To help implement this land reform, measures were also to be taken for "the most rapid organization of landless laborers and in general the proletarian part of the village into a separate union of agricultural workers." The local soviets, based solidly on poor and middling peasants, were to struggle against "the village bourgeoisie, kulaks, moneylenders and other enemies of the working people." Finally, the proposal called on all laborers to rally around their soviets and help them to restore more quickly the ruined economy, to overcome hunger, the absence of manufactured goods, "and most quickly to achieve the world rule of socialism, which alone can completely satisfy all laborers' needs."[19] A more idealistic and less realizable land reform would be difficult to imagine.[20]

The Left SRs' spokesman, Alekseev, criticized two aspects of this proposal: first, that it did not give peasants the land, but replaced the many landlords with the state as one new, more powerful lord; and second, that it sought to exploit peasants' labor on the collective types of farms. Alekseev noted that in Valky district, Kharkiv province, there were two large sugar plantations; under the communists' land policy these estates would be converted into Soviet farms. Thus, the peasants of Valky district would receive almost no land as a result of the communists' proposal.

The Ukrainian SRs, who had on almost all other issues supported the communists, agreed with the Left SRs on the land issues. They argued that soviet farms at that time were simply impossible without the great exploitation of peasants' labor. Instead, they called for the "socialization" of the land, allowing peasants to divide up all the land equally among those willing to cultivate it. Both Ukrainian and Left SRs stressed that collective forms of agriculture were possible only on a voluntary basis, and that forcing peasants onto communes would be disastrous. The Ukrainian SRs' resolution put it this way: "Nationalization of the land, by which the landlord will be replaced by the state, contradicts the land law accepted at the Second All-Ukrainian Congress of Soviets in Katerynoslav and cannot be permitted, because the landless and land-poor peasantry would be forced to implement their blood right to the land by aggressive, revolutionary means, which could introduce disorganization and weaken the socialist revolution."[21]

At various points in the speeches of the Ukrainian SRs and Left SRs, the stenographer recorded supportive ovations and shouts from the deputies, suggesting that support for their criticisms was growing. But there were no serious disruptions until the debate ended and the SR Alekseev proposed that, because the land reform issue was so important, the voting should be carried out not by party fraction but by calling out the name of each deputy, who would then cast his vote individually (*poimennym golosovaniem*). Communist Yan countered that all the questions the congress had to resolve were important and that one should not privilege one by putting it to a different kind of vote. He confidently declared, "the communists' fraction is in an absolute majority here. For the Left SRs it must be clear that, as with our whole party, the fraction is so disciplined that all its comrades will vote for this resolution (noise)... which was voted on in the fraction, passed and introduced here at the congress (voices from the public: "that is the question!")." Yan continued: "Not one communist here at the congress belonging to our fraction, not one of these communists will reject the fraction to which he belongs." Noting that time was running out and that voting by individual name would take two or three hours, he concluded that it would be "completely unnecessary," and proposed that they vote by fraction.[22]

When the chairman attempted to put to a vote whether to vote by fraction or individually on the land policy, a great din erupted as SRs and communists shouted at each other. The noise seems to have attracted the attention of Red Army soldiers, posted outside guarding the congress. They rushed in, leading the SRs to think that the communists were bolstering their numbers or intending to use force to pass their resolution. For a considerable period of time the chairman was unable to call the congress to order. In the end, however, the presidium managed to carry out the vote by fraction. The communists' resolution received 210 votes, the Left SRs' resolution, 88, and the Ukrainian SRs' resolution, 88.[23] Although the communists seemed to realize that this was not a very strong endorsement of their radical plans for "nationalizing" the land, the People's Commissar of Agriculture, Meshcheriakov, asked the congress to confirm the resolution. Noting that he could not possibly respond to all the 44 memos (*zapiski*) he had received from various deputies, he proposed to answer their questions about the land reform in the pages of the *Izvestiia Khar´kovskogo Sovieta rabochikh deputatov.*[24] Unfortunately, no issues of this newspaper from 1919 or any other evidence of the memos' contents have survived. One thing, however, is clear from this congress's proceedings. Although at this time communists enjoyed considerable sympathy among some peasant deputies (who were mostly members of the party or sympathetic to it), their resolutions received only qualified support. As with all such congresses, the deputies would now have to go back to their villages and attempt to gain their constituents' cooperation in implementing these radical changes in land relations.

The communist leadership seems to have taken little notice of the reservations expressed about its position on land reform. At the Third Congress of the KP(b)U (1–6 March 1919), party members passed a resolution on land policy identical to that proposed and accepted at the Kharkiv provincial congress of Soviets.[25] The party congress's resolution on food supply, full of similar ideological phrases, repeatedly suggested the application of "the rich experience of Soviet Russia."[26]

With these decrees in hand, the land departments quite enthusiastically embarked on a collectivization effort. The Kharkiv provincial land department (*zemotdel*) informed the districts that its "cardinal task" was "the construction of communes" and dispatched numerous instructors and agitators to the countryside.[27] These communes (*kommuny*) should not be confused with peasants' pre-revolutionary repartitional commune (*obshchina*, *mir*, or *hromada*, discussed in the introduction); the party's *kommuny* were idealistic attempts to move peasants directly to what it viewed as an economically much more advanced (that is, socialist) form of agricultural production. At the local level in Kharkiv province agitators for these *kommuny* quickly became frustrated, expressing great impatience with peasants' reluctance to take up collective forms of farming. A circular from the Izium district executive committee admitted that there had been "frequent cases, in which agitators, instead of explaining the advantages of agricultural communes, resort to the threat: 'We will drive you there [into the communes] with bayonets.'"[28] E. Evnitskii, reporting on his trip through Lebedyn district in March 1919, noted that because of the words of "excessively passionate communists" and also "under the influence of Left-SRs" and other "counterrevolutionaries," peasants "imagine that the commune will be introduced by force."[29] An Azbuka report from 22 March claims that the peasants' anti-Bolshevik mood was growing. The mood in the village could be defined quite simply: "the peasantry live with the singular desire to have their own land, though in a larger amount than it had previously." As representative of peasants' general position, the report quotes one "uncultivated peasant," who spoke at the Third Ukrainian Congress of Soviets in Kharkiv in mid-March: "If you bring the commune to us, then we will smash you in the mug."[30]

Remarkably, at this very time when party leaders were attempting to implement such revolutionary changes in the countryside, they were receiving clear indications that their support among peasants was rapidly declining. In early March 1919 the Worker-Peasant Government announced the mobilization of 19- and 20-year old males in Kharkiv province. As a first test of the new regime, it failed miserably. Both in the city and in the countryside the order was met with hostility. Peasants complained about Bolshevik agitators and commissars, accusing the latter of arriving to take their "land, children, and grain"—their land for the communes, their sons to fight in the Red Army, and grain to send to Soviet Russia. According to one Azbuka report from March 1919, peasants responded negatively to all these attempts to interfere in their lives and to force them to make sacrifices for "Soviet power." They directly and openly declared that "they will give up nothing," and any attempts to take their "land, children, and grain" would be met with all possible force up to and including "severe and bloody mob judgments [*samosudy*]." On this basis uprisings had already been sparked in neighboring Kursk province, where a detachment of fifty Red Army soldiers had been "slaughtered." In Valky district, where the so-called nationalization of landlords' sugar beet plantations threatened to leave peasants with little land for redistribution, peasant insurgents had formed detachments totaling about 10,000 soldiers.[31] A graphic display of resistance to mobilization occurred on 6 March 1919 in Kharkiv itself, when new peasant recruits reporting for mobilization announced that they refused to take part in the civil war and demanded that they be issued weapons and then be allowed to go home. When Soviet officials arrived and attempted to persuade them to obey the army commander, the recruits responded with cries of "Beat the Jews!" and a hail of rocks and bottles.[32] The insubordinate peasants marched to the train station, intending to return home, but were met there by an armored car and a detachment of Red Junkers. After the armored car fired off several rounds of machine gunfire, mostly in the air, the insurgents dispersed. That evening the Red Junkers encircled the train station, screening for deserters, and caught at least three hundred peasant-soldiers attempting to return to their villages.[33]

On 27 March the government leader Rakovskii declared, "We do not ever have to consider the internal enemy especially closely, because he will exhaust himself." Just a few days later, Rakovskii had a change of heart, arguing that "the counter-revolution could triumph not through the help of foreign bayonets and the volunteers [VA soldiers]; [rather] the kulak elements of the village could carry it out." Rakovskii noted further that, although the first mobilization in Kharkiv province had given "brilliant [!!] results," he had to admit that "the mobilization is an extremely unpopular measure among the peasants, especially when the war is not taking place directly near them in the district and when the mobilized are assigned for dispatch to other fronts."[34]

Peasants were also at this time beginning to express disagreement with and resist attempts to requisition their grain. On 23 March the Cheka reported that a "disturbance" had broken out along the Kursk-Kharkiv railway line in response to requisitioning. Noting that "measures had been taken" to halt the disturbance, the Cheka stated, "On the basis of the extraction [*razverstka*] of the grain obligation, peasants are noticeably dissatisfied, among whom counter-revolutionary agitation is being carried out." Quite misguided about the causes of peasants' discontent and resistance, the Cheka reported that it had taken measures for "fishing out the agitators."[35]

One of the most informative documents on Kharkiv peasants under Soviet rule in 1919 was provided by one VA agent named Vetchenko, who managed—quite easily, it seems—to slip across the front lines to the Soviet side and travel around Kharkiv and Poltava provinces from February to April 1919. Vetchenko had much to say about his experience living under what he called "the power of the Soviet of People's Commissars of Ukraine." He observed that there were three main centers of power: the executive committees, both at the provincial and district level, the Cheka, and at the most local level, the committees of poor peasants. Vetchenko stressed (and probably exaggerated) the growing disorder in the countryside. Finding that even well-off peasants were taking an active part in the plundering of landlords' estates, Vetchenko concluded, "rapacious propensities and brutality have gripped everyone like the plague."[36]

Such uncontrolled pillaging certainly crossed purposes with the government's plans for collectivizing agriculture. Indeed, Vetchenko argued that it was the communists' attempts to stop the plunder that had pushed the population to "an appropriate sobering-up" about the nature of Soviet power. While landless and land-poor peasants had received some land, the communists had taken into account much of the estates' land, produce, grain and livestock. Peasants greatly resented that government officials had appeared in their villages and declared many of the larger estates to be state property. Outrages committed against the church also helped to "sober up" the peasants from the "drunken euphoria" of Soviet power's early days. Many peasants, women in particular, were already candidly criticizing the regime. At bazaars older women (*baby*) "fearlessly" argued with Bolsheviks and Red Army soldiers, openly cursing them and accusing them of cheating the people.[37]

Vetchenko also discussed the attempts at communization. In early March 1919 the government had held the Third Congress of Soviets in Kharkiv, at which it had proposed and passed its radical land policy. According to Vetchenko, however, many of the delegates gathering at the conference had "categorically rejected this proposal." The majority of peasant delegates demanded equal additional allotments of the confiscated lands, insisting on the continued independence of their farms. They found significant support for their position among the Left-SRs, while the congress's "ringleaders" strove to convince peasant deputies that it was not possible to return to the old ways. Vetchenko presented figures expressing peasants' reluctance to take up new forms of collective farming: by mid-May 1919, out of the five million desiatynas of land and more than 3,000 villages of Kharkiv province only 79 socialist communes (*kommuny*) had been formed, on which only about 5,000 people farmed collectively an area of 31,000 desiatynas.[38] At the same time, attempts to communize were having significant, negative effects on peasant agriculture. Because peasants feared that these communes or the soviet authorities would take from them any excess grain they produced, and because of the great decrease in available working cattle, many of which had been taken for use on the communes, in the spring of 1919 peasants had sown about half as much land as in the previous year.[39]

Vetchenko credited much of the limited peasant support for the Soviet regime to its propaganda machine, reporting that "the whole Red Army and the population are soaked in Soviet publications and appeals." By contrast, he noted, the VA did not utilize propaganda as effectively.

"Unfortunately, peasants are not informed about the activities or goals of the Volunteer Army. No VA appeals or publications have reached them." During the recent anti-mobilization uprisings in Valky, Okhtyrka and Sumy districts, this had been the obvious deficiency that allowed the authorities to subdue the insurgents. "The anti-Bolshevik spirit of the peasantry is supported by nothing and no one." Noting repeatedly how many resources the Soviet government and army expended on propaganda, he concluded by stressing the need to inform the peasants about the VA and its goals in all ways possible. He recommended that, as the VA occupied new territories, civil authorities be immediately installed and that they become the VA's most active propagandists: "It is necessary that the governor and his assistants without pomp quickly visit the peasant population and personally explain to them the goals and tasks of the Volunteer Army."[40]

The Communist Party leaders eventually seem to have realized the negative effects of their efforts to communize the peasants. On 11 April 1919 the KP(b)U's Executive Committee published a directive categorically declaring that "any uniting of peasants into communal farms can proceed only on completely free bases, voluntarily," only when they realized the value of communal farms. Party organizations were ordered to watch closely that "provocateurs, who attach themselves to Soviet power, or people not understanding what they are doing, do not violate the policies of the party and the Central Soviet power in the area of land relations, immediately arresting and handing over to the court for counterrevolutionary crimes those who carry out a policy of forced creation of communes."[41] This was, however, too little too late.

A report from Colonel Tarasevich, the assistant chief of the VA's Kharkov Center,[42] that was based on information from an Azbuka agent who had returned from Kharkiv on 23 May, provides additional information on the region's villagers. Tarasevich noted that although at the time of its arrival in Kharkiv the Soviet government had very much expected the peasants' support, "its hopes had not proven justified." A recent very modest attempt to mobilize only twenty soldiers per volost "had suffered a complete defeat." Now, government officials no longer wished to announce mobilizations, because these announcements in some cases had led to peasants responding with "severe reprisals" against local commissars. Peasants had recently staged a series of uprisings across the province. In Izium, Kup'iansk, Chuhuïv, Zmiïv, and Sumy districts, armed peasant-insurgents roamed freely along the roads. In Starobilsk district peasant-insurgents fought pitched battles against Red Army soldiers, resulting in at least 600 casualties. The Soviet authorities strove to put down these uprisings with great severity. The VA agent reported peasants as saying, "When soviet power was solidly in place, the Bolsheviks, paying no attention to peasants' opinion, forcibly imposed commissars, and now, when the front has cracked, they [Bolsheviks] are begging them [the peasants] to come to the defense of these same commissars." At a meeting of the Kharkiv Soviet it was openly admitted that the Red Army itself no longer enjoyed sympathy among the peasant masses. At the same time, peasants worried about the Volunteer Army's advance, fearing reprisals for land they had seized from landlords.[43]

Even among Red Army soldiers dissatisfaction with the regime was increasing. On 12 May 1919 Colonel Riazhinskii, chief of the VA's intelligence agency, reported on the supposed anti-Semitic character of this discontent. The Red Army's infantry had been organized almost "accidentally"; the troops were undisciplined and could never be stopped from plundering newly conquered territory or carrying out pogroms against Jews. Dismissing the Red Army's earlier successes against Petliura's forces as resulting from the latter's weaknesses, Riazhinskii noted that desertion among Soviet troops was rising rapidly. Mobilizations were never successful, because after new recruits had received their guns, uniforms, and supplies at one recruitment point, they would immediately desert, sell the matériel, and go to another recruitment point to repeat their actions. Such behavior was greatly decreasing the army's supplies. Numerous detachments, "especially partisan detachments, of which there are more than regular detachments, consider everything seized from the enemy their personal property and frequently not only do not allow these items to be collected, but do not even provide information about them." Concerning "the spirit and mood of the troops," Riazhinskii found matters to be yet worse. Under the influence of the general dissatisfaction embracing the masses, some troops were even hostile toward Soviet power. He listed several causes of this dissatisfaction: "Jewish dominance in Soviet institutions"; hunger despite an abundance of foodstuffs; weariness concerning the civil war, in which "Christians were killing each other"; Soviet power's persecution of religion; and "in general a regime under which it is unbearably difficult not only for the intelligentsia, but for the worker and peasant to breathe." This general mood was being transferred to the troops, "who consider the 'Yids [*zhidy*]' responsible for all disasters and see as the only exit from the emerging situation the removal of Jews from all government institutions and in pogroms."[44] Very likely, Riazhinskii was reading more anti-Semitism into the troops' attitudes than truly existed.

One can find, however, even Soviet sources revealing the negative (though not anti-Semitic) mood among Red Army soldiers. On 4 June 1919, the commander of the 14th (formerly Second Ukrainian) Army, K. E. Voroshilov,[45] reported that recently the so-called Insurgent Brigade of Nestor Makhno was by telegraph and radio inviting individual soldiers and whole detachments to gather at his headquarters in Huliai-Pole for a congress. Pointing out that Makhno's Insurgent Brigade was in fact a part of the 14th Army and located in the front-line zone, Voroshilov declared, "Not any kind of congresses in the mentioned region will be permitted." Furthermore, he decreed, "Without a direct order no detachments or units have the right to change their location. Individual Red Army soldiers who attempt without authorization to quit their units and transfer to the region of the 'Insurgent' Brigade will be considered deserters; any violation of this order will be considered an action equal to treason against the Worker-Peasant State and will be punished with all the severity of laws of military time." As if this were not enough to suggest the Red Army command's concern with deserters, Leon Trotskii, who was then in Kharkiv attempting to rekindle local support for Soviet power, also issued an order commanding all Soviet troops and institutions "immediately to take all measures for the most strict execution" of Voroshilov's order.[46] Another Azbuka agent reported that at this time there was "no discipline" in the Red Army: "All commands concerning discipline and subordination provoke indignation among Red Army soldiers."[47]

At about the same time, Azbuka's Kharkov Center reported that the government's recently declared mobilizations had provoked a whole series of uprisings among those mobilized, particularly in Left-Bank Ukraine. Such district towns as Valky, Bohodukhiv, Okhtyrka, and Sumy had been seized by the mobilized peasants when they gathered at recruitment centers. Punitive detachments were sent to put down these uprisings. Kharkiv province was, however, relatively less hostile to the mobilization than other areas: out of fear of violent uprisings, the Soviet authorities did not even attempt to mobilize peasants in Poltava province or in Right-Bank Ukraine.[48]

These uprisings were provoked primarily by communist policies, especially the attempts to impose communal farms, requisition food, and recruit peasant boys to fight, but they were not expressly "anti-Soviet"; nor were the insurgents in general rising up to fight for the Ukrainian nation. In a recent study of the "anti-communist insurgent movement" in Left-Bank Ukraine, Pavlo Isakov has calculated that in 1919 no fewer than fifty-seven insurgent detachments with about 22,000 members rose up against this second Soviet government. Isakov notes that the insurgents' ideology included "a certain collection of uncoordinated slogans that were advanced depending on the situation." Thirty-two of these fifty-seven detachments "had no clearly defined political coloring." Another nine Isakov characterizes as "Makhnovite"—that is, followers of the anarchist Nestor Makhno. However, he describes these insurgents as rising up against the policy of "war communism" and the state's intervention in peasants' affairs, while loyally adhering to the "Soviet form of power." This does not appear to be very different from those insurgents without any political position. Indeed, he asserts that the main slogan of the 1919 insurgency was "For Soviet power, but without communists or communes."[49] Iurii Kotliar's findings corroborate the nonpolitical nature of the insurgents; he notes that in southern Ukraine the influence of political parties was small: most peasant uprisings in this region were very local, operating only within their own volost and motivated by what he describes as "local interests."[50]

Peasants' and peasant-soldiers' open hostility toward and resistance against the Communist regime, provoked by its attempts to introduce radical policies in the countryside, could not have come at a worse time for the Soviet government. In his 18 June report on the Red Army's retreat, VA commander Colonel Fon-Goerts noted that, despite the efforts of the Soviet command to organize counterattacks against the advancing Volunteer Army, Red Army soldiers continued to withdraw and were deserting in droves. Moreover, the number of insurgent towns and villages was "increasing with each day, in particular in Malorossiia [Ukraine]; Soviet power does not have the forces to suppress the uprisings, and most recently is not even attempting to do so, the more so because the most reliable units—sailors, Chinese, Latvians—are kept as close as possible to the general staff and [Soviet] institutions with the goal of their own salvation [*v tseliakh sobstvennogo spaseniia*]."[51] Thus ended the brief rule of the second Soviet government in Ukraine.

Ukraine under the Volunteer Army

With these kinds of attitudes and actions in mind, it is not difficult to understand why the Volunteer Army under the supreme command of General Anton Denikin was able to advance quickly across Left-Bank Ukraine in the late spring and summer of 1919, taking Kharkiv itself on 25 June. The VA's intelligence agents were quite aware of peasants' current dispositions, as reflected in their frequent reports. And yet, the most striking feature of the Volunteer Army's brief rule in Kharkiv province was the stark contrast between its knowledge about the local inhabitants' desires, fears, and recent experiences, and its inability to act on this knowledge.

Already in late May 1919, Azbuka agents, who had crossed the front line that then bisected the province, provided ample information about peasants' needs and demands, and proposed quite reasonable recommendations. In a report to the VA General staff from late May Colonel Tarasevich noted that in conversations with peasants, an Azbuka agent had learned that they were both interested in the VA and afraid that its arrival might bring reprisals against them for seizing the lords' estates, land, and inventory. Tarasevich worried that in those districts already occupied by the VA there was an absence of "solid authority able to explain to the peasants the goals and tasks of the Volunteer Army and immediately to embark on establishing order in the organs of village and city administration." Peasants had been left in complete ignorance about the VA, and at the same time, "not seeing solid authority, they easily succumb to Bolshevik agitation." In many villages already occupied by the VA the local authorities elected under the Bolsheviks remained in place; some peasants complained of this to Azbuka agents. Tarasevich reported that in some districts (Izium, Zmiïv, and Chuhuïv) the peasants' mood had been so transformed (no doubt mostly by news of the VA's advance) that they rushed to pay rent to landlords whose land they had not long ago seized. "Only the absence of power in those places liberated from Bolshevism hampers the restoration of normal life in the villages and district cities."[52]

Not surprisingly, Tarasevich recommended the "immediate, swift establishment of solid civil-military authority" in occupied areas. Although the Red Army was in retreat, local Bolsheviks were burying their weapons and communist cells were taking cover in newly liberated areas. The absence of civil authority was provoking the population's "complete confusion." Peasants feared that the VA's civil authority would be like Hetman Skoropads'kyi's rule, when "with the help of German rifles the landlords retrieved stolen property at two to three times more than its real value."[53] Since the VA sought its main support among the peasant masses, it was crucial that the civil administration treat them, as Tarasevich put it, "justly and impartially, because the peasants themselves say that they will without a problem return that which was stolen." In fact, peasants claimed that it had often been arriving Red Army soldiers who had carried out (probably more accurately *led*) the plundering of estate lands and the redistribution among the local inhabitants. In some cases, peasants had even begun to pay rent for this stolen land. Tellingly, Tarasevich thought it necessary to issue a secret order to local civil authorities demanding "the humane treatment of peasants." At the same time, he called for the most decisive measures against communists. Noting the mistakes of the Propaganda Department's officials, focusing almost entirely on counterintelligence rather than on informing the local inhabitants about the VA, he again stressed the importance of the latter. "Despite the fact that peasants of the most remote villages thirst to learn something about the goals of the Volunteer Army, literature does not even reach villages near the railway lines, and that which does happen to end up there is not explained but simply posted on fences."[54] Clearly, the VA's approach to propaganda differed from that of the Bolsheviks.

What exactly this literature said is difficult to uncover now, because so few VA documents of this type have survived. We can, however, learn something about the VA's land and food supply policies more generally. In the spring of 1919, as the VA was embarking on its most important offensive, Denikin issued a declaration concerning the agrarian question. While cautioning that only newly elected legislative institutions could conclusively solve the land question, Denikin declared, "Life does not wait. It is necessary to save the country from famine and to take those urgent steps that must be implemented immediately." He laid down five principles for local land organs to follow: (1) the interests of "the laboring population" were to be safeguarded; (2) consolidated, small- and medium-sized farms were to be created "at the expense of state and privately owned lands"; (3) some land was to be left to the former owners "with rights of incontrovertible ownership"; and (4) the rest was to be transferred to land-poor peasants "by voluntary agreements or by forced alienation, but without fail for compensation." Finally, (5) all new landowners were to receive "the utmost assistance by means of technological improvements of the land, agronomic help, credit, means of production, supplies of seeds, living and non-living inventory, and others." Denikin stressed that there was not time to work out a conclusive land law. "It is necessary now to take these measures to ease the transfer of land to the land-poor and to raise the productivity of agricultural labor. In all this, revenge and class hostility must not be allowed." In other words, class interests were to be subordinated to "the well-being of the state."[55]

Denikin's declaration, while promising some land eventually to land-poor and landless peasants, would likely not have been very satisfactory to most peasants. Those who seized land in 1917, defended it from other villages' peasants, were forced to return some of it in 1918 and then took it again in early 1919, would hardly have wanted to return their plots to their former owners and await an orderly redistribution of these lands, for which they would then have to pay.

A decree issued by the VA command in late July further reinforced peasants' fear about the VA's restorationist tendencies. Concerned with the gathering of the harvest, this decree proclaimed that in the absence of a former landowner or renter, the Administration of Agriculture and Land Reorganization was entrusted to harvest and thresh the grain. The administration was authorized to then take half of the threshed grain into its possession and set aside the other half for the absentee landlords. The administration was also entrusted "to take full economic control" over farms left by "snatchers [*zakhvatchiki*]" until the farms were returned to their owners.[56] One can imagine how the peasants who had cultivated these plots in the spring of 1919 would feel about giving up the harvest of their labors to the VA and the land's former owners.

Of course, as far as the VA had a political platform, it was not the restoration of the old regime, either in government or in the countryside. As Anna Procyk has pointed out, "With the exception of denying the non-Russian peoples of the former empire the right to self-determination, the VA's political objectives coincided rather closely with the Provisional Government's."[57] Peter Holquist has stressed that the VA's serious attention to surveillance was not backward-looking, reactionary, or anti-revolutionary, but rather quite modern in organization, if not in execution.[58] With the above-discussed decrees in mind, however, it is not difficult to see how peasants might have come to associate the VA's return with that of the old regime. More important, as with other aspects of the Volunteers' rule, the real problem was that many inhabitants saw them as "White Guards," "restorationists," "monarchists," and "counter-revolutionaries," largely as a result of Bolshevik propaganda. That this may not have been the case in fact is beside the point, because the VA largely failed to provide peasants with an alternative explanation of their decrees and policies. Holquist, who makes considerable effort to describe the VA's extensive surveillance and propaganda apparatus, admits that the effort was not successful: "The anti-Soviet movement failed spectacularly at winning widespread popular support."[59]

Documents on the VA's rule in Kharkiv province bear this out. A report from early July 1919 by the head of Azbuka's Kharkov Center, Colonel Fedorov, stressed that, while the peasants were decidedly against the Bolsheviks and related negatively toward Petliura, they also distrusted the Volunteer Army. Fedorov blamed part of this mistrust on the actions of "officer detachments, formed under the hetman, which the peasants confuse with the Volunteer Army." He also stressed "the complete absence of agitation" by the VA in Ukraine; this lack of engagement meant that peasants who had risen up against the Bolsheviks often joined "various local *otomany*, pursuing partly personal interests and partly only narrow provincial ones."[60]

On 5 July 1919, the Kharkov Center presented a more complete picture of what was needed. Making the surprisingly rarely expressed claim that the most essential and vital question for the VA's success was peasants' attitude toward it, the Center stressed, "how the village meets the VA depends on what kind of policy it introduces concerning the peasantry." Tellingly, the center felt compelled to justify and stress the importance of peasants' attitudes, as though this was not the accepted opinion of the VA's leadership. The Center claimed that the village throughout its political life had never proposed slogans of its own; rather it examined closely the slogans of any authorities who approached it and, if dissatisfied, almost immediately initiated an armed uprising against them. Noting some other causes, the report argued that the main reason that peasants came to hate Soviet power was its attempt to introduce the commune, which "the peasants saw as a means of taking their legally owned lands from them." In the numerous villages where peasants had risen up, they had also chased away the committees of the poor and the Soviet executive committees, and in place of them they had elected elders from their more prosperous co-villagers. The report stressed the importance of the land question, "which must be resolved immediately upon the arrival of the Volunteers [VA soldiers], because already now concerning the land reform the peasants say: 'Through winter the land is ours, come spring the devil knows whose land it will be.'" Those authorities who rationally resolved the land issue would win the peasants' support and this required above all "transferring the land as unconditional property to the peasantry." The question about who should pay for the land was secondary, because the village was (supposedly) "overflowing with money." Peasants' claims to the lands they had seized in the past years had to be recognized and confirmed by official papers with stamps and signatures, which the peasants had apparently come increasingly to respect in this anarchic period of civil strife. The Kharkov Center concluded that the Bolsheviks had been thrown out because of their attempts to introduce the communes; the peasants had responded to this attempt as to an orator they did not like at a village assembly, shouting "Enough, get lost!" To avoid the same fate, the Center argued that "Our policy in *Malorossiia* must be such that to us they will say 'Correct!'"[61]

In its brief occupation of the region, the VA managed to do little to implement such recommendations and much more to turn peasants against it. There are a few documents that suggest that a restorative approach was taken toward land relations at the local level. For example, on 31 August 1919 General V. Z. Mai-Maievskii, the VA's commanding officer in the province and across Left-Bank Ukraine, issued a decree ordering that all seized property be returned. Noting that during the Bolsheviks' rule in Kup'iansk, Vovchansk, and Starobilsk districts "several villages had carried away from fields and taken from barns already milled, privately owned grain," he ordered that "the plundered grain be immediately seized and returned to its owners, and those guilty be brought to trial." Local authorities were ordered to take "all measures for the immediate collection of that plundered," not hesitating before "taking punitive measures [*repressii*]."[62] In the absence of a significant number of such documents, and bearing in mind the above-mentioned decree noting the absence of landowners, one is tempted to conclude that actual attempts to restore seized plots to their former owners were rare. On the other hand, considering peasants' predisposition to fear the VA's restorationist tendencies, only a few cases of actual restoration would have been necessary to confirm peasants' fears.

Documents on peasants' attitudes toward the VA are difficult to find and few in number, but those we do have suggest that the VA's neglect of peasants' concerns and unwillingness to make concessions to them had serious consequences. For example, an instructor with clear communist sympathies, Gerasim Shevkun, travelling around Kharkiv province in July 1919 reported that peasants (already) held a hostile attitude toward "the White Guardists." Peasants readily described numerous "unceremonious deeds" (mostly requisitions) committed by VA troops and Cossacks, with the hardest hit being the poor peasants, from whom these troops took the last horse or cow. In conversations in Okhtyrka district, Shevkun heard peasants say that, although the communists had provoked peasants' disapproval and hostility, especially by attempting to implant the communes, "in any case Soviet power…is our power [*nasha vlada*], from our midst, and thus it is close to us and does not wish us evil. And now behind the Cossacks come the power of the landlords, and hence to us again life will not be. Enough already! Chase them away and we will help you."[63]

At about the same time an assistant procurator reported to the provincial procurator that, at least in Vovchansk district, "the overwhelming majority of peasants relate sympathetically toward the Bolsheviks; toward the VA's declarations they relate very mistrustfully." And this was not a newly emerging set of attitudes: peasants, at least in this district, had met the VA's troops "rudely." These feelings had then been strengthened by "separate army units and even individuals [soldiers]" arbitrarily requisitioning hay, cattle, and grain from peasants in the name of the Volunteer Army. The procurator suggested that these individuals were not VA soldiers, but merely evil-minded persons striving to rob peasants and blacken the VA's reputation. The assistant procurator also reported that the population "in every way strives to hide Bolsheviks," who were apparently carrying out secret agitation in the district. In the village of Bolshaia Babka it was impossible to get anyone to indicate where Bolsheviks might be hiding; nor would they say anything about the "deeds of those who had been arrested." Much evidence of Bolshevik agitation in the form of brochures, books, and appeals had also been found. The state guards were threatening to send all those accused to military field courts, but they seemed to be having little success.[64] In mid-September a VA food supply official reported to the Kharkiv governor that peasants in Zmiïv district refused to deliver grain and forage as stipulated in the VA's "Regulation about a one-time military collection." Complaining that he had appealed to the district commander several times without result, the official asked the governor to issue an order "forcing the population of the mentioned district to transport the obligatory grain to the collection points immediately."[65]

One document from Vovchansk district dated 29 September provides a more detailed description of relations between peasants and the VA authorities in one village, Shypuvate. According to a lengthy report by a local VA propaganda worker named Shevtsov, on 1 September 1919, a constable named Zelenskii had ordered the starshina of Shypuvate volost, Pustovar, to gather a contribution of 200,000 rubles from the villagers for the landlord Zadonskii within two days, in order to repay the landlord for the plundering of his orchard and horse farm when the Bolsheviks had arrived at the village in January. In response the villagers selected four elders representing the volost's four precincts and sent them to Zadonskii and the volost's chief to ask for more time. The peasants were given until 8 September to find those guilty and present lists of those who had taken part in the plunder. On 8 September the villagers sent just two peasants to take responsibility, and, not surprisingly, the authorities rejected them as solely guilty, soon returning them to the village. Instead, the volost *starshina* received a new order, this time assessing a contribution of 310 rubles on each household, regardless of guilt in stealing Zadonskii's property. Apparently, the peasants did their best to comply. By 21 September they had surrendered almost 140,000 rubles, and the rest was to be collected on 22 September, probably chosen because it was to be a new holiday, the Day of the Volunteer Army. But on that day, constable Zelenskii, arriving at the volost administration building, did not demand the rest of the money from the gathering crowd, but instead moved straight to reprisals for noncompliance with his order. According to an eyewitness, Zelenskii ordered that a loaded machine gun be set up in front of the administration building and pointed at the gathered peasants. Several village elders were then whipped in front of the crowd (at least nineteen of them were later examined by the precinct doctor).[66] It is important to note that Shevtsov, the VA's local propaganda worker, did not question Zelenskii's act of assessing the contribution on the village, only the methods by which it was extracted.

There is evidence that such behavior was more widespread. An unnamed VA colonel, the commandant of Kup'iansk, reported on 4 October that some Bolshevik proclamations signed by a "Ukrainian revolutionary committee" had been discovered in the area. He noted that he had at his disposal information "definitely corroborating that the mood in the villages of Kup'iansk district had recently sharply worsened and in some cases is clearly hostile to the VA and the government." Besides Bolshevik propaganda, the colonel named three main causes of this change of mood: first, "the very tactless and sometimes criminal behavior of officials of the state guard"; second, information reaching the villages about "the imaginary successes of Petliura and Makhno"; and third, the actions of a Chechen cavalry division stationed in the district. The Chechens, while "expressing very energetic and beneficial measures in relation to true Bolsheviks, in passing have caused irreparable harm to many guiltless inhabitants, which has naturally undermined the population's faith in the fairness of the VA."[67] It is, of course, problematic to accept the veracity of documents published in the Soviet period on the "counter-revolutionary" VA, but in this case the evidence is corroborated by the Volunteer Army's own documents.

On 28 October 1919, Colonel Fedorov, then head of Azbuka's Kharkov Center, provided a comprehensive summary of the VA's propaganda efforts and the reasons for its failure, and discussed the Kharkiv branch as characteristic of the VA's Department of Propaganda (OSVAG) in general. Formed on June 14, the Kharkiv OSVAG's staff included nine military and twelve civilian employees; within three days they acquired another forty civilians, among whom, it turned out, were several Bolsheviks: "Insufficient filtration of candidates during recruitment of new employees was a characteristic peculiarity of OSVAG and repeatedly placed it in the foolish position of involuntary accomplice to Bolshevik intelligence."[68] By the end of July the center employed 57 military staffers and 381 civilians, but this proved insufficient to keep up with the VA's advance. Indeed, it appears that most of the center's employees preferred the safer confines of Kharkiv to propaganda work in the villages "liberated" as the VA marched north. As a result, Fedorov reported, millions of people in the countryside, "thirsting for any kind of information about the Volunteer Army" were left uninformed. The VA thereby missed an "extraordinarily opportune moment, when the population presented itself as raw, very impressionable material" for OSVAG's propaganda. Instead, the population's hearts and minds were filled with "first, Bolshevik propaganda and, second, our own 'anti-propaganda'—that is, the behavior of our military detachments and the 'activity' of our administration." By the time OSVAG agents reached the population, they met not receptiveness, but "deaf opposition."[69]

Fedorov then laid out the many insufficiencies of OSVAG's various departments. The Information Department's summary reports were compiled by an assistant manager named Iurasov, who wrote his summaries "through the prism of the latest declarations," telling the VA's leaders just what they wanted to hear. This greatly biased the VA leadership's understanding of the mood in the civilian population. The Literature Publication Department wasted a great deal of time and energy searching for suitable printing paper because of extreme shortages and price speculation in Kharkiv. As a result, the department had published only a few modest brochures, mostly about the "worker question" and the "land question,"[70] as well as about four million portraits of Generals Kolchak, Denikin, and Kornilov. While Fedorov thought these portraits useful, their prioritization is indicative of the VA's misguided approach to propagandizing the population: what they really needed, apparently, was to see pictures of the new leaders. Moreover, many of those brochures remained in the cities, partly because of OSVAG employees' reluctance to engage peasants, and partly because there simply were not enough employees to leaflet rural areas. Fedorov observed that oral communication among illiterate peasants was much more effective than simply pasting leaflets and placing newspapers in volost government offices, and explained OSVAG's lack of personnel as a result of its own hiring rules. Propagandists and agitators had to take a course and pass an exam to gain employment. Of the 496 who signed up for the course, only 54 took the exam, of which only 34 passed. Of those 34 individuals only 26 were accepted in OSVAG. The educational level of those completing the course was, according to Fedorov, "not high," and 10 of the 26 accepted had only primary education, and many lacked any understanding of peasant life. Fedorov also noted the "criminal negligence ruling in the Technical Department" that was charged with distributing literature: incredibly, leaflets about the VA's land policy were distributed to mine workers, while the villages were supplied with flyers only about "the worker question."[71]

Fedorov concluded that the abundance of red tape and formalities had transformed "a vital, young issue [i.e. propaganda] into some kind of official 'presence'...there are many young people in jackets, surrounded by 'incoming' and 'outgoing' books, but very little real propaganda." The situation was no better at OSVAG's various propaganda "points" or centers in the localities: "If a 60-year-old general stands at the head of a point, then the whole point is wasted on stagnant routine." Peasants skeptically called this "Generals' propaganda." Alternatively, if a young student was in charge, then he was too subservient. According to Fedorov, peasants seemed to feel instinctively that at these "points" sit "the authorities." The results of all this were "in truth, terrible":

> With each day OSVAG diverges more and more from the population and our propaganda hangs in the air [*visnet v vozdukhe*]. Our Department of Propaganda copied the Bolsheviks' organization of the propaganda issue but did not take from them the main and most important thing: the Bolsheviks in their propaganda knew how to approach the population earnestly. The significance of this circumstance is unbelievably great: only thanks to it the Bolsheviks are now reducing our strategic successes to nothing.[72]

One of the most enlightening documents on the situation in the countryside near the end of the VA's rule was provided by a delegate to the South Russian conference of the Party of People's Freedom, which took place in Kharkiv in early November 1919. A. I. Ershov reported to the leading members of the political party most closely associated with the Volunteer Army movement that the people's once friendly attitude toward the VA had turned "visibly unfriendly, sometimes even hostile or apathetic." Ershov saw as the main cause of this change of mood "the observed discord between the tasks of declarations and the actions of the administration," especially concerning the land question. The people expressed a sharply negative attitude toward the VA's failure to resolve this crucial issue. The most frequently heard desire expressed in the countryside was that Petliura would return: "Let Petliura come. He can lift this burden off of us." Peasants stated that the VA fought "in vain" with Petliura and that the simple peasants (*muzhiki*) did not fear Petliura, though the lords (*pany*) did. At the same time, peasants had explained to Ershov that they did not think Petliura was dangerous as a separatist, because "he had already come twice as a separatist and not one soul had supported him nor will support him [as a separatist]." Peasants' hopes in Petliura rested on the belief that he would privilege land reform over any strivings for national independence.

Ershov also stressed the crucial role of peasant soldiers returning from the front. These soldiers complained to Ershov, "At the front they promise us one thing and here they are doing something else; they are returning the land to the rich in order to enrich the *pany* and we landless poor peasants remain without land." The soldiers claimed that they had greeted "the Volunteers [VA soldiers]" positively and helped them to fight the Bolsheviks, but they would not give up the land they had taken from the lords and already redistributed among themselves. When asked why they had destroyed the lords' estates, they replied that they had "burned the nests so that the crows would not find their way back," and threatened, "If they take our [land] now, we will smash the bird." The VA's treatment of peasant soldiers, who complained of abuses such as beatings with birch rods, had filtered back to noncombatants. This helped to turn the population against the army. Ershov also reported that peasants' complaints were frequently accompanied by comments that they were hoping for the Bolsheviks' return.[73] It is not surprising that Ershov saw no contradiction in peasants wishing for the return of both Petliura and the Bolsheviks. Many centrist and right-wing politicians, as well as VA informants, saw little difference between these two radical groups, one stressing national, the other class, distinctions.

Ershov asserted that in general the peasants were exhausted from years of rude treatment and beatings, and "although they quietly listen to all kinds of threats and insults, they will not forgive these offenses." They were becoming increasingly hostile toward the VA. They complained very often and were seriously offended by VA soldiers plundering and seizing "their property"; VA officers responded to their complaints with threats of beatings with ramrods. People also expressed great dissatisfaction with the VA's bureaucratism and complained about the administration's arbitrariness, especially in rehiring former tsarist police officers and firing left-leaning employees. Ershov concluded that, based on his numerous conversations with peasants, soldiers and others, "the history of the last year before the revolution is being repeated and the current time has much in common with the Hetmanate." The Volunteer Army's great mission of restoring "One, indivisible Russia"—the one VA policy that was unequivocally restorationist—was being destroyed by the "bureacratic-landlord regime" that had arrived in its wake. He concluded, "The rude activities of the emerging old-regime bureaucratic structure are pushing the people more strongly to the left than ever before for the whole three years of revolution."[74]

*

There is a strange irony in the insights of this member of the Kadet party, the unofficial ruling political party under the VA's rule, into peasants' experience of the Civil War. Whether the VA regime was in its intent reactionary or counter-revolutionary turned out to be irrelevant. In its inaction behind the frontlines, not providing sufficient positive propaganda to counter the Bolsheviks' efforts, and allowing some local officials and VA soldiers to behave badly, the VA left the peasants, exhausted by three years of revolution and civil war, to draw their own conclusions, sometimes with the help of communist underground workers. Peasants may have violently opposed the previous Worker-Peasant Government's attempts to introduce the communes, requisition their grain, and mobilize their remaining men, but compared to the VA's rule, or their perceptions of that rule, they now again found "Soviet power" more acceptable. At least, they now thought it the lesser evil, at least in the short run.

5 Compromise and Conviction, Peasants and Party: Groping toward "Soviet Power" in the Village

There was a moment in early 1920 when a rapprochement between villagers and the newly reformed Worker-Peasant Government seemed quite possible. Following a series of party debates in Moscow, the "Ukrainian" Communists resolved to return to Ukraine with a new policy more sensitive to peasants' desires. They denounced the previous Soviet government's forced communization, the brazenly expressed Russian chauvinism, and general ignorance of local conditions and the inhabitants' aspirations. For their part, peasants expressed a willingness to cooperate with the new regime, especially at the numerous non-party peasant conferences held across the province in February 1920. At the same time, they strongly asserted their own positions: they articulated their persistent demand for local autonomy, distrust of non-peasants (especially city-dwellers and the intelligentsia), and misgivings about the regime's food requisition (*prodrazverstka*) policy. Strangely, party leaders seem to have considered these non-party conferences to be merely publicity stunts. It was probably impossible (or unimaginable) for any government interested in modernizing Ukraine and Russia to satisfy peasants in their desire to be left alone. But the policies of this Worker-Peasant Government did much to antagonize and little to smooth over the difficult and inevitable transition to modernity. With the land question basically resolved, peasants came to focus on the food supply issue; they soon began to resist the food-requisition detachments and the latter's often crude and unfair attempts to extract food and fuel from the village. These detachments' expeditions more often than not proved unsuccessful; running into determined resistance, they sometimes provoked peasants to large-scale uprisings, which first appeared already in early March 1920. In response, the regime resorted to violent measures, eventually employing regular Red Army troops, but peasants continued to resist the regime's efforts to impose its authority, and especially the *prodrazverstka*, over them. Only after the KP(b)U's reluctant and delayed implementation of the New Economic Policy in the summer of 1921 did peasants begin to deliver their grain to market to feed the cities. Even after this, they continued to resist other Soviet policies, sometimes violently; and outbreaks of what the authorities termed "banditry" were reported in Kharkiv province as late as 1924.

The Second Return of Soviet Power

There is no doubt that, following the debacle of June 1919, the leaders of the Russian Communist Party (Bolsheviks) and, following closely, those of the Communist Party (Bolsheviks) of Ukraine, sought to make amends in Ukraine. On 29 November 1919 a plenary session of the RKP(b)'s central committee passed the resolution "On Soviet Power in Ukraine," which laid out the party's new position. Supposedly drafted by Lenin himself, the resolution reaffirmed the federation of Soviet Republics proclaimed on 1 June 1919, but demanded that Communists take all possible measures to eliminate anything hindering the development of Ukrainian language and culture. Ukrainians were now to be educated in the Ukrainian language and to be able to use it in dealing with all state institutions. In addition, great effort was to be made to win over poor and middling peasants. Affirming its food supply policy of state procurement of grain at set prices and compulsory quotas (*prinuditel′naia razverstka*), the resolution stressed that the extraction of peasants' surpluses be limited to that strictly necessary for the poor, workers, and the army, "paying special attention to the interests of the middle peasantry." The resolution called for "the complete liquidation of the landlord ownership restored by Denikin with the transfer of these lands to the landless and land-poor." Concerning the communes and other collective forms of agriculture, the party stressed that "no force would be permitted" and that party members should depend entirely on the "free decision of the peasants themselves," threatening severe punishments "for any attempts to implement this matter by the use of force."[1] Closely following suit, on 21 December the newly created All-Ukrainian Revolutionary Committee in its proclamation of victory over Denikin stressed that it would "decisively cut short any intervention in the life of the peasantry that pursues as its aim the forcing upon the peasants of economic organizations that are not the result of their own initiative."[2]

Such decrees do not tell us how those Soviet troops moving into Ukraine in late 1919 actually behaved, and such information is difficult to find. What I have found suggests that they behaved like almost all occupying armies—badly. A report from the Zmiïv district Revolutionary Committee (*revkom*) about the food supply situation in the district shortly after the Red Army's arrival reveals some of the ravages of the civil war. The grain collection points used under the previous Soviet regime had almost all been "ruined." All information gathered about and documents concerning Soviet state farms had been eliminated and the farms "destroyed" (probably by peasants), because these symbolized the hated policies of the previous Soviet regime. Under the rubric "the results of Denikin's plundering," the Zmiïv revkom reported that retreating VA troops had carried away almost 100 wagons of grain, along with "all property of any value," from telephones to blacksmith's tools. However, the revkom also noted that "both the retreating and the invading troops [i.e. Soviet troops] had seized, by an approximate accounting, 35–40 percent of the grain and forage from the peasants, not counting the estates on which nothing remains except straw."[3] The chairman of the Valky district revkom later remarked that frontline soviet troops "contributed much to the absence of property available to be confiscated" from landlords' estates.[4] A report from the People's Commissariat of Internal Affairs on Kharkiv province noted that still in early February 1920 there was considerable "friction between the district revkoms and Red Army detachments, because of the latter's arbitrary requisitions of foodstuffs."[5] Very likely, once Soviet institutions became established they were not inclined to have recorded complaints about pillaging by the arriving "victorious Red Army" or have desired to investigate them further.

Despite Red Army soldiers' bad behavior, many peasants soon expressed a desire to work with the new regime. The protocol of a provincial congress of district agitational-propaganda department managers, meeting in Kharkiv in mid-January 1920, presented a quite favorable picture of peasants' attitudes toward the new regime. The representative from Kharkiv district reported to the congress that "the mood in the volosts is very good: the peasantry in general, and the peasant youth in particular, stand for Soviet power; the attitude toward Makhno and Petliura is sharply negative, in eight volosts Communist cells were organized spontaneously." The Vovchansk district representative noted that there were revkoms in fifteen of nineteen volosts; in ten volosts Communists headed these committees, in the rest, those sympathizing with the party. It was, however, the representative from Chuhuïv district who provided the most revealing comment on peasants' attitudes at this moment: "The village is very revolutionarily inclined, greedily listening to all kinds of rumors emanating from the city, attentively following all the authorities' actions and insistently demanding literature and agitators, who could clearly explain those questions interesting them."[6]

The Non-Party Peasant Conferences of Early 1920

The most illuminating sources on peasants' attitudes and intentions toward the Soviet regime at this crucial juncture are the records of the non-party peasant conferences held in February 1920. These conferences have been largely overlooked as a source. Soviet historians either mentioned them only in passing as evidence of the peasants' support for the new regime,[7] and the new land law in particular, or dismissed them as poorly organized, "kulak-infested" affairs that did not express the views of the poor and middling peasantry.[8] Indeed, this latter interpretation sprang from the official protocols and reports produced after the conferences. But if one looks a little deeper, quite a different picture emerges. These conferences were in some sense "non-party," or more literally "without party" (*bezpartiinaia konferentsia*), which did not mean that no parties were represented, but that all legal parties were. The term "non-party" seems to have referred only to the presumed political mindset of the peasants and not to the content or subject matter of the conferences themselves. Party representatives from the KP(b)U, Borot′bists, Bor′bists and LSR-Internationalists spoke at these conferences, presenting the peasants with political alternatives on the current situation, the new land law, and food requisition policies. More important, unlike most later large assemblies, these conferences were not well orchestrated affairs. Thus, the conferences' stenographic records reveal much about peasants' attitudes toward the authorities and their own ideas about Soviet power.

The reasons the KPU(b) gave for calling these conferences were expressed in a circular letter to all party organizations from the head of the Department for Work in the Village (Otrabsel′), V. Nevskii, dated 26 December 1919. Nevskii explained that "a necessary condition for our successes in the rear and at the front is the participation of the wide laboring masses in Soviet construction and our party life." The first and most important theme to be explained at the conferences was that "the existence of Soviet power is a necessary and unavoidable condition of social revolution." The conferences were to be both a forum for propagandizing to the masses the importance of Soviet power and for drawing the masses into Soviet construction, the rebuilding of the economy and the implementation of the regime's policies.[9] The conferences were also a way to determine the mood of the peasantry and the degree of influence of various layers within the village.[10]

In his letter, Nevskii also explained in great detail how the conferences were to be initiated, stressing intensive preparation. Before calling the conferences, party workers were to determine local conditions and attitudes, and to consider the more general military and political situation. They were to carry out exhaustive agitation and propaganda before and during the election of delegates. District party leaders were to prepare reports well in advance that stressed all the good that Soviet power was doing for the people, the importance of the Red Army's victory over the counterrevolution, that its defeat meant the return of the *pany*, and finally, that only with the peasants' energetic help and support could the Red Army accomplish this task.[11]

Unfortunately for the party, these instructions appear to have had very little impact on the conferences' progress. Ambiguity over what the party center meant by "non-party" gave peasants the opportunity to employ their own interpretations. A report on the Bohodukhiv district conference noted that the peasants had not been familiarized beforehand with the goals of the conferences. This "unfamiliarity expressed itself in such an undesirable form that even the name 'non-party' was by them interpreted in the sense that it was necessary to elect to the conference *only* 'non-party' [*bezpartiinykh*] peasants. As a result the overwhelming majority of the conference's composition emerged from the kulak elements."[12]

Of course, only those who wrote this report knew what they meant by "kulak elements." As Moshe Lewin has suggested, the term "kulak" [*kurkul* in Ukrainian] "meant, in any particular period, different things amongst the Bolsheviks themselves."[13] In general, the Soviet regime used the term to label and criminalize any peasants who resisted or challenged Soviet power, regardless of those peasants' economic or social position.[14] It is impossible to know exactly what percentage of peasant delegates were "kulaks" in some economic sense, but clearly many of the delegates believed that the conferences would truly be "non-party." The party organizers had quite different directions from the center about how to lead the conferences.

The clearest example of this clash of interpretations occurred right after the district conferences began. At the opening of every conference the local party organizers presented to the peasant delegates a presidium composed of the leaders of the district's party organizations (mostly communists), and in every case the peasants rejected it. The most emphatic example occurred at the Kharkiv district non-party peasant conference, opened in Kharkiv on 8 February 1920. In his opening speech, the leading Bolshevik, identified in the proceedings as Comrade Nakonechnii, informed the peasant delegates that this conference had been called "in order to hear the voice of the peasants, to observe here those shortcomings which were made in the localities and to take measures on this account to solve these questions as the peasants express them." The conference was called from "the thick of those non-party peasant masses who, closest of all, clash with the very question of life." According to Nakonechnii, the peasants were to discuss the most crucial questions in order that the authorities might better resolve those questions, so that the peasants would come to understand that "worker-peasant power is their own authentic power. And that it was created for them, by them and from them. Hence, comrades, I wish you happy success in the resolution of our questions (applause)."[15]

Nakonechnii then announced the proposed presidium's members, who had been nominated "by the agreement of the [party] fractions" in advance and who included three Communist-Bolsheviks, two Communist-Borot′bists, two from the "group of non-party delegates" [*gruppa bezpartiinykh*],[16] and one left SR Bor′bist.[17] Having presented the presidium, Nakonechnii stated, "In order that we do not spend a lot of time here on these elections, I propose to you to confirm this presidium."[18]

The clamorous melee that Nakonechnii's words provoked cannot be recounted here in detail; it lasted the entire first day, late into the night of the evening session.[19] Most peasant delegates opposed the presidium that the parties had proposed, and in expressing their opposition they revealed much about their interpretations of the conferences' purpose and the political situation in general. A few quotations here will suffice:

> From a seat [*S mesta* —i.e., a peasant delegate]: Comrades, I myself think that if this is our peasant [*selianskaia*] conference which has gathered here, then we must ourselves elect the presidium, but we do not have to elect that [presidium] proposed to us. If we choose from our own midst, then we will know whom we elect....
>
> From a seat: I must respond to a previous speaker who indicated that non-party [peasants] have done nothing. I must say: Who did most of all, who suffered losses of forage and cattle, most of all non-party [peasants], who stayed at home and ran their farms....
>
> Chairman: That is not essential, you must speak about the presidium.
>
> From a seat: I will add to what the previous speaker said that if you [the party leaders] provided the freedom [*svobodu*] to gather today, then you must be good [*bud'te dobry*] and give us the will [*voliu*] to elect the members of the presidium from among ourselves, those who we ourselves propose. Once we, non-party [peasants], have gathered, then we must express our will. So, be good and give us the will to propose non-party [peasants] to the presidium....
>
> From a seat: We must elect those people who will express the voice of the people and not vote for any kind of party, and thus we should elect from the conference and not from parties.[20]

Reentering the fray and attempting to reestablish order, Nakonechnii tried to explain "normal conference procedure" to the peasant delegates. He pointed out that all conferences and congress were carried out in this way, noting the examples of the recent Kharkiv non-party workers' conference and the worker women's conference then taking place right next door. It was simply more efficient and less time-consuming to elect the predetermined presidium. Moreover, those already proposed were also "from the conference"; they were "just like you who have come forth here, but they can better conduct the meeting of our conference than just anyone." He noted that there were in fact two non-party delegates on the proposed presidium list. If the peasants simply elected from among themselves, then, he predicted, "from the thirty-six volosts there would be no fewer than thirty-six candidates" and in the end "random people [*sluchainye liudi*]," not capable of leading the conference, would end up on the presidium.[21]

Obviously not heeding Nakonechnii's plea for order, the very next speaker retorted from his seat: "It seems to me that this presidium that has been nominated now is not from this conference, but from separate groups, because many people did not participate [in their nomination]; everyone is here and we must elect the presidium from our own midst."[22] And the next peasant, after speaking at length, concluded, "We need those representatives who know our peasant life, those who will stand up for our peasant interests."[23] After several more attempts by Nakonechnii to control the debate, another peasant expressed what must have been a common feeling among the delegates: "The thing is that you [the party leaders] say that we [the peasants] or someone who we propose will not be able to direct the conference. But what sense is there in that if on the presidium will sit representatives of the parties, who will speak, and the people will sit and listen. You ask why are we afraid of party representatives whom we would approve, but we ask you, why are you afraid of those peasants whom we will elect [?]."[24]

Thus continued the debate for many hours, the peasants certainly not speaking in unison but universally opposing the party list. Moreover, they repeatedly drew a distinction between "we"—as in the peasants (or "the conference"), and "you"— meaning the parties. Eventually, peasant delegates began to propose alternative methods for electing the presidium: some suggested simply that each candidate from the proposed party list step forward and say who he was and where he was from, so that the peasants could determine if they were "of them" (*svoi*) or not. Others proposed that new non-party candidates be nominated "from the conference" and be voted on individually. Finally, some proposed that a recess be declared so that the representatives from each volost could gather together and select one candidate from among themselves; then those thirty-six volost representatives would gather and select the presidium. When Nakonechnii managed to stop the debate and put these four resolutions to a vote, the first three received very few votes, and the last—to elect by volost—was "accepted unanimously."[25] It would seem that the delegates were not only suspicious of the parties, but also of peasants from other volosts.

After the recess, Nakonechnii presented the new presidium, composed of seven non-party delegates, to the conference.[26] Not only all party leaders, but even the two peasant delegates representing the non-party group in the originally proposed presidium were not elected, perhaps tainted by their association with the parties' list. And yet, many peasants were still not satisfied, complaining that of the thirty-six volost representatives chosen, only seven ended up on the presidium. Expressing the fear that those seven delegates would speak and fight only for the interests of their own volosts, several peasants demanded that each of the newly proposed presidium's members step up to the podium, say who he is and "recount his own biography," as one peasant put it.[27] Nakonechnii seems to have picked up on this idea. Perceiving that the peasants feared electing unknown delegates, and that there was less possibility of a "kulak" "sneaking" into the presidium if each proposed member stood up to the podium and stated who he was, Nakonechnii and Sosnovskii, another member of the district revkom, repeatedly reminded the peasants that voting for this presidium as a whole was indeed "voting in the dark." This tactic dragged out the debate further, but in the end the overwhelming majority of the delegates confirmed the non-party presidium as a whole. (Actually, this was not quite the end of it. After a short break, the party leaders convinced the newly elected presidium to ask the conference to allow five party members [three Bolsheviks, two Borot´bists and one Bor´bist] onto the presidium, preserving the chair for a non-party peasant. After more debate, the parties' "additions" were confirmed unanimously with seven abstentions.)[28]

Local party leaders proved somewhat more tactful at the Kup'iansk district non-party peasant conference. On 10 February 1920 the chairman of the district revolutionary committee, Sazonov, opened the assembly of 370 peasant delegates with the proposal to sing the "International," Shevchenko's "Testament," and to play the death march "in memory of the fallen fighters for the liberation from the yoke of capitalists and landlords." He then proposed for the purpose of "conducting the assembly" the confirmation of a presidium composed of four members from the district revkom and three representatives from the peasants. Neverthless, some peasant delegates introduced a proposal to elect the presidium solely "from the conference." Two of the leading Bolsheviks, Liuksenburg and Golovin, explained to the delegates that the presidium would be the executive organ of the assembly and that the revkom had proposed its own candidates only in order to provide "fully experienced" people to lead the conference.[29]

These attempts to allay a major confrontation over the presidium were to little avail. A raucous debate erupted with the participation of many peasant delegates, using the same logic as in Kharkiv: If the presidium was truly to be non-party, then it must be elected from the peasants. When Sazonov finally brought the assembly to a vote, the results were already clear: the proposed presidium was rejected by a majority, and instead, a proposal to elect a presidium of nine people "whom the assembly itself would propose" was accepted. And yet, after the delegates elected these representatives, the party leaders managed to convince them also to elect Sazonov and Liuksenburg; then these two party leaders were able to convince the peasant members of the presidium that they should lead the assembly's proceedings.[30]

The peasant delegates elected to the Zmiïv district conference were also confused about the meaning of the term "non-party." As with the Bohodukhiv conference, an official report on this conference claimed that this misunderstanding was manipulated by "kulaks" to sneak their representatives into the conference, thus explaining the undesirable outcome. Strangely, this same report provided data that contradicted the "kulak" label by listing the party affiliation and social composition of the delegates: ten Communist-Bolsheviks with twenty-five sympathizers; five Borot′bists with five sympathizers; three Bor′bists with five sympathizers; the rest were "non-party" and described as twenty poor peasants; thirty "kulaks," and "about 150 middling peasants." The report claimed that because the mandate forms of many of the delegates had not yet been confirmed in the localities, it was not possible to confirm how many kulaks "concealed their property positions."[31] During the elections to the presidium these "kulaks" had supposedly argued that, since the conference was composed of non-party delegates, the presidium must be designated as "non-party" as well. The conference delegates rejected the list of candidates proposed by the three party fractions (Bolsheviks, Borot′bists and Bor′bists), and instead elected what the report termed "unsuitable people" to the presidium. The deputy chairman, Bocharov, was described as "an old man, a speculator from Chuhuïv volost, who constantly complained about a wagon of salt that had been taken from him."[32] The term "old man" was frequently employed as a euphemism for "kulak," probably because most of the better off people in the village who controlled the *skhod* were older men. Those using the label may also have hoped in this way to appeal to younger men who were anxious to get away from their old patriarchs. A separate report noted, "all Communist-Bolsheviks were deliberately rejected, because before the election each candidate was asked about party membership [*partiinost ′*]."[33] In fact, two party leaders were elected to the presidium: Lobanov (a Communist), chair of the district revkom, and Levchenko (a Bor′bist). However, "under complicated circumstances," the peasant delegates denounced them, shouting, "Go away! There is the road." Lobanov and Levchenko were forced to quit the presidium.

The protocol produced by the newly elected presidium secretary also reflected the peasants' attitude toward the communists. Describing a party leader's speech at the start of the conference, the secretary simply wrote: "The comrade from Kharkiv gave a speech, and talked very, very much [*vystupal tovarishch iz Khar′kova govoril mnogo mnogo*]." The next day, 7 February, at the party leaders' insistence, "almost in the form of an ultimatum," a compromise was reached and the delegates reelected the presidium. The new presidium was composed of two Bolsheviks, one Borot′bist, one Bor′bist, and three "non-party".[34] That some of these conferences eventually accepted a presidium that included party members probably suggests that these peasants wished to be heard, to feel they were in control of the conference, but that they also saw a need to compromise with party leaders.

After the peasant delegates finally elected their own presidiums, the district conferences moved on to discussing what was referred to as "the current moment." With this topic Communist Party leaders sought the peasants' confirmation of Soviet power and their ruling position, but the debate often widened into a discussion of how power should be organized in Ukraine. The most radical position on this issue was taken at the Bohodukhiv conference, about which regrettably little information has survived, probably because its resolutions ran contrary to the Communists' line. Revealing the great influence of the Ukrainian Borot′bists in this district, the conference resolved that "Ukraine, with its socioeconomic and politico-national particularities, should constitute itself as a separate national economic organism and can be developed successfully only when it has its own Ukrainian ruling center."[35] The first task of the

Ukrainian proletariat and poor peasantry was proclaimed "the creation of a united Ukrainian ruling center, which will be subordinate only to the Third Communist International and a United Ukrainian Communist Party."[36] It should, perhaps, be made clear that this was the only district conference at which national independence played an important role.

At all the other conferences, for which we have much better documentary records, debate on the "current moment" centered around whether to trust the new Soviet government, the KP(b)U, "the Bolsheviks," and party intellectuals in general. At the Valky district conference, after the Communists had laid out their position and the other party leaders had criticized them at length, peasant delegates launched into a protracted and serious debate.[37] In the end two resolutions were proposed, one put forward by the combined forces of the Communists and Borot′bists, and the other by the LSRs-Bor′bists and Internationalists. Peasant delegates refused to accept either resolution, instead proposing to elect a commission of five delegates to work out a separate resolution. Expressing confidence in the Red Army's eventual victory and the defeat of both the internal and international "counterrevolution," the peasants in their resolution proposed a rather eclectic set of new measures: the complete abolition of the death penalty; the establishment of a united revolutionary front of political and economic equality for workers and laboring peasants; the creation of a "united revolutionary front of left-socialist Soviet parties" (clearly bemoaning the party leaders' mutual mudslinging); the recruitment of real workers and peasants into Soviet institutions, warning against attempts to appoint officials "from above"; and the establishment of a barter system (*tovaroobmen*) and labor exchange (*trudoobmen*) between the city and the village. In addition, this resolution recognized as "essential the existence of a strong regular Red Army under the united supreme command of Soviet Ukraine and Russia, tightly bound in a single, revolutionary discipline." Almost all peasant delegates accepted their commission's resolution, though the Communists and Borot′bists abstained from voting.[38] Delegates attending the Izium district conference expressed similar distrust toward the Communists and the district revkom, also drafting and passing their own resolution on the current moment.[39]

One of the most revealing debates occurred at the Kup'iansk district non-party conference, following a speech on the current moment by the leading communist, Sazonov. Sazonov called on poor and middling peasants "to unite in fraternity with the workers" in reconstructing the ruined economy and helping to consolidate Soviet power.[40] The peasants' responses suggest that they either had other priorities or were not listening very closely to the party leaders' speeches. Delegate Evremenko, the first to speak after Sazonov, asked the party leaders why Kup'iansk district remained under martial law and proposed that the conference pass a resolution for the swift election of executive committees of soviets to replace the imposed revolutionary-military committees. Delegate Khymchenko proposed that they organize a "people's regiment," presumably to defend the district. Delegate Honchar declared, "Tsarism has ended, but in place of tsarism someone is again oppressing us worse than tsarism." Delegate Popov disagreed, stressing that under tsarism they had been treated like cattle. The power of the people had been proclaimed in 1917, but in fact it still did not exist; he warned that if workers continued to act separately from peasants, "then there will never be any understanding." Obviously perplexed by the proceedings, delegate Grigorenko then asked to what purpose had the congress been called. Delegate Shapovalov complained that, though the dictatorship of the proletariat had been ruling (*tsarstvuet*) since October 1917, peasants continue to be oppressed. He stated, "Peasants were oppressed by the Whites, they were oppressed by the Reds. Peasants are like cattle," and insisted that the revkoms stand "on the side of the revolution, and not the dictatorship. We peasants have not seen freedom since 1 October 1917." Demanding that the peasant conference not disperse until it had called for the immediate election of executive committees, he concluded, "As long as there will be a military dictatorship, there will be evil."

One peasant delegate complained about "the merciless requisitions" of food supply agents; another that party members were receiving privileges, such as riding in the heated cars on trains. Party leaders then tried to call peasants to unity and to support the new regime. The Communist Bondarenko asserted that his party was "the vanguard of the revolution." "The party has given us peasants the possibility to gather here," and thus, it deserves "only gratitude." According to Bondarenko, all attacks on the party were unfounded.[41]

After a supper break, the debate continued with the peasants criticizing the Communists and bringing up issues not closely related, and the party leaders attempting to defend the party and get the debate back on track. The final word was given to the Communist Liuksenburg, who tried to explain why the military-revolutionary committees could not yet be replaced by Soviet executive committees. The assembly reportedly expressed its gratitude for Liuksenburg's "unusually clear and comprehensible explanation," but when the presidium put the two resolutions (from Communists-Borot′bists and LSRs) to a vote, peasant delegates immediately proposed that a commission be elected to draw up a resolution from the assembly. Tellingly, the party leaders, probably feeling confident that they had brought the presidium's nine peasant delegates under their control, immediately suggested a compromise to entrust the presidium to amend the Communists' resolution. The delegates, however, refused this proposal as well and voted "unanimously to entrust a commission to draft a resolution."[42]

This commission's resolution called for an "All-Ukrainian non-party conference" including workers' deputies; the removal of martial law in the district and the election of executive committees at all levels; the organization of a militia, in no case permitting former tsarist police into service; an end to the civil war; that no monopoly be imposed on agricultural products until factories were able to provide "all that was necessary for peasants"; recognition of Ukraine as a "free republic with its own administration," though in federation with Russia; the publication of a law Ukrainianizing the state, schools and the church; land reform, taking into account "the customs and traditions of the Ukrainian people"; and repayment at market prices for all foodstuffs seized by Red Army troops. At the same time, the peasants expressed their "sincere gratitude to the Red Army for its labors…in the liberation of Ukraine from the yoke of its oppressors."[43] More peasant delegates voted for this resolution than for the two party resolutions combined.

Immediately after the voting, the party leaders began to denounce the peasants' resolution. Calling it "counterrevolutionary," especially the call to end the civil war, they demanded a second vote. The presidium soon acquiesced, and then the assembled peasant delegates unanimously rejected their own resolution. And yet, when the parties' resolutions were put to a second vote, only a minority of delegates voted for either. Noting that more than half the deputies had not participated in this vote, Liuksenburg called for another. It was, however, very late at night, and so the presidium closed the assembly without accepting any resolution on the current moment.[44] Eventually, the Communist leaders managed to convince the presidium to hold a secret ballot on the current moment, arguing that many poor peasants were afraid to vote for the Bolshevik resolution. The majority of delegates still did not vote for the Bolshevik resolution, however, despite the fact that the vote was held immediately after the peasants had almost unanimously accepted the Communists' resolution on the new land law. A majority of delegates voted for the LSRs' resolution, which had incorporated some aspects of the peasants' resolution (including the call for the immediate election of local soviets to replace the revkoms). But delegates may have preferred this resolution simply because it was not the Communists'.[45]

The third crucial issue discussed at these conferences, the land question, was the one question on which peasants expressed general agreement with the party leaders. This is not surprising, because the new land law, enacted by the All-Ukrainian Revolutionary Committee on 5 February 1920, basically gave the peasants what they had wanted all along. The law asserted that "henceforth, on the territory of Ukraine only laborers [*trudiashchiesia*] possess the right to use the land." All currently existing working farms (farms employing only the peasant household's labor) would remain inviolable and were allowed to use their land "in the manner in which they had used it until now," whether as part of a commune or as independent farmers (*otrub* or *khutor*). The lands of landowners, the state, the royal court and monasteries, whether already confiscated or not, were to be transferred without any payment "to the use of all Ukrainian laboring people," first of all to satisfy the land needs of landless and land-poor peasants. (These lands' farming equipment was to be similarly redistributed.) All former non-laboring owners, whether they were nobility or not, were to be immediately removed from their estates. The law also reversed the party's position on collective agriculture: all "soviet farms" formed in early 1919 from former landlord estates were to be transferred to the direct use of landless and land-poor peasants, except for those plots that local peasants agreed to leave intact, as model or experimental farms, useful for demonstrating improved agricultural techniques. The distributive process was to be carried out by land departments set up under the revkoms: "no soviet institutions nor private individuals" were allowed to use any land at all "without the appropriate permission of the land departments." These land departments were to determine norms of land redistribution per person (termed "eater") established at the district level, giving some flexibility for "local practices," and were to carry out the registration and redistribution of all these lands and inventory within one month from the day the law was published.[46] Almost all non-party peasant delegates across the province approved of the new land law, though a few did express concern about confiscating lands belonging to "kulaks."

At all district non-party conferences it was the government's next position, concerning food supply, to which peasants most unequivocally objected. Communist leaders stressed the ruined state of the economy and the sacrifices peasants had to make to restore it, mainly by supplying food to workers to enable them to rebuild old and construct new industries. The leaders proposed three crucial measures: (1) a monopoly on all major necessities; (2) the elimination of speculation and free trade on these items; and (3) the well planned, state-controlled distribution of all these items among workers and laboring peasants. They stressed that much of what was requisitioned would be used to feed Red Army soldiers and "the starving workers of the Donets basin," and that the burden placed on poor and middling peasants would not be great, "because the grain and forage will be taken mainly from the kulaks' surpluses."[47]

When party leaders opened up the issue to debate, however, they found little support for their proposals. Peasants immediately began listing numerous arbitrary and unjust actions already committed by food supply agents. At the Kup'iansk district conference, for example, delegate Dralov complained that agent Stadnik had shot for meat one of his volost's best breeding bulls. Delegate Shapovalov lamented the district food supply committee's decision to close all creameries, making butter and oil production impossible. He suggested that all such problems should be resolved by the local authorities and the people and not by the district food supply committee. Delegate Pleskach reported that in his volost, agents had seized grain from poor peasants, arrested the chairman of the volost's revkom and held him hostage in a cold barn until peasants delivered all the requisitioned grain. Others confirmed his story, especially noting the activities of one agent, Galygin, who had repeatedly seized grain from the poor and arrested those who refused to give. Delegate Sazonov complained that the "agents seize almost everything and, besides, do not protect the people's wealth." Warning that the agents' behavior would only lead to disaster, he accused the authorities of ignoring these abuses. Emboldened by these complaints, delegate Gerasimov declared, "all agents are the same." In Vilshanka volost agent Subbotin had behaved very recklessly, seizing the hay from some stacks and leaving the rest scattered about on the snow to spoil. Gerasimov insisted that agents should be accompanied by representatives from the volost revkom. He especially objected that, when the agents arrived, they did not allow the peasants to call an assembly to decide whether to give grain or not.[48]

The Communist party leaders at the Kup'iansk conference became increasingly frustrated with the delegates' complaints and unwillingness to debate what they thought the central points of the issue. Communist Ruban demanded that delegates stop conversing among themselves and focus on the food supply question. At the same time, party leaders seemed to be learning peasants' limits. Communist Liuksenburg admitted that mistakes had been made and that many of the delegates' complaints and censures were "just." He stressed, however, that Soviet power was poised at a crucial moment, when it will be determined whether "Soviet power will remain on the map or not." District food supply committee head Zhiliabin also acknowledged that mistakes had been made. Claiming that the most severe measures would be taken against bad agents, he pleaded with peasants to give up their grain for the Red Army: "If you will go out to greet the food supply organs in requisitioning, then you will make your army much more battle-ready." Granted the final word in the debate, Communist Sazonov claimed that the delegates had not criticized the essence of his party's position. Addressing some delegates who had mentioned the need for free trade, Sazonov unequivocally declared that this would mean "to sign the death sentence of Soviet power." He then read out the Communists' resolution on food supply, noting the three main points, and concluded with a call to "all for whom Soviet power, the power of peasants and workers, is dear, to execute their sacred duty before the valiant Red Army and all laborers and to surrender surplus grain to the state food supply organs."[49]

Delegate Tur, who had assumed the role of the peasants' leading spokesman, then stepped up to the podium and pointed out that the Communists' resolution would install "the laws of Great Russia, but in Ukraine these laws are not acceptable to us." He proposed (as usual) that the delegates form a committee to work out their own resolution. The Communists reacted with great frustration. Liuksenburg insisted, "we must decidedly know whether you support Soviet power's policy on the food supply question or not. Once you recognize Soviet power and state that you will support it in everything, clearly you must accept and implement all the principles for the construction of Soviet power and in particular the food supply question." In the face of this near ultimatum, the majority of delegates seem to have acquiesced, though a few delegates still insisted on changes and noted other agents' abuses. The conference soon accepted the Communists' resolution with one amendment, allowing peasants to keep some food-processing shops (such as creameries) open until a goods exchange system had been fully implemented.[50]

At other conferences intensive debate on the food supply question led to some concessions, but when Communist leaders insisted, the delegates gave in. The peasant delegates at the Izium district conference refused to vote for the Communists' resolution and instead elected a forty-eight-member commission to draft their own resolution. This commission was unable after twelve hours to produce a resolution. A second commission was then elected of twenty-seven members, which managed to draft a resolution proposing that free trade be allowed, with intensive struggle against speculation. However, when the district revkom leaders (all Communists) pushed peasants to decide between their resolution and "the return of the counterrevolution," most delegates rejected their own resolution and voted for the revkom's, although they gained acceptance of a few important amendments: food supply agents were to calculate the requisition quota of a volost based on the amount of land sown for that harvest, not the volost's total arable land; and they were to take into account Red Army detachments' requisitions and to determine universal standards for requisitioning raw versus milled grains.[51] In a sense, the peasant delegates had forced the party leaders to regulate the requisitions with greater precision, and let the authorities know that demands they considered unjust would not be tolerated.[52]

At the Valky district conference the peasant presidium also drafted its own resolution and, after a long and noisy debate, the majority of delegates accepted it; its terms included allowing free trade in foodstuffs and excusing Valky district from fulfilling its requisition quota because of the confiscations committed by "Denikin bands" in the past year. In response the Communist leaders declared that "since the resolutions of the Communists-Bolsheviks was rejected and the accepted resolution is counterrevolutionary," they would take no further part in the conference. The Borot´bists soon joined them. The peasants then backed down. The final resolution recognized the great need for peasants to make all efforts possible "without requisitions" to satisfy the needs of the Red Army and "starving workers and their families," but insisted that, because of Denikin's forced requisitions, the peasants of Valky district "at the present moment do not have the forces to fulfill the quotas ordered by Soviet power." The resolution asked that the quotas be reexamined, taking into account local conditions, the area sown and the poor quality of peasants' seeds. Agreeing to do everything possible to complete the revised quotas and to sell their grain at the government-set prices, the peasants asked that Soviet power do all possible to stop speculation and to improve the delivery of manufactured goods to local soviet organs, which would sell the goods at government-set prices to peasants. Finally, the delegates resolved "to petition the All-Ukrainian revkom about sending to the starving workers and peasants of Petrograd and Moscow part of the grain, at the discretion of local soviet authorities, at the expense of the assigned quotas."[53] In essence, though peasant delegates made some concessions to party leaders, they accepted a quite locally centered, peasant resolution.

The food supply question was also hotly debated at the Kharkiv district conference. Peasant delegates insisted so strongly on consulting with their constituents that eventually the conference was forced to take a week's break from its work so that delegates could go home and discuss the food supply question with their voters. After this recess and party leaders' failed attempt to regain control of the conference's presidium, the peasant delegates proposed and then accepted their own resolution, which placed numerous conditions on the Communists' proposals. Eventually, however, district revkom member Sosnovskii managed to convince the peasants to accept the necessity of fulfilling the food supply quotas as an amendment to the resolution. But the debate did not end there. On 25 February, the peasant-chairman, Tomakh, managed to get one further amendment into the final resolution, which read: "those volosts which do not possess the forces to fulfill the assigned requisition quota will have the right to petition about the lessening of the quota or about its complete removal."[54]

The sources on these conferences reveal several aspects of peasants' attitudes toward the new regime at the moment of its third assumption of power in Ukraine. First, at these conferences peasants sought to take the new regime's propaganda at its word. The conferences were supposed to be "non-party," and peasant delegates repeatedly resisted the election of a presidium preselected from among the party leaders. Second, the delegates' resistance to these party leaders' rule over the conferences suggests their great and continuing distrust of non-peasants, and the intelligentsia in particular. Third, the peasants expressed near-universal approval of the new land law, because it gave them most of the land, did not force them to redistribute their own land, and forbade all coercion in the creation of collective farms. Fourth, the peasants strongly resisted the food requisition policy proposed at the conference, often obtained major concessions, and sometimes replaced it with their own resolution. And, finally, when party leaders demanded that peasants choose between their numerous disagreements with Soviet power, and support for the latter, they consistently chose Soviet power. Although peasants disagreed with a number of the new regime's policies and actions, they still preferred it to the most easily imaginable alternatives—the return of Denikin's Volunteer Army or the Germans.

Unfortunately, Communist Party leaders seem to have paid very little attention to these peasant delegates' many and varied criticisms, comments and protests of their policies and, at the same time, did not sufficiently appreciate peasants' willingness to compromise for the sake of Soviet power. As official summaries of the non-party peasant conferences suggest, these leaders wrote off these conferences as "kulak-infested," unwilling to believe that poor and middling peasants would consciously object to their policies or have different ideas of how Soviet power should be organized. For example, in late spring the head of the Kharkiv provincial soviet's information department sent the People's Commissariat of Internal Affairs a report on these conferences, claiming that they had been characterized by "the struggle of kulaks with the poor." He boldly stated that the clearest evidence that most of the conferences' delegates were "kulaks" was their "attitude toward the Communists during the election of the conference's presidium." In other words, class position did not determine one's political views; rather, one's political views determined one's class. The department head noted that the Communists' food supply resolutions in particular had provoked "bitter arguments and in the majority of cases, if they were not outright rejected, then they were accepted with great changes, mainly concerning the necessity to preserve free trade, supposedly temporarily." Claiming that the main reason for the problems at these conferences was that "the village was still not differentiated" between poor peasants and kulaks, he recommended intensive work in the village and the organization of Committees of Not-Well-Off Peasants (*komitety nezamozhnykh selian*, hereafter KNS), instead of a second attempt at the non-party peasant conferences.[55]

The Struggle for the Grain

On 26 February 1920 the recently proclaimed new government, the Council of People's Commissars of Ukraine,[56] issued a law on grain delivery quotas (*khlebnaia razverstka*) stipulating that all peasant households farming more than three desiatynas of land had to deliver a certain amount of grain to collection points. Peasants would then be paid at government-set prices (usually below market prices). Although the party's policy at this time called for the requisition of all grain over that needed for peasants' own consumption and for seed, the government, considering the ruined state of peasant farms and the agricultural infrastructure, decreed to requisition a little more than one quarter of the projected total 1920 grain harvest for Ukraine, or 160 of 600 million poods. In addition, 25 percent of this collected grain was to be preserved at volost food supply centers for "the most needy rural population." Though this law might have gained some poor peasants' support for requisitions against the "kulaks," it would also have alienated the majority of peasant households farming more than three desiatynas of land; it also seems to have been at odds with the party's resolution "On Soviet power in Ukraine." Kharkiv province's peasants were assigned to deliver only 9.76 million poods of grain.[57]

Peasants' most widespread reaction to the government's insistence on these grain requisition quotas and food supply agents' often unfair actions was an increasing reluctance to surrender and slowness in delivering grain. When a food supply agent arrived to a village, peasants would often call a village assembly to decide whether they should fulfill the demanded quota. This was the way they understood Soviet power: radically democratized local control.[58] From the authorities' perspective this was a delaying technique that had to be stopped at all costs. In late February the Bohodukhiv district revkom called a meeting of representatives from its volost revkoms to discuss peasants' sluggish efforts to fulfill requisition quotas and the hauling obligation. Emphasizing the importance of fulfilling the district's quota, the revkom leader Varnavskii stated, "the Red Army cannot wait for village assemblies to decide whether to give grain or not; it is starving and needs grain." He instructed the volost representatives to ask the peasants directly whether they supported Soviet power. If so, then they should not call village assemblies "to decide the fate of the starving army." Varnavskii continued, "Village assemblies will never give us anything, since at present the poor are still under the influence of kulakdom and we need to gather the grain from all kulaks immediately in order to deliver swift sustenance to the Red Army." The revkom resolved to take "the most decisive measures for the fulfillment of the food supply quotas," also asking that a suitable number of agitators be sent to explain to the peasants "the demands of Soviet power." Concerning the hauling obligation, the revkom instructed the volost representatives "to watch assiduously" that peasants fulfilled their obligation to haul all requisitioned grain to the railroad stations, where trains could conveniently pick them up. Peasants were to be pushed to decide their loyalties most clearly and to prove them by satisfying "the demands of Soviet power," as defined by the center. For this, the revkom argued, they need not consult with their co-villagers.[59]

A most revealing account of the effects of implementing these policies was provided by the chairman of the Valky district revkom in a fairly detailed report on the situation in his district in the early spring of 1920. Arriving in the district in mid-January, he had been informed that, politically, the entire local population was content with Soviet power. He noted, however, that many were satisfied only because of the Red Army's recent decisive victories and because Soviet power and its policies had not yet been put into practice. By default free trade was still the norm, and large-scale requisitioning had yet to begin. Only after party members initiated this work did the actual "shocking picture" emerge: the district's military commissariat had only two hundred guards and their "progressiveness" was "doubtful"; among the militia only two officers were considered reliable. With such meager forces it was almost impossible to combat the home-brewing and drunkenness rampant among local troops at the time. Soldiers from the Fourth Brigade, briefly stationed in Valky, were drinking to excess, leading them to hurl threats and abuse at members of the district revkom. When the revkom arrested one drunken soldier, the brigade's commander ordered his immediate release; the soldier turned out to be the commander's driver. The revkom chairman blamed the work of several "actual members of the party of Borot′bists," who were agitating among the soldiers and spreading rumors across the countryside about the arrival of "eighty *kommunisty-katsapy*" intending to oppress Ukraine.[60] More important to our discussion (though the chairman put this point in parentheses), the revkom had just received two orders from Kharkiv: one forbidding the hauling of grain and livestock out of the district, and the other completely banning free trade. Fearful of peasants' reactions, the district party committee resolved not to publish the latter decree.

The chairman described the volatile state of affairs in Valky district. "In the absence of sufficient support, the food supply requisitions, the hauling obligation, the ban on free trade, and the disarming of peasants are creating an extremely unstable situation in the district." He cited a passage from the resolution on food supply accepted at the recently held district non-party peasant conference, which many local soviets and peasants sympathetic to the party had supported: "Ask, request the grain from the peasants, but do not send armed detachments to take the grain, then all will be lost, [our] trust in Soviet power, and, mainly [you] will not receive any grain. The Ukrainian peasant will bury the grain in the earth, hide [it], and disappear, but under the pressure of force he will not surrender it." The chairman also asked Kharkiv to provide directives about "our policy" concerning the food supply question. "If this is a policy of understanding with the peasant, then the provincial food supply committee needs to be instructed.... To the present moment our approach to the peasant has been on the basis of understanding and reasonable accord." He wondered, however, whether the policy had changed. He had recently received a decree stating that the requisition "must be executed, those not executing it should be arrested; if there is resistance, call for armed force." The decree was labeled "urgent [*boevym*]."[61] The chairman asked for immediate instructions, "because I completely do not agree with this decree." Calling it "mistaken," he boldly stated, "the comrades signing this decree have lost their grasp of reality and have not studied either the actual situation in the localities or the mood of the very peasantry, as truly expressed in the resolutions of the non-party conference." Recalling the party's experience in Russia, he noted that such decrees would have the opposite of the intended effect, provoking uprisings, not providing even a minimum of bread, and leaving the land unsown out of fears of further requisitions. "If we are condemned to repeat the mistakes that were committed on the Don and in Russia, then it is crucial that authoritative minds of the party and the Central Committee publish a precise circular and secondly insure the district with military force, because even party members in our district are not armed."[62] Insisting that the solution to the emerging crisis lay in compromise and understanding between the peasants and the party, he asked that, if this solution were not to be pursued, then more weapons be sent, "at least for arming party members."[63]

Kharkiv provincial party leaders received similar reports from other districts. The head of Zmiïv district revkom's information department, Vorob′ev, reported that in Beretska volost the population still supported Soviet power, but was "greatly dissatisfied with the ban on free trade" and that grain requisitions were being imposed unfairly. The peasants declared: "First, take all the grain into account and then determine whether to take grain from us." He noted that peasants were burying their grain, but that this did not matter, because the requisitions were determined by area of land, not grain on hand.[64] In Oleksiïvka volost the mood was also "unconditionally for Soviet power," though desertion was on the rise. Complaining about rampant drunkenness especially among the local militia, Vorob′ev stressed that the population's greatest complaint was the ban on free trade and the seemingly unplanned, unequal, and erratic requisitions. For example, in late February peasants arriving to sell their grain at market in Oleksiïvka instead were forced to surrender it to food supply agents, provoking "complete misunderstanding among the population." Peasants began to gather in groups, grumbling about the requisitions and the ban on free trade. Party workers claimed that some "speculators" arrived, calling themselves "Red Guards," and began to agitate among the grumbling peasants. Peasants complained that their grain had been requisitioned at government-set prices, while at the same market boots were being sold at inflated prices, and a box of matches cost 130 rubles. Far from calling for an end to food requisitions, these peasants declared that such manufactured necessities should be requisitioned as well and sold to them at set prices. Fortunately for the local authorities, two members of the district's revkom, Vorob′ev and Krylov, were in town at the time and helped the local Communists to persuade the menacing crowd to disperse. Vorob′ev recommended that efforts be made to sell goods to peasants at set prices and that the authorities avoid announcing the grain ration system to peasants, which would "unconditionally dissatisfy them" and set them against Soviet power. The system heavily favored city workers and Red Army soldiers.[65]

The perceived unequal and unfair impositions and the arbitrary actions and bad behavior of food supply agents contributed much to peasants' decreasing willingness to compromise with the new regime. The authorities' typical reaction to peasants' refusal to give up their grain was to demand greater vigilance from local authorities and the use of armed force. On 13 April a joint meeting of the Kharkiv district revkom and party committee passed a decree aimed at improving the increasingly sluggish grain deliveries. Noting the great lack of armed force at the disposal of the district military command and food supply commission, the meeting resolved to make use of all available armed forces, including those appointed for rounding up deserters; to request military forces from the provincial food supply committee; and to order all party workers in the district, regardless of assignment, "to carry out the widest agitation concerning the grain requisition quotas and to coordinate their activities with food supply agents arriving to their areas."[66]

The requisitions and the government's efforts to enforce them at first led only to passive resistance, widespread unwillingness to fulfill quotas, or slowness in delivering the grain. However, the repeated requisitions, imposed hauling obligations, and party workers' less than democratic attempts to get themselves elected to local soviets greatly antagonized peasants. The final straw for many peasants was the government's April 1920 announcement of a new mobilization of all men born between 1896 and 1900 in Kharkiv province. The overwhelming majority of peasants responded very negatively to this conscription, which provoked a sharp increase in desertions among those already serving and especially those who were newly mobilized.[67] As one informational report [*informatsionnaia svodka*] noted, a large part of the peasantry reacted to the announced mobilization "very unsympathetically." Although by 7 May more than 25,000 peasants had reported to recruitment points across the province, many of these new recruits soon deserted; they reported for mobilization only to receive the weapons and gear, and then deserted to the insurgents. The report concluded that the main result of the attempted mobilization was that in several districts "significantly large-scale uprisings have appeared."[68] This was the beginning of Kharkiv province's version of the Greens movement.

The Peasants' Insurgency

The largest and best organized uprising occurred in Valky district. An initial, smaller uprising had broken out already in mid-April in Khomlia and Martova volosts, provoked by party workers' "undemocratic methods" of conducting the volosts' elections to the soviets. The insurgents were able to acquire numerous weapons because they were located near Pechenihy, a center of partisan activities during the VA's rule. Their slogan was: "Long live Soviet power, down with the Communists [*Nekhai zhyve Radians´ka vlada, het´ komunisitiv*]!"[69] This uprising was soon suppressed, but the mobilization decree, making its way across Valky district on 23 April, provoked a much larger revolt, led and manned by former Red Army soldiers and new recruits. By 25 April pro-Soviet forces were searching for deserters instead of training new recruits; lacking the necessary forces, they had little success. A large group of deserters, hiding out in the forests of Perekip volost, was able to detain—voluntarily or not—numerous other recruits on their way to the mobilization center in Valky. By 27 April the number of deserters in such "bands" had reached, by the conservative estimate of the party's information department, at least 1,500 men, and were armed with pitchforks, axes, some rifles, and two machine guns. The leader of the uprising appears to have been the former commander of a Red Army cavalry regiment, Colonel Sorokin-Belets´kyi. The insurgents, referred to by party and state information suppliers as "bandits," soon occupied the Kov'iahy railroad station and managed to commandeer a train from Poltava, confiscating twelve wagons of fuel and two wagons of tobacco. On 27 April a detachment of one hundred insurgents with machine guns attacked a convoy train carrying about five hundred new recruits to Valky. The convoy leaders were either killed or taken prisoner (a few escaped); the majority of recruits joined the insurgents; the rest ran away.

News of the insurgents' bold actions in Valky district reached Kharkiv very quickly, and greatly alarmed party and government leaders; after all, Valky was only about forty kilometers from the city where the new republic's government then resided. The Valky district military commandant, A. N. Bondarenko, immediately reported to Kharkiv that the number of deserters had reached 1,500 and that they had taken control of the towns of Kov'iahy, Perekip, and Vysokopillia, along with the surrounding villages and forests.[70] On 28 April the Kharkiv provincial military command dispatched to Valky the 223rd battalion of the Troops for Internal Defense of the Republic (VOKhR), led by commander Podzolov. Encountering no insurgents when they pulled into Kov'iahy station, the battalion continued on toward Valky, but soon was caught in an ambush of insurgent troops who managed to cut off the battalion's retreat. Only after a long battle and the arrival of a 120-man detachment from Valky did the battalion break through and head for cover in Valky. Podzolov reported to his commander that "the insurgents operate with good organization, the capable leadership of specialists is noticeable"; they had clearly established communication among the various "bands." "The mood of the population is obviously hostile to Soviet power." Though he pointed out that there were among the insurgents "old men, obviously kulaks," he also admitted, "deserters compose the main mass of the insurgents."[71] As Kotliar has found for southern Ukraine, it was the less well-off villagers incensed by the *prodrazverstka*, restrictions on their economic behavior, and the mobilization that tended to join the insurgency.[72] Podzolov asked that reinforcements, more machine guns, cavalry, and ammunition be sent immediately. The Kharkiv provincial military commandant promptly petitioned to dispatch these forces as soon as possible to ensure there were "sufficient forces for a decisive and swift suppression of the uprising." The troops left for Valky the following day.[73]

The one historian who has studied this uprising in depth, Ievhen Sivachenko, stresses that the uprising was well organized and carried a Ukrainian nationalist character. Supposedly, the insurgent peasants even elected their own "Ukrainian People's Government," which called on peasants to fight for "the complete independence of Ukraine from Moscow," the removal of "all Muscovite troops from Ukraine," and "full self-recognition and self-administration of the Ukrainian people with its culture and traditions."[74] While there may be some truth to his interpretation, especially concerning the organized nature of the uprising, Sivachenko bases his entire description of the "Ukrainian People's Government" on one document cited in a memoir written thirteen years after the uprising by the Valky district military commandant, Bondarenko. Not only is this account written in a polemical tone, stressing the meddling of Ukrainian Borot′bists, but it contains numerous factual errors and is in many ways a celebration of the revolution and reminiscent of Soviet historians' most ideologized works.[75] Moreover, though other more contemporary sources stress how well the peasants were organized, no other document mentions that the uprising possessed a nationalist component.

Regardless of its exact character, the uprising certainly spread rapidly, embracing the entire southern half of Valky district and including at least 1,500 armed men. As Sivachenko rightly points out, this is probably an underestimate, because these very volosts were some of the most heavily populated in the province; it is likely that insurgents were well supported by non-fighters.[76] According to Soviet agents, "the insurgents live in the villages, but at the necessary moment run into ravines and forests." During the attack on 28 April agents noticed that peasants were shooting out of their homes at Soviet troops. The insurgents had acquired a field kitchen and were "receiving arms and reinforcements from the town of Murafa, Bohodukhiv district."[77] Reporting to Kharkiv from Valky, Commander Podzolov presented a more alarming picture, noting, "The bandits are carrying out serious agitation and provocations. They whisper from lips to ears that almost all of Ukraine is rising up. The population sympathizes with the uprising and old men, women, and children actively participate in it." Besides the regions already occupied, the insurgents had now seized the railroad line from Ohultsi to Kolomak (along with at least one locomotive), located about forty versts from their base. They were clearly moving into other volosts, threatening Kolomak, and gathering more weaponry along the way. Podzolov claimed that almost all the insurgents were now armed with Russian-made rifles and sabers.[78]

Podzolov eventually conceded that he could not suppress the uprising with the forces at his disposal and complained to Kharkiv that he lacked above all the artillery necessary to bombard the villages where the insurgents were hiding. He argued that artillery fire would have a devastating influence on morale, because peaceful villagers, greatly fearing their villages' destruction, would refuse to help the "bandits." He concluded, "Decisive measures are needed, because the uprising is embracing an ever greater area. The bandits' insolence is great."[79]

In the early morning of 1 May 1920 the insurgents launched a bold attack on the district center of Valky itself. One section of the insurgent army attacked from the south, under Bilets´kyi's command, and the rest from the north, their combined forces amounting to at least 2,000 armed men. The Soviet troops stationed in Valky along with Podzolov's forces amounted to about 850 men, though they were better armed and equipped. In the course of this protracted battle, involving a great deal of hand-to-hand street fighting, the insurgents managed to take a large section of the city. Eventually, however, they were beaten back and forced to retreat to the north to Kov'iahy.[80]

This attempted takeover of one of the province's largest district centers provoked yet greater alarm in Kharkiv. The authorities declared the district to be in a state of siege and dispatched yet more forces to Valky: another armored train with its company; a detachment of student recruits (100 plus two machine guns); a detachment from the Special Department of the Southwestern Front; and a significant cavalry unit (at least 130 men). Poltava's military command also sent a detachment, and on 2 May the commander in chief of the rear of the southwestern front, R. P. Eideman, arrived in another armored train to take command of suppressing the revolt. The insurgents, now seeing themselves outnumbered and outgunned, began to disperse to neighboring provinces.[81]

Even with superior numbers and armament it took Soviet troops a considerable amount of time to put down the uprising, and the actions of punitive detachments often sparked new, smaller scale revolts. The district's entire population was subjected to a harsh regime of arrests, administrative decrees, and demonstrative cruelty. For example, a revolutionary tribunal was held on 12 May condemning twenty-nine people to be shot for active participation in the uprising; thirty-five were condemned to forced labor with deprivation of their freedom; twenty-two were exiled to penal detachments; and three were imprisoned in a concentration camp.[82] It is likely that such officially reported measures underestimated the final death count.

At about the same time in the region of Okhtyrka and Sumy districts a large band of 350–400 men appeared, also provoked by the mobilization. These insurgents were "well armed and organized," possessing "a large reserve of ammunition cartridges." Ranging quite a distance from home, they carried out raids on the villages of Viazovaia and Kolotulovka in neighboring Kursk province (inside the RSFSR), killing nine militiamen and two Red Army soldiers. Their slogan was: "Smash the Communists and the deserter-hunting detachments!" In an attempt to liquidate the uprising, a detachment of fifty infantry soldiers, along with fifteen cavalrymen and two machine guns, were dispatched from Sumy. On 21 April, they managed to defeat the insurgents and suppress the uprising after a long battle. At least forty insurgents were killed, unknown numbers injured, and forty-five taken prisoner. The rest managed to split up and escape. In early May a band of about 1,000 deserters that had been mobilized in Chuhuïv district also staged an uprising; they were well armed, possessing machine guns, and they were led by an obviously experienced military commander. Kharkiv authorities sent out a cavalry reconnaissance detachment, but the insurgents soon disarmed it. Then, all Communists in Chuhuïv were mobilized and sent out "to take the most decisive measures toward the swift suppression of the uprising." They were eventually successful. The same report noted numerous cases of railroad lines being cut, fires being set, explosions erupting, bandits attacking, and "anti-Soviet agitation."[83]

Across Left-Bank Ukraine, peasant insurgent uprisings against the new Worker-Peasant Government took on a massive scale in 1920. One historian has recently calculated that no fewer than 214 insurgent detachments with an average of 350 men per detachment, amounting to about 75,000 insurgents in all, appeared in the region. They were also better armed than in the past, possessing in total eleven artillery guns and 172 machine guns. In 1920, the peasants of Kharkiv province rose up less frequently than those of Chernihiv or Poltava provinces. In fact, of the 214 detachments in 1920, 159 were based in the latter province (Chernihiv had 58; Kharkiv, 39). In 1921, however, the number of detachments in Kharkiv province rose sharply to 74 (more than 40 percent of all the detachments on the Left Bank).[84] As in 1919 most of these rural insurgents lacked (or did not express) a clear political program. Almost 70 percent of these detachments did not associate themselves with any political movement, not even the anarchist Nestor Makhno, though his ideas were very close to their own. A widely held and consistent demand among insurgents remained an equitable redistribution of the land, while the slogans "Down with the Commune!" and "For Soviet Power, but without Communists and Communes" of 1919 were replaced with "Down with the *prodrazverstka*!"[85]

The Party's Reactions

The party leaders' predominant reaction to these peasants' actions expressing clear hostility toward them and their policies was state- and party-sanctioned violence; those who opposed the communists' rule were often labeled "counterrevolutionary" and violently suppressed. Basically, all peasants who resisted the regime openly, from desertion to organized uprisings, were labeled "bandits," and their activities "banditry [*banditizm*]." As social historians of other times and countries have pointed out, terms such as "bandits" and "banditry" were often employed to refer to those who did not fit into the generally accepted social order.[86] In its April 1920 "Brief Instruction for Fighting Banditry and Kulak Uprisings," the Radnarkom gave Soviet forces the right to take hostages (usually those deemed "kulaks") in villages sympathetic to local bands and even to punish villages collectively for such behavior. The instruction stipulated that if the population expressed "open hostility" to "Soviet power" and refused to surrender insurgents, punishment could be "very severe, up to the elimination of the village."[87] The "Instruction" in hand, numerous armed forces were dispatched to suppress the insurgents. One historian has determined that about 80 percent of the 164 military questions discussed by the higher party organs in Ukraine in 1921 concerned the struggle with the peasant insurgency. Another has calculated that by the end of 1921 the government was employing about 1.2 million men to fight the insurgency.[88] To cite one example, in early May 1920 Radnarkom chair Khristian Rakovskii at the Kharkiv Provincial Congress of Soviets proudly recounted the recent brutal suppression of the "disturbance" in Valky district "as an example of the successful struggle of Soviet power with counterrevolutionary risings."[89]

Violence was not, however, the authorities' only response. Party leaders also renewed their efforts to split the village community in two, clearly reflecting their Marxist (and Manichean) worldview. On 9 May 1920 the All-Ukrainian Central Executive Committee and the Radnarkom issued a law on the KNS. The law basically allowed anyone who stood to gain through the implementation of Soviet policies to join the KNS, including peasants who were deemed land-poor or landless and therefore were to receive land according to the land law's redistribution rules; those who had been freed from the grain requisition quotas (those holding less than three desiatynas); those who out of poverty were supposed to receive grain or foodstuffs from the volost food supply committee; and all those "forced to sell their labor force." Former landlords, local tsarist officials, "kulaks," "speculators," shop owners, factory owners, "counterrevolutionaries, and all those exploiting human labor" were excluded. KNS members were given three main tasks: (1) the swift implementation of the land law, distributing land and inventory to landless and land-poor peasants (often KNS members); (2) the fulfillment of grain requisition quotas, leaving a portion to the village poor (often KNS members);[90] and (3) assisting Soviet power in asserting its authority in the village, especially in the struggle with "banditry," illiteracy, and "kulak dominance."[91] The committees were supposed to sow class discord between the poor to middling peasants and the "kulaks"—that is, in communist rhetoric, to "differentiate the village."[92] It is, however, more probable that they pitted one section of a village—those left out of the traditional village leadership roles and now empowered—to fight against those who had formerly been more powerful, which often included the more prosperous members of the village.

In a sense, the new regime was attempting to make classes where they did not exist; and these classes were to be essentially defined by allegiance or nonallegiance to the regime. On 28 May, the People's Commissar of Land Affairs, Dmytro Manuïl´s´kyi, called on Communists to do all possible "to activate the KNSs," instructing agitators to stress that the committees should seize "kulak" land and livestock, that the grain obligation would be borne by "kulaks," and that KNS members first of all would be supplied with manufactured goods. "In one word, we must make of the rural poor the same kind of 'privileged estate [*privillegirovannoe soslovie*]' in a certain sense as is the working class in the city in the eyes of the worker-peasant state. And only in this case will we create a solid base for Soviet power in the countryside. Only then will our slogan, already thrown out by the All-Ukrainian Revkom, about the 'muzhik-ization [*omuzhichenie*]' of Soviet power not remain only an empty phrase, but take form in flesh and blood."[93]

Initially, the KNSs seem to have had some success in Kharkiv province. In mid-June the Chuhuïv district executive committee reported that KNSs had been set up across the district, though grain requisitioning continued to go poorly.[94] An 8 July report from the People's Commissariat of Internal Affairs noted that at least 1,000 committees had been formed in the last month across Ukraine, many in Kharkiv province. Indeed, the report's author seemed surprised that "in some districts (Chuhuïv and Izium) the committees are welcomed by the population."[95] On 20 July Kup'iansk district reported that 8,750 peasants had signed up as KNS members.[96] By the time of the calling of the All-Ukrainian Congress of KNS on 10 November the Kharkiv provincial KNS organization reported having created 1,190 committees with 86,930 registered members.[97] One might question whether this was a significant number in a province of at least two million peasants.[98] In addition, it was soon reported that the KNSs were provoking hostility among some peasants. A late 1920 report revealed that 152 heads of village KNSs had been killed in 1920.[99] Moreover, the regime itself soon questioned the quality of these organizations' membership.

In late November 1920 the provincial KP(b)U committee issued a telegram to all district party committees and executive committees ordering the reregistration of all KNSs in Kharkiv province by 5 December. Lamenting the presence in the KNSs of "kulak, semi-kulak and anti-Soviet elements, delaying the growth of consciousness and organizational skills," the committee laid out the method of reregistration in great detail.

Party workers were warned not to strive to increase KNS membership at the expense of quality and to take special care that no "kulak, semi-kulak or anti-soviet elements" were reregistered. If a particular KNS showed itself to be very capable, it was not to be reregistered. The party committee repeatedly stressed the importance of implementing this decree, calling the reregistration an "immediate, military, urgent task of the party"; workers were "to concentrate all attention and energy on it."[100] In the next few years, however, the KNSs would be subjected to numerous reregistrations.[101] Indeed, the KNS never managed to take a dominant or leading position in the village, despite the party's great efforts, and they were eventually liquidated.

While attempting to sow discord within the village, the government also continued to take serious violent measures to combat overt resistance to the regime. The already mentioned April 1920 "Brief Instruction for Fighting Banditry and Kulak Uprisings" created provincial Permanent Councils for the Struggle with Banditry, and the Kharkiv branch held its first meeting on 7 June 1920. Reporting on the situation in Kharkiv province, the commission's chair, Fedotov, recalled the mistakes made in the struggle to date, especially in Izium district, and stressed that it was essential to conduct this battle in a more organized fashion. At this point, the commission's main problem was a lack of accurate information and inadequate connections with the localities; thus, it resolved to improve these as its first priority.[102] These problems plagued the commission's early activities; at the 26 June meeting, Fedotov was still complaining about the poor flow of information to the commission, making its work impossible. The commission blamed the provincial executive committee, claiming that the committee was not forwarding the information it received from the localities.

At the same meeting the commission discussed how to suppress a recent outbreak of "banditry" in Rublivska volost (Bohodukhiv district), thereby revealing its tasks and methods. Apparently, the peasants of Rublivska volost had refused to report for mobilization, only very weakly fulfilled their grain quota, refused to surrender their weapons, and concealed deserters and "bandits." They had also murdered the volost's military commandant and the executive committee's chairman, attacked and opened fire on the premises occupied by the district food supply committee, as well as those occupied by the commission sent out to investigate the murders. In an effort to suppress these "clearly anti-Soviet actions," the commission ordered a series of repressive measures: it imposed a *kontributsiia* (the same word used by German troops in 1918) of 20,000 poods of grain and five million rubles on the volost's inhabitants; and 15 persons were to be seized, along with all their property, as hostages until the contribution was paid. The peasants were ordered to give up within twenty-four hours all weapons, deserters, "bandits," and the murderers of these Soviet officials. After this period, the military and civil authorities were to carry out mass searches to uncover any remaining weapons or deserters. The commission stressed that during the implementation of these measures, the authorities were "to adhere strictly to the foundations of our policy"—that is, to implement "the differentiation of the village, widely drawing into the very procedure of punishments the KNS, or, where there were no KNSs, the poor in general." The commission also noted the importance of developing political work "to the maximum in the volost, explaining the essence and significance of the imposed punishments."[103]

On 1 July the permanent commission heard a report on the implementation of these measures in Rublivska volost. Noting that the operation to liquidate the "band" operating in the volost was not "crowned with success," the commission blamed Poltava province's military commandant, whose "sluggishness of action" had allowed the main forces of the "bandits" to escape encirclement and hide themselves in that province's forests. The commission then considered a proposal from the Bohodukhiv district military command "about the removal of the entire male population between the ages of 18 and 45 from Rublivska volost." The commission resolved not to act on this proposal until the already imposed penalties had been fully implemented, but it is clear that the commission was empowered and prepared to take all measures necessary to quell such "anti-Soviet uprisings."[104]

The commission also took measures against one the major centers of anti-Soviet resistance. The people of Murafa (Bohodukhiv district) were accused of a whole series of anti-Soviet actions: non-appearance for mobilization, harboring deserters and bandits, "the persistent non-fulfillment of the food supply quota, and the non-fulfillment of orders and decrees of Soviet power." Bearing in mind these accusations, the provincial commission sanctioned all the repressive measures proposed by the district commission: "To arrest ten prominent kulaks and bandit leaders," confiscating all their property; to confiscate all horses that peasants had concealed from being registered; to announce and post an ultimatum demanding the appearance of all deserters, threatening for non-appearance the confiscation of better-off peasants' property. The commission stressed that all local commissions for the struggle with banditry should employ the principle of "collective responsibility" and all the measures introduced in Rublivska volost.[105] This basically summed up the permanent commission's methods and approach to peasants' resistance and set the tone for the future relations of many peasants with the increasingly powerful state. At the same time, the resolution revealed the commission's major weakness, that of an insufficient number of forces: it resolved to defer operations against Murafa until after it had completely suppressed the Rublivska uprising.[106]

If such repressive measures had any wider pacifying effects, they were short-lived. At its 20 August 1920 meeting the provincial permanent commission admitted that "banditry" was greatly increasing across the province. While blaming much of this on the "insufficiency of armed forces," the commission recognized that the more immediate cause was the recently proclaimed new grain quotas, extending the requisition burden to include those households farming less than three desiatynas. In response, whole volosts were taking up arms against the regime. The commission's reaction was characteristically simple, resolving "insistently to petition the Rear Command of the Southwestern Front about the immediate assignment to the Kharkiv provincial rear command of sufficient real forces for the liquidation of existing bands and for the successful fulfillment of the immediate food supply tasks of the center."[107] The close connection between "banditry" and the requisitions was rarely made clearer.

At its 9 September meeting the commission discussed which measures to take to prevent "possible uprisings" flaring up in response to the impending, intensified requisition campaign. The commission resolved to ask the provincial party committee to form immediately "detachments of special assignment" composed of Communists and "loyal Soviet workers, who must be completely reliable" to use as "a militant force in the struggle with the larger expressions of banditry." Second, the commission petitioned for reinforcements for the garrison. Third, it ordered Kup'iansk, Zmiïv, Izium, Lebedyn and Okhtyrka district military commandants to free all their food supply agents, workers and detachments from other work in order to focus all energies on "delivery operations." Finally, the commission resolved to arm all food supply agents and detachments, declaring this "urgently necessary."[108]

All these weapons and men seem not to have solved the increasingly widespread "banditry" or the still worsening food supply problem. In early October the provincial commission for struggle with banditry complained that Kharkiv had recalled cavalry troops from its command to serve directly under various punitive detachments. Calling the provincial center "greedy," the commission stressed that this recall came at a time "when in several districts...the most furious struggle with smaller bandit gangs is being carried out." The removal of these cavalrymen was not only premature, "but extraordinarily dangerous, depriving the districts of the most reliable force, a real force in the struggle with banditry, and granting the latter the possibility almost with impunity to stroll about and do evil things."[109]

In late November a "kulak band" attacked a food supply detachment working in Nizhnia Orel (now Lyhivka) volost, Zmiïv district. Half of the detachment's members were hacked to death, the other half were left naked. The district executive committee demanded that at least a battalion be sent "for carrying out food supply work and restoring order." In Lebedyn district a local peasant band led by Shtepenko was constantly harassing food supply detachments. Soviet authorities organized a large detachment of 400 men from the Lebedyn and Okhtyrka garrisons, along with 150 cavalrymen and 35 other horsemen from the district's militia. In a large battle this detachment managed to kill Shtepenko, his assistant Rubak, and about 30 other "bandits," but the majority of the "bandits" escaped into the nearby thickly wooded forest.[110] The ease with which insurgents could launch sudden raids, seize weapons, then escape and find refuge in forests and often in villages prolonged the struggle considerably. Insurgents did not need to win individual battles in wide open spaces in order to survive or avoid capture; they could always retreat, hide, and prepare for another day, being well supplied with food, horses, and hiding places. They often enjoyed local villagers' support.

Like the "struggle with banditry," the closely connected "struggle for the grain" experienced more failures than successes in 1920. Rich evidence of how poorly the food requisitions were being fulfilled can be found in the proceedings of the Bohodukhiv district conference of food supply detachments that took place in early December 1920. These detachments were composed almost entirely of workers from Moscow and Kharkiv; they were committed Communists who saw their mission somewhat like fighting a holy war. Opening the conference, chairman Shatalov set the tone by requesting that the conference take a moment to remember all those food supply agents and workers "killed on the food supply front in Bohodukhiv and other districts." All in attendance stood to honor their fallen comrades and then sang the funeral march.[111] One party leader, Ashten, explained to the food supply workers how to approach the peasants, noting the differences between Ukrainian and Russian villages and peasants. Workers should not offend the peasants or their "national feeling," recommending that agents strive to speak with them in Ukrainian. If agents did not know the language, then at least, he pleaded, "do not ridicule it." He asked that agents relate courteously toward peasants and give them no pretext to support "counterrevolutionary elements" in the countryside.[112]

One of the conference leaders, comrade Bondarenko, then discussed ways to improve quota fulfillment. He claimed that agents were already carrying out "more peaceful and systematic work in the localities," working "honestly and conscientiously" as "the defenders of the poor peasantry and enemies of the kulaks." He called all food supply workers to "united and conscientious work, since food supply is the most important work and the entire success of the revolution depends on it."[113] However, when the agents working in the villages finally were granted the opportunity to report on their experiences, a quite different picture emerged. Comrade Veselov reported that his food supply detachment (the seventh) had initially had considerable success, mainly because it had been assigned to work in a state-owned sugar refinery, where the detachment's numerous metalworkers were of great use. But when the detachment was transferred to Kolontaïv region (southwest of Bohodukhiv) its fortunes greatly changed, because the region was replete with "bandits." The detachment was compelled to be constantly on guard against attacks. Because there were no regular troops stationed in the area, it became in effect the region's police force, deprived of any time or opportunity to rest, let alone enforce or help collect grain requisitions.

Comrade Rodiman then reported on his work in the tenth detachment in the area of the Rublivska uprising. Working at a "feverish" pace, the detachment had strived "to seize as much grain as possible from the peasants," who were "completely uninterested" in the detachment's work. He complained, "the malicious-minded peasants often helped the bandits."[114]

Some agents reported positive results, stressing that it was specifically in those volosts where the detachments worked most energetically that the quotas were fulfilled. Other agents criticized the local food supply commissars for obstructing their work. Comrade Filatov claimed that his region's food supply commissar Progonnyi "was too humane with the peasants," repeatedly granting them more time to fulfill the quotas. Filatov's detachment would arrest a local "kulak" for not fulfilling his quota, but Progonnyi would soon have him released. Filatov claimed that "if the detachment were given freedom of action, it would long ago have completed the quota in Polkova Mykytivka region." As a summary of some agents' reports admitted, "clashes with peasants had occurred." In the village of Iamne a detachment's work had almost provoked an uprising. In Velyka Pysarivka peasants had attempted to arrest and disarm one detachment, "but the detachment always remained on top of the situation and suppressed all these outbursts at their roots."[115]

Reading these agents' reports, one gathers that food supply agents rarely tried to find accommodation with peasants, poor, rich or middling, but rather viewed their work as a battle against the peasants for the grain. The conference's resolution unapologetically asserted, "Soviet power's food supply policy is correct. Neither the raising of set prices nor free markets will feed the starving workers. The peasantry must surrender their surpluses to the starving urban proletarians, since they [the workers?] obtained 'LAND and FREEDOM' for them [the peasants]." The resolution concluded that until peace and order had been fully established in the country, the workers' food supply detachments had to play "the leading role in completing quotas."[116] No doubt this situation led to greater antagonisms and alienation between workers and peasants.

In addition to open opposition to the regime or resistance to fulfilling quotas, many peasants chose a less confrontational path: complaining to the authorities about the behavior of food supply agents. In early December the head of the Kharkiv district Worker-Peasant Inspection, comrade Tsykhmistro, reported to the district executive committee on its work in the countryside. He noted that "in the localities there is observable friction with the organs of Soviet power, and especially the food supply organs," and reported receiving 175 complaints from peasants (just in Kharkiv district since 8 July 1920), most of them concerning the abuses of food supply detachments and other armed forces.[117]

Thus peasants resisted the "demands of Soviet power" in various ways, from complaints to open armed violence. Their most successful efforts were aimed at resisting the government's attempts to wrest grain and other foodstuffs from them. Although there is plenty of evidence scattered throughout the archives suggesting that the requisition quotas of 1920 were not being fulfilled, the strongest evidence of the government's failing food supply policy was presented at the Fifth Congress of Soviets of Ukraine in mid-February 1921. The People's Commissar of Food Supply, Myron K. Vladymyrov, reported that for all of Ukraine only 9,721,000 poods of grain and other foodstuffs were collected in 1920. The target quota for Ukraine's spring 1920 harvest, initially set at 160 million poods, had by December been reduced to 35 million. All the food supply detachments' work—propaganda, enlistment of local poor peasants, hostage-taking and violence—had managed to extract only 28 percent of this severely downgraded target. It is not likely that this great shortfall was due to a decreased harvest. According to a recent study of peasant economy in the early Soviet period, Ukraine's total gross yield of grain for 1920 was 513.5 million poods, almost all of which came from peasant farms. This was as much as a 55 percent drop in gross yield since 1913, but if peasants had been willing to give even 25 percent of this to food supply detachments, the gross collected grain would have been 128 million, or about 13 times the amount actually collected.[118] Vladymyrov noted that in the first nine months of 1920 about one thousand food supply agents had been killed by peasants, not including the Red Army soldiers killed in clashes with "partisans."[119]

The Party's Retreat

Although one should be careful not to exaggerate their importance, it seems clear that peasant uprisings across Ukraine and Russia, especially the "Antonovshchina" then sweeping across Tambov province, and the non-fulfillment of the requisition quotas contributed greatly to Lenin's and then the Politbiuro's decision to end "war communism" and introduce those policies that came to be called the New Economic Policy.[120] At the Tenth Congress of the RKP in mid-March 1921, the move to NEP was officially initiated. Lenin made clear the root cause of this important policy change. Opening up the discussion on the key change to agricultural policy, replacing requisitions with a "tax-in-kind" on peasants' harvests, he stated that there was no need to dwell on the reasons for replacing the requisition quotas with the tax. "You all, of course, know perfectly well which sum of events—particularly owing to the extreme aggravation of poverty, provoked by the war, ruin, demobilization and crop failure—which sum of circumstances have made the peasantry's situation especially difficult, critical, and have unavoidably strengthened its alienation from the proletariat to the bourgeoisie."[121]

After Lenin's lengthy speech and a modicum of debate, the congress resolved to replace the requisition quotas (*razverstka*) with the tax-in-kind (*prodnalog*), giving as reasons the need to ensure the "economy's correct and peaceful operation," to strengthen the peasant economy, improve its productivity, and finally, to establish exactly the peasants' obligations to the state. The tax-in-kind was intended to be less burdensome than the requisitions, amounting to only what was needed "to cover the minimal necessary demands of the army, city workers and the non-agricultural population." The tax was to be decreased gradually as the restoration of transport and industry allowed Soviet power to receive foodstuffs by "normal means—that is, in exchange for factory and handcrafted products." In calculating the tax rate, the state was to consider a farm's harvest yield, as well as how many people and livestock it had to feed; the tax was also to have a "progressive character," with poorer and middling peasants paying a lower percentage.[122] At the same time, clearly appealing to peasants' economic self-interest, the resolution stipulated that "diligent peasant farm heads," who increased their sown area and productivity, would receive "privileges," either a decreased tax rate or "partial liberation from the tax." After paying the tax-in-kind, peasants were granted "free command" of the rest of their foodstuffs, raw materials, and forage, which could be used for improving their farms, increasing consumption, or to exchange for manufactured products, "within the borders of local economic circulation."[123]

Considering the violent extremes to which KP(b)U leaders in particular had resorted in their efforts to extract grain from the countryside, it is not surprising that they expressed little enthusiasm for this policy change, widely perceived among party members as a step back. In fact, at the Tenth RKP Congress, as delegates were about to vote for Lenin's resolution on the tax-in-kind, Dmytro Manuïl's'kyi, a leading KP(b)U member and People's Commissar of Land Affairs, was given the podium to ask for some latitude for Ukraine's "peculiarities." Claiming that the "literal application" of Lenin's resolution in Ukraine would deal a "severe blow" to the KNSs, Manuïl's'kyi declared that, in agreement with the

RKP's leadership, the KP(b)U would, while voting for the resolution, "reserve for itself the right to introduce this or that change, evoked by local conditions."[124] The Tenth Congress's debate and resolution on the tax-in-kind were published in Kharkiv in the KP(b)U's leading organ, *Kommunist*, just two days after the decision in Moscow,[125] but the party's leaders remained ambivalent. They claimed that the "kulaks" were too strong in the Ukrainian village and that local organs of soviet power, especially the KNS and village soviets, were too weak to compel peasants to pay the tax-in-kind. At an emergency meeting on 27 March the All-Ukrainian Executive Committee accepted the resolution on the tax-in-kind, but still demanded that the fall 1920 *razverstka* be completed, although with a decrease of the overall target to 50 million poods. The committee also ruled that peasants were only to be informed of their new "right" to dispose of the rest of their harvest as they wished *after* they had fulfilled their quotas; the committee ordered the Food Supply and Internal Affairs commissariats to work out measures "for the regulation of markets, bazaars, and fairs, and for the struggle with middlemen and speculators."[126]

At about the same time, KP(b)U leaders reinvigorated their efforts to foment "class struggle" in the village. On 13 April the Executive Committee proclaimed the KNSs to be "organizations of state significance," granting them sweeping rights: free use of land, forest, rivers, agricultural implements and livestock; the right to receive grain and sowing equipment from a special state fund; priority in receiving agronomic supplies and advice, manufactured goods (steel, salt, gas, and so on), medical and veterinary help, education (including priority in entering universities) and government employment. They were also granted the power to seize the land and property of "kulaks," landlords, "bandits," families of deserters, and other "enemies of Soviet power." The KNSs were instructed to resettle these "enemies," redistribute their land, and even organize them into forced labor detachments; they were entrusted to arrest "the especially wicked" ones and send them to concentration camps.[127]

Ukrainian party leaders' attitude toward the Tenth Party Congress' resolutions was most clearly expressed at the First All-Ukrainian Party Conference in early May 1921, which was specifically called to figure out how to implement those resolutions. The tension inside the KP(b)U between the impetus to follow Moscow's "retreat" and the party's desire to win the war against the "kulaks" can be illustrated most clearly in its resolution “On the Tax-in-kind and KNS.” The resolution admitted that the proletariat’s dictatorship was in “crisis,” that “millions of petty proprietors”—that is, peasants—were stubbornly resisting “the Communist transformation of old social relations,” and that this threatened “to rip the peasantry from under the proletariat’s influence, [and] to prepare fertile ground for the strengthening and development of the peasant counterrevolution.” Hence, the party felt it was faced with a choice: “either, not waiting for help from the West European proletariat…, to enter into open civil war with the mass of the peasantry and to lay the whole weight of the Russian Revolution on the shoulders of the Russian proletariat—numerically weak, physically exhausted, and bled white by three years of war—or to make economic concessions to the peasantry, to strengthen through agreement with it the social base of Soviet power and the revolution, making it invincible in the near future from any counterrevolutionary internal attacks.”[128] The conference accepted the Tenth Congress’s concessions to the peasantry, but it is doubtful that the KP(b)U really gave up on the need for “civil war with the mass of the peasantry.” While acknowledging the need to introduce the tax-in-kind, the party’s resolution insisted that “the state must preserve in its own hands surveillance and control over large-scale goods-exchange operations.” Moreover, it stressed the need to provide the KNSs with all possible “advantages” to help them overcome any disadvantages resulting from the tax-in-kind. Indeed, it could be argued that the party’s repeated attempts to strengthen the position of the KNSs in the village, granting them wide-ranging rights and even giving them the power to redistribute the tax burden away from their members, allowed the KP(b)U to travel both paths: granting concessions to the majority of peasants who had resisted all food supply policies to date, and at the same time continuing the civil war on the “kulaks,” however the party defined the term. The party stressed that only by bolstering the KNSs and their influence in the village would “Soviet power be able truly to implement the tax-in-kind,” especially since the new law eliminated the use of collective responsibility to collect the tax. Only when the KNSs were solidly established in the villages could Soviet power “overcome the banditry corroding the Ukrainian village and facilitate the rebirth of the peasant economy.”[129]

Considering the unwillingness of party leaders to stop fighting peasants for grain and their reluctance to accept the turn to NEP, it is not surprising that they continued to push for the completion of the requisition quotas of 1920 into the summer of 1921, even though they were at this very time receiving reports that "banditry was expanding with great force." In mid-June 1921 the Kharkiv Provincial Commission for the Struggle with Banditry reported that formerly small "bands" pursuing only plunder had now coalesced into "large bands with political coloring," noting that these bands' large-scale appearance in the province coincided with the movement of Makhno's troops into the region.[130]

Party leaders continued to demand the completion of the 1920 quotas even as they published articles about the approaching implementation of the tax-in-kind.[131] At a meeting on 4 July 1921 of the Politburo of the TsK KP(b)U, Stanislav Kosior proposed a series of measures to increase food procurement. The Politburo resolved "in principle to recognize as expedient the use of mobile sessions of the Revolutionary tribunal in the most urgent places for the condemnation of individual masters [*khoziaeva*] who are not completing the requisition quota." Ordering the People's Commissariat of Food Supply to reach an agreement with the military command "about insuring the tribunals with sufficient armed forces," the Politburo also resolved to sanction as a repressive measure the collection of the equivalent in goods or money at market prices from those not fulfilling the requisition quota.[132]

Such measures appear to have had little effect on the fulfillment of the quotas, and the KNSs do not seem to have helped. On 30 July 1921 the All-Ukrainian Central Executive Committee ordered a Ukraine-wide re-registration of KNSs. While stressing that the KNS was Soviet power's "most faithful leader of political and economic activities in the village," the committee admitted that "a significant majority of KNSs display insufficient firmness and energy and take little part in Soviet construction in the village and in defense of the poor's interests." The committee considered the main cause of this insufficiency that "village *kurkuli* [kulaks], speculators, deserters, and bandits" had penetrated into the KNSs and were "carrying out their disintegrative work in the midst of the very committees." Just two months later, on 30 September 1921, the KP(b)U's central committee ordered a "severe purge [*suvora chystka*] of the KNS, leaving in them only semi-proletarian elements."[133] In the absence of serious studies of the KNSs at the local level, we can only say that such re-registrations and claims of "infiltration" by "enemies of the people" suggest that the KNSs were not faithfully implementing "the demands of Soviet power" and were probably frustrating them in some places.

The party's attempts to fulfill the fall 1920 requisitions had little success, especially because the peasants quickly learned through unofficial means about the transition to a tax-in-kind. As a report on requisitions in Poltava province put it, "the dragging out of the requisition quota is perniciously reflected in the campaign for harvesting grain. The peasantry is extraordinarily indifferent to our appeals. They do not believe us. There are cases of kulaks burning the crops."[134]

We do not know exactly when party leaders gave up on completing the 1920 requisition quota or what percentage they managed to obtain,[135] but by early August 1921 the party organ, *Kommunist*, was rallying its readers to struggle for the most rapid completion of the tax-in-kind, not only to provide food to Ukraine's cities, but to areas of Russia and Ukraine hit hard by famine.[136] In late September there was also a wholesale replacement of the party presidium's members. No further mention was made of completing the fall 1920 requisition quotas.[137]

In general, peasants of Kharkiv province responded positively to the implementation of the tax-in-kind. A report to the Radnarkom from 27 September 1921 noted that in the countryside, no "outstanding counter-revolutionary actions" had been noticed. There were still some incidents of "banditry" in the province, but these were having "no influence on the collection of the tax-in-kind."[138] A report from 30 September confirmed this description, claiming that with the defeat of Makhno in late-August, peasants' attitudes toward Soviet power had somewhat improved. The "kulak element" reportedly was distributing "all possible provocative rumors" in an attempt to undermine the tax collection, but peasants were paying the tax "without delays" or coercion.[139] On 10 October 1921 the Kharkiv provincial party committee's information department reported that peasants had fulfilled 45 percent of the tax imposed; daily deliveries for the whole province fluctuated between 100 and 150 poods.[140] This positive response was not limited to Kharkiv province; for example, the peasants of Volyn province were the first to fulfill their tax-in-kind quotas for 1921. And, according to Soviet officials, the peasants of Podillia province had as a result of the introduction of the tax-in-kind "begun to believe in the possibility of the renewal of their farms."[141] The tax-in-kind and goods exchange system seem to have been sufficient concessions for many peasants to give up their grain—a sacrifice of 25 percent or less for the right to do what they wanted with the rest of their harvest.

Unfortunately, for many inhabitants of the former Russian Empire, this was too little too late. The revolutions, three years of civil war, the forced requisitions of the previous years by the state and various armies that had led to peasants decreasing their sown area, and finally, drought conditions in several provinces in the spring of 1921 led to famine in many areas of Ukraine and Russia that lasted in some provinces into 1923.[142] Although peasants of Kharkiv province seem to have produced enough grain for themselves and to pay their portion of the tax-in-kind, many peasants in other provinces suffered greatly. From 1921 to 1932, between 1.5 million and 2 million peasants died of famine in the UkSSR and some 4–5 million died in the Soviet Union overall.[143] Although the famine did not play a central role in Kharkiv province, some Ukrainian historians have argued that the famine greatly helped the Cheka's efforts to end the peasant insurgency.[144]

The completion of the tax-in-kind lessened but did not end some peasants' protests against the Soviet regime. Outbreaks of "banditry" were reported into late 1924. The authorities in charge of its liquidation often declared that they were winning. A September 1921 report from the frequently rebellious Valky district claimed that "banditry in the district had taken on a criminal character in the full sense of the word." The distinction made between "political" and "criminal" banditry suggests how flexibly the term was employed. Labeling all those who resisted the Soviet regime and its policies "bandits" delegitimized these peasants' efforts to create their own version of "soviet power," but the regime still was compelled to distinguish between those who were resisting for political reasons, and those who were mostly out for plunder, though they may have at times been involved in such activities. Larger "territorial bands" with "political colorings" had been forced by the strong presence of soviet forces to disperse into smaller groups. The "bandits" in general expressed few political slogans, though some had been agitating for peasants not to fulfill the tax-in-kind. The report insisted that "all layers and classes" were hostile toward "banditry," stating, "even that element of the population which at some time nourished the hope that the bandits would help or prepare the basis for the overthrow and elimination of Soviet power had now lost confidence in the force of banditry." The report provided as a basic explanation for the peasants' loss of faith in these "bandits" the ever-growing "certainty of the might of Soviet power, a brilliant example of which serves the comparatively successful fulfillment of the tax-in-kind."[145] This "might" was expressed not in a growing number of civil authorities, but in the presence of numerous armed forces, including four Cheka detachments (127 armed men and five machine guns); Red Army detachments (315 armed men and eight machine guns); and Valky's cavalry squadron of KNS peasants (83 armed with sabers, 36 unarmed). Noting the population's recent realization of the "impotency and harmfulness of banditry and the might of Soviet power," the report concluded that these "armed forces make it possible to strengthen the volost authorities and workers."[146]

Certainly, the increased and fortified presence of military forces decreased the likelihood of outbreaks of large-scale "banditry," and the Red Army's victories over all "external enemies" probably convinced many peasants that this "worker-peasant government" was here to stay. "Banditry" did not end so quickly, however. In early July 1922 the "group for the struggle with banditry" under the provincial GPU (*Gosudarstvennoe politicheskoe upravlenie*; the Cheka's successor) presented a lengthy report, arguing that a new, better organized and conspiratorial type of "banditry" was on the rise in the province. This new type seemed so well organized and careful in all its activities that the GPU suspected "outside forces" under the guidance of Simon Petliura were at work in the province.[147] The report listed raids, robberies, and other activities of "bandits" in almost all the province's districts, suggesting that anti-Soviet actions were increasing. Predicting that this "regeneration of banditry… is unconditionally strengthening a fully developing political banditry of a new type," the GPU expressed the fear that this banditry could disastrously upset the approaching harvest.[148]

The difference between "bandits" and peasants rising in protest remained unclear. Some peasants, especially Red Army deserters, took an active part in these groups; others joined temporarily. Although those fighting the "bandits" were reluctant to admit that some non-"bandits" sympathized with and joined them, in some cases they could not avoid it. One report noted that during the Smeian band's attack on what remained of the Krinichanska estate (Okhtyrka district), local peasants provided "plenty of assistance," cutting the telephone lines in advance of the attack and burning down the estate's buildings. The report attributed the peasants' assistance to the fact that they had seized much of the estate's land in 1917–18 and wished to eliminate their "hated neighbor."[149] At the same time, there were many peasants who probably wanted nothing to do with these "bandits," especially the most notorious ones, fearing reprisals by the authorities. And some peasants, especially members of the KNSs, took an active part in finding, attacking, catching, and killing "bandits."

Although political forms of peasant "banditry" seems to have died out across Ukraine by the end of 1923,[150] Kharkiv police agencies were still encountering small-scale, apolitical cases in late 1924. In November of that year the provincial branch of the GPU reported that "bandits" had carried out 41 armed raids and robberies, 37 horse thefts, intentionally set 19 fires, committed 26 burglaries, and murdered one soviet official and 27 private individuals. The report concluded, however, that these acts were not "of a threatening kind," and did not require any "special measures." They represented in fact a 20 percent decrease from those of the previous month. Ambiguity remained, but gradually these "bands" became smaller and smaller in number and size, and "non-bandit" peasants became less and less tolerant of them. The same report noted that some peasants from Sumy district had even carried out a *samosud* against the bandit leader known as Iarov.[151]

Eventually, "banditry" and peasants' open resistance to the regime died out, largely as a result of several factors: the move to NEP removed some of peasants' most pressing grievances; the regime's military forces violently suppressed most of the larger insurgent groups, dispersing them into smaller, less effective "bands"; propaganda efforts labeling all forms of resistance "banditry," "criminal" and "anti-Soviet" also contributed to the demise of "banditry"; and finally, the growing might and presence of "Soviet power" in the countryside encouraged peasants increasingly to acquiesce to (if not accept) the center's definition of that term and its rule.

Perhaps the best characterization of Soviet authorities' efforts to bring their version of "Soviet power" to the village is that an uneasy and ambiguous truce slowly and unevenly took shape between the new authorities and the rural inhabitants of the Ukrainian Socialist Soviet Republic. Peasants did not ever obtain what they called "soviet power"—that is, control over their daily lives and work, "free trade," and the right to dispose of the fruits of their labor as they saw fit. And they certainly did not receive freedom from outside interference. Such anarchistic dreams could not have been fulfilled by any of the governments pretending to power in this space and time. Indeed, the peasants of Ukraine and Russia had no choice but to become modern citizens and come to grapple with an intrusive and pervasive state, whether it was of the communist or capitalist variety. However, the approach and methods of this

Worker-Peasant Government, even this revised, reformed, and more conciliatory version, did little to appease and much to provoke peasants. In response, peasants complained loudly, resisted fulfilling and delivering the desparately needed and insistently demanded foodstuffs, deserted the Red Army, and when pushed sufficiently, rose up against the government that they had once thought shared their understanding of soviet power. The regime responded with violence, greater attempts to infiltrate and divide villagers against themselves, and eventually, begrudgingly, the introduction of the NEP, a less than complete compromise. The violence eventually waned, but a real understanding between peasants and party was never achieved. This temporary truce would not last through even the first renewed attempts to force peasants onto collective farms, the results of which would prove disastrous, most of all for the peasants themselves, so many of whom died of starvation in the Great Famine of 1932–33.

Conclusion

As the preceding chapters make clear, this attempt to extract from the archives a representative picture of peasants' experiences of war and revolution in one Ukrainian province of the Russian Empire has not been easy. Most of the people who created the documents on which this book is based were not peasants, nor did they share peasants' understanding of the world, nor their hopes for the revolution. These nonpeasants brought diverse ideological baggage to their perceptions and interpretations of peasants' statements and actions. Tsarist police officials, landlords, SR party agitators, Hetmanate district starostas, Communist party leaders, Azbuka intelligence agents, Soviet food supply workers, and Cheka agents interpreted peasants' behavior through their various and varied ideas about "the peasant," "class struggle," the revolutionary process, and the role that peasants should or could play in it. For the most part, they strove to control and administer peasants, and to compel them to sell or give up their grain to the cities, their armies, and themselves. Sometimes, especially in 1917, they sought peasant participation in the revolution, or even (later) to transform them into "communists" and their farms into collective farms; other authorities tried to induce them to return to their former, more passive, modes of behavior, and to return the land and property they had seized in 1917. But few of these nonpeasants endeavored to understand peasants, to gain insight into their perceptions and expectations of the revolution. Certainly, they did not ask the questions a historian would pose. The answers to such questions had to be teased out of the documents, cobbled together and transformed into a coherent narrative of this tumultuous and contradictory set of events.

Nevertheless, a representative picture of these peasants' experiences has emerged and one might best sketch that picture in the following way. The mobilizations of World War I took from many peasant households of Kharkiv province their only male worker and their last horse. Peasant women—especially the soldatki—adapted, taking on most of the socially prescribed "men's work." With their men at the front, these women then played an active and leading role in stopping the implementation of the Stolypin land reform in their villages, the most violent expression of which was the riot in Nyzhna Syrovatka. Soon after this event, Minister Krivoshein was forced to lay aside the reform, but peasants did not return to their earlier relative docility. In 1916 they carried out numerous protests against attempts by local officials to impose set prices on their produce for sale at market. Though these disturbances quieted down on the eve of the revolution, underlying animosities between peasants and police (and other government) officials remained. Moreover, the disturbances over set prices gave peasants an important reason to hesitate before hauling their surplus foodstuffs to market towns, where they probably suspected that government officials and town-dwellers awaited the opportunity to take from them whatever they could for as little as possible. Indeed, a central preoccupation of all the subsequent governments to claim power in the province and across Ukraine over the revolutionary period was to get peasants to bring their grain to market or give it up to feed the cities and their armies' soldiers.

News of the February Revolution took a long time to trickle down to the village, but once peasants realized how free they had become, they embarked on a modified version of the great Black Repartition. In contrast to the interpretations of many Soviet and some Western scholars, however, this book demonstrates how little this "agrarian revolution" had in common with "class struggle" or the revolutions taking place in the capitals and other cities. Peasants cleverly exploited the numerous committees newly proclaimed by the Provisional Government in order to justify and legitimize their seizures of land, forest, and farming equipment; and they took land not just from landlords, but from all nonpeasants. Moreover, they soon realized that their main competitors for the land were not the landlords, who in the absence of tsarist authorities were quite powerless to resist, but the peasants from the next village, who wished to possess the same estate lands. Indeed, the struggle to obtain as much as possible of the rather meager spoils of this agrarian revolution, revealed in the many intervillage conflicts of 1917, can only have strengthened peasants' primary identification with their covillagers and further distanced them from everyone outside the village. This very local view of the world was also revealed in their unwillingness to sacrifice for larger ideas of community, such as the broader concepts of Ukraine or Russia. In fact, there is strong evidence to suggest that peasants did not identify even with those newly founded revolutionary institutions that claimed to speak on their behalf, such as the Kharkiv Provincial Soviet of Peasants' Deputies. This evidence brings into question some of the findings of those social historians who have relied on these supposedly "popular" institutions, especially the soviets, for their understanding of peasants' attitudes and desires. Moreover, the finding that peasants primarily identified with their village undermines the often assumed and sometimes asserted claim that most Ukrainian peasants supported the Central Rada and its efforts to bring about a national revolution in Ukraine.

In fact, one could argue that, at least to this point in the revolutionary process, the experiences of these Ukrainian-speaking peasants differed relatively little from those of Russian-speaking peasants, particularly those cultivating similar, fertile, black soil in neighboring Kursk and Voronezh provinces. But in 1918 these peasants' paths diverged quite sharply, after the Central Rada's delegation signed a peace treaty with the Central Powers at Brest-Litovsk. During the consequent occupation peasants experienced the frequently brutal and arbitrary actions of German soldiers, apparently left by their commanders to plunder the countryside as they wished, abusing peasants and imposing contributions on them. As a result, the German occupation did much to tarnish the Ukrainian national idea in the eyes of many Ukrainian-speaking peasants, while preserving their idealized understanding of "Soviet power"—an understanding that had little in common with the experiences of Russian-speaking peasants living under "war communism" just to the north. The same two processes led most peasants of Kharkiv province to reject the return of the UNR under the Directory's leadership in late 1919, especially after experiencing the brief rule of Otaman Petro Bolbochan. Within this context, it is not difficult to see why many of these peasants came to call themselves "bolsheviks" in late 1918, to demand "All power to the soviets!" and to provide considerable assistance, men, and food to the returning Ukrainian Soviet Divisions of the Red Army.

The reward for their sacrifices was to have to endure in 1919 the rule of two regimes, both of which did little to please and much to provoke them. The leaders of the second Soviet regime to claim authority in the province, the Temporary Worker-Peasant Government of Ukraine, seem not to have understood why peasants supported the Red Army or what they meant by "soviet power," and soon (unintentionally or not) did almost everything possible to turn them against the regime. Attempts to force peasant villages into communes, requisition their grain, and mobilize their men incited numerous uprisings, which greatly facilitated the advance of Denikin's Volunteer Army (VA) into the region in June 1919. The VA, however, kept its sights on Moscow, rarely looking to its rear. In its efforts to restore "Russia—One and Indivisible," the VA left many peasants victim to the arbitrary whim of returning landlords and former tsarist bureaucrats, doing almost nothing to discourage and much to encourage peasants' perception that General Denikin was the leader of the "White Guards" and "the counterrevolution," as Bolshevik agitators and their propaganda often claimed.

Hence, it is not entirely surprising that when the Red Army, the leaders of the KP(b)U, and the recently reformed Worker-Peasant Government returned in December 1919, peasants articulated a more sober but clear willingness to work with them. At the numerous "nonparty" peasant conferences of early 1920 they revealed their understanding of "soviet power," rebuffing party leaders' attempts to take control of their conferences. Peasant delegates expressed their distrust of nonpeasants, their approval of the government's new land law, a strong desire for local autonomy and, above all, a complete rejection of the party's food supply policy. Party leaders refused to listen, instead exerting all available forces to requisition grain from peasants, impose their authority over the countryside, and mobilize peasant men into the Red Army. Peasants resisted, at first passively but soon actively, especially after the regime attempted yet one more mobilization of young peasant men. The regime eventually managed to suppress the resulting violent uprisings by resorting to greater violence, but many peasants still refused to surrender their grain. Only the replacement of the grain requisition quotas with the tax-in-kind, and the allowance of some degree of free trade, along with peasants' realization of the growing strength of soviet forces in the countryside, finally convinced most of them to begin giving up their grain. Even then, the regime had to exert a great deal of effort—weapons, men, propaganda, and time—to put an end to the frequent outbreaks of peasant "banditry."

One hesitates to identify a concluding point to such a chaotic series of events, because the narrative lacks a dramatic finale. Some historians have argued that the "uneasy truce" described above in chapter five was no peace at all, but a brief respite between the revolutionary struggles of 1917–21 and the clashes over collectivization beginning in late 1928.[1] In 1923, however, the Soviet government saw some evidence that a turbulent period had come to a definitive end. In that year the People's Commissariat of Land Affairs of Ukraine (Narkomzem) published a rather triumphant pamphlet, entitled *The Results of the Agrarian Revolution in Ukraine.*[2] This document declared in both Ukrainian and Russian to the Ukrainian Socialist Soviet Republic's citizens that with the publication of the Land Codex on 14 December 1922, which was supposed to regulate land relations in the postrevolutionary countryside, it was time "to sum up the results of the agrarian revolution in Ukraine." Proposing that the basic task posed by the October Revolution was "the elimination of landlords' land ownership and the transfer of all land to the hands of the laboring peasantry," Narkomzem claimed that the Communist Party had fulfilled this task completely and that "the hopes of the peasantry had finally received their complete realization." Of the republic's 33,956,633 desiatynas of arable land, peasants had received for their direct use 31,168,346 desiatynas, or about 92 percent. And half of the remaining eight percent had been set aside to distribute to those peasants willing to migrate from overpopulated to less populated regions. Narkomzem proudly declared that in place of the 19.4 million desiatynas held by peasants prior to 1917, they now were able to make use of 32.6 million desiatynas, a 68 percent increase. The appended tables and diagrams purportedly revealed with all clarity "the gains achieved by the revolution."[3]

Although this widely distributed document gave far too much credit to the party and "the revolution" for successful land reform, its statistics revealed a significant change in the nature of land and power relations in the Ukrainian countryside: the former owners (nonpeasants) of much of the land had fled or been removed, and most of the land was under peasant control. One might wonder, though, how much peasants had really gained. As noted in chapter two, an equal redistribution of all arable land among the republic's peasant households would not have allowed them to do much more than eke out an existence. If these 32.6 million desiatynas of land were distributed equally among all of the new republic's 4,011,000 peasant households, each household would have had at its disposal no more than 8.1 desiatynas of arable land. As Holubnychy has pointed out, this would have been a gain of only about one and a half desiatyna per household.[4] In Kharkiv province matters stood somewhat worse. If all of the 2,559,754 desiatynas that Narkomzem claimed had been granted to the province's peasants were distributed equally among their 450,644 households, each farm would have ended up with less than six (5.68) desiatynas, or about 15 acres.[5] Employing their traditional farming methods and tools, these peasant households would have only continued to subsist, sometimes selling their limited surpluses at local markets in exchange for a few manufactured goods. More intensive and efficient farming techniques were needed to solve "the agrarian problem" conclusively. In the 1920s the Soviet government made serious efforts to increase the productivity of some peasant farms, though its fear of strengthening the "kulaks," along with peasants' distrust of nonlocal Soviet authorities attempting to tell them how to farm, greatly inhibited and often disrupted these efforts.[6] Moreover, these limited attempts to improve peasant farming methods were cut short when the regime turned to collectivization in 1927.

Does this book, then, conclude somewhere in the middle of a larger story? In one sense it does. In another sense, though, its terminal point *does* conclude one period of open, violent revolution and civil war. As Ol′ha Hanzha has shown, peasants' open resistance to the regime waned in 1922–23, and was redirected into more peaceful forms of protest.[7] Moreover, considering how many studies of the revolution have focused solely on 1917, this study's time frame does much to provide a longer perspective on these villagers' travails.

Although the experiences of these peasants were many and varied, several consistent themes run through this investigation. The first is the persistent efforts by peasants to protect and improve their perceived economic interests. Petr Stolypin may have been correct that, in the long run, land consolidation would benefit the peasantry as a whole, but most peasants saw in consolidation only a serious threat to their narrow, widely dispersed, but familiar strips of land, and World War I only exacerbated their fears. It also might have made better economic sense to preserve the more agriculturally advanced estates as model farms, as the Bolsheviks attempted in 1919, but villagers preferred to divide up these estate lands and property among their households. Perceptions mattered far more than the sometimes reasonable propositions of outsiders. Indeed, it is somewhat paradoxical to observe how poorly many of these outsiders, especially the communists, understood and were able to take advantage of peasants' tendency to act primarily on their perceived economic interests.

Closely bound up with this theme is peasants' very local understanding of the world, and their identification with the village, or volost at most. This localness was most clearly expressed in 1917, during the intervillage struggles over newly seized lands and when the Provisional Government and Central Rada repeatedly asked villagers to make sacrifices for Russia and Ukraine. But it can also be seen in peasants' stubborn resistance to attempts by various food supply agents to take their grain and forage during the civil war and afterward. Considering that throughout this period most peasants of Kharkiv province never really starved, one is struck by their unwillingness to give up or even sell their grain (at below market prices) to fulfill quotas to feed Red Army soldiers, workers, and even starving peasants in other provinces. Throughout this turbulent period most of this province's peasants continued to think of themselves primarily as members of a village community—for example, Sokolivtsy or Ostroverkhivtsy.

Of course, over this period some peasants did move outside their village-worlds. The Valky uprising of 1920 seems to have embraced about half of that district's peasants; a few other uprisings achieved a similar scale. Now and then some peasants also expressed an identification with Ukraine; some called for Ukrainian autonomy, others asked only that the communists pay greater attention to "local peculiarities." While these expressions of sympathy with the Ukrainian national idea are significant, they were not very widespread and often seem to have been initiated by Ukrainian Borot′bists (mostly nonpeasants) agitating in the area. Other studies corroborate this finding. Pavlo Isakov, for example, has shown that most peasant insurgents in Left-Bank Ukraine during the civil war did not adhere to any political tendency at all, neither pro-Ukrainian Directory or pro-Makhno, though he insists they were all "anti-communist."[8] Doubtless, the national question played a role in the larger events of the revolutionary period, but it was not crucial (at least not yet) to these peasants, and probably not to many other peasants of the crumbling empire.

In his dissertation on Ukrainian peasants in Right-Bank Ukraine, where, in contrast to Kharkiv province, the repartitional commune was barely present, Graham Tan argues that throughout the period from 1917 to 1923 peasants carried out their revolutionary actions primarily through their village community (*hromada*): "For many the boundaries of the village or local volost represented the limits of their world." Tan concludes that the village community played "a fundamental role in organising peasant villages and expressing peasant beliefs in much the same way as community organisations throughout the Russian Empire."[9] His findings contrast to some extent with two other works on the peasants of Right-Bank Ukraine. Oleksandr Nesterov, in his more narrowly focused study of the 1919 anticommunist peasant insurgency on the Right Bank, found that in the movement's early stages most insurgents were active only within their own volost or district, "without the Directory's leadership, without any common program or tactics, without a united plan." But as the struggle continued, some of the leading otamans established links ("though not tight") with the UNR's military staff. Through the work of Ukrainian political parties, this peasant insurgent movement "gradually took on a more national content."[10] Nesterov coauthored another study that makes similar assertions.[11] While these historians argue that peasants on the Right Bank were developing in 1919 a wider sense of national consciousness (at least in 1919), I find their argument somewhat problematic. The authors often cite the words of the insurgent leaders and Ukrainian political party representatives, and rarely the words or actions of the rank-and-file peasant insurgents themselves. At the same time, they admit that among the insurgents "traditional peasant localness [*mistechkovist´*]" remained a problem. Their argument is also somewhat circular: On the Right Bank political parties with a Ukrainian national coloring had influence among the peasantry; these parties at various times proclaimed themselves for the creation of a Ukrainian state; therefore, the peasants took up arms against the soviet regime for the Ukrainian state. No evidence is presented to prove that peasants shared the goals of party activists; the connection is assumed. In fact, the authors provide considerable evidence that on the Right Bank, as in Kharkiv province, the land question was most important, concluding that the cause of the insurgency was the Soviet government's land policy (not even mentioning nationalism as a cause).[12] Dmytro Mykhailychenko asserts in his study of the 1919 anticommunist peasant uprising in all regions of Russian-ruled Ukraine that a "characteristic peculiarity of the peasant insurgency remained "localism" and that the influence of Ukrainian political parties on the peasant movement remained relatively small."[13]

One can find further evidence of peasants' localness in Iurii Kotliar's work on the peasant insurgencies in southern Ukraine. Describing the two largest uprisings against the VA's rule,[14] in which the peasants of two villages, Vysuns´ka and Poltavka-Bashtanka, actually declared their villages to be "republics," Kotliar concludes that they failed partly because of the absence of any broader goal: in his analysis, these "republics" never went beyond "local interests." In fact, Kotliar agrees with Isakov that most peasant insurgents, typically the more vocal and worldly members of their communities, held no strong political allegiances, and switched sides in the civil war "more than once," though all shared the desire "to defend the interests of their villages and neighborhoods."[15] Summing up these various recent studies, one can draw a broader conclusion about the importance of peasants' local community in Ukraine, thereby bringing into question the tendency of many historians to treat the revolution in the non-Russian regions of the empire (and especially in Ukraine) as primarily a national struggle between the centralizing Muscovites and the national minorities.

Contesting the other side of that old historiographical equation, Sarah Badcock has found that the Russian-speaking peasants of Nizhegorod and Kazan provinces also organized primarily through their village and communal councils and were very locally minded. These villagers repeatedly confounded the representatives of the Provisional Government (including many socialists) by their consistent tendency to sacrifice national interests for their local ones.[16] Donald Raleigh, in his engaging study of Saratov province during the civil war, cites numerous examples of peasant efforts "to rebuff the state's intrusion into the village." He stresses, however, that Saratov peasants tended to resist in a nonconfrontational manner, unlike the peasants of Kharkiv province.[17] Historians working on other revolutions have found a similar local-mindedness.[18]

Peasants' predominantly local village identity was resistant not only to attempts by outsiders to get them to think of and sacrifice for a broader community, but also to attempts to divide the village from within. One might usefully compare the findings of this book to those of Orlando Figes, especially concerning how Soviet power was consolidated at the local level. Figes argues that the breakdown of urban-rural market relations, the massive influx of urban residents into the countryside, and the impoverishment of the rural population greatly weakened the social cohesion of the village community and placed great burdens on local soviets. Many stable peasant farmers, who often dominated the village communes, responded to these changes by striving to isolate themselves from the outside world and from the soviets, which were seen increasingly as organs of central power. Here lay the base of resistance to the establishment of centralized power in the countryside. Figes asserts, however, that the marginalized elements of rural society (ex-servicemen, rural laborers, craftsmen, migrants, youths, and sometimes women) saw in the new soviet institutions a way "to break out of a traditional stifling peasant society." These groups joined the ranks of the burgeoning state apparatus in the volost towns. The Soviet regime was consolidated through the institutionalization of these divisions within rural society.[19]

While this book accords with some of Figes's findings about the Volga peasants, it differs considerably on this point. There is no evidence that those village "elements" left out of the traditional power structure in Kharkiv province's villages were co-opted into new Soviet institutions or that, indeed, Soviet power was ever very well established in the Ukrainian countryside before collectivization. The intervillage land conflicts of 1917–18 reinforced peasants' sense of village identity. The more brutal and violent character of the German occupation and the civil war in Ukraine pushed peasants ever further into their localness, strengthening village cohesion. Hence, when in 1920–21 the victorious Soviet regime attempted to impose its authority in the village contrary to peasant wishes, it ran into serious and repeated resistance. Unlike the Volga villages examined by Figes, those of Kharkiv province proved far more resiliently (though imperfectly) united.[20] Attempts to create Committees of Not-Well-Off Peasants (KNSs) in the Ukrainian countryside failed repeatedly in "differentiating the village" and extracting the grain. Rather, only the combined effects of the introduction of NEP, a great deal of violence, and the regime's persistent and growing presence in the countryside eventually led peasants to give up their grain and stop supporting the numerous "bandits" roaming across the province. Even then, the evidence does not clearly show that the regime was ever able to differentiate the village or to create a solid base of support there to fight the so-called kulaks. For example, a 1928 official report on the work of the soviets in Kharkiv province admitted that "the huge mass of the poor are still not attracted to the KNS." Having just carried out yet another reregistration of KNS members to clean out those "elements foreign to the poor and hostile to Soviet power," the report counted as of 10 October 1928 only 27,894 KNS members across the entire province.[21] Hence, it appears that on the eve of Stalin's drive to force peasants into collective farms, most were still not incorporated into the Soviet system. Perhaps only collectivization or some similar, violent, transformative, modernization project could accomplish that.

*

For most of the peasants of Kharkiv province this period of war and revolution was also one of great hope followed by greater disappointments. Mobilized by the social turmoil unleashed by the Great War and set free to do as they pleased after the February Revolution, peasants actively participated in and made their own revolutions in 1917, enamored with the dream of improving their lives and those of their children. They were soon to be disillusioned. Neither the Central Rada, nor the Provisional Government, nor the Temporary Worker-Peasant Governments of Ukraine proved capable of retaining the support of the masses or giving them what they really wanted. Perhaps none of the governments and parties contending for power over this period could have done that, no matter what their policies and actions. Class and national revolution in a peasant country was surely a dubious undertaking at best. Having seized all nonpeasant land in 1917, many peasants wished above all to be left alone. None of the serious contenders for power in Ukraine could even consider this alternative. The Central Rada and the Sovnarkom promised them liberation as a nation and a class, progress, prosperity and enlightenment, but gave them instead the quite brutal occupation of German troops, zealous communist party members attempting to force them into more "progressive" forms of agriculture, and food supply detachments employing armed force to requisition the fruits of their labor. From 1918 onward those pretending to power in Ukraine resorted primarily to violent methods to extract food, forage, and men from the countryside, pushing peasants further and further into isolation and repeatedly confirming their long-held suspicions about outsiders. In this regard, the uneasy and unequal truce that gradually took shape in Ukraine in the early 1920s could be described as an unspoken, but in some sense mutual, agreement between the peasants and party leaders to stop fighting openly, while continuing to disagree about how "soviet power" should be organized at the local level. Collectivization conclusively broke the truce and destroyed those local identities.

Notes

Introduction

1. Sarah Badcock, *Politics and the People in Revolutionary Russia: Two Volga Provinces during 1917* (Cambridge, 2007), 10.
2. Kate Brown, *A Biography of No Place: From Ethnic Borderland to Soviet Heartland* (Cambridge, Mass., 2004), 40. In Ukrainian the word most often used to describe a "local" was *tuteshnii* (of here), although *mistsevyi* (of this place) and *lokal´nyi* were also used.
3. John-Paul Himka, "The National and the Social in the Ukrainian Revolution of 1917–1920: The Historiographical Agenda," *Archiv für Sozialgeschichte* 34 (1994): 95–110.
4. Himka, "The National and the Social in the Ukrainian Revolution," 96–99. The classic studies are Dmytro Doroshenko, *Istoriia Ukraïny, 1917–1923 rr.*, 2 vols. (Uzhhorod, 1930–32; New York, 1954); Pavlo Khrystiuk, *Zamitky i materiialy do istoriï ukrains´koï revoliutsiï, 1917–1920 rr.*, 3 vols. (Vienna, 1921); Oleh S. Pidhainy, *The Formation of the Ukrainian Republic* (New York, 1966); John S. Reshetar, *The Ukrainian Revolution, 1917–1920: A Study in Nationalism* (Princeton, 1952); Mykyta Iu. Shapoval, *Velyka revoliutsiia i ukraïns´ka vyzvol´na programa* (Prague, 1928); less scholarly, more literary, more left-leaning, but still interesting to read is the work of Volodymyr K. Vynnchenko, *Vidrodzhennia natsiï*, 3 vols. (Kyiv, 1920).
5. See the well-crafted and provocative essays in Taras Hunczak, ed., *The Ukraine, 1917–1921: A Study in Revolution* (Cambridge, Mass., 1977); and Roman Szporluk's review of that collection in *Annals of the Ukrainian Academy* 14, nos. 37–38 (1978–1980): 267–71.
6. The most important exceptions are the excellent works of Steven L. Guthier, "The Popular Base of Ukrainian Nationalism in 1917," *Slavic Review* 38, no. 1 (March 1979): 30–47; idem, "The Roots of Popular Ukrainian Nationalism: A Demographic, Social and Political Study of the Ukrainian Nationality to 1917" (PhD diss., University of Michigan, 1990); as well as H. R. Weinstein,

"Land Hunger and Nationalism in the Ukraine, 1905–1917," *Journal of Economic History* 2 (1942): 24–35; and Graham Tan, "Peasant Action and Village Social Organization: The Peasantry of Right-Bank Ukraine during the Revolution, 1917–1923" (PhD thesis, University of London, 1999); Andrea Gratsiozi [Graziosi], *Bol′sheviki i krest′iane na Ukraine, 1918–1919 gody: Ocherk o bol′shevizmakh, natsional-sotsializmakh i krest′ianskikh dvizheniiakh* (Moscow, 1997); and Andrea Graziosi, *The Great Soviet Peasant War: Bolsheviks and Peasants, 1917–1933*, Harvard Papers in Ukrainian Studies (Cambridge, Mass., 1996).

7. Himka, "The National and the Social in the Ukrainian Revolution," 102.
8. I. V. Khmil′, *Trudiashche selianstvo Ukraïny v borot′bi za vladu rad* (Kyiv, 1977), 8. One Soviet historian, V. V. Kabanov, attempted an in-depth investigation of rural social relations during the revolutionary period, although he focused on Russian peasants. Kabanov, "Oktiabr′skaia revoliutsiia i krest′ianskaia obshchina," *Istoricheskie zapiski* 111 (1984): 100–150.
9. For example, see Viacheslav F. Verstiuk, et al., comps., *Ukraïns′ka Tsentral′na Rada: Dokumenty i materialy u dvokh tomakh* (Kyiv, 1996–1997).
10. For example, from 1991 to 2002 *Ukraïns′kyi istorychnyi zhurnal* published 80 articles on the Ukrainian National Revolution and another 28 on Hrushevs′kyi; of these only eight touch on the broader masses in any substantial way. The rest focus explicitly on the leading national figures and their institutions, especially the Ukrainian Central Rada.
11. Oleh Pavlyshyn, "Istoriohrafiia ukraïns′koï revoliutsii 1917–1921 rr.," in *Ukraïns′ka istoriohrafiia na zlami XX i XXI stolit′: zdobutky i problemy*, ed. Leonid Zashkilniak (Lviv, 2004), 181.
12. Mykhailo Hrushevs′kyi, *Khto taki ukraïntsi i choho vony khochut′* (Kyiv, 1991), 162.
13. See, for example, *Ukraïns′kyi selianyn: Zbirnyk naukovykh prats′ vypusk* 8 (2004): 184–221. Unfortunately, I have found only three issues of this journal (at Harvard's Widener Library), the last one in 2008, but it appears to have been started in 2000 at Cherkasy State University and includes on its editorial board some of the leading Ukrainian historians.
14. Pavlyshyn, "Istoriohrafiia ukraïns′koï revoliutsiï 1917–1921 rr.," 171. N. I. Zemziulina, "Selians′ke pytannia v Ukraïni 1917–1918 rr. (istoriohrafiia problemy)" (Avtoreferat dysertatsii na zdobuttia naukovoho stupenia kandydata istorychnykh nauk, Kyïvs′kyi universytet imeni Tarasa Shevchenka, 1998).
15. The most pertinent studies include O. I. Hanzha, *Ukraïns′ke selianstvo v period stanovlennia totalitarnoho rezhymu (1917–1927 rr.)* (Kyiv, 2000); and the various works of Iaroslav Malyk, most recently, Iaroslav Malyk and

Oleh Bereza, *Zaprovadzhennia radians'koho rezhymu v ukraïns'komu seli (1917–1920)* (Lviv, 2001).

16. This finding contradicts in particular the works of Iaroslav Malyk, especially Malyk and Bereza, *Zaprovadzhennia radians'koho rezhymu v ukraïns'komu seli*, 314–20.

17. Iu. V. Kotliar, *Povstanstvo: Selians'kyi rukh na Pivdni Ukraïny (1917–1925)* (Mykolaïv and Odesa, 2003); Petro Zakharchenko, Nataliia Zemziulina, and Oleksandr Nesterov, *U pokhodi za voleiu (selians'ko-povstans'kyi rukh na pravoberezhnii Ukraïni u 1919 rotsi)* (Kyiv, 2000); Pavlo Isakov, "Povstans'kyi antykomunistychnyi rukh na livoberezhnii Ukraïni (berezen' 1919–lystopad 1921 rr.): Heohrafiia poshyrennia, dynamika kil'kisnykh zmin, ideolohiia," *Moloda natsiia: al'manakh* (Kyiv, 2000); P. M. Isakov, "Selians'kyi povstanches'kyi antykomunistychnyi rukh na Livoberezhnii Ukraïni (berezen' 1919–lystopad 1921 rr.)" (avtoreferat dysertatsiï na zdobuttia naukovoho stupenia kandydata istorychnykh nauk, NANU, Instytut Istoriï Ukraïny, Kyiv, 2001); O. V. Nesterov, "Selians'kyi povstans'kyi rukh na pravoberezhnii Ukraïni (1919 r.)" (avtoreferat dysertatsiï na zdobuttia naukovoho stupenia kandydata istorychnykh nauk, Kyïvs'kyi universytet imeni Tarasa Shevchenka, 2001); D. Iu. Mykhailychenko, "Polityka 'Voennoho komunizmu' i ukraïns'ke selianstvo, 1919 r." (avtoreferat dysertatsiï na zdobuttia naukovoho stupenia kandydata istorychnykh nauk, Kharkivs'kyi national'nyi universytet im. V. N. Karazina, 2002); I. V. Kutashev, "Selians'kyi rukh v Ukraïni (berezen' 1917 r.–kviten' 1918 r.)" (avtoreferat dysertatsiï na zdobuttia naukovoho stupenia kandydata istorychnykh nauk, Natsional'nyi pedahohichnyi universytet imeni M. P. Drahomanova, Kyiv, 2003).

18. Malyk and Bereza, *Zaprovadzhennia radians'koho rezhymu v ukraïns'komu seli*, 319.

19. O. I. Hanzha, "Selians'kyi povstans'kyi rukh," in *Istoriia ukraïns'koho selianstva: Narysy v 2-kh tomakh*, ed. V. M. Lytvyn et al., vol. 2 (Kyiv, 2006), 8.

20. Murray Frame, comp., *The Russian Revolution, 1905–1921: A Bibliographic Guide to Works in English* (Westport, Conn., 1995), 105–7. Admittedly, Frame lists some sources more than once.

21. D. J. Raleigh, *Revolution on the Volga: 1917 in Saratov* (Ithaca, 1985); idem, "Revolutionary Politics in Provincial Russia: The Tsaritsyn 'Republic' in 1917," *Slavic Review* 40 (1981): 194–209; and idem, *Experiencing Russia's Civil War: Politics, Society, and Revolutionary Culture in Saratov, 1917–1922* (Princeton, 2002). Also see R. C. Elwood, *Russian Social Democracy in the Underground: A Study of the RSDRP in the Ukraine, 1907–1914* (Assen, 1974); R. Pethybridge, *The Spread of the Russian Revolution. Essays on 1917* (London, 1972); Rex A. Wade, *Red Guards and the Workers' Militias in the*

Russian Revolution (Stanford, 1984); Michael C. Hickey, "Local Government and State Authority in the Provinces: Smolensk, February–June 1917," *Slavic Review* 55 (1996): 863–81.

22. John Channon, "The Peasantry in the Revolutions of 1917," in *Revolution in Russia: Reassessments of 1917*, ed. Edith Rogovin Frankel, Jonathan Frankel, and Baruch Knei-Paz (Cambridge, 1992), 105. Other important studies of the Russian peasantry include: Orlando Figes, *Peasant Russia, Civil War: The Volga Countryside in Revolution (1917–1921)* (Oxford, 1989); O. Radkey, *The Unknown Civil War in South Russia: A Study of the Green Movement in the Tambov Region, 1920–1921* (Stanford, 1976); M. Frenkin, *Tragediia krest′ianskikh vosstanii v Rossii 1918–1921 gg.* (Jerusalem, 1987); G. Gill, *Peasants and Government in the Russian Revolution* (London, 1979). More recently, see Aaron B. Retish, "Creating Peasant Citizens: Rituals of Power, Rituals of Citizenship in Viatka Province, 1917," *Revolutionary Russia* 16 (2003): 47–67; and Badcock, *Politics and the People in Revolutionary Russia*.
23. Frame, *Russian Revolution*, 39–53; 102–3; 111–12.
24. Figes, *Peasant Russia, Civil War*, 2.
25. Figes, *Peasant Russia, Civil War*, 5.
26. By the 1897 census the total population of the empire, not including the Grand Duchy of Finland, was 122,666,500, of which the majority (55.7 percent) were non-(Great) Russians. Moreover, the criteria used to determine nationality, native tongue (*rodnoi iazyk*), inflated the proportion of Russians, since some of those who gave Russian as their native tongue were Russified non-Russians. *Pervaia Vseobshchaia Perepis′ Naseleniia Rossiiskoi Imperii, 1897 g.*, vol. 2 (St. Petersburg, 1905), 1–19.
27. Ronald Grigor Suny, *The Revenge of the Past: Nationalism, Revolution, and the Collapse of the Soviet Union* (Stanford, 1993), 77.
28. Suny, *Revenge of the Past*, 77.
29. There are some important exceptions: Theodore H. Friedgut, *Iuzovka and Revolution*, vol. 2, *Politics and Revolution in Russia's Donbass, 1869–1924* (Princeton, 1994); Hiroaki Kuromiya, *Freedom and Terror in the Donbas: A Ukrainian-Russian Borderland, 1870s–1990s* (Cambridge, 1998), Lars T. Lih, *Bread and Authority in Russia, 1914–1921* (Berkeley, 1990); Vladimir N. Brovkin, *Behind the Front Lines of the Civil War: Political Parties and Social Movements in Russia, 1918–1922* (Princeton, 1994); Vladimir Brovkin, ed., *The Bolsheviks in Russian Society: The Revolution and the Civil Wars* (New Haven, 1997); Peter Holquist, "A Russian Vendee: the Practice of Revolutionary Politics in the Don Countryside, 1917–1921" (PhD diss., Columbia University, 1995); idem, *Making War, Forging Revolution: Russia's Continuum of Crisis, 1914–1921* (Cambridge, Mass., 2002); Raleigh, *Experiencing Russia's Civil War*; Joshua A. Sanborn, *Drafting the Russian Nation: Military Conscription,*

Total War, and Mass Politics, 1905-1925 (Dekalb, Ill., 2003); and Aaron B. Retish, "Peasant Identities in Russia's Turmoil: Status, Gender, and Ethnicity in Viatka Province, 1914–1921," (PhD diss., Ohio State University, 2003).

30. M. V. Kurman and I. V. Lebedinskii, *Naselenie bol'shogo sotsialisticheskogo goroda* (Moscow, 1968), 17–18.
31. D. I. Bagalei and D. P. Miller, *Istoriia goroda Khar'kova za 250 let ego sushchestvovaniia (s 1655-go po 1905-i god)* (Kharkiv, 1905), 1:53–54.
32. *Pervaia Vseobshchaia Perepis' Naseleniia Rossiiskoi Imperii, 1897 g.*, vol. 47, *Khar'kovskaia guberniia* (Moscow, 1904), 1, 102. These figures probably underestimate the number of inhabitants of non-Russian nationality (*natsional'nost'*). Many native Ukrainian in-migrants felt forced to learn and interact in Russian in the city. Of the 173,100 census-registered inhabitants of Kharkiv in 1897, two-thirds gave their place of birth in predominantly Ukrainian provinces (Kharkiv: 96,000; Poltava: 5,000; Kyiv: 4,500; Katerynoslav: 2,500; and Podillia: 1,500). Kurman and Lebedinskii, *Naselenie bol'shogo sotsialisticheskogo goroda*, 122.
33. *Pervaia Vseobshchaia Perepis' Naseleniia Rossiiskoi Imperii, 1897 g.*, vol. 47, *Khar'kovskaia guberniia*, xiv.
34. *Pervaia Vseobshchaia Perepis' Naseleniia Rossiiskoi Imperii, 1897 g.*, vol. 47, *Khar'kovskaia guberniia*, 1, 102. Other nationalities populating the province included Jews (12,650 or 0.51 percent), Belarusians (10,258 or 0.41 percent), Germans (9,080 or 0.36 percent), and Poles (5,910 or 0.24 percent).
35. For example, in his otherwise quite informative article on the progress of the Stolypin reforms in Kharkiv province, V. S. Maistrenko agrees with the statement of the Kharkiv governor in 1909 that the province's peasants were "by their nature inclined toward individual forms of ownership," adding that "thanks to the correspondence of the Stolypin agrarian laws with the *internal convictions of Kharkiv province's native population* the success of the matter could be guaranteed." Emphasis added. V. S. Maistrenko, "Stolypins'ka ahrarna reforma na Kharkivshchyni ta ïï rezul'taty (1906–1915 rr.)," *Visnyk Kharkovs'koho derzhavnoho universytetu* 29, no. 396 (1997): 88. On the governor's report to the tsar, Maistrenko cites: Derzhavnyi arkhiv Kharkivs'koï oblasti [hereafter: DAKhO], f. 3, op. 285, spr. 7, ark. 6; also see V. S. Maistrenko, "Konfliktni sytuatsii v khodi provedennia stolypins'koï ahrarnoï reformy v Kharkivs'koi hubernii (1906–1915 rr.)," *Visnyk Kharkivs'koho derzhavnoho universytetu* 31, no. 441 (1999): 156–64.
36. Tsentral'nyi statisticheskii komitet MVD, *Statistika zemlevladeleniia 1905 g.*, vol. 33, *Khar'kovskaia guberniia* (St. Petersburg, 1906), 10–11.
37. The benefits peasants saw in the commune are well described in Judith Pallot, *Land Reform in Russia, 1906–1917: Peasant Responses to Stolypin's Project of Rural Transformation* (Oxford, 1999), 69–94, 104–5.

38. Tsentral′nyi statisticheskii komitet MVD, *Statistika zemlevladeniia 1905 g.*, 10–13.
39. M. P. Avdusheva et al., comp., *Khar′kov i Khar′kovskaia guberniia v pervoi russkoi revoliutsii 1905–1907 gg.: Sbornik dokumentov i materialov* (Kharkiv, 1955).
40. M. A. Siroshtan, et al., eds. *Istoriia mist i sil Ukraïns′koï RSR: Kharkivs′ka oblast′* (Kyiv, 1967), 19.
41. Scott J. Seregny, "Peasants and Politics: Peasant Unions during the 1905 Revolution," in *Peasant Economy, Culture, and Politics of European Russia, 1800–1921*, eds. E. Kingston-Mann and T. Mixter (Princeton, 1991), 351.
42. See Figes' somewhat exaggerated paraphrase of Seregny's more even-handed article in his *A People's Tragedy: A History of the Russian Revolution* (New York, 1996), 183.
43. Seregny, "Peasants and Politics," 356–57. Stressing that the union's leaders advocated mainly nonviolent means for peasants to achieve their demands, Seregny points out that "serious agrarian disorders began in Sumy only after the union was crushed" (ibid., 357).
44. Adrian Neil Jones, "The Peasants of Late Imperial Russia: Economy and Society in the Era of the Stolypin Reform" (PhD diss., Harvard University, 1988), 225–26.
45. On peasants' more covert yet stubborn forms of resistance to the Stolypin land reform's implementation, especially in the reform's earlier years, see Pallot, *Land Reform in Russia, 1906–1917*, 156–88; for peasants' more overt actions against the reform's implementation, see chapter 1.
46. P. N. Zyrianov, *Krest′ianskaia obshchina Evropeiskoi Rossii 1907–1914 gg.* (Moscow, 1992), 98. The average size of these consolidated farms was only 5.7 desiatynas, while the provincial average was 7.3 desiatynas.
47. Maistrenko, "Stolypins′ka ahrarna reforma na Kharkivshchyni," 92. Maistrenko confuses peasants' declarations of a desire to gain title to their strips *within* the commune with a desire to leave the commune.
48. For all of European Russia only about 20 percent of communal peasant households had by this time declared a desire to consolidate. Maistrenko, "Stolypins′ka ahrarna reforma na Kharkivshchyni," 92.
49. Pallot, *Land Reform in Russia, 1906–1917*, 106–7. Many of the households who petitioned to gain title to their plots had lost members since the last repartition and stood to lose in the next (ibid., 110–11).
50. Rossiiskii Gosudarstvennyi Istoricheskii Arkhiv, fond 408, 1909, opis 1, no. 113, 536, 225, and 22; as cited in Pallot, *Land Reform in Russia, 1906–1917*, 118.
51. Pallot, *Land Reform in Russia, 1906–1917*, 126, 171–72. Pallot stresses that many communes that declared for consolidation never intended to

implement it, but did so rather to delay the land reorganization committees' work.

Chapter 1

1. For in-depth discussions of the war's social impact in Western European countries, see Richard Wall and Jay Winter, eds., *The Upheaval of War: Family, Work and Welfare in Europe, 1914–1918* (Cambridge, 1988); John Horne, ed., *State, Society and Mobilization in Europe during the First World War* (Cambridge, 1997); Frans Coetzee and Marilyn Shevin-Coetzee, eds., *Authority, Identity and the Social History of the Great War* (Oxford, 1995). The path-breaking studies are Arthur Marwick, *The Deluge: British Society and the First World War* (London, 1965); and Jean Jacques Becker, *The Great War and the French People*, trans. Arnold Pomerans (Leamington Spa, 1985).
2. Until February 1918 Russia adhered to the Julian (Old Style) calendar, which ran thirteen days behind the Gregorian (New Style) calendar used in Western Europe. The Soviet government changed to the Gregorian calendar at midnight on 31 January 1918; the next day was 14 February 1918. In the first two chapters of this dissertation dates are in the Old Style, thereafter they are in the New Style. Where there is a possibility of confusion, I have given both.
3. Khar′kovskoe gubernskoe statisticheskoe biuro, *Vserossiiskaia sel′sko-khoziaistvennaia i gorodskaia perepis′ 1917 g. Khar′kovskaia gub. Itogi po uezdam, gubernii i gorodam. Predvaritel′nyi podschet* (Kharkiv, 1920), 2–3.
4. My calculations, based on Tsentral′noe statisticheskoe upravlenie [hereafter TsSU], *Rossiia v mirovoi voine, 1914–1918 goda (v tsifrakh)* (Moscow, 1925), 22; and Khar′kovskoe gubernskoe statisticheskoe biuro, *Vserossiiskaia sel′sko-khoziaistvennaia i gorodskaia perepis′ 1917 g. Khar′kovskaia gub.*, 2–3.
5. P. F. Reshod′ko, *Selians′kyi rukh u Kharkivs′kii hubernii (berezen′ 1917–sichen′ 1918 r.)* (Kharkiv, 1972), 12; cites: *Pogubernskie itogi Vserossiiskoi sel′skokhoziaistvennoi i pozemel′noi perepisi 1917 goda po 52 guberniiam i oblastiam*, vol. 5, pt. 1 (Moscow, 1921), 34–35.
6. Khar′kovskoe gubernskoe statisticheskoe biuro, *Vserossiiskaia sel′sko-khoziaistvennaia i gorodskaia perepis′ 1917 g. Khar′kovskaia gub.*, 2–3. This figure includes both those households without any adult male family members and without any other unrelated adult male workers. According to an earlier summary of the 1917 agricultural census results, there were 174,600 households (37.7 percent) with no male workers. For twenty-nine provinces and six oblasts of the empire, the overall figure was lower: 27.7 percent of all peasant households had no male workers. Tsentral′noe statisticheskoe upravlenie, *Predvaritel′nye pogubernskie itogi vserossiiskoi*

sel′sko-khoziaistvennoi i pozemel′noi perepisi 1917 g. po 29 guberniiam i 6 oblastiam (Moscow, 1919), 35, 42–43.

7. P. Bilyk, "Volneniia v Khar′kovskoi gubernii v gody imperialisticheskoi voiny," *Krasnyi arkhiv* 76 (1936): 17. For other examples of peasants' complaints about unfair mobilization practices, see Josh Sanborn, "The Mobilization of 1914 and the Question of the Russian Nation: A Reexamination," *Slavic Review* 59 (Summer 2000): 278–79, 288–89.
8. TsSU, *Rossiia v mirovoi voine, 1914–1918 goda (v tsifrakh)*, 22.
9. A. M. Anfimov, "Krest′ianskoe khoziaistvo Rossii v gody pervoi mirovoi voiny," *Istoriia SSSR*, no. 3 (July–August 1957): 63.
10. Khar′kovskaia gubernskaia zemskaia uprava, *Vserossiiskaia sel′sko-khoziaistvennaia perepis′ za 1916 god: Naselenie, skot i posevy itogo po uezdam (Predvaritel′nyi podschet′)* (Kharkiv, 1916), found in DAKhO, f. 304, op. 1, spr. 2065, ark. 2–4.
11. Khar′kovskoe gubernskoe statisticheskoe biuro, *Vserossiiskaia sel′sko-khoziaistvennaia i gorodskaia perepis′ 1917 g. Khar′kovskaia gub.*, 8–9. For comparative statistics see Anfimov, "Krest′ianskoe khoziaistvo Rossii," 63. Anfimov provides comparative data for thirteen provinces, including Kharkiv, with prewar statistics from censuses completed between 1909 and 1913 and a total for all of them.
12. Rossiiskii gosudarstvennyi voennyi arkhiv [hereafter RGVA], f. 2000, op. 111, d. 2433, l. 155v; cited in Anfimov, "Krest′ianskoe khoziaistvo Rossii," 61–62.
13. RGVA, f. 2000, op. 111, d. 2433, l. 152; cited in Anfimov, "Krest′ianskoe khoziaistvo Rossii," 62; Anfimov also cites another example: ibid., d. 2509, l. 23.
14. RGVA, f. 2000, op. 111, d. 2507, l. 332; cited in Anfimov, "Krest′ianskoe khoziaistvo Rossii," 62.
15. Published in: A. L. Sidorov, ed., *Ekonomicheskoe polozhenie Rossii nakanune velikoi oktiabr′skoi sotsialisticheskoi revoliutsii: Dokumenty i materialy*, vol. 3, *Sel′skoe khoziaistvo i krest′ianstvo* (Leningrad, 1967), doc. 46, 102–3, and fn. 1, 464.
16. *Obzor Khar′kovskoi gubernii za 1914 g.* (Kharkiv, 1915), 6. Unfortunately, this source does not give breakdowns by *soslovie* or size of farm and includes animals owned by urban inhabitants as well, though the latter group owned no more than seven percent of any type of livestock in 1914 (ibid., 5); 1916 data is from: *Vserossiiskaia sel′sko-khoziaistvennaia perepis′ za 1916 god*; and St. Zhilkin, *Ukraina v tsifrakh, 1913–1920 gg.* (Kharkiv, 1922), 25; 1917 figures are from: Khar′kovskoe gubernskoe statisticheskoe biuro, *Vserossiiskaia sel′skokhoziaistvennaia i gorodskaia perepis′ 1917 g. Khar′kovskaia gub.*, 8–9.
17. Khar′kovskoe gubernskoe statisticheskoe biuro, *Vserossiiskaia sel′sko-khoziaistvennaia i gorodskaia perepis′ 1917 g. Khar′kovskaia gub.*, 8–9.

18. Anfimov, "Krest´ianskoe khoziaistvo Rossii," 65.
19. TsSU, *Predvaritel´nye pogubernskie itogi vserossiiskoi sel´sko-khoziaistvennoi i pozemel´noi perepisi 1917 g. po 29 guberniiam i 6 oblastiam*, 35.
20. The figures for 1913 are calculated from: Khar´kovskaia gubernskaia zemskaia uprava, *Sel´skoe khoziaistvo, fabrichnaia promyshlennost´ i zaniatiia naseleniia Khar´kovskoi gubernii* (Kharkiv, 1917), 4; for 1917 they are based on Khar´kovskoe gubernskoe statisticheskoe biuro, *Vserossiiskaia sel´skokhoziaistvennaia i gorodskaia perepis´ 1917 g. Khar´kovskaia gub.*, 12–13.
21. My calculation, based on Khar´kovskoe gubernskoe statisticheskoe biuro, *Vserossiiskaia sel´skokhoziaistvennaia i gorodskaia perepis´ 1917 g. Khar´kovskaia gub.*, 2–3. See also M. P. Avdusheva et al., comp., *Krest´ianskoe dvizhenie v Poltavskoi i Khar´kovskoi guberniiakh v 1902 g.: Sbornik dokumentov* (Kharkiv, 1961), vii. Based on data gathered in the summer of 1917 in neighboring Poltava province, zemstvo economists calculated that even households farming 3–6 desiatynas were losing on average 118 rubles per year. M. A. Iakymenko, "Zemel´na orenda na Ukraïni v period kapitalizmu," *Ukraïns´kyi istorychnyi zhurnal* (1991), no. 2, 62; cites: Poltavskoe gubernskoe zemstvo, Statisticheskoe biuro, *Statisticheskii spravochnik po Poltavskoi gubernii na 1917 g.* (Poltava, 1917), 210, 212.
22. Statistics calculated from Khar´kovskii kreditnyi soiuz´ kooperativov, Statisticheskoe biuro, *Promysly i zaniatiia zemledel´cheskago naseleniia Khar´kovskoi gubernii* (Kharkiv, 1919), 29, 85–87; and Khar´kovskoe gubernskoe statisticheskoe biuro, *Vserossiiskaia sel´skokhoziaistvennaia i gorodskaia perepis´ 1917 g. Khar´kovskaia gub.*, 2–3, 12–13.
23. Sidorov, *Ekonomicheskoe polozhenie Rossii nakanune velikoi oktiabr´skoi sotsialisticheskoi revoliutsii*, table no. 71, between pp. 158 and 159.
24. S. G. Wheatcroft and R. W. Davies, "Agriculture," in *The Economic Transformation of the Soviet Union, 1913–1945*, eds. R. W. Davies, Mark Harrison, and S. G. Wheatcroft (Cambridge, 1994), 108.
25. N. D. Kondrat´ev, *Rynok khlebov i ego regulirovanie vo vremia voiny i revoliutsii* (Moscow, 1991), 122, table 19. Also see Alessandro Stanziani, "Spécialistes, bureaucrates et paysans les approvisionnements agricoles pendant la premiere guerre mondiale 1914–1917," *Cahiers du Monde russe* 36, nos. 1–2 (1995): 86.
26. TsSU, *Predvaritel´nye pogubernskie itogi vserossiiskoi sel´sko-khoziaistvennoi i pozemel´noi perepisi 1917 g. po 29 guberniiam i 6 oblastiam*, 39.
27. Compared to 1913, the sown area in 1916 had decreased by 8.5 percent from 1,499,100 desiatynas to 1,371,300 desiatynas. See Anfimov, "Krest´ianskoe khoziaistvo Rossii," 68. According to Kondrat´ev, on average between 1909 and 1911 Kharkiv province exported 31,872,500 poods of grain beyond its

borders, 22,521,300 poods (70.7 percent) of which was purchased within Russia by consuming provinces, the rest being exported to foreign markets. Kondrat′ev, *Rynok khlebov i ego regulirovanie vo vremia voiny i revoliutsii*, 106.

28. Compiled from a rough draft of the zemstvo's report based on the peasant correspondents' responses; contained in: DAKhO, f. 304, op. 1, spr. 2065, ark. 27–33.
29. DAKhO, f. 304, op. 1, spr. 2065, ark. 27–33. These were, of course, the result of the Stolypin reforms began in 1907.
30. Land rent rates decreased substantially during the war, largely as a result of the lack of work hands. See DAKhO, f. 304, op. 1, spr. 2058, ark. 6–7.
31. DAKhO, f. 304, op. 1, spr. 2065, ark. 28–33.
32. DAKhO, f. 304, op. 1, spr. 2065, ark. 10.
33. Judith Pallot, "Khutora and Otruba in Stolypin's Program of Farm Individualization," *Slavic Review* 43 (Summer 1984): 242–56. For a fuller discussion of the whole interdepartmental struggle over the reform see George L. Yaney, *The Urge to Mobilize: Agrarian Reform in Russia, 1861–1930* (Urbana, Ill., 1982). The most reliable and widely accepted Soviet view is S. M. Dubrovskii, *Stolypinskaia zemel′naia reforma: Iz istorii sel′skogo khoziaistva i krest′ianstva Rossii v nachale XX veka* (Moscow, 1963).
34. DAKhO, f. 304, op. 1, spr. 2065, ark. 29. Emphasis added. As Judith Pallot has pointed out, the very fact that even those who separated from the commune referred to themselves as a collectivity ("among us") suggests "the continuing relevance of collective action" among peasants. Pallot, *Land Reform in Russia, 1906–1917*, 166.
35. DAKhO, f. 304, op. 1, spr. 2065, ark. 31–32; also see ark. 32–33 for other claims that *otrubshchiki*'s farms were prospering, while communal farms, those stuck in their "old ways," were being ruined.
36. Kimitaka Matsuzato, "Stolypinskaia reforma i russkii agrotekhnologicheskii perevorot," *Acta Slavica Iaponica* 10 (1992): 39; the quotation is taken from A. N. Minin's report to the First All-Russian Agricultural Congress: *Trudy pervogo Vserossiiskogo sel′sko-khoziaistvennogo s″ezda v Kieve 1–10 sentiabria 1913 goda*, pt. 2 (Kyiv, 1913–1914), 131.
37. For examples, see Richard Pipes, *The Russian Revolution* (New York, 1990), 236–37; Figes, *People's Tragedy*, 298–99; A. N. Antsiferov et al., eds., *Russian Agriculture during the War* (New Haven, 1930), 140 and 151–52. A more nuanced account is provided in John Keep's *The Russian Revolution: A Study in Mass Mobilization* (New York, 1976), 28–41. The classic Soviet example is A. M. Anfimov, *Rossiiskaia derevnia v gody pervoi mirovoi voiny* (Moscow, 1962).
38. On Marx's definition of class and class struggle, see Tom Bottomore, ed., *A Dictionary of Marxist Thought* (Oxford, 1983), 74–81.

39. The Great War's tremendous impact on gender roles in the West European context has been quite thoroughly researched and substantiated; see Margaret Higonnet and Jane Jenson, eds., *Behind the Lines: Gender and the Two World Wars* (New Haven, 1987); Margaret Higonnet, ed., *Lines of Fire: Women's Vision of World War I* (New York, 1999); Ruth Harris, "The Child of the Barbarian: Rape, Race and Nationalism in France during the First World War," *Past and Present*, no. 141 (1993): 170–206; Philippa Levine, "Walking the Streets in a Way No Decent Woman Should: Women Police in World War One," *Journal of Modern History* 66 (1994): 34–78; Susan K. Kent, *Making Peace: the Reconstruction of Gender in Interwar Britain* (Princeton, 1993); Ute Frevert, *Women in German History: From Bourgeois Emancipation to Sexual Liberation*, trans. Stuart McKinnon-Evans (Oxford, 1989); Mary-Louise Roberts, *Civilization Without Sexes: Reconstructing Gender in Postwar France, 1917–1927* (Chicago, 1994). For a promising beginning in the Russian context, see Barbara Alpern Engel, "Not by Bread Alone: Subsistence Riots in Russia during World War I," *Journal of Modern History* 69 (December 1997): 696–721.
40. Alan K. Wildman, *The End of the Russian Imperial Army: The Old Army and the Soldiers' Revolt (March–April 1917)* (Princeton, 1980), 89, 107–10, 113–20.
41. See, for example, the report of the deputy chief of the provincial gendarme administration, Lieutenant Colonel Levanevskii: Tsentral′nyi derzhavnyi istorychnyi arkhiv Ukraïny u m. Kyievi [hereafter TsDIA], f. 336, op. 2, spr. 124, ark. 2v.
42. Beatrice Farnsworth, "The Soldatka: Folklore and Court Record," *Slavic Review* 49 (spring 1990): 58–73.
43. Richard Stites, *The Women's Liberation Movement in Russia: Feminism, Nihilism, and Bolshevism, 1860–1930* (Princeton, 1978), 223.
44. Rose L. Glickman, "The Russian Factory Woman, 1880–1914," in *Women in Russia*, eds. Dorothy Atkinson, Alexander Dallin, and Gail Warshofsky Lapidus (Stanford, 1977), 82–83.
45. DAKhO, f. 3, op. 287, spr. 4707, ark. 1 and 4v. For a report on the conditions in which the soldatki left the surveyor's apartment and office, see ibid., ark. 6.
46. DAKhO, f. 3, op. 287, spr. 4707, ark. 1v. The exact date on this document has been torn off, but it is probably the same date as the arrest decree (ibid., ark. 2), which states that on 28 July 1914 these four "main instigators" were arrested under article 21 of the rules of Extraordinary Safeguard. According to ark. 15, by the governor's decree of 4 August 1914 (no. 13269) Molchanov, Vinnik, and Pugach were sentenced to sixty days each from 28 July to 26 September 1914.
47. DAKhO, f. 3, op. 287, spr. 4709, ark. 3. According to Judith Pallot, the quite common protest action of removing the surveyor's boundary markers was

largely a symbolic act, intended to restore peasants' sense of community and express their desire to keep the commune together. Pallot, *Land Reform in Russia, 1906–1917*, 181.

48. DAKhO, f. 3, op. 287, spr. 4709, ark. 1 v.
49. The village starosta was the leader of a village community, usually elected by the village assembly of male heads of households.
50. DAKhO, f. 3, op. 287, spr. 4709, ark. 10. On peasants' use of the village gathering to delay the land reform's implementation, see Pallot, *Land Reform in Russia, 1906–1917*, 171–80.
51. DAKhO, f. 3, op. 287, spr. 4709, ark. 6v. The fact that she had no children was mentioned repeatedly in the police protocol.
52. DAKhO, f. 3, op. 287, spr. 4709, ark. 1–2. The governor's final decision was to give Ignatenko ninety days under arrest, and Lavrenkova and another sixty days. He did not explain why Ignatenko received the harsher sentence, but Lavrenkova's gender may have played a role. DAKhO, f. 3, op. 287, spr. 4709, ark. 12.
53. DAKhO, f. 3, op. 287, spr. 4710, ark. 1v.
54. DAKhO, f. 3, op. 287, spr. 4710, ark. 6–7.
55. DAKhO, f. 3, op. 287, spr. 4710, ark. 12.
56. DAKhO, f. 3, op. 287, spr. 4710, ark. 15 and 18.
57. For other similar actions against the Stolypin reforms, see DAKhO, f. 3, op. 287, spr. 4704, 4709, 4710, 4485, 4725, 4772, 4796, 4827, 4833, 4900, 5100, 5106, 5148, 5194; and TsDIA, f. 336, op. 2, spr. 141.
58. See B. D. Hrinchenko, *Slovar′ ukrainskago iazyka*, vol. 1 (Kyiv, 1907), 342.
59. DAKhO, f. 3, op. 287, spr. 5038, ark. 8.
60. This account was taken from a report by the regional gendarme chief, Captain Mkurnali, to the provincial gendarme chief, Rykovskii: TsDIA, f. 336, op. 2, spr. 141, ark. 23v; the report includes ibid., ark. 22–23; and see DAKhO, f. 3, op. 2, spr. 5038, ark. 8. For a slightly different version of events, which downplays Masal′skii's role, see Rykovskii's paraphrase of Mkurnali's report: TsDIA, f. 336, op. 2, spr. 141, ark. 29.
61. Pallot, *Land Reform in Russia, 1906–1917*, 160.
62. TsDIA, f. 336, op. 2, spr. 141, ark. 45.
63. TsDIA, f. 336, op. 2, spr. 141, ark. 45v.
64. DAKhO, f. 3, op. 287, spr. 5038, ark. 10.
65. TsDIA, f. 336, op. 2, spr. 124, ark. 21v; the quotation is from ark. 23.
66. TsDIA, f. 336, op. 2, spr. 124, ark. 2. The real reason that Katerinich left his post is unknown. The next governor, Nikolai Vasil′evich Protas′ev, was appointed on 8 June 1915: S. I. Posokhov and A. N. Iarmysh, *Gubernatory i general-gubernatory* (Kharkiv, 1997), 96.
67. "Priostanovka vydelov na otruba," *Iuzhnyi krai*, no. 12693, 8 May 1915.

68. See DAKhO, f. 3, op. 287, spr. 5212; and TsDIA, f. 336, op. 2, spr. 142, ark. 63–65.
69. One might note here that no study of the Stolypin land reform to date has paid attention to the bold and open actions of the soldatki against the reforms during the war, or to the crucial role they seem to have played in the reform's cessation. Even Judith Pallot's otherwise thorough and sophisticated study of peasants' responses to the reform makes no mention of the soldatki or these disturbances, though her study goes up to 1917; she does not even mention Krivoshein's May 1915 announcement. Pallot, *Land Reform in Russia, 1906–1917*, especially 180–88.
70. According to the Kharkiv provincial zemstvo's statistics, between February 1915 and February 1917 prices rose as follows: a pood of rye from 100 kop. to 205 kop.; wheat from 117 kop. per pood to 272 kop. per pood; potatoes, from 30 to 101 kop.; eggs from 22 kop. for ten to 106 kop.; chickens from 53 kop. each to 235 kop. V. Kachinskii, "Krest′ianskoe dvizhenie," in *1917 god v Khar′kove: Sbornik statei i vospominanii*, eds. V. Morgunov and Z. Manul′skaia (Kharkiv, 1927), 181.
71. See the path-breaking study of E. P. Thompson, "The Moral Economy of the English Crowd in the Eighteenth Century," *Past and Present*, no. 50 (February 1971): 76–136.
72. TsDIA, f. 336, op. 2, spr. 193, ark. 56.
73. See TsDIA, f. 336, op. 2, spr. 193, ark. 56–57 for the fullest report.
74. TsDIA, f. 336, op. 2, spr. 193, ark. 70.
75. TsDIA, f. 336, op. 2, spr. 193, ark. 71.
76. Lih, *Bread and Authority in Russia, 1914–1921*, 20.
77. Kondrat′ev, *Rynok khlebov i ego regulirovanie vo vremia voiny i revoliutsii*, 235. According to a report by the Economic Department of the Union of Cities, of the 250 cities for which data was available, 228 (from 67 different provinces) complained of inflation and had taken measures against it (usually by imposing tariffs). Vserossiiskii Soiuz Gorodov, *Anketa o dorogovizne 1915 g.* (Moscow, 1915), 12–13.
78. TsDIA, f. 336, op. 2, spr. 124, ark. 68v.
79. Vserossiiskii Soiuz Gorodov, *Anketa o dorogovizne 1915 g.*, 154; and Kondrat′ev, *Rynok khlebov i ego regulirovanie vo vremia voiny i revoliutsii*, 236–38.
80. TsDIA, f. 336, op. 2, spr. 193, ark. 63 and 66–67.
81. TsDIA, f. 336, op. 2, spr. 193, ark. 72.
82. A. M. Anfimov, ed., *Krest′ianskoe dvizhenie v Rossii v gody pervoi mirovoi voiny (iiul′ 1914 g.–fevral′ 1917 g.): Sbornik dokumentov* (Moscow and Leningrad, 1965), doc. 239, 404.
83. TsDIA, f. 336, op. 2, spr. 193, ark. 87.

84. See Kondrat′ev, *Rynok khlebov i ego regulirovanie vo vremia voiny i revoliutsii*, 241–43.
85. Most of this data comes from the files of the Kharkiv governor's "sekretnyi stol"; DAKhO, f. 3, op. 287, cross-checked with gendarme and police reports. One Soviet historian claims that there were more peasant disturbances in Kharkiv province during the war, and that they included more participants and were of greater severity, than in any other Ukrainian province. A. P. Korotenko, "Revoliutsionnaia rabota bol′shevikov Khar′kovshchiny v period pervoi mirovoi imperialisticheskoi voiny," *Sbornik nauchnykh rabot kafedr obshchestvennykh nauk vuzov g. Khar′kova*, pt. 1 (1956): 99.
86. See DAKhO, f. 3, op. 287, vol. 4, 1917. In all my research on the World War I period I have not found a single incident of peasants' collective action concerning which there was not a file in the governor's "sekretnyi stol" collection. It is also unlikely that such files were lost, since those on workers and students striking in the city of Kharkiv in January and February 1917 are well preserved.
87. A. T. Vasil′ev, "Svodka direktora departamenta politsii po tsirkuliarnoi telegramme tov. Ministra vnutrennikh del ob obshchestvennom nastroenii," in *Burzhuaziia nakanune fevral′skoi revoliutsii*, ed. B. B. Grave (Moscow-Leningrad, 1927), 137; originally cited in Pipes, *Russian Revolution*, 237. In his introduction, Vasil′ev stressed the great similarities among the reports from regions across the empire (136).
88. Sarah Badcock well describes the causes of women's absence from political positions in 1917 in Kazan and Nizhegorod provinces. Badcock, *Politics and the People in Revolutionary Russia*, chapter 4.
89. On the post–World War I return of soldiers to the factories and fields, forcing many women back into the private sphere, see note 39 above.
90. Thompson, "Moral Economy of the English Crowd in the Eighteenth Century," 122.
91. Holquist, *Making War, Forging Revolution*, 45.
92. TsDIA, f. 336, op. 2, spr. 124, ark. 2v. and 11.
93. TsDIA, f. 336, op. 2, spr. 124, ark. 2v. For other examples of soldiers' letters from Kharkiv province, see O. A. Chaadaeva, comp., "Soldatskie pis′ma v gody mirovoi voiny (1915–1917 gg.)," *Krasnyi arkhiv* 65–66 (1934): 125, 127, 130, 135, 138, 144–45, 159.
94. TsDIA, f. 336, op. 2, spr. 124, ark. 60.

Chapter 2

1. On 5 March 1917 the Provisional Government dispatched a circular that removed all governors, replacing them with the chairmen of provincial zemstvos, now called "provincial commissars of the Provisional Government." Holquist, *Making War, Forging Revolution*, 55.

2. V. Kachinskii, "Krest′ianskoe dvizhenie," 197. Kachyns′kyi was an SR at the time of the February Revolution and was the first elected chairman of the Kharkiv Soviet of Peasants' Deputies. In March 1919, Kachyns′kyi became a leading member of the Ukrainian Party of Left-SRs (Borot′bists). Unfortunately, such telegrams are completely absent from the archives, and we can only rely on Kachyns′kyi's account for much of the earliest period of the revolution in the village.
3. *Zemlia i volia*, 18 March 1917; cited in Kachinskii, "Krest′ianskoe dvizhenie," 194.
4. *Zemlia i volia*, 20 June 1917; cited in Kachinskii, "Krest′ianskoe dvizhenie," 202.
5. Tsentral′nyi derzhavnyi arkhiv vyshchykh orhaniv vlady ta upravlinnia Ukraïny [hereafter TsDAVO], f. 1327, op. 1, spr. 52, ark. 56.
6. TsDAVO, f. 1327, op. 1, spr. 52, ark. 71.
7. TsDAVO, f. 1327, op. 1, spr. 52, ark. 85.
8. *Izvestiia Khar′kovskago Soveta rabochikh deputatov*, no. 1, 4 March 1917, p. 1. This newspaper was later renamed *Izvestiia Iuga*.
9. *Izvestiia Khar′kovskago Soveta rabochikh deputatov*, no. 36, 15 April 1917, p. 2.
10. *Slobozhanets* refers to a person from Slobids′ka Ukraïna, which was in the seventeenth century a frontier zone of the Russian Empire. Peasants and Cossacks were encouraged to settle in the region to help defend the empire against incursions by the Crimean and Nogai Tatars. The name derives from the word *sloboda*, a Slavic word for "freedom" or "liberty."
11. *Robitnycha hazeta*, no. 33, 11 May 1917, p. 1.
12. *Iuzhnyi krai*, no. 13959, 9 May 1917, p. 2.
13. TsDAVO, f. 1400, op. 1, spr. 1, ark. 1a. This document is a broadside announcing the congress's resolutions, printed in parallel columns with Ukrainian on the left and Russian on the right. At the top there is a brief chart explaining how to read Ukrainian, which suggests that the authors assumed that many readers only read Russian.
14. Khrystiuk, *Zamitky i materiialy do istorii ukrainskoi revoliutsii,* 1:36–41. The program of the All-Ukrainian National Congress (6–8 April) did not even mention the land question. See I. V. Khmil′, "Na shliakhu vidrodzhennia ukraïnskoï derzhavnosti (Ukraïns′kyi natsional′nyi konhres-z'ïzd 6–8 kvitnia 1917 r.)," *Istorychni zoshyty* (Kyiv, 1994): 6–7.
15. *Robitnycha hazeta*, no. 36, 16 May 1917, p. 2.
16. Ibid. I should stress the certainty of the last sentence, the verb in its perfective form: "*Zdobudemo zemliu i voliu!*"
17. *Robitnycha hazeta*, no. 36, 16 May 1917, p. 2.
18. TsDAVO, f. 1400, op. 1, spr. 1, ark. 1a.
19. Ibid.

20. On 25 March 1917 the Provisional Government replaced its tsarist predecessor's wartime grain levy system, from which some peasants and landlords had profited, with a state monopoly on grain surpluses. All grain was supposed to be turned over to the state (at prices set by the state), excepting a minimum left to grain producers. See *Sobranie uzakonenii i rasporiazhenii Pravitelstva, izdavaemoe pri Pravitelstvuiushchem Senate* (St. Petersburg, 1917), otd. 1, 487; and *Vestnik Vremennogo pravitelstva*, 30 March 1917; cited in V. A. Vakhromeev, "Sovety i prodovol′stvennyi vopros v 1917 g. (mart–oktiabr′)," *Istoricheskie zapiski* 116 (1988): 8.
21. *Izvestiia Khar′kovskogo Soveta rabochikh i soldatskikh deputatov,* no. 52, 6 May 1917, p. 2. "Aronov" thought these speeches "extraordinarily characteristic" of the peasantry's attitude toward the monopoly.
22. TsDAVO, f. 1400, op. 1, spr. 1, ark. 1a.
23. *Izvestiia Khar′kovskogo Soveta rabochikh i soldatskikh deputatov,* no. 54, 9 May 1917, p. 4.
24. For a good general overview of the All-Russian peasant revolution of 1917–18, see Channon, "Peasantry in the Revolutions of 1917," 105–30. For a somewhat outdated but still useful discussion of the Ukrainian context, see Vsevolod Holubnychy, "The 1917 Agrarian Revolution in Ukraine," in *Soviet Regional Economics: Selected Works of Vsevolod Holubnychy*, ed. Iwan S. Koropeckyj (Edmonton, 1982), 3–65.
25. Figes, *Peasant Russia, Civil War*, 47.
26. I. I. Mints, *Istoriia Velikogo Oktiabria*, vol. 2 (Moscow, 1967–1972), 838, 1125, 1122–23; A. D. Maliavskii, *Krest′ianskoe dvizhenie v Rossii v 1917 g., mart–oktiabr′* (Moscow, 1981), 378, 376.
27. TsDAVO, f. 1326, op. 1, spr. 11, ark. 100.
28. Reshod′ko, *Selians′kyi rukh u Kharkivs′kii hubernii̇ (berezen′ 1917–sichen′ 1918 r.)*, 99; my calculations based on ibid., 54–57, 68–73.
29. TsDAVO, f. 1326, op. 1, spr. 25, ark. 193–94, 201.
30. TsDAVO, f. 1326, op. 1, spr. 25, ark. 202.
31. TsDAVO, f. 1326, op. 1, spr. 25, ark. 193–94.
32. TsDAVO, f. 1326, op. 1, spr. 25, ark. 192.
33. TsDAVO, f. 1326, op. 1, spr. 25, ark. 195; capitalization as in the original.
34. V. I. Kostrikin, *Zemelnye komitety v 1917 godu* (Moscow, 1975), 101. The rent was to be paid to the land's owner.
35. See TsDAVO, f. 1400, op. 1, spr. 1, ark. 41.
36. TsDAVO, f. 1326, op. 1, spr. 25, ark. 197–200.
37. TsDAVO, f. 1326, op. 1, spr. 27, ark. 52–53. For the provincial authorities' repeated appeals to peasants to sow all the land, see ibid., ark. 56, 73, and especially ark. 75–76.
38. TsDAVO, f. 1326, op. 1, spr. 25, ark. 201.
39. TsDAVO, f. 1326, op. 1, spr. 25, ark. 208.

40. *Ukraïns′ka Tsentral′na Rada: Dokumenty i materialy*, 2 vols. (Kyiv, 1996–1997), vol. 1, doc. 187, p. 400.
41. TsDAVO, f. 1326, op. 1, spr. 25, ark. 214.
42. TsDAVO, f. 1326, op. 1, spr. 25, ark. 216. It is interesting that the provincial land administration continued to cite the Third Universal, though by this time forces loyal to the Bolsheviks' Sovnarkom in Petrograd were in firm control of Kharkiv.
43. TsDAVO, f. 1326, op. 1, spr. 90, ark. 143.
44. TsDAVO, f. 1326, op. 1, spr. 90, ark. 145.
45. TsDAVO, f. 1327, op. 1, spr. 53, ark. 126.
46. TsDAVO, f. 1327, op. 1, spr. 53, ark. 124.
47. TsDAVO, f. 1326, op. 1, spr. 90, ark. 118.
48. TsDAVO, f. 1326, op. 1, spr. 90, ark. 119.
49. TsDAVO, f. 1326, op. 1, spr. 90, ark. 120.
50. TsDAVO, f. 1326, op. 1, spr. 90, ark. 127.
51. TsDAVO, f. 1326, op. 1, spr. 90, ark. 132; also see ark. 121, 127, and 131.
52. The characterization of these peasants' actions as "class struggle" has proved surprisingly persistent. See, for example, I. V. Khmil′, *Ahrarna revoliutsiia v Ukraïni: berezen′ 1917 r.–kviten′ 1918 rr.* (Kyiv, 2000), 45: "The agrarian movement in Ukraine was accompanied by severe class struggle."
53. V. Holubnychy calculated that, even if all 42 million desiatynas of arable land in Ukraine were distributed equally among all 4,011,000 peasant households, the average household would have gained only 1.49 desiatynas and would have remained "merely a subsistence farm." Holubnychy, "The 1917 Agrarian Revolution in Ukraine," 4–5.
54. See, for example, TsDAVO, f. 1326, op. 1, spr. 90, ark. 154.
55. Maureen Perrie, "Folklore as Evidence of Peasant Mentalité: Social Attitudes and Values in Russian Popular Culture," *Russian Review* 48, no. 2 (1989): 124–28.
56. *Izvestiia Khar′kovskago Soveta rabochikh i soldatskikh deputatov*, no. 22, 29 March 1917, p. 3; no. 27, 5 April 1917, p. 5; also see TsDAVO, f. 1326, op. 1, spr. 90, ark. 37–42; and TsDAVO, f. 1400, op. 1, spr. 1, ark. 90.
57. TsDAVO, f. 1326, op. 1, spr. 90, ark. 147–51; for other petitions by *otrubshchiki*, see ibid., ark. 37–42, 190–96, 374–75, 434–35.
58. V. Kachinskii, *Ocherki agrarnoi revoliutsii na Ukraine: Uravnitel′nyi razdel zemli* (Kharkiv, 1922), 54–56. Kachinskii notes that because of the German occupation and civil war, a small number of *otruba* and *khutora* remained in Ukraine until 1920, when their "final liquidation was completed" (55).
59. TsDAVO, f. 1326, op. 1, spr. 90, ark. 30.
60. TsDAVO, f. 1326, op. 1, spr. 90, ark. 31.
61. TsDAVO, f. 1326, op. 1, spr. 90, ark. 124.
62. TsDAVO, f. 1326, op. 1, spr. 90, ark. 125. For more on the land committee's

powerlessness, see Kachinskii, "Krest′ianskoe dvizhenie," 219; Reshod′ko, *Selians′kyi rukh u Kharkivs′kii hubernii̋*, 103; and TsDAVO, f. 1326, op. 1, spr. 11, ark. 67.

63. TsDAVO, f. 1326, op. 1, spr. 25, ark. 20.
64. TsDAVO, f. 1326, op. 1, spr. 25, ark. 19.
65. TsDAVO, f. 1326, op. 1, spr. 25, ark. 171.
66. TsDAVO, f. 1326, op. 1, spr. 25, ark. 174. This is the receipt given to Maslivka's representatives on 10 August, certifying that they had paid the military commissar 2,600 rubles in rent for those 520 desiatynas of state land.
67. TsDAVO, f. 1326, op. 1, spr. 25, ark. 171. The committee also noted that some of Maslivka's peasants had already plowed and sown the land seized by Tahanka's peasants, as a result of which they were left not only without land, but without any winter seed.
68. TsDAVO, f. 1326, op. 1, spr. 25, ark. 177.
69. For more examples of intervillage conflict, see TsDAVO, f. 1326, op. 1, spr. 25, ark. 19–26, 61–66, 71, 80, 183–84; f. 1326, op. 1, spr. 52 and 90 in passim.
70. Figes, *People's Tragedy*, 364.
71. Vakhromeev, "Sovety i prodovol′stvennyi vopros v 1917 g.," 5–42. On the old regime's failure to solve the food supply problem, see especially: Kimitaka Matsuzato, "The Role of Zemstva in the Creation and Collapse of Tsarism's War Effort During World War One," *Jahrbücher für Geschichte Osteuropas* 46, no. 3 (1998): 321–37; and idem, "Inter-Regional Conflicts and the Collapse of Tsarism: The Real Reason for the Food Crisis in Russia after the Autumn of 1916," in *Emerging Democracy in Late Imperial Russia*, ed. Mary Schaeffer Conroy (Niwot, Colo., 1998), 243–300.
72. In Kharkiv province the government-set prices, even after Kerenskii doubled them on 27 August 1917, remained far below the local market price. Kondrat′ev, *Rynok khlebov i ego regulirovanie vo vremia voiny i revoliutsii*, 400–407.
73. Holquist, *Making War, Forging Revolution*, p. 97.
74. For the empire as a whole, grain deliveries to the army and civilian population decreased steadily from July to October 1917 from 50 to 19 percent of grain orders. Vakhromeev, "Sovety i prodovol′stvennyi vopros v 1917 g.," 32–33. In late August 1917 Kerenskii assented to doubling the fixed prices on grain, but this did little to increase grain deliveries. Holquist, *Making War, Forging Revolution*, 103–4.
75. *Nova hromada*, no. 18, 2 [15] December 1917, 1.
76. TsDAVO, f. 1400, op. 1, spr. 1, ark. 217 and 215v.
77. TsDAVO, f. 1400, op. 1, spr. 1, ark. 216v. Rubinsky was no doubt speaking here through a very class-conscious understanding of the revolution. He provided no evidence that "kulaks" in particular were hiding grain, and I have not found any in my research.

78. TsDAVO, f. 1400, op. 1, spr. 1, ark. 216–17.
79. TsDAVO, f. 1400, op. 1, spr. 1, ark. 216.
80. TsDAVO, f. 1400, op. 1, spr. 1, ark. 215.
81. TsDAVO, f. 1400, op. 1, spr. 1, ark. 263–64. Compared to 1913, the sown area in 1916 had decreased by 8.5 percent from 1,499,100 desiatynas to 1,371,300 desiatynas. This was not a substantial decrease—certainly not enough to account for the food supply committee's failure to receive grain. See Anfimov, "Krest´ianskoe khoziaistvo Rossii," 68.
82. TsDAVO, f. 1400, op. 1, spr. 1, ark. 262v and 263.
83. The main distinction Ukrainian Central Rada supporters stressed was that their land law was to be worked out in a more orderly fashion by the land committees. For a rather unsuccessful attempt to make clear why the Central Rada's land law was "more well thought out" than the Sovnarkom's, see Ol. Sokolovs´kyi, "Universal Ukraïns´koï Tsentral´noï Rady i zemel´na sprava," *Nova hromada*, no. 3, 12 [25] November 1917, 2.
84. Badcock, *Politics and the People in Revolutionary Russia*, 312–24. In Kazan province, one frustrated food supply committee worker noted of villagers' resistance, "Russia is forgotten: the word *rodina* (motherland) is understood only as their village." Badcock, *Politics and the People in Revolutionary Russia*, 316.
85. Holquist, *Making War, Forging Revolution*, 105–6.
86. For an example, see Michael Melancon, "The Syntax of Soviet Power: The Resolutions of Local Soviets and Other Institutions, March–October 1917," *Russian Review* 52 (October 1993): 486–505. While Melancon presents a cogent and sophisticated analysis of some of the resolutions received from local soviets by the Executive Committee of the Petrograd Soviet (later, the All-Russian Executive Committee of the Soviets), he does not question the degree to which these resolutions and the institutions that generated them expressed the will of "the masses," whom they claimed to represent.
87. For example, on 30 July the provincial soviet resolved "to applaud the Provincial Land Committee's activities." TsDAVO, f. 1400, op. 1, spr. 1, ark. 110.
88. TsDAVO, f. 1400, op. 1, spr. 1, ark. 150v; and TsDAVO, f. 1326, op. 1, spr. 90, ark. 60.
89. The one extensive Western study of the soviets only mentions how much the Petrograd Soviet received from March to June 1917, but does not discuss from where this money came. Oskar Anweiler, *The Soviets: The Russian Workers, Peasants, and Soldiers Councils, 1905–1921*, trans. Ruth Hein (New York, 1974), 108. Anweiler does not discuss the funding of local soviets.
90. TsDAVO, f. 1400, op. 1, spr. 1, ark. 3. Comrade Rubinsky was sent to the provincial zemstvo to request funds for the soviet.
91. TsDAVO, f. 1400, op. 1, spr. 1, ark. 11.

92. Only in the months of May and July did the EC stay under this budget estimate. In fact, later in 1917 the EC revised this estimate to 141,600 rubles per month, though it only found sufficient funds to spend on average 68,000 rubles for each of the months from May to November 1917. Most of these funds came from loans from the Union Bank and the provincial zemstvo. TsDAVO, f. 1400, op. 1, spr. 4, ark. 36–38.
93. TsDAVO, f. 1400, op. 1, spr. 1, ark. 13v.
94. TsDAVO, f. 1400, op. 1, spr. 1, ark. 33.
95. Narodnii komisariiat zemel´nykh sprav, *Pidsumky ahrarnoï revoliutsiï na Ukraïni* (Kharkiv, 1923), 6.
96. TsDAVO, f. 1400, op. 1, spr. 4, ark. 33, and ibid., spr. 1, ark. 111.
97. TsDAVO, f. 1400, op. 1, spr. 1, ark. 130. The Randava volost case in particular suggests that peasants equated local soviets with other prerevolutionary peasant organizations.
98. TsDAVO, f. 1400, op. 1, spr. 1, ark. 132.
99. TsDAVO, f. 1400, op. 1, spr. 1, ark. 142v.
100. TsDAVO, f. 1400, op. 1, spr. 1, ark. 158.
101. The label of "defensist" usually denoted those who supported a defensive position in the war effort, as opposed to a separate peace, which the Sovnarkom was at this time negotiating with the Central Powers at Brest-Litovsk. Here it may have referred more generally to those who opposed the Bolshevik takeover and attempted to remain loyal to the Provisional Government, which had espoused a defensist position toward the war.
102. TsDAVO, f. 1400, op. 1, spr. 1, ark. 207.
103. TsDAVO, f. 1400, op. 1, spr. 1, ark. 225.
104. TsDAVO, f. 1400, op. 1, spr. 1, ark. 289 and 308.
105. TsDAVO, f. 1400, op. 1, spr. 1, ark. 262v. A further indication that peasants possessed the means to pay the tax is found in their ability to pay money to rent land. According to the 1913 peasant household census, in Kharkiv province 87.3 percent of rented land was paid for with money and 36.7 percent of peasant households rented land. Khar´kovskaia gubernskaia zemskaia uprava, *Sel´skoe khoziaistvo, fabrichnaia promyshlennost´ i zaniatie naseleniia Khar´kovskoi gubernii*, 8–9. Moreover, by 1917, because local land committees significantly lowered the rent on the lands they confiscated and because of the decrease in manufactured goods for peasants to purchase, they likely had more money on hand than previously. In addition, because of the prohibition on alcoholic drink during World War I, peasants had still more money at hand. See Holquist, *Making War, Forging Revolution*, 32–33.
106. According to the 1917 agricultural census, there were 450,644 peasant households in Kharkiv province in 1917. Khar´kovskoe gubernskoe statiticheskoe biuro, *Vserossiiskaia sel´skokhoziaistvennaia perepis´ 1917 g. Kharkovskoi gub.*, 12–13.

107. For example, following the shutdown of *Slovo*, Vynnychenko was forbidden by administrative order to live in Kharkiv city and province. TsDIAK, f. 336, op. 2, spr. 124, ark. 91v.
108. TsDIAK, f. 336, op. 2, spr. 124, ark. 79v. For the whole report, see ibid., ark. 79–83.
109. *Ridne slovo*, no. 1, 1 April 1917, 4. Hnat Khotkevych was Kharkiv's leading Ukrainian political figure in the pre- and postrevolutionary period, a prolific playwright and later a renowned bandura player. He perished during the Iezhov terror. See I. Koshelivets, "Khotkevych, Hnat," *Encyclopedia of Ukraine*, 2:491.
110. *Ridne slovo*, no. 1, 1 April 1917, 3.
111. *Ridne slovo*, no. 1, 1 April 1917, 1. This weekly only lasted through mid-July 1917, which is not surprising, considering the intense competition for the Kharkiv reading public in 1917. During the period from March to December 1917, at least forty-two different newspapers were published in the province; twenty-nine in Kharkiv itself. Of these only four were Ukrainian-language newspapers; the most successful was *Nova hromada*, which appeared after the Central Rada's declaration of the Third Universal, was published by the Rada Slobidskoï Ukraïny and edited jointly by Ukrainian Social-Democrats, Socialist-Revolutionaries, and Socialist-Federalists. These figures are based on a thorough search of all Ukrainian archives and libraries containing materials relating to Kharkiv province. The largest collection of newspapers published in Kharkiv province during the revolution is held not in Kharkiv, but in Kyiv at Naukovo-Dovidkova Biblioteka Tsentral′nykh Derzhavnykh Arkhiviv Ukraïny [hereafter, NDBTsDAU], located at Ukraine's central archive building (vul. Solomonska, 25).
112. Guthier, " Roots of Popular Ukrainian Nationalism," 14.
113. Guthier, "Popular Base of Ukrainian Nationalism in 1917," 37, 46.
114. The classic study is Oliver H. Radkey, *Russia Goes to the Polls: The Election to the All-Russian Constituent Assembly, 1917* (Ithaca, 1950; repr. 1989); see also the more recent L. G. Protasov, *Vserossiiskoe uchreditel′noe sobranie: istoriia rozhdeniia i gibeli* (Moscow, 1997).
115. *Izvestiia Khar′kovskogo Soveta rabochikh deputatov*, no. 1, 4 March 1917, 1. The Petrograd Soviet of Workers' Deputies also saw it this way. Protasov, *Vserossiiskoe uchreditel′noe sobranie*, 31.
116. *Ridne slovo*, no. 1, 1 April 1917, 2.
117. TsDAVO, f. 1400, op. 1, spr. 1, ark. 87–88.
118. TsDAVO, f. 1400, op. 1, spr. 1, ark. 96.
119. TsDAVO, f. 1400, op. 1, spr. 1, ark. 104, 106.
120. TsDAVO, f. 1400, op. 1, spr. 1, ark. 108.
121. TsDAVO, f. 1400, op. 1, spr. 1, ark. 110v.
122. TsDAVO, f. 1400, op. 1, spr. 1, ark. 112v and 113.

123. The "Maximalists" were a radical offshoot of the PSR, who advocated violent actions not only against tsarist government officials, but "economic terror" against landlords and industrialists. In the tsarist period they were also notorious for carrying out numerous "expropriations"—a euphemism for robberies—in order to finance their political program. When the PSR disowned them in 1906, they formed their own Union of Socialists-Revolutionaries Maximalists. Pipes, *Russian Revolution*, 148.
124. TsDAVO, f. 1400, op. 1, spr. 1, ark. 176.
125. Ekaterina K. Breshko-Breshkovskaia was one of the most well known heroes of the revolutionary movement and later a vehement anti-Bolshevik. It is very likely that the platform of these soldiers' candidate was less radical than that of the Soviet-PSR/UPSR list, and certainly included a pro-war stance; in the local press they were referred to as "defensists [*oborontsy*]." See Jane E. Good and David R. Jones, *Babushka: The Life of the Russian Revolutionary Ekaterina K. Breshko-Breshkovskaia (1844–1934)* (Newtonville, Mass., 1991), 151–53; and Joseph L. Wieczynski, ed., *The Modern Encyclopedia of Russian and Soviet History*, vol. 5 (Gulf Breeze, Fla., 1977), 168.
126. TsDAVO, f. 1400, op. 1, spr. 1, ark. 178. At the same meeting it was learned that Breshko-Breshkovskaia would soon arrive in Kharkiv province to agitate for the soldiers' list.
127. TsDAVO, f. 1400, op. 1, spr. 1, ark. 183.
128. According to the incomplete figures provided by Executive Committee's treasurer, the Soviet spent at least 22,878 rubles on agitators, literature and campaigning for the Constituent Assembly elections. TsDAVO, f. 1400, op. 1, spr. 4, ark. 36-37.
129. *Zemlia i volia*, no. 176, 4 (17) November 1917, p. 3. In fact, less than half of the volosts (18 of 42) were represented at the conference.
130. *Zemlia i volia*, no. 176, 4 (17) November 1917, 3.
131. Ibid.
132. *Nova hromada*, no. 1, 10 November 1917, 3.
133. Protasov, *Vserossiiskoe uchreditel′noe sobranie*, 195.
134. *Nova hromada*, no. 9, 19 November (2 December) 1917, p. 3.
135. *Nova hromada*, no. 6, 16 (29) November 1917, 3.
136. *Russkaia zhizn′*, 20, 25, and 30 November 1917; cited in Reshod′ko, *Selians′kyi rukh u Kharkivsk′ii hubernii*, 114–15. In Sumy district list no. 5 received only 59,065 votes or 64.1 percent; list no. 15 received far greater support than in any other area: 15,634 votes or 17 percent.
137. Concerning the Constituent Assembly elections in the Don region, Holquist notes that "voters ascribed different meaning to their votes than did the parties for whom they voted." Holquist, *Making War, Forging Revolution*, 117. Sarah Badcock has found a similar local-mindedness in her study of the

CA elections in Kazan and Nizhegorod provinces. Badcock, *Politics and the People in Revolutionary Russia*, 162.

138. Graham Tan also traces the importance of peasants' village community and identity on Right-Bank Ukraine in 1917. For example, one village assembly decreed, "all power to the people, that is to say the village, immediately. We will not carry out any other decrees except the resolutions of the *skhod*." Tan, "Peasant Action and Village Social Organization," 286. Hiroaki Kuromiya notes a similarly strong sense of local-mindedness in the Donbas region of Ukraine, especially among colliers. Kuromiya, *Freedom and Terror in the Donbas*, 90. In fact, Theodore Friedgut, in his thorough study of the workers of Iuzovka (now Donetsk, Ukraine), suggests that peasants who became workers transferred their "parochial tendencies" from the village to the factory or mine. Friedgut, *Iuzovka and Revolution*, 2:464–65; see also 55.

Chapter 3

1. Beginning with this chapter, dates are given according to the Gregorian calendar. On Russia's shift to the Gregorian calendar, see chapter 1, note 2, above.
2. Already on 21 January 1918 the Soviet government in Petrograd seems to have believed that Kyiv was theirs for the taking. In a memorandum of that date from the People's Commissariat of Military Affairs concerning the personnel composition of the Military District Councils (Soviets), "Kiev district" ("Kievskii okrug") was listed as one of the twelve military districts under the commissariat's control. Note that there was not yet a Kharkiv [Kharkov] Military District. The Papers of the Red Army, reel 2, microfilm of fond 1, opis 1, delo 72, list 14v, from the Administration for Matters of the People's Commissariat of Military Affairs, located at RGVA.
3. Gratsiozi, *Bol′sheviki i krest′iane na Ukraine, 1918–1919 gody*, 43.
4. Oleh S. Fedyshyn, *Germany's Drive to the East and the Ukrainian Revolution, 1917–1918* (New Brunswick, N.J., 1971), 89–91. Also see Basil Dmytryshyn, "The German Overthrow of the Central *Rada*, April, 1918: New Evidence from German Archives," *Nationalities Papers* 23, no. 4 (December 1995): 751–66.
5. Ia. I. Malyk, *Ukraïns′ke selianstvo v period avstro-nimets′koï okupatsiï 1918 roku* (Lviv, 1996), 4; cites: Tsentral′nyi derzhavnyi arkhiv hromads′kykh ob'iednan′ Ukraïny (hereafter: TsDAHO), f. 6, op. 1, spr. 16, ark. 51.
6. Historians have paid very little attention to how peasants perceived and reacted to the occupation and the Hetmanate. Boris Malinovskii has pointed out that Soviet historians focused on what was called "the patriotic war of the Ukrainian people against the German occupants," while Western historians focused on German and Austro-Hungarian policy toward Ukraine. The

best of the former is N. I. Suprunenko, *Ocherki istorii grazhdanskoi voiny i inostrannoi voennoi interventsii na Ukraine: 1918–1920* (Moscow, 1966); and of the latter, Fedyshyn, *Germany's Drive to the East and the Ukrainian Revolution, 1917–1918*. Boris Malinovskii, "Vospriiatie deiatel′nosti avstro-vengerskikh i germanskikh voisk v Ukraine (1918 g.) Ukrainskim krest′ianstvom" (paper presented at the conference "Kriegserfahrungen in Osteuropa," Eberhard Karls Universität, Tübingen, Germany, October 2000).

7. On 28 March 1918 Berlin and Vienna divided up Ukraine into two occupied spheres; Kharkiv province fell to the German troops to occupy. Wolfram Dornik and Peter Lieb, "Die Besatzungsverwaltung," in *Die Ukraine zwischen Selbstbestimmung und Fremdherrschaft 1917–1922* (Graz, 2011), 251.
8. Kharkiv Bolsheviks were some of the most vehement opponents of the Brest-Litovsk peace treaties; this probably strengthened their resistance to the German occupation. I. D. Nazarenko et al., eds., *Ocherki istorii Kommunisticheskoi partii Ukrainy* (Kyiv, 1961), 225. On the stubborn resistance of pro-Bolshevik sources, see RGVA, f. 1, op. 2, d. 1, l. 73.
9. On 16 February 1918 the retreating Soviet government proclaimed the creation of the Donets–Kryvyi Rih Soviet Republic, renaming itself the Soviet of the People's Commissariats of that republic. However, this political entity existed mostly on paper and in the party's newspapers. I have found no traces of its decrees or influence at the local level in the countryside. P. Pavliuk, *Kharkivs′ka chervona hvardiia (liutyi 1917 r.–berezen′ 1918 r.)* (Kyiv, 1948), 90–91; also see Richard Pipes, *The Formation of the Soviet Union: Communism and Nationalism, 1917–1923* (Cambridge, Mass., 1964), 130–31.
10. TsDAVO, f. 1326, op. 1, spr. 7, ark. 19; at about the same time, the provincial land department received reports on "the massive felling of forest" in Bohodukhiv district and ordered the district's land department to permit the cutting of trees "only in cases of real necessity." TsDAVO, f. 1326, spr. 128, ark. 1.
11. TsDAVO, f. 1326, op. 1, spr. 7, ark. 19.
12. TsDAVO, f. 1400, op. 1, spr. 1 ark. 289; and TsDAVO, f. 1326, op. 1. spr. 7, ark. 51.
13. TsDAVO, f. 1326, op. 1, spr. 7, ark. 21. Non-laboring farms are those not worked by the owner's own hands.
14. [Colin Ross], "Doklad nachal′niku operatsionnogo otdeleniia germanskogo vostochnogo fronta o polozhenii del na Ukraine v Marte 1918 goda," *Arkhiv russkoi revoliutsii* 1 (1923), 288.
15. TsDAVO, f. 1400, op. 1, spr. 1, ark. 305. This is the last document in the protocols of the Provincial Soviet of Peasants' Deputies.
16. DAKhO, f. 10, op. 1, spr. 278, ark. 1. Surprisingly, at this time the Red Army was still finding considerable support among the local population. A report of 1 April 1918 to the People's Commissariat for Military Affairs noted that in

Kharkiv "work for the organization of the Red Army is going successfully." Locals had recently organized two detachments, into whose ranks had entered, among others, numerous prisoners-of-war. The Papers of the Red Army, reel 2, microfilm of f. 1, op. 1, d. 72, l. 99, fond of the Administration for Matters of the People's Commissariat of Military Affairs, located at RGVA, f. 1, op. 1, d. 72, l. 99.

17. TsDAVO, f. 1326, op. 1, spr. 7, ark. 84.
18. TsDAVO, f. 1326, op. 1, spr. 7, ark. 100.
19. TsDAVO, f. 1326, op. 1. spr. 7, ark. 101.
20. As other historians have noted, no protests were provoked by the Central Rada's replacement, either among intellectuals or the wider masses. Dmytro Doroshenko, *Istoriia Ukraïny 1917–1923 rr.*, vol. 2, *Ukraïns'ka Het'mans'ka Derzhava 1919 roku* (Uzhhorod, 1930), 39. In my own research I found no evidence of dismay at the Rada's passing.
21. P. P. Skoropads'kyi, "Uryvok zi 'Spomyniv' Het'mana Pavla Skoropads'koho," *Khliborobs'ka Ukraïna*, book 5, (1924–1925): 71.
22. Malyk, *Ukraïns'ke selianstvo v period avstro-nimets'koï okupatsiï 1918 roku*, 12–13.
23. Fedyshyn, *Germany's Drive to the East and the Ukrainian Revolution, 1917–1918*, 184; cites telegram no. 474 from German Ambassador to Ukraine, Baron Mumm, to the German Foreign Office, dated 30 April 1918, found in German Foreign Office Archives, no. 37.
24. TsDAVO, f. 1325, op. 1, spr. 33, ark. 129 and 131.
25. TsDAVO, f. 1325, op. 1, spr. 33, ark. 175.
26. For more examples, see TsDAVO, f. 1325, op. 1, spr. 33, ark. 101–28. Another document in this file lists the property losses from eight peasants in Starobilsk district, the total damage amounting to 38,621 rubles (ibid., ark. 36). One might note that, even in the midst of serious inflation, this was a considerable amount of money to peasants.
27. The local leaders' desire to have their district included in Kharkiv province was never realized. After the civil war Graivoron district was not included in the UkRSR, but became part of Belgorod oblast, RSFSR, during the redivision of oblasts in 1923. See Siroshtan et al., *Istoriia mist i sil UkRSR: Kharkivs'ka oblast'*, 8. Interestingly, another district of Kursk province, Fatezhskii uezd, just a short time later sent an appeal to the Kursk Provincial Executive Committee of United Soviets of Workers' and Peasants' Deputies, insisting just the opposite. Concerned about the ongoing negotiations in Kyiv with the Russian Federation's delegation over the proper division between Ukraine and Russia, the representatives of the Fatenskii district soviet asked the peace delegation to make every effort "to defend the territory of Fatenskii district from the pretensions of Ukrainian autocracy," insisting that it "remain under the control of Soviet Power." Papers of the Red Army, reel 6, microfilm of

f. 1, op. 1, d. 236, l. 1, fond of the Administration for Matters of the People's Commissariat of Military Affairs, located at RGVA. A report from 31 July 1918 from Nizhnedevitsk district, Voronezh province, stresses that "across the whole district at assemblies resolutions about recognizing Soviet power are being issued and the population does not in any case want to be united to Ukraine." Ibid., l. 8.

28. TsDAVO, f. 1326, op. 1, spr. 33, ark. 394.
29. Malinovskii, "Vospriiatie deiatel′nosti avstro-vengerskikh i germanskikh voisk v Ukraine (1918 g.) Ukrainskim krest′ianstvom," 3.
30. TsDAVO, f. 1326, op. 1, spr. 33, ark. 395.
31. Cited in full in Doroshenko, *Istoriia Ukraïny 1917–1923 rr.*, 2:49–53.
32. *Kievskaia mysl′*, 12 May 1918; cited in Iaroslav Malyk, "Zemel′ne pytannia v ukraïns′kii het′mans′kii derzhavi," in *Ostannii het′man: Iuvileinyi zbirnyk pam'iati Pavla Skoropads′koho, 1873–1945*, ed. Oleksandr Lupanov et al. (Kyiv, 1993), 98–99.
33. Malyk, "Zemel′ne pytannia v ukraïns′kii het′mans′kii derzhavi," 99. No documents have survived from the temporary land commissions.
34. Malinovskii, "Vospriiatie deiatel′nosti avstro-vengerskikh i germanskikh voisk v Ukraine (1918 g.) Ukrainskim krest′ianstvom," 5.
35. Malyk, "Zemel′ne pytannia v ukraïns′kii het′mans′kii derzhavi," 104; and Malyk, *Ukraïns′ke selianstvo v period avstro-nimets′koï okupatsiï 1918 roku*, 40–41. Doroshenko, *Istoriia Ukraïny 1917–1923 rr.*, 2:290–91. Of course, Skoropads′kyi had to clear any such decrees with the German military authorities in Ukraine.
36. Malyk, *Ukraïns′ke selianstvo v period avstro-nimets′koï okupatsiï 1918 roku*, 14–17; V. Vynnychenko, *Vidrodzhennia natsiï*, part 4 (Kyiv, 1920), 47–48.
37. N. N. Popov, ed., *Osvoboditel′naia voina ukrainskogo naroda protiv nemetskikh okkupantov: Dokumenty i materialy* (Moscow, 1937), doc. 219, p. 288.
38. Popov, *Osvoboditel′naia voina ukrainskogo naroda protiv nemetskikh okkupantov*, doc. 283, p. 393.
39. Suprunenko, *Ocherki istorii grazhdanskoi voiny i inostrannoi voennoi interventsii na Ukraine*, 61–63. Unfortunately, I was not able to verify these events in Ukrainian archives.
40. M. Ivanov, comp., "Ot vlasti otkazyvaius′ (Dokumenty o Getmanshchine iz arkhiva Khar′kovskogo gubernskogo starosty)," *Letopis′ revoliutsii* (1924), no. 2, 226. In fact, German soldiers also imposed onerous requisitions and exactions on the estates.
41. Ivanov, "Ot vlasti otkazyvaius′," 231.
42. Malinovskii, "Vospriiatie deiatel′nosti avstro-vengerskikh i germanskikh voisk v Ukraine (1918 g.) Ukrainskim krest′ianstvom," 8; and Popov, *Osvoboditel′naia voina ukrainskogo naroda protiv nemetskikh okkupantov*,

docs. 100–103, p. 155; and doc. 122, p. 172.
43. TsDAVO, f. 1325, op. 1, spr. 31, ark. 1.
44. TsDAVO, f. 1325, op. 1, spr. 31, ark. 2.
45. TsDAVO, f. 1325, op. 1, spr. 31, ark. 3, for quotation and the rest from ark. 2.
46. TsDAVO, f. 1325, op. 1, spr. 31, ark. 4–5.
47. TsDAVO, f. 1325, op. 1, spr. 31, ark. 4a; the starosta's response was typed on the back of the peasants' petition.
48. TsDAVO, f. 1325, op. 1, spr. 31, ark. 11.
49. TsDAVO, f. 1325, op. 1, spr. 31, ark. 21.
50. TsDAVO, f. 1325, op. 1, spr. 31, ark. 54.
51. TsDAVO, f. 1325, op. 1, spr. 31, ark. 6.
52. TsDAVO, f. 1325, op. 1, spr. 31, ark. 9. One might add that at no time did anyone suggest, even the Kolomak villagers, that the Germans were to blame for the violence.
53. TsDAVO, f. 1325, op. 1, spr. 31, ark. 6.
54. TsDAVO, f. 1325, op. 1, spr. 31, ark. 10, 16, and 54.
55. TsDAVO, f. 1325, op. 1, spr. 31, ark. 54.
56. TsDAVO, f. 1325, op. 1, spr. 31, ark. 55. The Directory's rule in Kharkiv was overthrown by Kharkiv workers just three days later. On Kharkiv workers' actions, see Mark Baker, "How to Make Kharkiv Workers into Bolsheviks: Lessons from the Hetmanate and Directory, 1918," *Canadian-American Slavic Studies* 40, no. 1 (Spring 2006): 49–63.
57. TsDAVO, f. 1325, op. 1, spr. 32, ark. 38.
58. TsDAVO, f. 1325, op. 1, spr. 32, ark. 41.
59. TsDAVO, f. 1325, op. 1, spr. 32, ark. 38.
60. TsDAVO, f. 1325, op. 1, spr. 31, ark. 18–19. The spelling "Kokh" is transliterated directly from the original Russian-language document. Of course, there is a common German surname, Koch, but I prefer to use the document's spelling. I was unable to find out more about this starosta's identity. He might have been a recent German immigrant who was faithful to the Ukrainian state, but he might also have been the offspring of German settlers under Catherine the Great, several generations removed from Germany, and completely Russified.
61. TsDAVO, f. 1325, op. 1, spr. 31, ark. 17.
62. TsDAVO, f. 1325, op. 1, spr. 33, ark. 37.
63. TsDAVO, f. 1325, op. 1, spr. 31, ark. 23; dated 24 August 1918.
64. TsDAVO, f. 1325, op. 1, spr. 33, ark. 38; dated 28 August 1918.
65. TsDAVO, f. 1325, op. 1, spr. 31, ark. 37–38.
66. Grelka, "Deutsche Militarverwaltung in der Ukraine im Erstern und Zweiten Weltkrieg," 8–9; cites Politisches Archiv des Auswartigen Amtes Bonn, Ukraine nr. 1, bd. 8.
67. Ross, "Doklad nachal′niku," 288. Wolfram Dornik and Peter Lieb have

recently stressed the great attention Ross's report received in the German Foreign Office, Economics Department and the Supreme Army Command (OHL). Hoffman in fact also agreed with Ross's report. Dornik and Lieb, "Die militärischen Operationen," in *Die Ukraine zwischen Selbstbestimmung und Fremdherrschaft 1917–1922* (Graz, 2011), 212n39.

68. Grelka, "Deutsche Militarverwaltung in der Ukraine im Erstern und Zweiten Weltkrieg," 13; cites Heeresgruppe Eichorn-Kiew, Abt. Ic 20128, 14.4.1918, BA-MA, N46/172. Fedyshyn makes passing reference to the deleterious effects of German soldiers—by requisitioning food and other necessities for their own consumption—in disrupting their leaders' plans; Fedyshyn, *Germany's Drive to the East and the Ukrainian Revolution, 1917–1918*, 186.
69. TsDAVO, f. 1325, op. 1, spr. 33, ark. 151.
70. TsDAVO, f. 1325, op. 1, spr. 33, ark. 150.
71. TsDAVO, f. 1325, op. 1, spr. 33, ark. 200.
72. TsDAVO, f. 1325, op. 1, spr. 33, ark. 202.
73. Prince Maximilian von Baden, *The Memoirs of Prince Max of Baden*, trans. W. M. Calder and C. W. H. Sutton (New York, 1928), 2:23.
74. Maximilian, *Memoirs of Prince Max von Baden*, 2:35, 41–42. Fedyshyn (*Germany's Drive to the East and the Ukrainian Revolution, 1917–1918*, 231) cites this speech as the one Maximilian actually delivered in the Reichstag on 5 October, but Maximilian clearly states that he "gave up" this speech and instead made a far more general and conciliatory one, not defining the government's understanding of the Fourteen Points, but only speaking in broad generalities about his hopes for "an early, honest peace of justice and reconciliation." Auswärtiges Amt. Germany, *Amtliche Urkunden zur Vorgeschichte des Waffenstillstandes 1918 (auf Grund der Akten der Reichskanzlei, des Auswärtigen Amtes und des Reichsarchivs herausgegeben vom Auswärtigen Amt und vom Reichsministerium des Innern)* (Frankfurt am Main, 1988), doc. 34a, pp. 75–76.
75. Fedyshyn, *Germany's Drive to the East and the Ukrainian Revolution, 1917–1918*, 231; cites Report of the Foreign Armies Division of the General Staff of the Army, Secret, no number, 6 October 1918, German Foreign Office Archives, no. 99.
76. Winfried Baumgart, ed., *Von Brest-Litovsk zur Deutschen Novemberrevolution: Aus den Tagebüchern, Briefen und Aufzeichnungen von Alfons Paquet, Wilhelm Gröner und Albert Hopman, März bis November 1918* (Göttingen, 1971), 442. Groener was chief of staff of the Kyiv Army group under Field Marshall von Eichhorn, but, after the latter's assassination (30 July 1918), he became de facto chief military commander in Ukraine for the rest of 1918. In early November Groener left Kyiv to replace General Ludendorff as First Quartermaster General.

77. Fedyshyn, *Germany's Drive to the East and the Ukrainian Revolution, 1917–1918*, 247.
78. A. I. Burik et al., eds, *Khar'kovshchina v period grazhdanskoi voiny i inostrannoi voennoi interventsii 1918–1920 gg.: Sbornik dokumentov i materialov* (Kharkiv, 1973), doc. 62, pp. 47–48; and TsDAVO, f. 1325, op. 1, spr. 3, ark. 40. The law on extraordinary safeguard (*chrezvychainaia okhrana*) was first promulgated in 1881 by Alexander III, following the assassination of his father, Alexander II. Richard Pipes, *Russia under the Old Regime* (New York, 1974), 305–7. The 1916 law provided yet greater powers to the person ruling over an administrative unit proclaimed to be in such a state of siege.
79. TsDAVO, f. 1325, op. 1, spr. 3, ark. 31.
80. TsDAVO, f. 1325, op. 1, spr. 5, ark. 194.
81. The decree is provided in full in Doroshenko, *Istoriia Ukraïny 1917–1923 rr.*, 2:414–15.
82. See Iaroslav Shtendera, *Zasudzhenyi do rozstrilu* (Lviv, 1995), 83; and Doroshenko, *Istoriia Ukraïny 1917–1923 rr.*, 2:417.
83. Doroshenko, *Istoriia Ukraïny 1917–1923 rr.*, 2:418.
84. Shtendera, *Zasudzhenyi do rozstrilu*, 84. At some point in 1918 the division was divided into two regiments and the Second Zaporozhian Regiment was dispatched to Chernihiv province.
85. Serhii Shemet, "Polkovnyk Petro Bolbochan (Zamitky do istoriï Zaporozhs'koho Korpusu 1917–1919 rr.)," *Khliborobs'ka Ukraïna*, bk. 4 (1922–1923): 211–12.
86. Shtendera, *Zasudzhenyi do rozstrilu*, 80.
87. Shemet, "Polkovnyk Petro Bolbochan," 213.
88. Matvii Stakhiv stressed that Bolbochan was not brought into the confidence of the planners of the uprising until the end of October 1918. Matvii Stakhiv, *Ukraïna v dobi Dyrektoriï UNR* (Scranton, Penn., 1962), 1:32.
89. "Lyst sot. I. Baryla do hen. Omelianovycha-Pavlenka," *Batkivshchyna* (Toronto), no. 6, 27 March 1971.
90. Petro Solukha, *Dohovir z Moskvoiu proty het'mana Pavla Skoropads'koho* (n.p., 1973), 63. Solukha claimed that it was widely known among Kyivans "that Bolbochan was against making Petliura 'Marshal' of the Ukrainian Army; they [also] knew that Bolbochan did not consider Konovalets [commander of the Sichovi stril'tsi] his superior." Ibid., 64.
91. "Lyst sot. I. Baryla do hen. Omelianovycha-Pavlenka," *Batkivshchyna* (Toronto), no. 8, 1 May 1971.
92. Shemet, "Polkovnyk Petro Bolbochan," 213; and Shtendera, *Zasudzhenyi do rozstrilu*, 87. Tymoshenko was a member of the Ukrainian Social-Democratic Workers' Party and its representative in the Ukrainian National Union. Ibid., 212.

93. Burik, *Khar′kovshchina v period grazhdanskoi voiny i inostrannoi voennoi interventsii 1918–1920 gg.*, doc. 77, pp. 57–59.
94. German troops' role in Bolbochan's seizure of power in Kharkiv is not revealed in the sources; we know that as of 17 November, three days after Bolbochan's arrival, the Council of German soldiers in Kyiv signed an agreement with the Directory that all German troops in Ukraine were to observe strict neutrality and return to pro-Directory troops any seized weapons. For the complete text see TsDAVO, f. 1078, op. 1, spr. 20, ark. 1. With the arrival of French Consul Enno to Odesa, German troops were ordered on 30 November to maintain order in the country and "with arms in hand to render resistance to insurgents, Bolsheviks and in general all anarchic elements." M. Gor′kii, I Mints, and R. Eideman, eds., *Krakh germanskoi okkupatsii na Ukraine (po dokumentam okkupantov)* (Moscow, 1936), doc. 103, p. 191.
95. Burik, *Khar′kovshchina v period grazhdanskoi voiny i inostrannoi voennoi interventsii 1918–1920 gg.*, doc. 77, pp. 57–59.
96. TsDAVO, f. 1325, op. 1, spr. 33, ark. 180; for a particularly nasty example, see ibid., ark. 177–78 and 181–82.
97. See Gratsiozi, *Bol′sheviki i krest′iane na Ukraine, 1918–1919 gody*, 88–89.
98. Malyk, "Zemel′ne pytannia v ukraïns′kii het′mans′kii derzhavi," 105.
99. *Biulliuten poslednikh sobytii: Ezhednevnoe izdanie* (Kharkiv), no. 2, 25 November 1918, 1.
100. *Nash golos: Ezhednevnaia Rabochaia Sotial-demokraticheskaia gazeta*, no. 26, 17 December 1918, 5.
101. *Nash golos*, no. 26, 17 December 1918, 5.
102. This description is derived from three independent accounts of the event, the most comprehensive of which appeared in V. A. Antonov-Ovseenko, "V bor′be protiv Direktorii (Na Ukraine v kontse 1918 goda)," *Litopys revoliutsiï*, nos. 38–39 (veresen–hruden′ 1929): 150. The other two accounts are in *Nash golos*, no. 27, 18 November 1918, 4; and *Bednota*, no. 222, 24 December 1918, as quoted in S. M. Korolivskii, N. K. Kolesnik, and I. K. Rybalka, eds., *Grazhdanskaia voina na Ukraine, 1918–1920: sbornik dokumentov i materialov* (Kyiv, 1967), vol. 1, book 1, doc. 581, p. 507.
103. Popov, *Osvoboditel′naia voina ukrainskogo naroda protiv nemetskikh okkupantov*, doc. 446, p. 575.
104. Popov, *Osvoboditel′naia voina ukrainskogo naroda protiv nemetskikh okkupantov*, doc. 479, p. 611.
105. Antonov-Ovseenko, "V bor′be protiv Direktorii (Na Ukraine v kontse 1918 goda)," 181.
106. Popov, *Osvoboditel′naia voina ukrainskogo naroda protiv nemetskikh okkupantov*, doc. 480, p. 612. Hrytsenko summarizes the same document

in A. P. Hrytsenko, *Politychni syly u borot′bi za vlady v Ukraïni (kinets′ 1917 r.-pochatok 1919 r.)*, Istorychni zoshyty (Kyiv, 1993), 74–75. She cites TsDAVO, f. 1078, op. 2, spr. 24, ark. 115.

107. Isakov, "Selians′kyi povstanches′kyi antykomunistychnyi rukh na Livoberezhnii Ukraïni (berezen′ 1919–lystopad 1921 rr.)," 10.
108. As Andrea Graziosi has pointed out, the most successful actions of the "Kharkiv government"—that is, the first pro-Moscow "Worker-Peasant government of Ukraine" (1917–18)—were that it proclaimed loud and far Lenin's Decree on the Land, that it rendered serious resistance to the Germans, and that, most importantly, it "quickly disappeared." Gratsiozi, *Bol′sheviki i krest′iane na Ukraine, 1918–1919 gody*, 53.

Chapter 4

1. Few of the leading members of the Communist Party (Bolsheviks) of Ukraine considered themselves to be Ukrainian by nationality, nor did they care that they were not.
2. Here my findings support the interpretation of Gratsiozi, *Bol′sheviki i krest′iane na Ukraine, 1918–1919 gody*, 95–168.
3. On Kharkiv workers' very independent actions to overthrow the Directory's short-lived rule in Kharkiv and establish pro-Bolshevik "Soviet Power" in the city, see Baker, "How to Make Kharkiv Workers into Bolsheviks."
4. Gratsiozi, *Bol′sheviki i krest′iane na Ukraine, 1918–1919 gody*, 95–96.
5. Because the occupying authorities lacked the troops to patrol the area, it became a place of refuge for those seeking to escape the Hetmanate.
6. Hoover Institution Archives, Vrangel Collection, box no. 41, file 2.
7. Burik, *Khar′kovshchina v period grazhdanskoi voiny i inostrannoi voennoi interventsii 1918–1920 gg.*, doc. 81, pp. 62–63. If one thinks about the implications of this document for the founding myth of Soviet history, it is quite remarkable that it was published in the Soviet Union in 1973.
8. Hoover Institution Archives, Vrangel Collection, box no. 52, file 7; "Svodka. Razvedyvatel′naia k 20 chasam 19 iiunia."
9. Hoover Institution Archives, Vrangel Collection, box no. 29, file 3; no title, begins, "Ukrainskaia sovetskaia armia sostoit iskliuchitel′no iz dobrovol′tsev…," fols. 1–2.
10. Figes, *Peasant Russia, Civil War*, 5, 9.
11. *Izvestiia Vremennogo raboche-krest′ianskogo pravitel′stva Ukrainy i Khar′kovskogo Soveta rabochikh deputatov*, no. 33, 31 January 1919; cited in full in Burik, *Khar′kovshchina v period grazhdanskoi voiny i inostrannoi voennoi interventsii 1918–1920 gg.*, doc. 112, pp. 89–90.
12. *Raboty Khar′kovskogo Gubernskogo S″ezda Soveta Rabochikh i Krestianskikh Deputatov ot 16 fevralia 1919 goda* (Kharkiv, 1919), 132–33. This published

stenograph of the congress is unique in its completeness, including the non-communist party leaders' speeches seriously criticizing the new Soviet government and the party's proposals.

13. Khristian Rakovskii, a Bulgarian and leading member of the Romanian Social-Democratic Party, was chairman of the Sovnarkom (Radnarkom) and the People's Commissar of Foreign Affairs from January 1919 with short breaks until July 1923. M. G. Stanchev and G. I. Cherniavskii, *Fars na krovi* (Kharkiv, 1997), 6.
14. *Raboty Khar′kovskogo Gubernskogo S″ezda Soveta Raboch. i Kr. Deputatov ot 16 fevralia 1919 goda*, 36.
15. The delegates shouted "Prosim, prosim, prosim!" suggesting that they wished to contest the presidium's decision. Ibid., 36.
16. Ibid., 46. It is not entirely clear how many deputies voted for the communists' resolution. The presidium put this resolution to a vote before those of the Left SRs and Ukrainian SRs, and then, declaring that a majority of deputies had voted for it, never put the other two resolutions to a vote.
17. Ibid., 74–75.
18. Ibid., 106.
19. Ibid., 106–7.
20. This proposal closely followed the "Statute on Socialist Land Organization," passed at about the same time in Moscow. Figes, *People's Tragedy*, 729–30.
21. *Raboty Khar′kovskogo Gubernskogo S″ezda Soveta Raboch. i Kr. Deputatov ot 16 fevralia 1919 goda*, 107–19; quotation from 119.
22. Ibid., 119–20.
23. According to the survey that deputies filled out upon arrival to the congress, there were 271 deputies either members of or sympathetic to the communists. Hence, Ian overestimated the party's solidarity. Ibid., 126.
24. Ibid., 121. These memos (*zapiski*) were a sort of substitute for real input; because the deputies were not given the opportunity to speak throughout most of the conference, they were allowed to submit these memos, which the party leaders would then use to gauge opinions and, perhaps, modify policies.
25. Compare: Instytut istorii partii TsK KP Ukraïny, *Komunistychna partiia Ukraïny v rezoliutsiiakh i rishenniakh z'ïzdiv i konferentsiï, 1918–1956* (Kyiv, 1958), 34–35; and *Raboty Khar′kovskogo Gubernskogo S″ezda Soveta Raboch. i Kr. Deputatov ot 16 fevralia 1919 goda*, 106–7.
26. Originally published in *Izvestiia vremennogo raboche-krest′ianskogo pravitel′stva Ukrainy i Khar′kovskogo Soveta rabochikh deputatov*, no. 62, 7 March 1919; quoted in Instytut istorii partii TsK KP Ukraïny, *Komunistychna partiia Ukraïny v rezoliutsiiakh i rishenniakh z'ïzdiv i konferentsiï, 1918–1956*, 37–38.

27. Suprunenko, *Ocherki istorii grazhdanskoi voiny*, 202. The Kyiv zemotdel set a similar task "to organize in the province the maximal number of one or another kind of collectives."
28. I. P. Voloshchuk, M. A. Rubach, et al., eds., *Radians′ke budivnytstvo na Ukraïni v roky Hromadians′koï viiny, 1919–1920: Zbirnyk dokumentiv i materialiv* (Kyiv, 1957), 281.
29. Surprunenko, *Ocherki istorii grazhdanskoi voiny*, 202–3.
30. Hoover Institution Archives, Vrangel Collection, box no. 30, file 10; "Soobshchenie Kievskago Otdeleniia 'Azbuka' ot 22 marta n. st.," fol. 1. This report from the Kyiv Azbuka agent noted that peasant deputies at almost all Kyiv Congresses of Soviets had shouted similarly abusive comments at the communists. Hatred of the communes was not limited to Ukraine. Donald Raleigh, for example, found a quite similar antipathy among the Russian-speaking peasants of Saratov province. Raleigh, *Experiencing Russia's Civil War*, 327–29. See also Figes, *Peasant Russia, Civil War*, 303–8.
31. As noted above, the Left SR Alekseev had pointed out the very negative impact of nationalization on the peasants of Valky district at the provincial congress of Soviets in February 1919. See *Raboty Khar′kovskogo Gubernskogo S″ezda Soveta Raboch. i Kr. Deputatov ot 16 fevralia 1919 goda*, 108.
32. The available sources make it very difficult to determine to what degree such exclamations were authentic expressions of peasants' anti-Jewish attitudes. The Volunteer Army's documents are peppered with such claims, basically implying that the peasants associated "the Bolsheviks" with "the Jews." There is no doubt that an anti-Jewish mood prevailed within the VA itself, and peasants in general held some quite intolerant attitudes toward Jews. I have yet to find in my research unpublished, archival documents that suggest that peasants made this association between "Bolsheviks" and "Jews," but the peasants of Kharkiv province had not, it should be remembered, had much interaction with Jews, because the province was outside the Pale of Settlement. There were some anti-Jewish pogroms in Kharkiv province during the civil war (about thirteen, according to Gergel, resulting in twenty-four deaths); these represented only 1.1 percent of all pogroms carried out in Ukraine over the period. N. Gergel, "The Pogroms in the Ukraine in 1918–1921," *YIVO Annual of Jewish Social Science* 6 (1951): 239, 249.
33. Hoover Institution Archives, Vrangel Collection, box no. 29, file 3; no title, begins, "Ukrainskaia sovetskaia armia sostoit iskliuchitel′no iz dobrovol′tsev," fols. 2–3.
34. Hoover Institution Archives, Vrangel Collection, box no. 40, file 25; "Donesenie Kievskago otdeleniia 'AZBUKA' ot 3-go aprelia n.s. 1919 g.," fol. 6.
35. RGVA, fond 33987, opis′ 3, delo 32, list 13 (original); cited in Alexis Berelovich

and V. A. Danilov, eds., *Sovetskaia derevnia glazami VChK-OGPU*, vol. 1, *1918–1922: Dokumenty i materialy* (Moscow, 1998), doc. 77, p. 125. The same "operative summary [*operativnaia svodka*]" reported on similar uprisings, also sparked by the requisition campaign in neighboring Kursk and Voronezh provinces. "Cheka" was the acronym for "Chrezvychainaia komissiia po bor′be s kontrrevoliutsiei i spekuliatsiei [Extraordinary commission for the struggle with the counter-revolution and speculation]."

36. Hoover Institution Archives, Vrangel Collection, box no. 41, file 1; "Doklad o polozhenii pri bol′shevikakh v Khar′kovskoi i Poltavskoi guberniiakh," fol. 3.
37. Ibid., fol. 4.
38. According to the data of the Soviet farms' subdepartment of Narkomzem USSR, the overall number of Soviet farms in July 1919 was 1,256 with a land area of 1,202,514 desiatynas, of which only 636,160 desiatynas were sown. *Pervoe soveshchanie predstavitelei rabochikh sovetskikh khoziaistv Ukrainy 11–13 iiulia 1919 g. v Kieve: 3-e soveshchanie gubzemotdelov Ukrainy 14–17 iiulia 1919 g. v Kieve* (Kyiv, 1919), 11; cited in Suprunenko, *Ocherki istorii grazhdanskoi voiny*, 198.
39. Hoover Institution Archives, Vrangel Collection, box no. 41, file 1; "Doklad o polozhenii pri bol′shevikakh v Khar′kovskoi i Poltavskoi guberniiakh," fols. 10–11. Vetchenko also provided the inflated prices for some livestock: a pair of oxen now cost as much as 30,000 rubles; horses, up to 5,000; and cows, up to 20,000.
40. Ibid., fol. 22.
41. *Bol′shevik*, 11 April 1919; cited in Suprunenko, *Ocherki istorii grazhdanskoi voiny*, 204.
42. I will use the Russian spelling for this organization, because the VA's personnel would not have spoken Ukrainian; in fact, most were quite intolerant of any manifestations of Ukrainian nationalism.
43. Hoover Institution Archives, Vrangel Collection, box no. 53, file 12; "'Raport' ot Pomoshchnika Nachal′nika Khar′kovskago Glavnago Tsentra, Polkovnika Tarasevicha," dated late May 1919.
44. Hoover Institution Archives, Vrangel Collection, box no. 53, file 3.
45. Kliment Efremovich Voroshilov (1881–1969; Ukr. Klyment Iefremovych Voroshylov) was a prominent Red Army commander during the civil war.
46. Hoover Institution Archives, Vrangel Collection, box no. 52, file 14; "Prikaz Revoliutsionnogo Voennogo Soveta XIV (byv. 2-I Ukr.) Armii."
47. Hoover Institution Archives, Vrangel Collection, box no. 29, file 2; "Politicheskii obzor za period s 1/14 iiunia po 15/28 iiunia 1919 g.," fol. 2.
48. Hoover Institution Archives, Vrangel Collection, box no. 29, file 2; "Malorossiia," fol. 10.

49. Isakov, "Selians′kyi povstanches′kyi antykomunistychnyi rukh na Livoberezhnii Ukraïni," 11–12. I should note that Isakov asserts that Chernihiv was the center of this insurgency, with 32 of the 57 detachments (each detachments contained about 400 insurgents on average).
50. Kotliar, *Povstanstvo: Selians′kyi rukh na Pivdni Ukrainy*, 41, 53.
51. Hoover Institution Archives, Vrangel Collection, box no. 52, file 7; "Svodka svedenii o protivnike deistvuiushchem protiv fronta Dobrovol′cheskoi armii s 12-go po 18 iiunia 1919 goda."
52. Hoover Institution Archives, Vrangel Collection, box no. 53, file 12; "'Raport' ot Pomoshchnika Nachal′nika Khar′kovskago Glavnago Tsentra, Polkovnika Tarasevicha," dated late May 1919.
53. The available sources do not reveal how often landowners' estates were in fact restored to them under the Hetmanate or VA. The fact that even Soviet historians rarely cited or published documents about such "restorationist" actions suggests that they were rarely carried out.
54. Hoover Institution Archives, Vrangel Collection, box no. 53, file 12; "'Raport' ot Pomoshchnika Nachal′nika Khar′kovskago Glavnago Tsentra, Polkovnika Tarasevicha," dated late May 1919.
55. Gosudarstvennyi arkhiv Rossiiskoi Federatsii (GARF), f. R-5827, op. 1, delo 106, l. 58–59; no date given, but from spring 1919; quoted in full in G. M. Ippolitov, *Kto Vy, General A. I. Denikin? Monograficheskoe issledovanie politicheskoi, voennoi i obshchestvennoi deiatel′nosti A. I. Denikina v 1890–1947 gg.* 2nd ed. (Samara, 1999), 227.
56. Hoover Institution Archives, Vrangel Collection, box no. 29, file 14; "Sobranie uzakonenii i rasporiazhenii pravitel′stva, izdavaemoe osobym soveshchaniem pri Glavnokomanduiushchem vooruzhennymi silami na iuge Rossii," no. 15, 31 July 1919, fol. 210.
57. Anna Procyk, *Russian Nationalism and Ukraine: The Nationality Policy of the Volunteer Army during the Civil War* (Edmonton, 1995), 139.
58. Holquist, *Making War, Forging Revolution*, 222–31.
59. Ibid., 231.
60. Hoover Institution Archives, Vrangel Collection, box no. 53, file 20; "Otdel politicheskii. Nastroenie krest′ian."
61. Hoover Institution Archives, Vrangel Collection, box no. 29, file 2, report titled "Malorossiia." The Odesa Azbuka center also called on the VA to pay great attention to peasants (as the key to rejuvenating and reuniting Russia) and to strive to create a solid base of support among those owning small- to medium-sized farms. See Hoover Institution Archives, Vrangel Collection, box no. 29, file 10.
62. Quoted in full in Burik, *Khar′kovshchina v period grazhdanskoi voiny i inostrannoi voennoi interventsii 1918–1920 gg.*, doc. 199, p. 161.

63. Quoted in full in ibid., 159–60.
64. TsDAVO, f. 4447, op. 1, spr. 1, ark. 16; quoted in full in Burik, *Khar′kovshchina v period grazhdanskoi voiny i inostrannoi voennoi interventsii 1918–1920 gg.*, doc. 198, pp. 160–61.
65. Quoted in Burik, *Khar′kovshchina v period grazhdanskoi voiny i inostrannoi voennoi interventsii 1918–1920 gg.*, doc. 200, p. 162.
66. Quoted in ibid., 162–65. More than nineteen peasants may have been whipped, but Shevtsov only mentioned in passing that he was submitting from the precinct's doctor reports on nineteen injured peasants.
67. Quoted in ibid., 166.
68. Hoover Institution Archives, Vrangel Collection, box no. 38, file 15, dated 28 October 1919, Khar′kov, fol. 1 of the report.
69. Ibid., fol. 2.
70. The VA's position on the land reform remained unresolved; not until November 1919 did the "special agrarian commission" present the first draft of the new land law, which contained 4,353 points and several appendices; it was published in leading VA newspapers and discussed, but never came close to enactment before defeat. Kotliar, *Povstanstvo: Selians′kyi rukh na Pivdni Ukraïny*, 44.
71. Hoover Institution Archives, Vrangel Collection, box no. 38, file 15, dated 28 October 1919, Khar′kov, fols. 3–5.
72. Ibid., fol. 7. The absence of VA propaganda work in the rear was not specific to Kharkiv province. An Azbuka report from Kyiv region, dated 19 October, noted "the complete absence of any sign of propaganda department work, especially in the village and pre-front area." Hoover Institution Archives, Vrangel Collection, box no. 49, file 16; "Obshchaia svodka agenturnykh svedenii po dokladam moim za oktiabr′ mesiats s.g."
73. Hoover Institution Archives, Vrangel Collection, box no. 28, file 49; "Doklad o nastroenii na mestakh dlia Iuzhno-Russkoi Konferentsii Partii Narodnoi Svobody," fol. 1.
74. Ibid., fol. 2.

Chapter 5

1. A. G. Egorov and K. M. Bogoliubov, eds., *Kommunisticheskaia partiia sovetskogo soiuza v rezoliutsiiakh i resheniiakh s″ezdov, konferentsii i plenumov TsK*, vol. 2, *1917–1922* (Moscow, 1983), 199–201; and M. I. Ksenzenko, *Zavershennia revoliutsiinykh zemel′nykh peretvoren′ na Kharkivshchyni (hruden′ 1919–berezen′ 1921 rr.)* (Kharkiv, 1968), 47–48. Two weeks later at the Eighth All-Russian conference of the RKP(b), 2–4 December 1919, the resolution "On Soviet Power in Ukraine" was unanimously approved.
2. Cited in Jurij Borys, *The Sovietization of Ukraine, 1917–1923: The Communist Doctrine and Practice of National Self-Determination*, rev. ed. (Edmonton,

1980), 256–57. The All-Ukrainian Revolutionary Committee was created in Moscow as Soviet troops were marching into Kharkiv on 11 December 1919 by a joint meeting of the Presidium of the All-Russian Executive Committee and the Council of People's Commissars of the USRR. This committee was to be the ruling body in Ukraine until the "Petliurists" and "White-Guardists" had been completely removed from Ukrainian territory. V. M. Volkovyns'kyi and S. V. Kul'chyts'kyi, *Khrystyian Rakovs'kyi: Politychnyi portret* (Kyiv, 1990), 125.

3. DAKhO, f. R-203, op. 1, spr. 139, ark. 22. This report was in fact requested by the Provincial Food Supply committee. Unfortunately, no reports from other districts have survived.
4. DAKhO, f. P-1, op. 1, spr. 141, ark. 26.
5. TsDAVO, f. 5, op. 1, spr. 289, ark. 1.
6. Burik, *Khar'kovshchina v period grazhdanskoi voiny i inostrannoi voennoi interventsii, 1918–1920 gg.* doc. 233, 198–200. For more expressions of peasants' willingness to work with the new regime, see TsDAHO, f. 1, op. 20, spr. 268, ark. 1–2.
7. For examples, see M. I. Kulichenko, *Bol'sheviki Khar'kovshchiny v Borbe za vlast' sovetov (1918–1920 gg.)* (Kharkiv, 1966), 188; and K. K. Shyian and S. Ia. Ostrovs'kyi, *Mynule i suchasne sela* (Kharkiv, 1963), 129.
8. See Ksenzenko, *Zavershennia revoliutsiinykh zemel'nykh peretvoren' na Kharkivshchyni*, 56.
9. *Spravochnik partiinogo rabotnika* (Moscow, 1921), 83–85; quoted in full in Voloshchuk et al., *Radians'ke budivnytstvo*, doc. 12, 31–35; here 31.
10. Hanzha, *Opir selian stanovlenniu totalitarnoho rezhymu v USRR*, Istorychni zoshyty (Kyiv, 1996), 12.
11. *Spravochnik partiinogo rabotnika*, 83–85; quoted in full in Voloshchuk et al., *Radians'ke budivnytstvo*, doc. 12, 31–35. Elections were to be carried out in phases, from the village assembly to the district conferences, with a ratio of one representative per 5,000 citizens.
12. DAKhO, f. R-202, op. 2, spr. 18, ark. 16. Emphasis added.
13. Moshe Lewin, "Who was the Soviet Kulak?" *Soviet Studies* 18 (October 1966): 191.
14. Donald Raleigh found a similar use of social labels in Saratov province during the civil war: "More and more, political allegiance determined social identity in Bolshevik external language; class was defined in *political*, not sociological terms." Raleigh, *Experiencing Russia's Civil War*, 64–65 (emphasis in the original).
15. DAKhO, f. R-202, op. 2, spr. 19, ark. 4.
16. It seems that a group of peasants had secured sufficient numbers before the conference opened to elect leaders to represent them.
17. This is not the place to discuss the intricate political and programmatic

differences among the political parties that the new regime allowed to operate legally at this time. But I should note that by early 1920 the KP(b)U had formed an alliance with the Left SRs and the Borot´bists. James E. Mace, *Communism and the Dilemmas of National Liberation: National Communism in Soviet Ukraine, 1918–1933* (Cambridge, Mass., 1983), 59. The Borot´bists' basic programmatic differences from the KP(b)U were their desire to create a truly independent Ukrainian Soviet republic with a separate army and administration. Borys, *Sovietization of Ukraine,* 271.

18. DAKhO, f. R-202, op. 2, spr. 19, ark. 4.
19. In the stenogram this took up forty-seven single-spaced, tightly typed pages: DAKhO, f. R-202, op. 2, spr. 19, ark. 4–51.
20. DAKhO, f. R-202, op. 2, spr. 19, ark. 5–7. As will become clear, to the peasants "the conference" meant the peasant delegates, and definitely not the party leaders.
21. DAKhO, f. R-202, op. 2, spr. 19, ark. 7–8.
22. DAKhO, f. R-202, op. 2, spr. 19, ark. 8. It seems that the conference organizers held a meeting the previous day at which the proposed presidium was chosen. However, most peasant delegates did not attend.
23. DAKhO, f. R-202, op. 2, spr. 19, ark. 10.
24. DAKhO, f. R-202, op. 2, spr. 19, ark. 11.
25. DAKhO, f. R-202, op. 2, spr. 19, ark. 13.
26. DAKhO, f. R-202, op. 2, spr. 19, ark. 14. These were: M. Kovalenko, D. Zakharchenko, S. Tomakh, D. Semenenko, F. Verizhenko, B. Derecha, and E. Dolgoruchenko.
27. DAKhO, f. R-202, op. 2, spr. 19, ark. 15.
28. DAKhO, f. R-202, op. 2, spr. 19, ark. 22–24, 51.
29. DAKhO, f. R-203, op. 1, spr. 144, ark. 136.
30. DAKhO, f. R-203, op. 1, spr. 144, ark. 136 and 136v. Liuksenburg, a representative from the provincial milrevkom, spoke at the conference on behalf of the party and Soviet power.
31. DAKhO, f. R-202, op. 2, spr. 18, ark. 19.
32. DAKhO, f. R-202, op. 2, spr. 18, ark. 19–19v.
33. DAKhO, f. R-202, op. 2, spr. 18, ark. 25.
34. DAKhO, f. R-202, op. 2, spr. 18, ark. 19v.
35. On the Ukrainian Borot´bists' influence in Bohodukhiv district, see DAKhO, f. R-431, op. 1, spr. 3., ark. 13. This fond should contain the protocols of the Bohodukhiv nonparty peasant conference, but they are missing; nor are they in f. R-203, op. 1, spr. 129, which is supposed to contain the protocols of meetings of Bohodukhiv district's soviet organs, conferences, congresses, etc. I was not able to find any further references to the Bohodukhiv nonparty conference anywhere in the opysy at DAKhO or TsDAVO.
36. DAKhO, f. P-1, op. 1, spr. 141, ark. 2.

37. TsDAHO, f. 1, op. 20, spr. 269, ark. 23.
38. DAKhO, f. R-89, op. 1, spr. 173, ark. 1–2.
39. TsDAVO, f. 2, op. 1, spr. 827, ark. 11–13; originally cited in Voloshchuk et al., *Radians'ke budivnytstvo*, doc. 114, 201.
40. DAKhO, f. R-203, op. 1, spr. 144, ark. 137.
41. DAKhO, f. R-203, op. 1, spr. 144, ark. 138.
42. DAKhO, f. R-203, op. 1, spr. 144, ark. 140 and 140v.
43. DAKhO, f. R-203, op. 1, spr. 144, ark. 142v.
44. DAKhO, f. R-203, op. 1, spr. 144, ark. 142v and 143.
45. DAKhO, f. R-203, op. 1, spr. 144, ark. 148.
46. TsDAVO, f. 2360, op. 1, spr. 10, ark. 17–19; cited in full in Voloshchuk et al., *Radians'ke budivnytstvo*, doc. 29, 59–61: "Zakon Vseukraïns'koho revoliutsiinoho komitetu pro zemliu, 5 liutoho 1920 r."
47. DAKhO, f. R-203, op. 1, spr. 144, ark. 150–150v.
48. DAKhO, f. R-203, op. 1, spr. 144, ark. 150v–151.
49. DAKhO, f. R-203, op. 1, spr. 144, ark. 151–152; quote from 152.
50. DAKhO, f. R-203, op. 1, spr. 144, ark. 152v and 153.
51. Voloshchuk et al., *Radians'ke budivnytstvo*, doc. 114, 201–2. "Informatsiia Kharkivs'koho hubkomu KP(b)U pro robotu povitovykh bezpartiinykh selians'kykh konferentsii Liutyi 1920 r." Cited from TsDAVO, f. 2, op. 1, spr. 827, ark. 11–13 and TsDAHO, f. 1, op. 2, spr. 366, ark. 4–6.
52. Voloshchuk et al., *Radians'ke budivnytstvo*, doc. 114, 203–4.
53. DAKhO, f. R-89, op. 1, spr. 173, ark. 2–2v.
54. TsDAVO, f. 5, op. 1, spr. 166, ark. 32; and DAKhO, f. 202, op. 1, spr. 21, ark. 102.
55. TsDAVO, f. 5, op. 1, spr. 166, ark. 32v.
56. On 20 February 1920 the All-Ukrainian Revolutionary Committee was replaced by the Council of People's Commissars of Ukraine (Radnarkom): Khristian Rakovskii was appointed its chairman and Commissar of Internal Affairs; D. Manuïl's'kyi, Land Affairs; Hryhorii Hryn'ko (Borot'bist), Education; Myron Vladymyrov, Food Supply; Terlets'kyi (Bor'bist), Justice; Paderin, Social Insurance; Nikolai Kost, Health; V. Ia. Chubar, Economy (Sovnarkhoz); V. P. Zatons'kyi, commissar without portfolio. *Izvestiia VTsIK*, 21 February 1920, no. 56, 1. Originally cited in Borys, *Sovietization of Ukraine*, 257; but corrected.
57. M. Vladimirov, "Zakon o khlebnoi razverstke," *Kommunist*, no. 50, 29 February 1920, 3.
58. In his work on the Don Territory Peter Holquist has described a similar gulf between local inhabitants' understanding of soviet power as local control (*vlast' sovetov*) and the center's "orthodox" interpretation. Holquist, *Making War, Forging Revolution*, 131. Similarly, Iurii Kotliar has found that the peasants of southern Ukraine understood the soviets as "fully legal

representative organs of local self-government," an understanding that clashed sharply with the Bolsheviks' vision of them as "organs for carrying out the will of the center." Kotliar, *Povstanstvo: Selians′kyi rukh na Pivdni Ukraïny*, 46.

59. DAKhO, f. R-203, op. 1, spr. 129, ark. 35.
60. The word "katsapy" was a term of abuse by which Ukrainians sometimes referred to Russians. It may have been taken from a word referring to an animal something like a billy goat, because peasants thought that all Russians wore longish beards. Orest Subtelny, *Ukraine: A History*, 2nd ed. (Toronto, 1988), 275.
61. DAKhO, f. P-1, op. 1, spr. 141, ark. 25 and 25v.
62. DAKhO, f. P-1, op. 1, spr. 141, ark. 25.
63. DAKhO, f. P-1, op. 1, spr. 141, ark. 26.
64. DAKhO, f. R-203, op. 1, spr. 139, ark. 13.
65. DAKhO, f. R-203, op. 1, spr. 139, ark. 13v–14.
66. DAKhO, f. R-203, op. 1, spr. 156, ark. 1.
67. Ievhen Sivachenko, "Spalakhy hnivu narodnoho: Z istoriï selians′koho povstans′koho rukhu na Kharkivshchyni (1920 r.)," *Zbirnyk Kharkivs′koho istoryko-filolohichnoho tovarystva*, new ser., vol. 5 (1995): 19.
68. DAKhO, f. P-1, op. 1, spr. 141, ark. 188.
69. A similar uprising was provoked by the same cause in Vovchansk district at about the same time; the slogan of this uprising, which had embraced three volosts of the district, was very similar.
70. DAKhO, f. P-1, op. 1, spr. 142, ark. 15v.
71. DAKhO, f. P-1, op. 1, spr. 34, ark. 22. Verstiuk cites data published in *Izvestiia Vseukrainskogo TsIK*, 24 April 1920, that in Valky district only 4.8 percent of the households were classified as "kulaks," 60 percent as poor peasants, and 35 percent as middling. V. F. Verstiuk, "Vnutrennii front: strategiia i taktika bor′by," in *Ukraina v 1917–1921 gg.: Nekotorye problemy istorii: Sbornik nauchnykh trudov*, ed. Iu. Iu. Kondufor (Kyiv, 1991), 170.
72. Kotliar, *Povstanstvo: Selians′kyi rukh na Pivdni Ukraïny*, 113.
73. DAKhO, f. P-1, op. 1, spr. 34, ark. 22.
74. Sivachenko, "Spalakhy hnivu narodnoho," 24.
75. Bondarenko's account can be found in DAKhO, f. P-10, op. 1, spr. 367, titled "A. N. Bondarenko. Istoriia Koviaskogo vosstaniia 1920 goda."
76. Sivachenko, "Spalakhy hnivu narodnoho," 24n10.
77. DAKhO, f. P-1, op. 1, spr. 354, ark. 142, 15 and 25. Murafa was known among Communists as a center of peasant insurgency. See, for example, DAKhO, f. R-203, op. 1, spr. 129, ark. 36 and 42.
78. DAKhO, f. P-1, op. 1, spr. 354, ark. 6.
79. DAKhO, f. P-1, op. 1, spr. 354, ark. 26.

80. DAKhO, f. P-1, op. 1, spr. 142, ark. 24; f. P-1, op. 1, spr. 354, ark. 27; and Sivachenko, "Spalakhy hnivu narodnoho," 25–26.
81. DAKhO, f. P-1, op. 1, spr. 142, ark. 24; f. P-1, op. 1, spr. 354, ark. 32.
82. DAKhO, f. P-1, op. 1, spr. 141, ark. 188–189; spr. 142, ark. 25; spr. 354, ark. 32.
83. DAKhO, f. P-1, op. 1, spr. 141, ark. 189.
84. Isakov, "Selians′kyi povstanches′kyi antykomunistychnyi rukh na Livoberezhnii Ukraïni," 17.
85. Ibid., 13–14; quotation from p. 14.
86. See, for example, Eric J. Hobsbawm, *Bandits* (London, 1969).
87. Hanzha, *Ukrains′ke selianstvo*, 137.
88. Ibid., 141. The party organs calculation was done by V. M. Volkovyns′kyi, *Bat′ko Makhno* (Kyiv, 1992), 40.
89. Verstiuk, "Vnutrennii front: strategiia i taktika bor′by," 141.
90. In poorer provinces as much as 25 percent of the requisitioned grain was to be retained in volost funds for the "rural poor"; in better off provinces, 10 percent. Part of this grain was to be reserved for seed. Mikhail Kubanin, *Makhnovshchina: Krest′ianskoe dvizhenie v stepnoi Ukraine v gody grazhdanskoi voiny* (Leningrad, [1927]), 135.
91. TsDAVO, f. 2, op. 1, spr. 576, ark. 128; cited in Voloshchuk, et al., *Radians′ke budivnytstvo*, doc. 53, pp. 95–97.
92. The inclusion of middling peasants was probably a reaction to the failure of the committees of poor peasants (*kombidy*) introduced under the previous (1919) Soviet government in Ukraine; authorities concluded from the experience of 1919 that in Ukraine the middling peasants represented too strong a social force to ignore. See, for example, Hanzha, *Ukrains′ke selianstvo*, 24–25.
93. D. Manuïl′s′kyi, "O nashei politike v derevne," *Kommunist*, 28 May 1920, no. 2, pp. 5–8; quotation from p. 8.
94. DAKhO, f. R-203, op. 1, spr. 7, ark. 15v.
95. DAKhO, f. P-1, op. 1, spr. 141, ark. 98.
96. DAKhO, f. R-203, op. 1, spr. 7, ark. 33.
97. TsDAVO, f. 257, op. 1, spr. 11, ark. 26; on the number of communists, see *Obzor organizatsii KNS s nachala organizatsii po 1 dekabria 1920 g.*, vyd. NKVS, 35; cited in Ksenzenko, *Zavershennia revoliutsiinykh zemel′nykh peretvoren′ na Kharkivshchyni*, 114–15. According to Chyhyryk, there were 9,599 KNSs across all of Ukraine by 10 November 1920. V. V. Chyhyryk, "KP(b)U v borot′bi za revoliutsiine peretvorennia ahrarnykh vidnosyn," *Ukraïns′kyi istorychnyi zhurnal*, 1958, no. 4:15.
98. Population figures for 1920 are understandably not very reliable, but according to the one available source there were 1,961,296 rural inhabitants in the province in 1920. Tsentral′noe statisticheskoe upravlenie, *Statistika*

Ukrainy: Naselenie Khar'kovskoi gubernii po dannym perepisi 1920 goda (Kharkiv, 1920), 16–17.

99. Hanzha, *Ukrains'ke selianstvo*, 144–45.
100. DAKhO, f. R-431, op. 1, spr. 20, ark. 127. Party leaders used the adjective "military" (*boevoi*) to connote crucial tasks or orders; it derives from the word for battle (*boi*), suggesting that the thing it modifies is crucial to winning the battle. Its frequent use in officially nonmilitary contexts suggests the party leaders' mindset, forged during the civil war.
101. See James E. Mace, "The *Komitety nezamozhnykh selyan* and the Structure of Soviet Rule in the Ukrainian Countryside, 1920–1933," *Soviet Studies* 35 (October 1983): 492. The failure of such efforts to "differentiate" the village was not peculiar to Ukraine. Donald Raleigh charts the complete rejection by Saratov province's peasants of the Bolsheviks' attempt to introduce Committees of Poor Peasants (*kombedy*) in 1918. Raleigh, *Experiencing Russia's Civil War*, 317–20. The difference lies in the KP(b)U's puzzling persistence throughout the 1920s.
102. DAKhO, f. R-200, op. 1, spr. 1, ark. 1.
103. DAKhO, f. R-200, op. 1, spr. 1, ark. 4v.
104. DAKhO, f. R-200, op. 1, spr. 1, ark. 5.
105. DAKhO, f. R-200, op. 1, spr. 1, ark. 5. The resolution referred specifically to the protocol on repressive measures against Rublivska volost.
106. The Rublivska operation was declared "completed" on 8 July, and the commission then moved to implement the measures against Murafa. DAKhO, f. R-200, op. 1, spr. 1, ark. 7.
107. DAKhO, f. R-200, op. 1, spr. 1, ark. 11. Emphasis added. Recognizing that "to eradicate banditry only with measures of a purely military character was inconceivable," the commission also resolved to order the provincial Cheka to work out a plan of struggle "with the help of informers and spies." Ibid., ark. 11v.
108. DAKhO, f. R-200, op. 1, spr. 1, ark. 13.
109. DAKhO, f. R-200, op. 1, spr. 1, ark. 14.
110. DAKhO, f. R-203, op. 1, spr. 7, ark. 87.
111. DAKhO, f. R-203, op. 1, spr. 129, ark. 108.
112. DAKhO, f. R-203, op. 1, spr. 129, ark. 109.
113. DAKhO, f. R-203, op. 1, spr. 129, ark. 110–110v.
114. DAKhO, f. R-203, op. 1, spr. 129, ark. 112.
115. DAKhO, f. R-203, op. 1, spr. 129, ark. 113 and 113v.
116. DAKhO, f. R-203, op. 1, spr. 129, ark. 110–110v. Capital letters in the original.
117. DAKhO, f. R-203, op. 1, spr. 156, ark. 65–67.
118. V. V. Kalinichenko, *Selians'ke hospodarstvo Ukraïny v period NEPu: Istoryko-ekonomichne doslidzhennia* (Kharkiv, 1997), 34. Soviet policy in this period,

the so-called *razverstka*, implied that all surplus foodstuffs not needed for personal consumption were to be requisitioned by the state.

119. Kubanin, *Makhnovshchina*, 127, 130; cites "Otchet Narkomproda USSR v sbornike otchetov V s″ezdu Sovetov USSR," *Sbornik otchetov narodnykh komissariatov USSR, upolnomochennykh narodnykh komissariatov RSFSR pri Sovnarkome USSR i tsentral′nykh uchrezhdenii Ukrainy k 5-mu Vseukrainskomu s″ezdu sovetov* (Kharkiv, 1921), 14–16.
120. See V. P. Danilov et al., eds., *Krest′ianskoe vosstanie v Tambovskoi gubernii v 1919–1921 gg. "Antonovshchina": Dokumenty i materialy* (Tambov, 1994), 14–15, 109–12; and Graziosi, *Great Soviet Peasant War: Bolsheviks and Peasants, 1917–1933*, 38.
121. *Stenograficheskii otchet X s″ezda Rossiiskoi Kommunisticheskoi Partii (8–16 marta 1921 g.)* (Moscow, 1921), 164.
122. Ibid., 175. The poorest peasants were to be excluded from some and, in exceptional cases, all forms of the tax-in-kind.
123. *Stenograficheskii otchet X s″ezda Rossiiskoi Kommunisticheskoi Partii (8-16 marta 1921 g.)*, 167.
124. Ibid., 174. From the wording of this statement, it seems that Manuïl′s′kyi had received the approval of the RKP's central committee in advance.
125. Surprisingly complete reports on the Tenth Party Congress almost immediately appeared in *Kommunist*, published in Kharkiv. The first article on Lenin's speech introducing the new policy appeared in the 17 March 1921 issue, no. 58 (352), 1.
126. *Kommunist*, no. 67 (362), 29 March 1921, 3; and O. M. Movchan, A. P. Ohins′ka, and L. V. Iakovlieva, comps., *Holod 1921–1923 rokiv v Ukraïni: Zbirnyk dokumentiv i materialiv* (Kyiv, 1993), 24–25. In fact, Kharkiv, Volhynia, Katerynoslav (now Dnipropetrovsk), and Chernihiv provinces were liberated from fulfilling part of the fall 1920 *razverstka*, because these provinces had already done their share and had borne much of the burden of the spring 1920 grain deliveries.
127. I. K. Rybalka et al., eds., *Komitety nezamozhnykh selian Ukraïny, 1920–1933: Zbirnyk dokumentiv i materialiv* (Kyiv, 1968), 119–31.
128. Institut istorii partii TsK KP Ukrainy, *Kommunisticheskaia partiia Ukrainy v rezoliutsiiakh i resheniiakh s″ezdov i konferentsii, 1918–1956* (Kyiv, 1958), 116. Part of this quotation was originally cited in Graziosi, *Great Soviet Peasant War: Bolsheviks and Peasants, 1917–1933*, 37.
129. Institut istorii partii TsK KP Ukrainy, *Kommunisticheskaia partiia Ukrainy v rezoliutsiiakh i resheniiakh s″ezdov i konferentsii*, 121.
130. DAKhO, f. P-1, op. 1, spr. 466, ark. 40. These Makhnovite troops were probably detachments in retreat from a failed attack on Poltava in June 1921. Makhno found some support in the southern districts of Kharkiv

province, near Starobilsk and Izium, but he did not stay there long. See V. A. Savchenko, *Makhno* (Kharkiv, 2005), 352–70; V. F. Verstiuk, *Makhnovshchyna: selians´kyi povstanches´kyi rukh na Ukraïni (1918–1921)* (Kyiv, 1992), 332–36.

131. See for example *Kommunist*, no. 142, 1 July 1921, 1, 3.
132. TsDAHO, f. 1, op. 6, spr. 16, ark. 7. At the same Politburo meeting a telegram from Lenin was heard demanding reinforced efforts to send grain "to the North."
133. Rybalka et al., *Komitety nezamozhnykh selian Ukraïny (1920–1933): Zbirnyk dokumentiv i materialiv*, 143–44, 149.
134. Movchan et al., *Holod 1921–1923 rokiv v Ukraïni*, 26; cites TsDAVO, f. 2, op. 2, spr. 339, ark. 83. Poltava province was supposed to deliver a large portion of the fall 1920 *razverstka*. Ibid., 24.
135. Unfortunately, for the period from mid-July to late September 1921 almost nothing has been preserved concerning the situation in Kharkiv province. Not only the Cheka reports, but also the protocols of the provincial executive committee, the provincial party committee, and the provincial commissariat of the economy have not survived. See, for example, TsDAVO, f. 2, op. 2, spr. 317, ark. 31–32, where the protocols of the presidium of the provincial executive committee skip from 11 July 1921 to 22 October 1921.
136. *Kommunist*, nos. 169–72 (463–67), 2–5 August 1921.
137. The introduction of NEP took still longer in southern Ukraine. Kotliar claims that it was not fully implemented there before mid-1923, largely delayed by the famine and local communists' insistence on fulfilling the last *prodrazverstka*. Kotliar, *Povstanstvo: Selians´kyi rukh na Pivdni Ukraïny*, 86–110.
138. TsDAVO, f. 2, op. 2, spr. 297, ark. 1.
139. TsDAVO, f. 2, op. 2, spr. 297, ark. 4.
140. DAKhO, f. P-1, op. 1, spr. 464, ark. 251.
141. Graham Tan, "Transformation versus Tradition: Agrarian Policy and Government-Peasant Relations in Right-Bank Ukraine 1920–1923," *Europe-Asia Studies* 52 (July 2000): 918; cites TsDAVO, f. 5, op. 1, spr. 620, ark. 57.
142. Movchan et al., *Holod 1921–1923 rokiv v Ukraïni*, 5–8, 24–39; and Roman Serbyn, "The Famine of 1921–1923: A Model for 1932–1933?" in *Famine in Ukraine, 1932–1933*, ed. Roman Serbyn and Bohdan Krawchenko (Edmonton, 1986), 147–78.
143. Serbyn, "Famine of 1921–1923," 169–70.
144. Kotliar, *Povstanstvo: Selians´kyi rukh na Pivdni Ukraïny*, 128–29; Stanislav Kul´chyts´kyi, *Komunizm v Ukraïni: pershe desiatyrichchia (1919–1929)* (Kyiv: Osnovy, 1996), 202; Hanzha, "Selians´kyi povstans´kyi rukh," 19.
145. DAKhO, f. R-200, op. 1, spr. 59, ark. 11.
146. DAKhO, f. R-200, op. 1, spr. 59, ark. 11v. For reports on other districts, where

similar claims were made that banditry was becoming less and less political, see: ibid., ark. 4–10 and 12.

147. DAKhO, f. R-200, op. 1, spr. 59, ark. 32v. The report named two gang leaders and one "new school teacher" as the Petliurist organizers.
148. DAKhO, f. R-200, op. 1, spr. 59, ark. 33–33v.
149. DAKhO, f. R-200, op. 1, spr. 59, ark. 29.
150. Kotliar, *Povstanstvo: Selians'kyi rukh na Pivdni Ukraïny*, 131; Hanzha also gives this date for the end of organized "banditry." Hanzha, "Selians'kyi povstans'kyi rukh," 19.
151. DAKhO, f. R-200, op. 1, spr. 59, ark. 131 and 133 (for statistics).

Conclusion

1. For example, see Graziosi, *Great Soviet Peasant War: Bolsheviks and Peasants, 1917–1933*.
2. Narodnii komisariiat zemel'nykh sprav (hereafter Narkomzem), *Pidsumky ahrarnoï revoliutsiï na Ukraïni*.
3. Narkomzem, *Pidsumky ahrarnoï revoliutsiï na Ukraïni*, 4.
4. Holubnychy, "1917 Agrarian Revolution in Ukraine," 4–5.
5. Khar'kovskoe gubernskoe statisticheskoe biuro, *Vserossiiskaia selsko-khoziaistvennaia perepis 1917 g. Khar'kovskoi gubernii*, 12–13.
6. See Tan, "Transformation versus Tradition."
7. Hanzha, *Ukrains'ke selianstvo v period stanovlennia totalitarnoho rezhymu*, 152–81.
8. Isakov, "Selians'kyi povstanches'kyi antykomunistychnyi rukh na Livoberezhnii Ukraïni," 15.
9. Tan, "Peasant Action and Village Social Organization," 277, 285; see also 273–75.
10. Nesterov, "Selians'kyi povstans'kyi rukh na pravoberezhnii Ukraïni," 12–13.
11. Zakharchenko, Zemziulina, and Nesterov, *U pokhodi za voleiu*.
12. Ibid., 90–91, 124, 125; on this circular argument see especially 122.
13. Mykhailychenko, "Polityka 'Voennoho komunizmu' i ukraïns'ke selianstvo, 1919 r.," 14.
14. Kotliar is the only Ukrainian historian to compare the anticommunist and anti-VA uprisings.
15. Kotliar, *Povstanstvo: Selians'kyi rukh na Pivdni Ukraïny*, 83–84, 34–35.
16. Badcock, *Politics and the People in Revolutionary Russia*, 29, 330.
17. Raleigh, *Experiencing Russia's Civil War*, 321. Strangely, though his study is in part about the countryside, Raleigh mostly discusses "localism" among party and soviet leaders in Saratov and the district towns, as well as the ways in which Moscow used the term "localism" to discredit these local elites and to further centralization. See, for example, 89–92, 105, 284, 403, and 409–11.
18. There is a great deal of evidence, for example, that during the revolutionary

events in Germany and Italy, localness was one of the main problems, from the socialist parties' perspectives. See for example, Geoff Eley, *Forging Democracy: The History of the Left in Europe, 1850–2000* (Oxford, 2002), 172–73; on pages 119–20 Eley describes some of the more radical German activists in the revolutionary actions of 1918–21 as rejecting parties and their centralized control, but they also seemed to be rejecting the center itself. One maverick later declared, "Away with centralism, the organizational principle of the ruling class. Away with all central corporate bodies." Taken from an anonymous autobiography, "Erlebnisse und Schlußfolgerungen eines Revolutionärs," in *Proletarischer Zeitgeist* 10 (1931); Eley got the quotation from Hans M. Bock, *Geschichte des "linken Radikalismus" in Deuschland: Ein Versuch* (Frankfurt, 1976), 97. Similarly, Stephen MacDonald asserts, "The foregoing sketch of selected workers' and soldiers' councils in the Kassel district suggests certain conclusions. Though products of a national revolution, the councils arose locally and reflected in their composition and political character the variety of local economic, political and cultural conditions. The economic structure of a given city or county played a major role in determining a council's membership and political goals, but similar economic preconditions did not mechanically, automatically produce similar councils." Stephen C. MacDonald, *A German Revolution: Local Change and Continuity in Prussia, 1918–1920* (New York, 1991), 37.

19. Figes, *Peasant Russia, Civil War*, 355.
20. This too, like localness, was not a peculiarity of Kharkiv province or Ukrainian-speaking peasants. Donald Raleigh found in his study of Saratov province during the civil war that "in general, the village remained a cohesive unit in which the dominant struggle took place between insiders and outsiders; when threatened by an outside force, peasants showed solidarity." Raleigh, *Experiencing Russia's Civil War*, 316.
21. *Khar′kovshchina v tsifrakh i faktakh (Materialy k otchetnoi kampanii sovetov)* (Kharkiv, 1928), 102–4. Similarly, Graham Tan describes the continuing insignificance of the KNSs in the Right-Bank Ukrainian countryside: poor peasants took part in villages' continuing seizures and redivision of land in the 1920s, "whilst the KNS looked on passively." Tan, "Peasant Action and Village Social Organization," 284. For a useful introduction to the KNSs in the 1920s Ukrainian countryside, see Mace, "The *Komitety nezamozhnykh selyan* and the Structure of Soviet Rule in the Ukrainian Countryside, 1920–1933."

Works Cited

1. Major Archives

Archives of the Hoover Institution on War, Revolution, and Peace, Stanford University, Palo Alto, Calif., USA.

Derzhavnyi arkhiv Kharkivs´koï oblasti (DAKhO), Kharkiv, Ukraine.

Rossiiskii gosudarstvennyi voennyi arkhiv (RGVA), Moscow, Russia.

Tsentral´nyi derzhavnyi arkhiv hromads´kykh ob'iednan´ Ukraïny (TsDAHO), Kyiv, Ukraine.

Tsentral´nyi derzhavnyi arkhiv vyshchykh orhaniv vlady ta upravlinnia Ukraïny (TsDAVO), Kyiv, Ukraine.

Tsentral´nyi derzhavnyi istorychnyi arkhiv Ukraïny u m. Kyievi (TsDIA), Kyiv, Ukraine.

2. Newspapers

Biulliuten poslednikh sobytii. Ezhednevnoe izdanie. Kharkiv, fall 1918.

Iuzhnyi krai. Kharkiv, 1914–1917.

Izvestiia Khar´kovskago Soveta rabochikh deputatov; later *Izvestiia Khar´kovskago Soveta rabochikh i soldatskikh deputatov*; later still *Izvestiia Iuga.* Kharkiv, 1917–1918.

Kommunist. Kharkiv, 1920–1922.

Nash golos. Ezhednevnaia Rabochaia Sotsial´-demokraticheskaia gazeta. Kharkiv, 1918–1919.

Nova hromada. Kharkiv, 1917–1918.

Ridne slovo. Kharkiv, 1917.

Robitnycha hazeta. Kyiv, 1917.

Zemlia i volia. Kharkiv, 1917–1918.

3. Statistical Sources

Khar′kovskaia gubernskaia zemskaia uprava. *Sel′skoe khoziaistvo, fabrichnaia promyshlennost′ i zaniatiia naseleniia Khar′kovskoi gubernii*. Kharkiv, 1917.

——. *Vserossiiskaia sel′skokhoziaistvennaia perepis′ za 1916 god. Naselenie, skot i posevy itogo po uezdam. (Predvaritel′nyi podschet′)*. Kharkiv, 1916.

Khar′kovskii kreditnyi soiuz kooperativov. Statisticheskoe biuro. *Promysly i zaniatiia zemledel′cheskago naseleniia Khar′kovskoi gubernii*. Kharkiv, 1919.

Khar′kovshchina v tsifrakh i faktakh (Materialy k otchetnoi kampanii sovetov). Kharkiv, 1928.

Khar′kovskoe gubernskoe statisticheskoe biuro. *Vserossiiskaia sel′skokhoziaistvennaia i gorodskaia perepis′ 1917 g. Khar′kovskaia gub. Itogi po uezdam, gubernii i gorodam. Predvaritel′nyi podschet*. Kharkiv, 1920.

Narodnii komisariiat zemel′nykh sprav. *Pidsumky ahrarnoï revoliutsiï na Ukraïni*. Kharkiv, 1923.

Obzor Khar′kovskoi gubernii za 1914 g. Kharkiv, 1915.

Pervaia Vseobshchaia Perepis′ Naseleniia Rossiiskoi Imperii, 1897 g. Vol. 47, *Khar′kovskaia guberniia*. Moscow, 1904.

Pervaia Vseobshchaia Perepis′ Naseleniia Rossiiskoi Imperii, 1897 g. Vol. 2. St. Petersburg, 1905.

Pogubernskie itogi Vserossiiskoi sel′skokhoziaistvennoi i pozemel′noi perepisi 1917 goda po 52 guberniiam i oblastiam. Vol. 5, pt. 1. Moscow, 1921.

Poltavskoe gubernskoe zemstvo. Statisticheskoe biuro. *Statisticheskii spravochnik po Poltavskoi gubernii na 1917 g.* Poltava, 1917.

Tsentral'noe statisticheskoe upravlenie. *Predvaritel'nye pogubernskie itogi vserossiiskoi sel'sko-khoziaistvennoi i pozemel'noi perepisi 1917 g. po 29 guberniiam i 6 oblastiam.* Moscow, 1919.

——. *Rossiia v mirovoi voine, 1914–1918 goda (v tsifrakh).* Moscow, 1925.

——. *Statistika Ukrainy. Naselenie Khar'kovskoi gubernii po dannym perepisi 1920 goda.* Kharkiv, 1920.

Tsentral'nyi statisticheskii komitet Ministerstva vnutrennikh del. *Statistika zemlevladeleniia 1905 g.* Vol. 33, *Khar'kovskaia guberniia.* St. Petersburg, 1906.

Vserossiiskii Soiuz Gorodov. *Anketa o dorogovizne 1915 g.* Moscow, 1915.

Zhilkin, St. *Ukraina v tsifrakh, 1913–1920 gg.* Kharkiv, 1922.

4. Published Documents

Anfimov, A. M., ed. *Krest'ianskoe dvizhenie v Rossii v gody pervoi mirovoi voiny (iiul' 1914 g.–fevral' 1917 g.): Sbornik dokumentov.* Moscow and Leningrad, 1965.

Auswärtiges Amt. Germany. *Amtliche Urkunden zur Vorgeschichte des Waffenstillstandes 1918 (auf Grund der Akten der Reichskanzlei, des Auswärtigen Amtes und des Reichsarchivs herausgegeben vom Auswärtigen Amt und vom Reichsministerium des Innern).* Frankfurt am Main, 1988.

Avdusheva, M. P., et al., comp. *Khar'kov i Khar'kovskaia guberniia v pervoi russkoi revoliutsii 1905–1907 gg.: Sbornik dokumentov i materialov.* Kharkiv, 1955.

Avdusheva, M. P., et al., comp. *Krest'ianskoe dvizhenie v Poltavskoi i Khar'kovskoi guberniiakh v 1902 g.: Sbornik dokumentov.* Kharkiv, 1961.

Baumgart, Winfried, ed. *Von Brest-Litovsk zur Deutschen Novemberrevolution: Aus den Tagebüchern, Briefen und Aufzeichnungen von*

Alfons Paquet, Wilhelm Gröner und Albert Hopman, März bis November 1918. Göttingen, 1971.

Berelovich, Alexis, and V. A. Danilov, eds. *Sovetskaia derevnia glazami VChK-OGPU*. Vol. 1, *1918–1922: Dokumenty i materialy*. Moscow, 1998.

Bilyk, P. "Volneniia v Khar′kovskoi gubernii v gody imperialisticheskoi voiny." *Krasnyi arkhiv* 76 (1936): 3–23.

Burik, A. I., et al., eds. *Khar′kovshchina v period grazhdanskoi voiny i inostrannoi voennoi interventsii 1918–1920 gg.: Sbornik dokumentov i materialov*. Kharkiv, 1973.

Danilov, V. P., et al., eds. *Krest′ianskoe vosstanie v Tambovskoi gubernii v 1919–1921 gg. "Antonovshchina": Dokumenty i materialy*. Tambov, 1994.

Egorov, A. G., and K. M. Bogoliubov, eds. *Kommunisticheskaia partiia sovetskogo soiuza v rezoliutsiiakh i resheniiakh s″ezdov, konferentsii i plenumov TsK*. Vol. 2, *1917–1922*. Moscow, 1983.

Gor′kii, M., I. I. Mints, and R. Eideman, eds. *Krakh germanskoi okkupatsii na Ukraine (po dokumentam okkupantov)*. Moscow, 1936.

Institut istorii partii TsK KP Ukrainy. *Kommunisticheskaia partiia Ukrainy v rezoliutsiiakh i resheniiakh s″ezdov i konferentsii, 1918–1956*. Kyiv, 1958.

Instytut istorii partii TsK KP Ukraïny. *Komunistychna partiia Ukraïny v rezoliutsiiakh i rishenniakh z'ïzdiv i konferentsiï, 1918–1956*. Kyiv, 1958.

Ivanov, M., comp. "'Ot vlasti otkazyvaius′ (Dokumenty o Getmanshchine iz arkhiva Khar′kovskogo gubernskogo starosty)." *Letopis′ revoliutsii* (1924), no. 2: 224–31.

Korolivskii, S. M., N. K. Kolesnik, and I. K. Rybalka, eds. *Grazhdanskaia voina na Ukraine, 1918–1920: Sbornik dokumentov i materialov*. 3 vols. Kyiv, 1967.

Movchan, O. M., A. P. Ohins′ka, and L. V. Iakovlieva, comps. *Holod 1921–1923 rokiv v Ukraïni: Zbirnyk dokumentiv i materialiv*. Kyiv, 1993.

Popov, N. N., ed. *Osvoboditel′naia voina ukrainskogo naroda protiv nemetskikh okkupantov: Dokumenty i materialy*. Moscow, 1937.

Raboty Khar′kovskogo Gubernskogo S″ezda Soveta Rabochikh i Krestianskikh Deputatov ot 16 Fevralia 1919 goda. Kharkiv, 1919.

[Ross, Colin]. "Doklad nachal′niku operatsionnogo otdeleniia germanskogo vostochnogo fronta o polozhenii del na Ukraine v Marte 1918 goda." *Arkhiv russkoi revoliutsii* I ([1923): 288–94.

Rybalka, I. K., et al., eds. *Komitety nezamozhnykh selian Ukraïny, 1920–1933: Zbirnyk dokumentiv i materialiv*. Kyiv, 1968.

Sidorov, A. L., ed., *Ekonomicheskoe polozhenie Rossii nakanune velikoi oktiabr′skoi sotsialisticheskoi revoliutsii: Dokumenty i materialy*. Vol. 3, *Sel′skoe khoziaistvo i krest′ianstvo*. Leningrad, 1967.

Skoropads′kyi, Pavlo. "Uryvok zi 'Spomyniv' Het′mana Pavla Skoropads′koho." *Khliborobs′ka Ukraïna*. Book 5 (1924–25): 31–92.

Stenograficheskii otchet X s″ezda Rossiiskoi Kommunisticheskoi Partii (8–16 marta 1921 g.). Moscow, 1921.

Trudy pervogo Vserossiiskogo sel′sko-khoziaistvennogo s″ezda v Kieve 1–10 sentiabria 1913 goda. Pt. 2. Kyiv, 1913–1914.

Ukraïns′ka Tsentral′na Rada: Dokumenty i materialy. 2 vols. Kyiv, 1996–1997.

Verstiuk, Viacheslav F., et al., comps. *Ukrains′ka Tsentral′na Rada: Dokumenty i materialy u dvokh tomakh*. 2 vols. Kyiv, 1996–1997.

Voloshchuk, I. P., M. A. Rubach, et al., eds. *Radians′ke budivnytstvo na Ukraïni v roky Hromadians′koï viiny, 1919–1920: Zbirnyk dokumentiv i materialiv*. Kyiv, 1957.

5. Secondary Sources

Anfimov, A. M. "Krest′ianskoe khoziaistvo Rossii v gody pervoi mirovoi voiny." *Istoriia SSSR*, no. 3 (July–August 1957): 57–86.

———. *Rossiiskaia derevnia v gody pervoi mirovoi voiny*. Moscow, 1962.

Antonov-Ovseenko, V. A. "V bor′be protiv Direktorii (Na Ukraine v kontse 1918 goda)." *Litopys revoliutsiï*, nos. 38–39 (veresen–hruden′ 1929): 142–86.

Antsiferov, A. N., et al., eds. *Russian Agriculture during the War*. New Haven, 1930.

Anweiler, Oskar. *The Soviets: The Russian Workers, Peasants, and Soldiers Councils, 1905–1921*. Translated by Ruth Hein. New York, 1974.

Badcock, Sarah. *Politics and the People in Revolutionary Russia: Two Volga Provinces during 1917*. Cambridge: Cambridge University Press, 2007.

Bagalei [Bahalii], D. I., and D. P. Miller. *Istoriia goroda Khar′kova za 250 let ego sushchestvovaniia (s 1655-go po 1905-i god)*. 2 vols. Kharkiv, 1905.

Baker, Mark. "How to Make Kharkiv Workers into Bolsheviks: Lessons from the Hetmanate and Directory, 1918." *Canadian-American Slavic Studies* 40, no. 1 (Spring 2006): 49–63.

Becker, Jean Jacques. *The Great War and the French People*. Translated by Arnold Pomerans. Leamington Spa, 1985.

Borys, Jurij. *The Sovietization of Ukraine, 1917–1923: The Communist Doctrine and Practice of National Self-Determination*, Rev. ed. Edmonton, 1980.

Bottomore, Tom, ed. *A Dictionary of Marxist Thought*. Oxford, 1983.

Brovkin, Vladimir N. *Behind the Front Lines of the Civil War: Political Parties and Social Movements in Russia, 1918–1922*. Princeton, 1994.

———, ed. *The Bolsheviks in Russian Society: The Revolution and the Civil Wars*. New Haven, 1997.

Brown, Kate. *A Biography of No Place: From Ethnic Borderland to Soviet Heartland*. Cambridge, Mass., 2004.

Chaadaeva, O. A., comp. "Soldatskie pis′ma v gody mirovoi voiny (1915–1917 gg.)." *Krasnyi arkhiv* 65–66 (1934): 118–63.

Channon, John. "The Peasantry in the Revolutions of 1917," in *Revolution in Russia: Reassessments of 1917*, edited by Edith Rogovin Frankel, Jonathan Frankel, and Baruch Knei-Paz, 105–30. Cambridge, 1992.

Chyhyryk, V. V. "KP(b)U v borot′bi za revoliutsiine peretvorennia ahrarnykh vidnosyn." *Ukraïns′kyi istorychnyi zhurnal* (1958), no. 4: 3–19.

Coetzee, Frans, and Marilyn Shevin-Coetzee, eds. *Authority, Identity and the Social History of the Great War*. Oxford, 1995.

Davies, R. W., Mark Harrison, and S. G. Wheatcroft. *The Economic Transformation of the Soviet Union, 1913–1945*. Cambridge, 1994.

Dmytryshyn, Basil. "The German Overthrow of the Central *Rada*, April, 1918: New Evidence from German Archives." *Nationalities Papers* 23, no. 4 (December 1995): 751–66.

Dornik, Wolfram, and Peter Lieb. "Die Besatzungsverwaltung." In *Die Ukraine zwischen Selbstbestimmung und Fremdherrschaft 1917–1922*. Graz, 2011.

———. "Die militärischen Operationen." In *Die Ukraine zwischen Selbstbestimmung und Fremdherrschaft 1917–1922*. Graz, 2011.

Doroshenko, Dmytro. *Istoriia Ukraïny, 1917–1923 rr*. 2 vols. New York, 1954.

Dubrovskii, S. M. *Stolypinskaia zemel′naia reforma: Iz istorii sel′skogo khoziaistva i krest′ianstva Rossii v nachale XX veka*. Moscow, 1963.

Eley, Geoff. *Forging Democracy: The History of the Left in Europe, 1850–2000*. Oxford, 2002.

Elwood, R. C. *Russian Social Democracy in the Underground: A Study of the RSDRP in the Ukraine, 1907–1914*. Assen, 1974.

Engel, Barbara Alpern. "Not by Bread Alone: Subsistence Riots in Russia during World War I." *Journal of Modern History* 69 (December 1997): 696–721.

Farnsworth, Beatrice. "The Soldatka: Folklore and Court Record." *Slavic Review* 49 (Spring 1990): 58–73.

Fedyshyn, Oleh S. *Germany's Drive to the East and the Ukrainian Revolution, 1917–1918*. New Brunswick, N.J., 1971.

Figes, Orlando. *Peasant Russia, Civil War: The Volga Countryside in Revolution (1917–1921)*. Oxford, 1989.

———. *A People's Tragedy: A History of the Russian Revolution.* New York, 1996.

Frame, Murray, comp. *The Russian Revolution, 1905–1921: A Bibliographic Guide to Works in English.* Westport, Conn., 1995.

Frankel, Edith Rogovin, Jonathan Frankel, and Baruch Knei-Paz, eds. *Revolution in Russia: Reassessments of 1917.* Cambridge, 1992.

Frenkin, Mikhail S. *Tragediia krest′ianskikh vosstanii v Rossii 1918–1921 gg.* Jerusalem, 1987.

Frevert, Ute. *Women in German History: From Bourgeois Emancipation to Sexual Liberation.* Translated by Stuart McKinnon-Evans. Oxford, 1989.

Friedgut, Theodore H. *Iuzovka and Revolution.* Vol. 2, *Politics and Revolution in Russia's Donbass, 1869–1924.* Princeton, 1994.

Gergel, N. "The Pogroms in the Ukraine in 1918–1921." *YIVO Annual of Jewish Social Science* 6 (1951): 237–52.

Gill, Graham. *Peasants and Government in the Russian Revolution.* London, 1979.

Glickman, Rose L. "The Russian Factory Woman, 1880–1914." In *Women in Russia*, edited by Dorothy Atkinson, Alexander Dallin, and Gail Warshofsky Lapidus, 63–83. Stanford, 1977.

Good, Jane E., and David R. Jones. *Babushka: The Life of the Russian Revolutionary Ekaterina K. Breshko-Breshkovskaia (1844–1934).* Newtonville, Mass., 1991.

Gratsiozi [Graziosi], Andrea. *Bol′sheviki i krest′iane na Ukraine, 1918–1919 gody: Ocherk o bol′shevizmakh, natsional-sotsializmakh i krest′ianskikh dvizheniiakh.* Moscow, 1997.

Grave, B. B., ed. *Burzhuaziia nakanune Fevral′skoi revoliutsii.* Moscow, 1927.

Graziosi, Andrea. *The Great Soviet Peasant War: Bolsheviks and Peasants, 1917–1933.* Harvard Papers in Ukrainian Studies. Cambridge, Mass., 1996.

Grelka, Frank. "Deutsche Militarverwaltung in der Ukraine im Erstern und Zweiten Weltkrieg: Aspekte einer komparatistischen Okkupationsforschung aus der Perspektive ukrainischer Selbstandigkeitsbestrebungen." Unpublished manuscript; sent to me by the author, April 2001.

Guthier, Steven L. "The Popular Base of Ukrainian Nationalism in 1917." *Slavic Review* 38, no. 1 (1979): 30–47.

———. "The Roots of Popular Ukrainian Nationalism: A Demographic, Social and Political Study of the Ukrainian Nationality to 1917." PhD dissertation, University of Michigan, 1990.

Hanzha, Oksana I. *Opir selian stanovlenniu totalitarnoho rezhymu v USRR*. Istorychni zoshyty. Kyiv, 1996.

———. "Selians′kyi povstans′kyi rukh." In *Istoriia ukraïns′koho selianstva: Narysy v 2-kh tomakh*, ed. V. M. Lytvyn et al., 2:7–19. Kyiv, 2006.

———. *Ukraïns′ke selianstvo v period stanovlennia totalitarnoho rezhymu (1917–1927)*. Kyiv, 2000.

Harris, Ruth. "The Child of the Barbarian: Rape, Race and Nationalism in France during the First World War." *Past and Present*, no. 141 (1993): 170–206.

Hickey, Michael C. "Local Government and State Authority in the Provinces: Smolensk, February–June 1917." *Slavic Review* 55 (1996): 863–81.

Higonnet, Margaret, ed. *Lines of Fire: Women's Vision of World War I*. New York, 1999.

Higonnet, Margaret, and Jane Jenson, eds. *Behind the Lines: Gender and the Two World Wars*. New Haven, 1987.

Himka, John-Paul. "The National and the Social in the Ukrainian Revolution of 1917–1920: The Historiographical Agenda." *Archiv für Sozialgeschichte* 34 (1994): 95–110.

Hobsbawm, Eric J. *Bandits*. London, 1969.

Holquist, Peter. "A Russian Vendee: The Practice of Revolutionary Politics in the Don Countryside, 1917–1921." PhD dissertation, Columbia University, 1995.

——. *Making War, Forging Revolution: Russia's Continuum of Crisis, 1914–1921*. Cambridge, Mass., 2002.

Holubnychy, Vsevolod. "The 1917 Agrarian Revolution in Ukraine." In *Soviet Regional Economics: Selected Works of Vsevolod Holubnychy*, edited by Iwan S. Koropeckyj, 3–65. Edmonton, 1982.

Horne, John, ed. *State, Society and Mobilization in Europe during the First World War*. Cambridge, 1997.

Hrushevs'kyi, Mykhailo, *Khto taki ukraïntsi i choho vony khochut'*. Kyiv, 1991.

Hrytsenko, A. P. *Politychni syly u borot'bi za vlady v Ukraïni (kinets' 1917 r.–pochatok 1919 r.)*. Istorychni zoshyty. Kyiv, 1993.

Hunczak, Taras, ed. *The Ukraine, 1917–1921: A Study in Revolution*. Cambridge, Mass., 1977.

Iakymenko, M. A. "Zemel'na orenda na Ukraïni v period kapitalizmu." *Ukraïns'kyi istorychnyi zhurnal* (1991), no. 2: 54–63.

Ippolitov, G. M. *Kto Vy, General A. I. Denikin? Monograficheskoe issledovanie politicheskoi, voennoi i obshchestvennoi deiatel'nosti A. I. Denikina v 1890–1947 gg.* 2nd ed. Samara, 1999.

Isakov, P. M. "Povstans'kyi antykomunistychnyi rukh na livoberezhnii Ukraïni (berezen' 1919–lystopad 1921 rr.): Heohrafiia poshyrennia, dynamika kil'kisnykh zmin, ideolohiia." *Moloda natsiia: al'manakh*, no. 1 (2000): 62–74.

——. "Selians'kyi povstanches'kyi antykomunistychnyi rukh na Livoberezhnii Ukraïni (berezen' 1919–lystopad 1921 rr.)." Avtoreferat dysertatsiï na zdobuttia naukovoho stupenia kandydata istorychnykh nauk, NANU, Instytut Istoriï Ukraïny, Kyiv, 2001.

Jones, Adrian Neil. "The Peasants of Late Imperial Russia: Economy and Society in the Era of the Stolypin Reform." 2 vols. PhD dissertation, Harvard University, 1988.

Kabanov, V. V. "Oktiabr'skaia revoliutsiia i krest'ianskaia obshchina." *Istoricheskie zapiski* 111 (1984): 100–150.

Kachinskii, V. "Krest'ianskoe dvizhenie." In *1917 god v Khar'kove: Sbornik statei i vospominanii*, edited by V. Morgunov and Z. Manul´skaia, 192–220. Kharkiv, 1927.

——. *Ocherki agrarnoi revoliutsii na Ukraine: Uravnitel´nyi razdel zemli*. Kharkiv, 1922.

Kalinichenko, V. V. *Selians´ke hospodarstvo Ukraïny v period NEPu: Istoryko-ekonomichne doslidzhennia*. Kharkiv, 1997.

Keep, John L. H. *The Russian Revolution: A Study in Mass Mobilization*. New York, 1976.

Kent, Susan K. *Making Peace: the Reconstruction of Gender in Interwar Britain*. Princeton, 1993.

Khmil´, I. V. *Ahrarna revoliutsiia v Ukraïni: berezen´ 1917–kviten´ 1918 r*. Kyiv, 2000.

——. "Na shliakhu vidrodzhennia ukraïnskoï derzhavnosti (Ukraïns´kyi natsional´nyi konhres-z'ïzd 6–8 kvitnia 1917 r.)." *Istorychni zoshyty*. Kyiv, 1994.

——. *Trudiashche selianstvo Ukraïny v borot´bi za vladu rad*. Kyiv, 1977.

Khrystiuk, Pavlo. *Zamitky i materiialy do istoriï ukraïns´koï revoliutsiï, 1917–1920 rr*. 3 vols. Vienna, 1921.

Kondrat´ev, N. D. *Rynok khlebov i ego regulirovanie vo vremia voiny i revoliutsii*. Moscow, 1991.

Korotenko, A. P. "Revoliutsionnaia rabota bol´shevikov Khar´kovshchiny v period pervoi mirovoi imperialisticheskoi voiny." *Sbornik nauchnykh rabot kafedr obshchestvennykh nauk vuzov g. Khar´kova*, pt. 1 (1956): 79–103.

Kostrikin, V. I. *Zemel´nye komitety v 1917 godu*. Moscow, 1975.

Kotliar, Iu. V. *Povstanstvo: Selians´kyi rukh na Pivdni Ukraïny (1917–1925)*. Mykolaïv and Odesa, 2003.

Ksenzenko, M. I. *Zavershennia revoliutsiinykh zemel´nykh peretvoren´ na Kharkivshchyni (hruden´ 1919–berezen´ 1921 rr.)*. Kharkiv, 1968.

Kubanin, Mikhail I. *Makhnovshchina: Krest´ianskoe dvizhenie v stepnoi Ukraine v gody grazhdanskoi voiny*. Leningrad, [1927].

Kul´chyts´kyi, Stanislav. *Komunizm v Ukraïni: pershe desiatyrichchia (1919–1929)*. Kyiv, 1996.

Kulichenko, M. I. *Bol´sheviki Khar´kovshchiny v Borbe za vlast´ sovetov (1918–1920 gg.)*. Kharkiv, 1966.

Kurman, M. V., and I. V. Lebedinskii. *Naselenie bol´shogo sotsialisticheskogo goroda*. Moscow, 1968.

Kuromiya, Hiroaki. *Freedom and Terror in the Donbas: A Ukrainian-Russian Borderland, 1870s–1990s*. Cambridge, 1998.

Kutashev, I. V. "Selians´kyi rukh v Ukraïni (berezen´ 1917 r.–kviten´ 1918 r.)." Avtoreferat dysertatsiï na zdobuttia naukovoho stupenia kandydata istorychnykh nauk, Natsional´nyi pedahohichnyi universytet imeni M. P. Drahomanova, Kyiv, 2003.

Levine, Philippa. "Walking the Streets in a Way No Decent Woman Should: Women Police in World War One." *Journal of Modern History* 66 (1994): 34–78.

Lewin, Moshe. "Who was the Soviet Kulak?" *Soviet Studies* 18 (October 1966): 189–212.

Lih, Lars T. *Bread and Authority in Russia, 1914–1921*. Berkeley, 1990.

Lupanov, Oleksandr, et al., eds. *Ostannii het´man: Iuvileinyi zbirnyk pam'iati Pavla Skoropads´koho, 1873–1945*. Kyiv, 1993.

MacDonald, Stephen C. *A German Revolution: Local Change and Continuity in Prussia, 1918–1920*. New York, 1991.

Mace, James E. *Communism and the Dilemmas of National Liberation: National Communism in Soviet Ukraine, 1918–1933*. Cambridge, Mass., 1983.

———. "The *Komitety nezamozhnykh selyan* and the Structure of Soviet Rule in the Ukrainian Countryside, 1920–1933." *Soviet Studies* 35 (October 1983): 487–503.

Maistrenko, V. S. "Konfliktni sytuatsii v khodi provedennia stolypins´koï ahrarnoï reformy v Kharkivs´koi hubernii (1906–1915 rr.)." *Visnyk Kharkivs´koho derzhavnoho universytetu* 31, no. 441 (1999): 156–64.

———. "Stolypins'ka ahrarna reforma na Kharkivshchyni ta ïï rezul'taty (1906–1915 rr.)." *Visnyk Kharkovs'koho derzhavnoho universytetu* 29, no. 396 (1997): 88–98.

Maliavskii, A. D. *Krest'ianskoe dvizhenie v Rossii v 1917 g., mart–oktiabr'*. Moscow, 1981.

Malinovskii, Boris. "Vospriiatie deiatel'nosti avstro-vengerskikh i germanskikh voisk v Ukraine (1918 g.) Ukrainskim krest'ianstvom." Paper presented at the conference "Kriegserfahrungen in Osteuropa," Eberhard Karls Universität, Tübingen, Germany, October 2000.

Malyk, Ia. I. *Ukraïns'ke selianstvo v period avstro-nimets'koï okupatsiï 1918 roku*. Lviv, 1996.

———. "Zemel'ne pytannia v ukraïns'kii het'mans'kii derzhavi," In *Ostannii Het'man: Iuvileinyi zbirnyk pam'iati Pavla Skoropads'koho, 1873–1945*, ed. Oleksandr Lupanov et al., 98–106. Kyiv, 1993.

Malyk, Ia. I., and Oleh Bereza. *Zaprovadzhennia radians'koho rezhymu v ukraïns'komu seli (1917–1920)*. Lviv, 2001.

Marwick, Arthur. *The Deluge: British Society and the First World War*. London, 1965.

Matsuzato, Kimitaka. "Inter-Regional Conflicts and the Collapse of Tsarism: The Real Reason for the Food Crisis in Russia after the Autumn of 1916." In *Emerging Democracy in Late Imperial Russia*, edited by Mary Schaeffer Conroy, 243–300. Niwot, Colo., 1998.

———. "The Role of Zemstva in the Creation and Collapse of Tsarism's War Effort During World War One." *Jahrbücher für Geschichte Osteuropas* 46, no. 3 (1998): 321–37.

———. "Stolypinskaia reforma i russkii agrotekhnologicheskii perevorot." *Acta Slavica Iaponica* 10 (1992): 33–42.

Maximilian, Prince of Baden. *The Memoirs of Prince Max of Baden*. Translated by W. M. Caulder and C. W. H. Sutton. New York, 1928.

Melancon, Michael. "The Syntax of Soviet Power: The Resolutions of Local Soviets and Other Institutions, March–October 1917." *Russian Review* 52 (October 1993): 486–505.

Mints, I. I. *Istoriia Velikogo Oktiabria*. 3 vols. Moscow, 1967–1972.

Morgunov, V., and Z. Manul′skaia, eds. *1917 god v Khar′kove: Sbornik statei i vospominanii*. Kharkiv, 1927.

Mykhailychenko, D. Iu. "Polityka 'Voennoho komunizmu' i ukraïns′ke selianstvo, 1919 r." Avtoreferat dysertatsiï na zdobuttia naukovoho stupenia kandydata istorychnykh nauk, Kharkivs′kyi national′nyi universytet im. V. N. Karazina, 2002.

Nazarenko, I. D., et al., eds. *Ocherki istorii Kommunisticheskoi partii Ukrainy*. Kyiv, 1961.

Nesterov, O. V. "Selians′kyi povstans′kyi rukh na pravoberezhnii Ukraïni (1919 r.)." Avtoreferat dysertatsiï na zdobuttia naukovoho stupenia kandydata istorychnykh nauk, Kyïvs′kyi universytet imeni Tarasa Shevchenka, 2001.

Pallot, Judith. "Khutora and Otruba in Stolypin's Program of Farm Individualization." *Slavic Review* 43 (Summer 1984): 242–56.

———. *Land Reform in Russia, 1906–1917: Peasant Responses to Stolypin's Project of Rural Transformation*. Oxford, 1999.

Pavliuk, P. *Kharkivs′ka chervona hvardiia (liutyi 1917 r.-berezen′ 1918 r.)*. Kyiv, 1948.

Pavlyshyn, Oleh. "Istoriohrafiia ukraïns′koï revoliutsiï 1917–1921 rr." In *Ukraïns′ka istoriohrafiia na zlami XX i XXI stolit′: zdobutky i problemy*, edited by Leonid Zashkilniak, 168–83. Lviv, 2004.

Perrie, Maureen. "Folklore as Evidence of Peasant Mentalité: Social Attitudes and Values in Russian Popular Culture." *Russian Review* 48, no. 2 (1989): 119–43.

Pethybridge, Roger. *The Spread of the Russian Revolution: Essays on 1917*. London, 1972.

Pidhainy, Oleh S. *The Formation of the Ukrainian Republic*. New York, 1966.

Pipes, Richard. *The Formation of the Soviet Union: Communism and Nationalism, 1917–1923*. Cambridge, Mass., 1964.

———. *The Russian Revolution*. New York, 1990.

———. *Russia under the Old Regime*. New York, 1974.

Posokhov, S. I., and A. N. Iarmysh. *Gubernatory i General-Gubernatory*. Kharkiv, 1997.

Procyk, Anna. *Russian Nationalism and Ukraine: The Nationality Policy of the Volunteer Army during the Civil War*. Edmonton, 1995.

Protasov, L. G. *Vserossiiskoe uchreditel′noe sobranie: Istoriia rozhdeniia i gibeli*. Moscow, 1997.

Radkey, Oliver H. *Russia Goes to the Polls: The Election to the All-Russian Constituent Assembly, 1917*. Ithaca, 1989.

———. *The Unknown Civil War in Soviet Russia: A Study of the Green Movement in the Tambov Region, 1920–1921*. Stanford, 1976.

Raleigh, Donald J. *Experiencing Russia's Civil War: Politics, Society, and Revolutionary Culture in Saratov, 1917–1922*. Princeton, 2002.

———. "Revolutionary Politics in Provincial Russia: The Tsaritsyn 'Republic' in 1917." *Slavic Review* 40 (1981): 194–209.

———. *Revolution on the Volga: 1917 in Saratov*. Ithaca, 1986.

Reshetar, John Stephen. *The Ukrainian Revolution, 1917–1920: A Study in Nationalism*. Princeton, 1952.

Reshod′ko, P. F. *Selians′kyi rukh u Kharkivs′kii hubernii (berezen′ 1917–sichen′ 1918 r.)*. Kharkiv, 1972.

Retish, Aaron B. "Creating Peasant Citizens: Rituals of Power, Rituals of Citizenship in Viatka Province, 1917." *Revolutionary Russia* 16 (2003): 47–67.

———. "Peasant Identities in Russia's Turmoil: Status, Gender, and Ethnicity in Viatka Province, 1914–1921." PhD dissertation, Ohio State University, 2003.

Roberts, Mary-Louise. *Civilization Without Sexes: Reconstructing Gender in Postwar France, 1917–1927*. Chicago, 1994.

Sanborn, Joshua A. *Drafting the Russian Nation: Military Conscription, Total War, and Mass Politics, 1905–1925*. Dekalb, Ill., 2003.

———. "The Mobilization of 1914 and the Question of the Russian Nation: A Reexamination." *Slavic Review* 59 (Summer 2000): 267–89.

Savchenko, V. A. *Makhno*. Kharkiv, 2005.

Serbyn, Roman. "The Famine of 1921–1923: A Model for 1932–1933?" In *Famine in Ukraine, 1932–1933*, edited by Roman Serbyn and Bohdan Krawchenko, 147–178. Edmonton, 1986.

Seregny, Scott J. "Peasants and Politics: Peasant Unions During the 1905 Revolution." In *Peasant Economy, Culture, and Politics of European Russia, 1800–1921*, edited by E. Kingston-Mann and T. Mixter, 341–77. Princeton, 1991.

Shapoval, Mykyta Iu. *Velyka revoliutsiia i ukraïns´ka vyzvol´na programa*. Prague, 1928.

Shemet, Serhii. "Polkovnyk Petro Bolbochan (Zamitky do istoriï Zaporozhs´koho Korpusu 1917–1919 rr.)." *Khliborobs´ka Ukraïna*. Book 4 (1922–1923): 200–36.

Shtendera, Iaroslav. *Zasudzhenyi do rozstrilu*. Lviv, 1995.

Shyian, K. K., and S. Ia. Ostrovs´kyi. *Mynule i suchasne sela*. Kharkiv, 1963.

Siroshtan, M. A., et al., eds. *Istoriia mist i sil Ukraïns´koï RSR: Kharkivs´ka oblast´*. Kyiv, 1967.

Sivachenko, Ievhen. "Spalakhy hnivu narodnoho: Z istorii selians´koho povstans´koho rukhu na Kharkivshchyni (1920 r.)." *Zbirnyk Kharkivs´koho istoryko-filolohichnoho tovarystva*, new series, vol. 5 (1995): 17–28.

Solukha, Petro. *Dohovir z Moskvoiu proty het´mana Pavla Skoropads´koho*. N.p., 1973.

Stakhiv, Matvii. *Ukraïna v dobi Dyrektoriï UNR*. Scranton, Penn., 1962.

Stanchev, M. G., and G. I. Cherniavskii. *Fars na krovi*. Kharkiv, 1997.

Stanziani, Alessandro. "Spécialistes, bureaucrates et paysans les approvisionnements agricoles pendant la premiere guerre mondiale 1914–1917." *Cahiers du Monde Russe* 36, nos. 1–2 (1995): 71–94.

Stites, Richard. *The Women's Liberation Movement in Russia: Feminism, Nihilism, and Bolshevism, 1860–1930*. Princeton, 1978.

Subtelny, Orest. *Ukraine: A History*. 2nd ed. Toronto, 1988.

Suny, Ronald Grigor. *The Revenge of the Past: Nationalism, Revolution, and the Collapse of the Soviet Union*. Stanford, 1993.

Suprunenko, N. I. *Ocherki istorii grazhdanskoi voiny i inostrannoi voennoi interventsii na Ukraine: 1918–1920*. Moscow, 1966.

Szporluk, Roman. Review of *The Ukraine, 1917–1921: A Study in Revolution*, edited by Taras Hunczak. *Annals of the Ukrainian Academy* 14, nos. 37–38 (1978–1980): 267–71.

Tan, Graham. "Peasant Action and Village Social Organization: The Peasantry of Right-Bank Ukraine during the Revolution, 1917–1923." PhD thesis, University of London, 1999.

———. "Transformation versus Tradition: Agrarian Policy and Government-Peasant Relations in Right-Bank Ukraine 1920–1923." *Europe-Asia Studies* 52 (July 2000): 915–37.

Thompson, E. P. "The Moral Economy of the English Crowd in the Eighteenth Century." *Past and Present*, no. 50 (February 1971): 76–136.

Vakhromeev, V. A. "Sovety i prodovol′stvennyi vopros v 1917 g. (mart–oktiabr′)." *Istoricheskie zapiski* 116 (1988): 5–42.

Verstiuk, V. F. *Makhnovshchyna: selians′kyi povstanches′kyi rukh na Ukraïni (1918–1921)*. Kyiv, 1992.

———. "Vnutrennii front: strategiia i taktika bor′by." In *Ukraina v 1917–1921 gg.: Nekotorye problemy istorii: Sbornik nauchnykh trudov*, edited by Iu. Iu. Kondufor, 102–72. Kyiv, 1991.

Volkovyns′kyi, V. M., *Bat′ko Makhno*. Kyiv, 1992.

Volkovyns′kyi, V. M., and S. V. Kul′chyts′kyi. *Khrystyian Rakovs′kyi: Politychnyi portret*. Kyiv, 1990.

Vynnchenko, Volodymyr K. *Vidrodzhennia natsiï*. 3 vols. Kyiv, 1920.

Wade, Rex A. *Red Guards and Workers' Militias in the Russian Revolution*. Stanford, 1984.

Wall, Richard, and Jay Winter, eds. *The Upheaval of War: Family, Work and Welfare in Europe, 1914–1918*. Cambridge, 1988.

Weinstein, H. R. "Land Hunger and Nationalism in the Ukraine, 1905–1917," *Journal of Economic History* 2 (1942): 24–35.

Wheatcroft, S. G., and R. W. Davies. "Agriculture." In *The Economic Transformation of the Soviet Union, 1913–1945*, edited by R. W. Davies, Mark Harrison, and S. G. Wheatcroft, 106–30. Cambridge, 1994.

Wildman, Alan K. *The End of the Russian Imperial Army: The Old Army and the Soldiers' Revolt (March–April 1917)*. Princeton, 1980.

Yaney, George L. *The Urge to Mobilize: Agrarian Reform in Russia, 1861–1930*. Urbana, Ill., 1982.

Zakharchenko, P. P., Nataliia Zemziulina, and Oleksandr Nesterov. *U pokhodi za voleiu (selians′ko-povstans′kyi rukh na pravoberezhnii Ukraïni u 1919 rotsi)*. Kyiv, 2000.

Zemziulina, N. I. "Selians′ke pytannia v Ukraïni 1917–1918 rr. (istoriohrafiia problemy)." Avtoreferat dysertatsiï na zdobuttia naukovoho stupenia kandydata istorychnykh nauk, Kyïvs′kyi universytet imeni Tarasa Shevchenka, 1998.

Zyrianov, P. N. *Krest′ianskaia obshchina Evropeiskoi Rossii 1907–1914 gg*. Moscow, 1992.

Index